# Bird Kiss

## VOLUME 1
## EUN AH PARK

**TOKYOPOP®**

HAMBURG // LONDON // LOS ANGELES // TOKYO

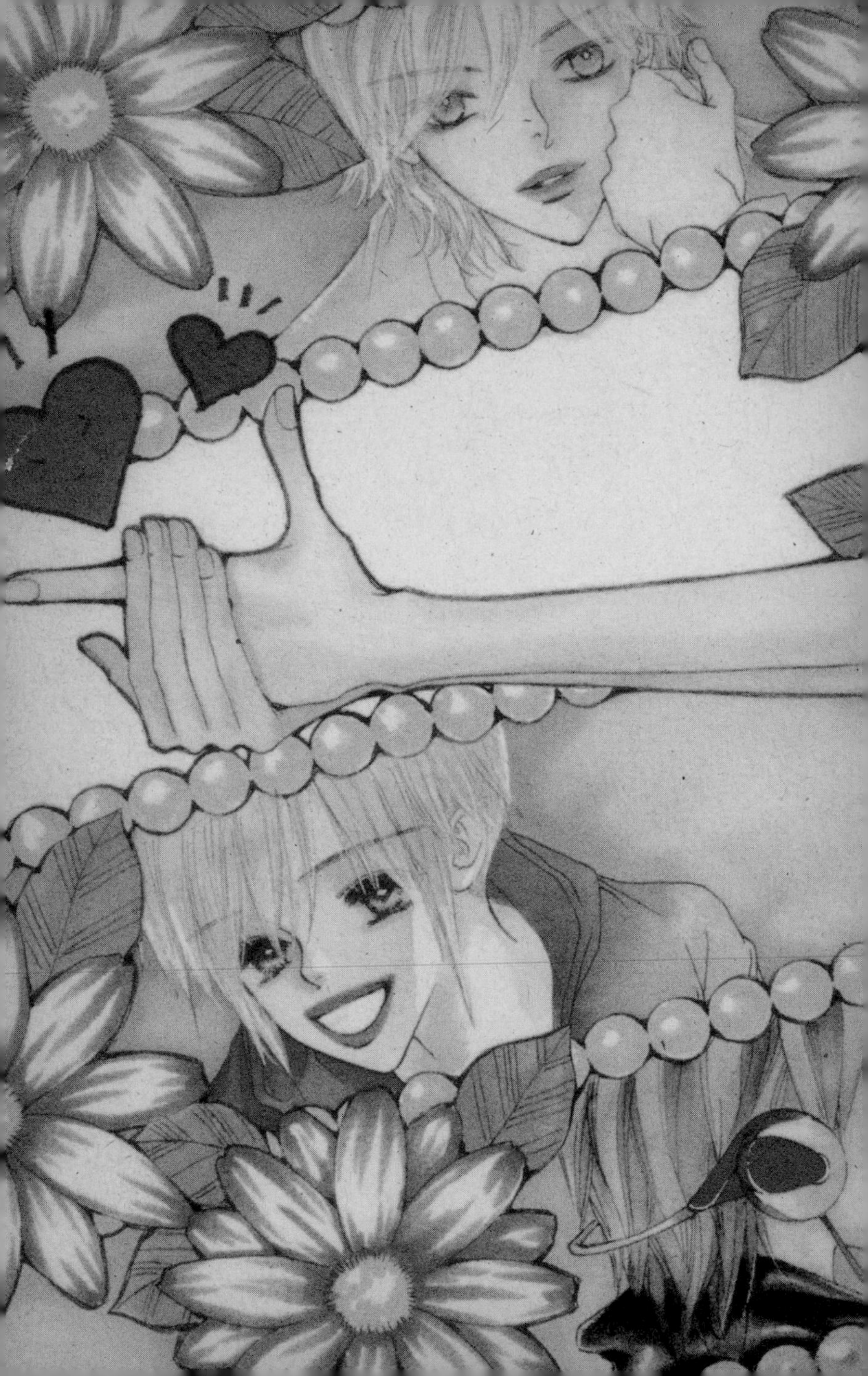

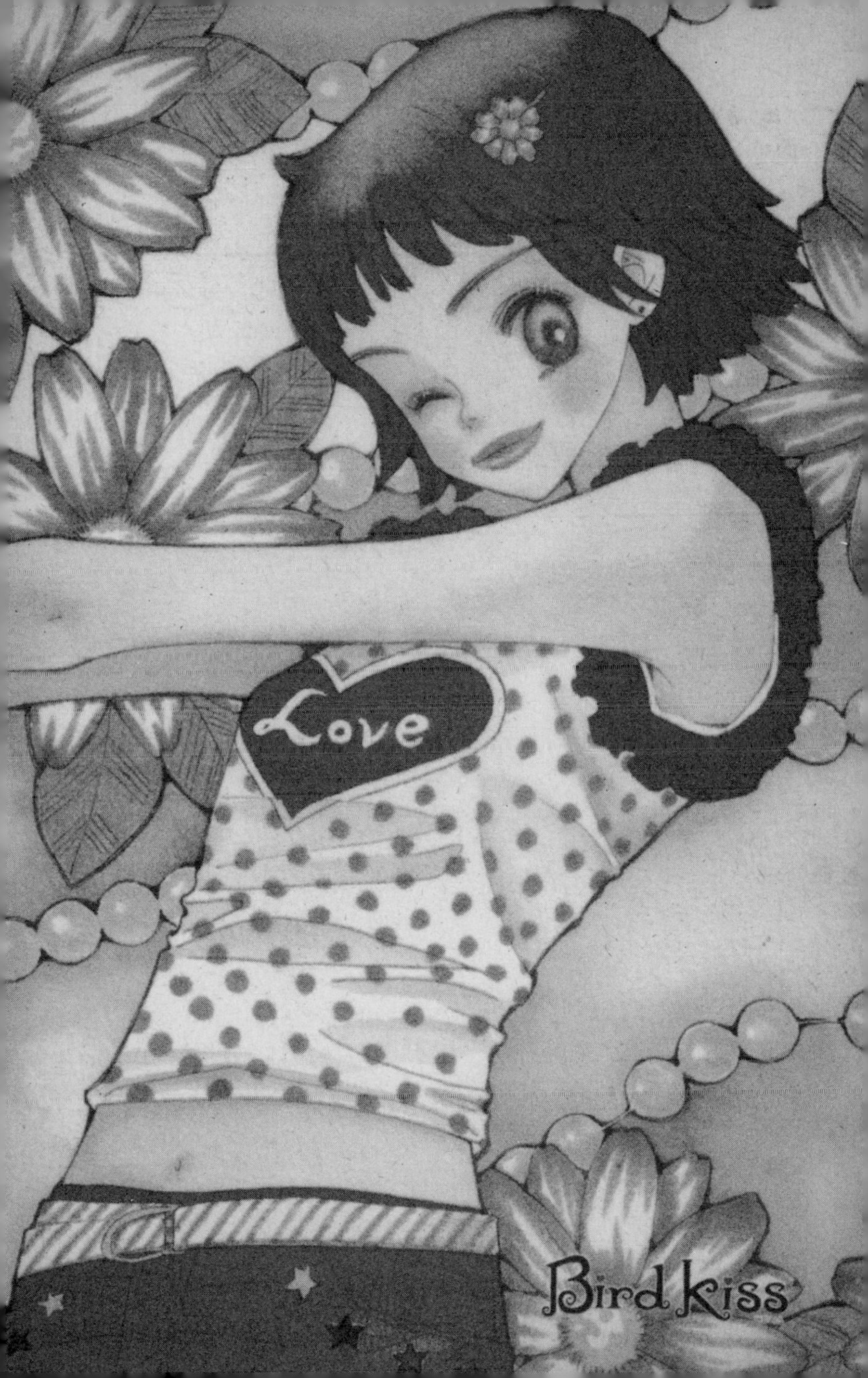
Love
Bird kiss

## *Bird Kiss Vol. 1*
## Created by Eun Ah Park

Translation - Jihae Hong
English Adaptation - Sarah Dyer
Retouch and Lettering - Mike Graniel
Production Artist - Bowen Park
Cover Design - Louis Csontos

Editor - Hope Donovan
Digital Imaging Manager - Chris Buford
Production Manager - Elisabeth Brizzi
Managing Editor - Sheldon Drzka
VP of Production - Ron Klamert
Editor-in-Chief - Rob Tokar
Publisher - Mike Kiley
President and C.O.O. - John Parker
C.E.O. and Chief Creative Officer - Stuart Levy

A  Manga

TOKYOPOP Inc.
5900 Wilshire Blvd. Suite 2000
Los Angeles, CA 90036

E-mail: info@TOKYOPOP.com
Come visit us online at www.TOKYOPOP.com

ISBN: 1-59816-491-0

First TOKYOPOP printing: August 2006
10 9 8 7 6 5 4 3 2 1
Printed in the USA

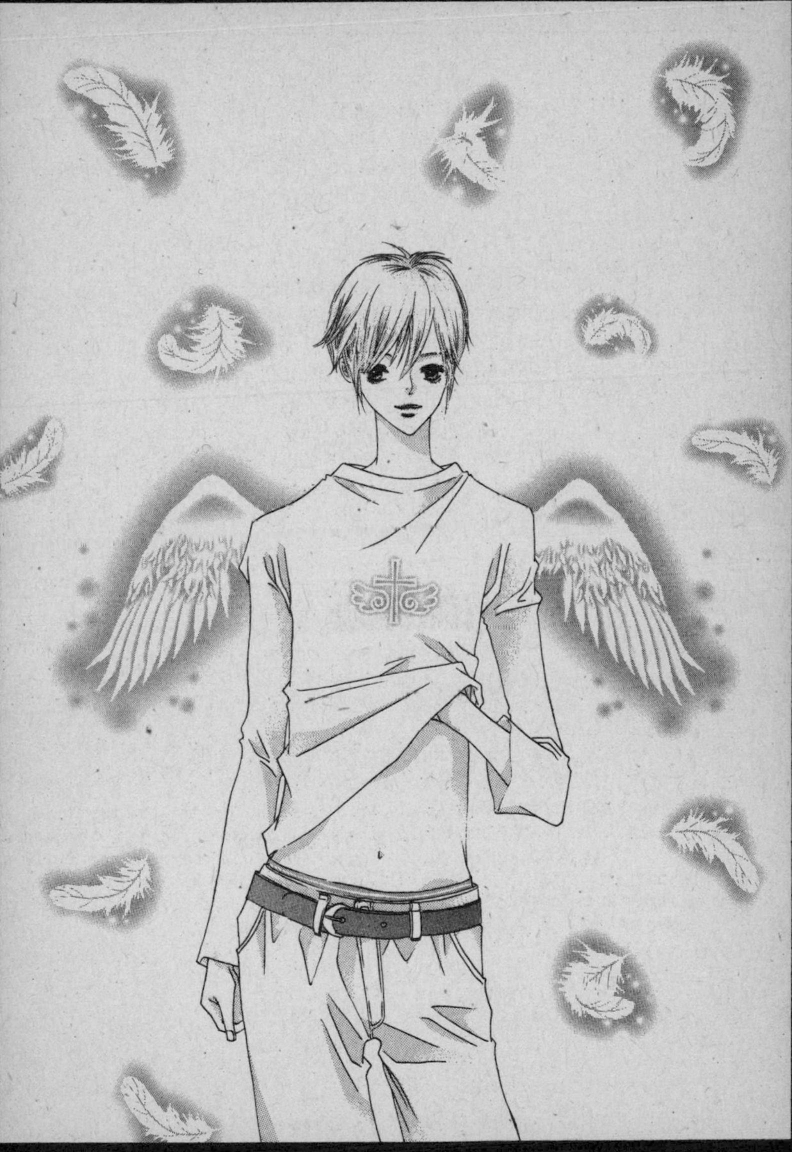

BIRD KISS 1

EUN AH PARK

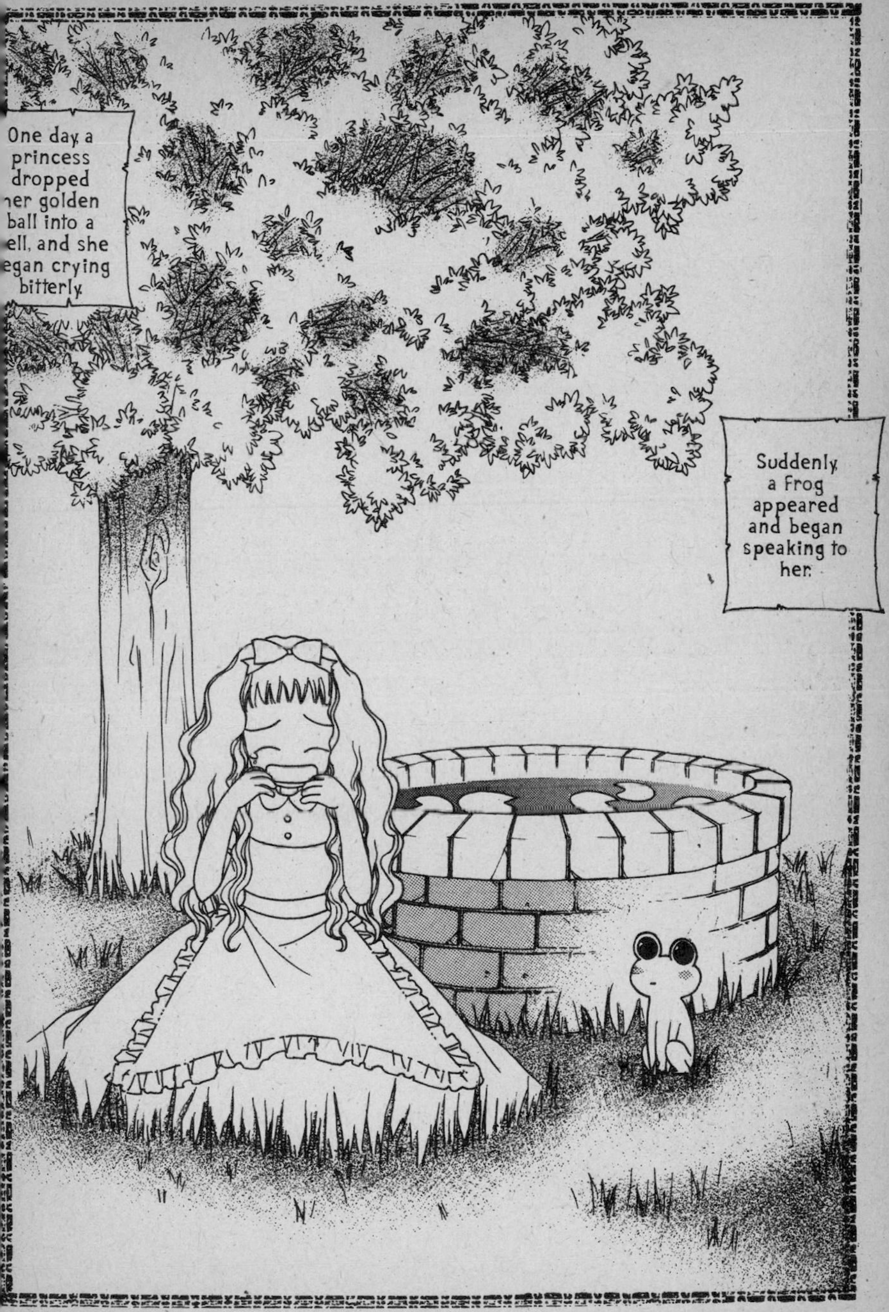
One day, a princess dropped ner golden ball into a ell, and she egan crying bitterly.
Suddenly, a Frog appeared and began speaking to her.

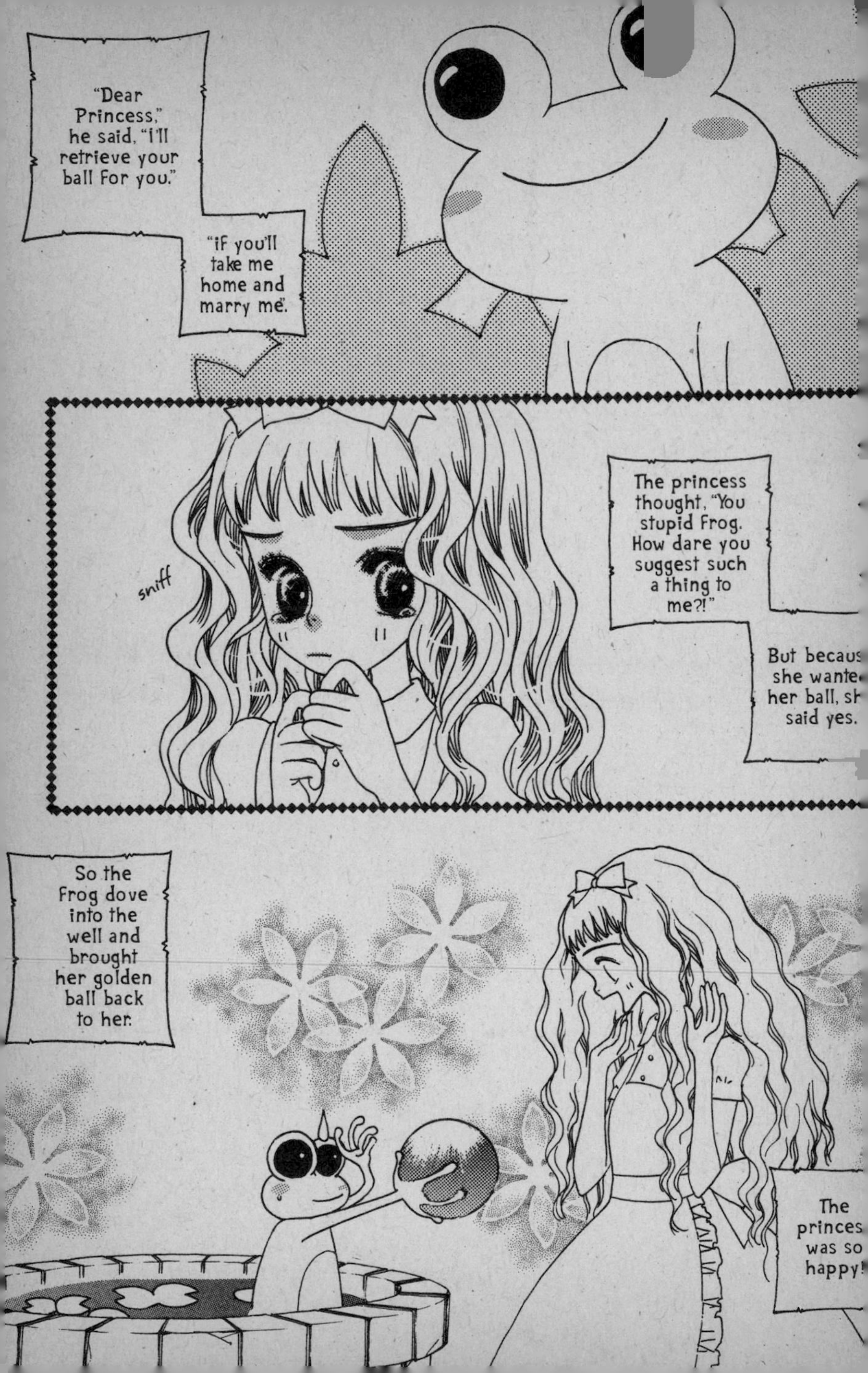
"Dear Princess," he said, "I'll retrieve your ball for you."
"if you'll take me home and marry me."
sniff
The princess thought, "You stupid frog. How dare you suggest such a thing to me?!"
But becaus she wante her ball, sh said yes.
So the frog dove into the well and brought her golden ball back to her.
The princes was so happy!

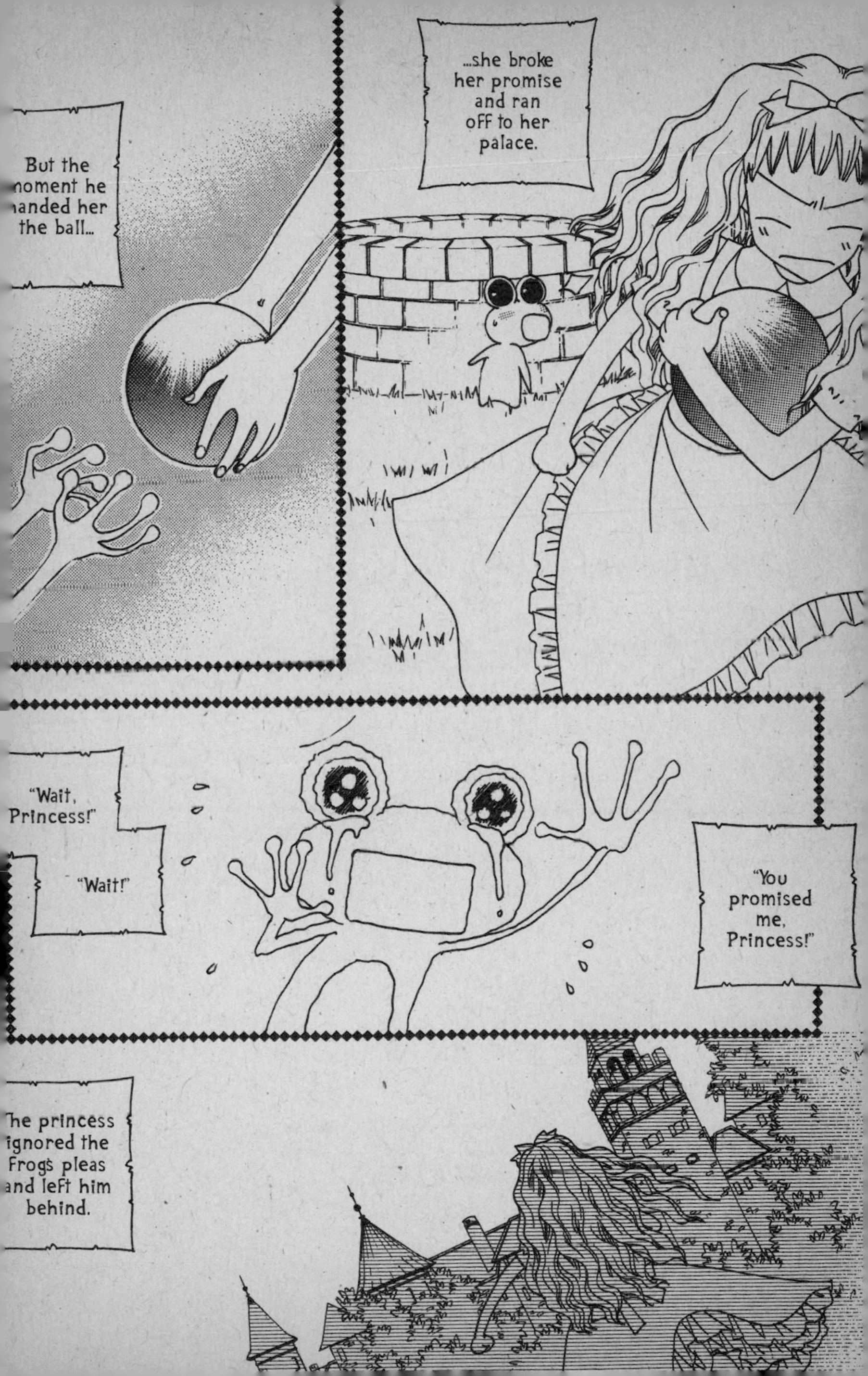
But the noment he anded her the ball...
...she broke her promise and ran off to her palace.
"Wait, Princess!"
"Wait!"
"You promised me, Princess!"
he princess ignored the Frog's pleas nd left him behind.

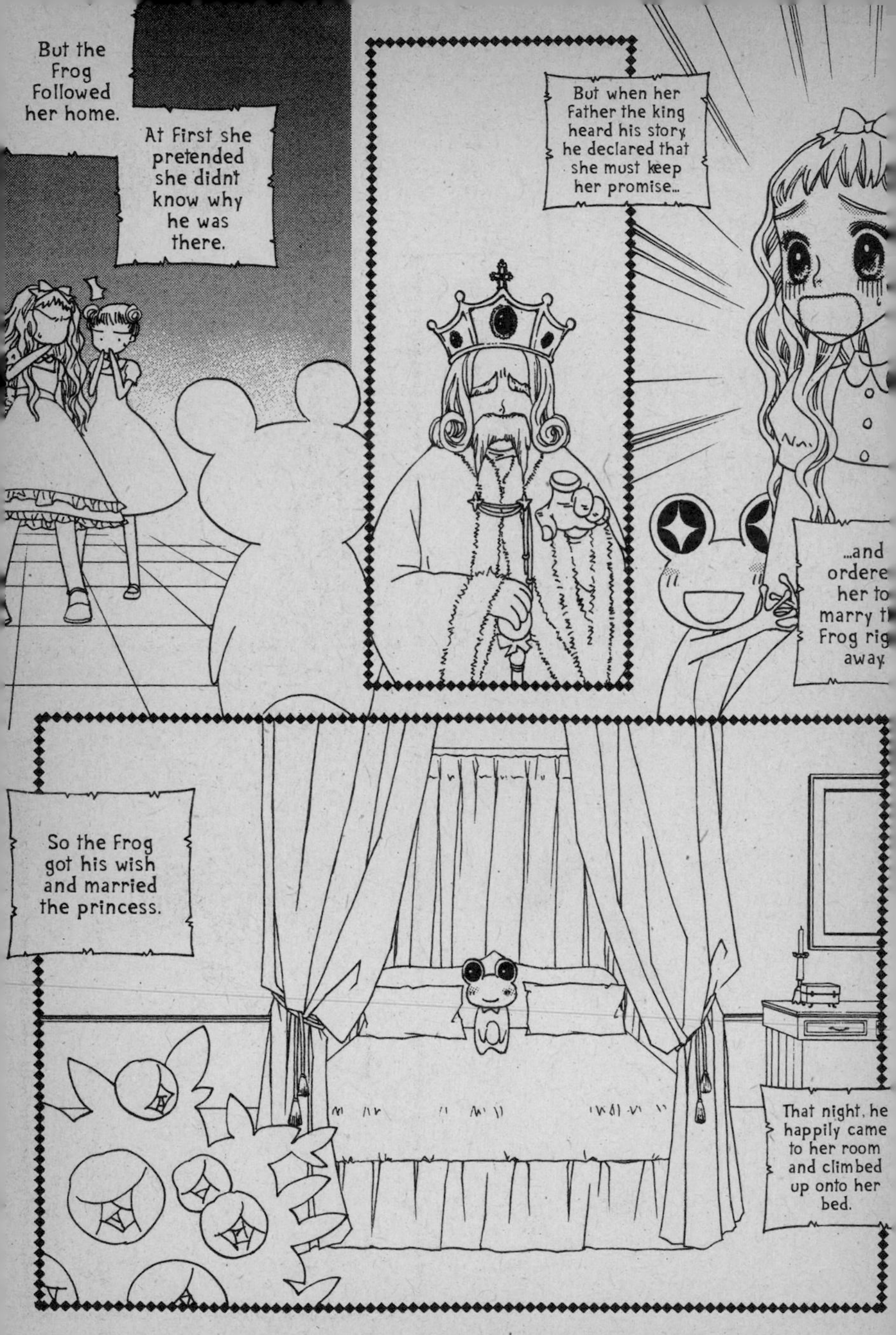
But the Frog Followed her home.
At First she pretended she didn't know why he was there.
But when her Father the king heard his story, he declared that she must keep her promise...
...and ordere her to marry t Frog rig away.
So the Frog got his wish and married the princess.
That night, he happily came to her room and climbed up onto her bed.

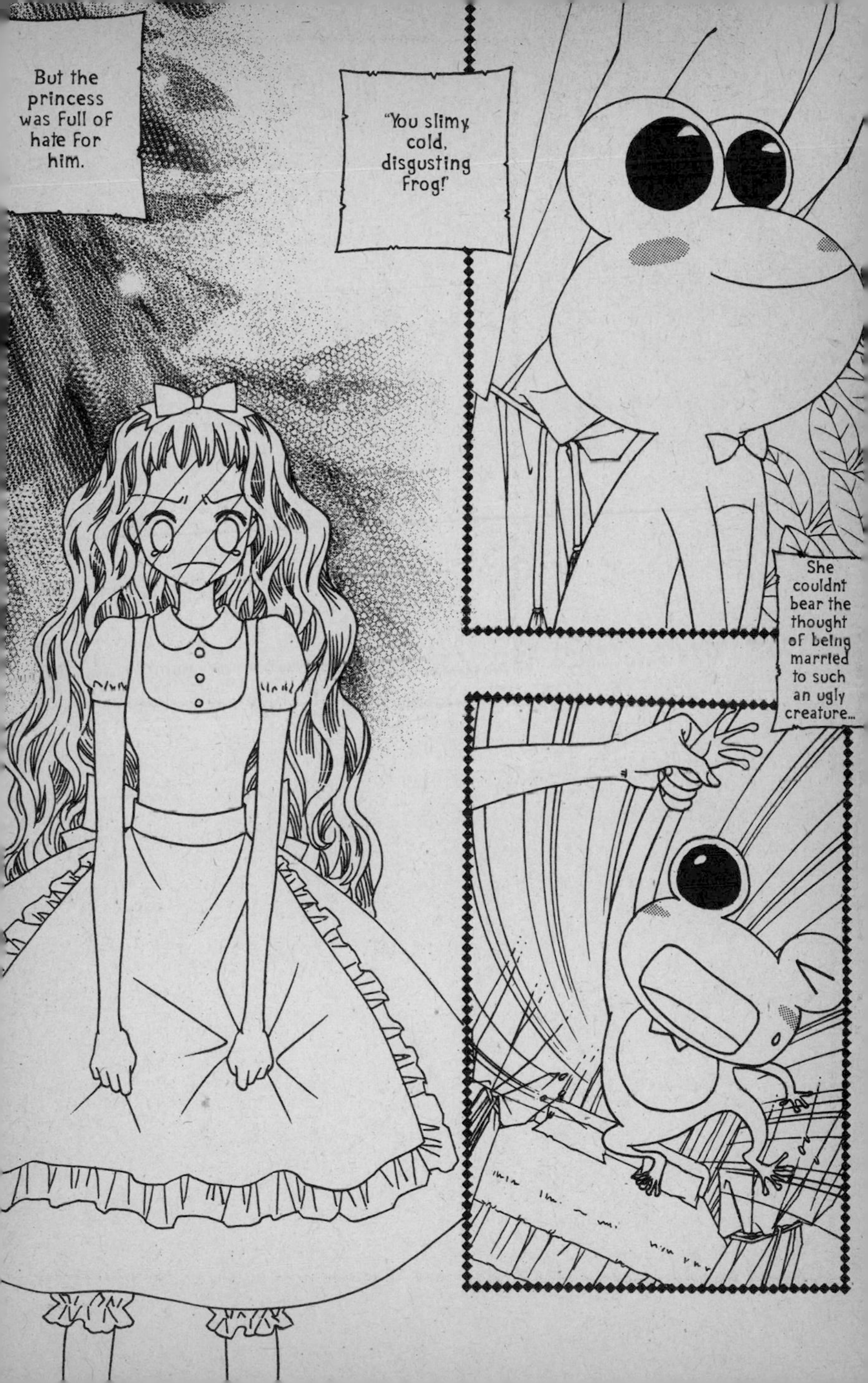
But the princess was Full of hate For him.
"You slimy, cold, disgusting Frog!"
She couldnt bear the thought of being married to such an ugly creature...

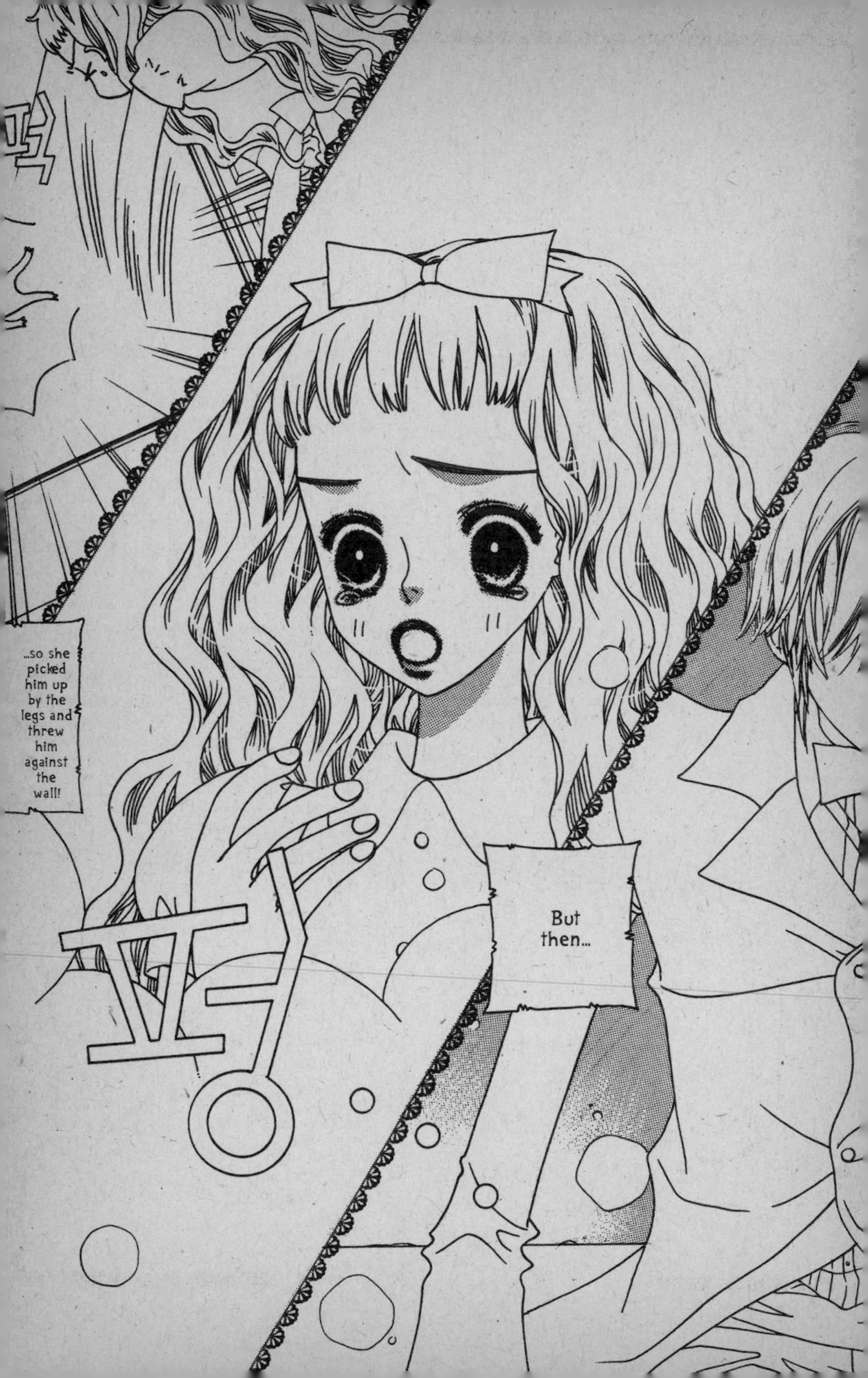
...so she picked him up by the legs and threw him against the wall!
But then...

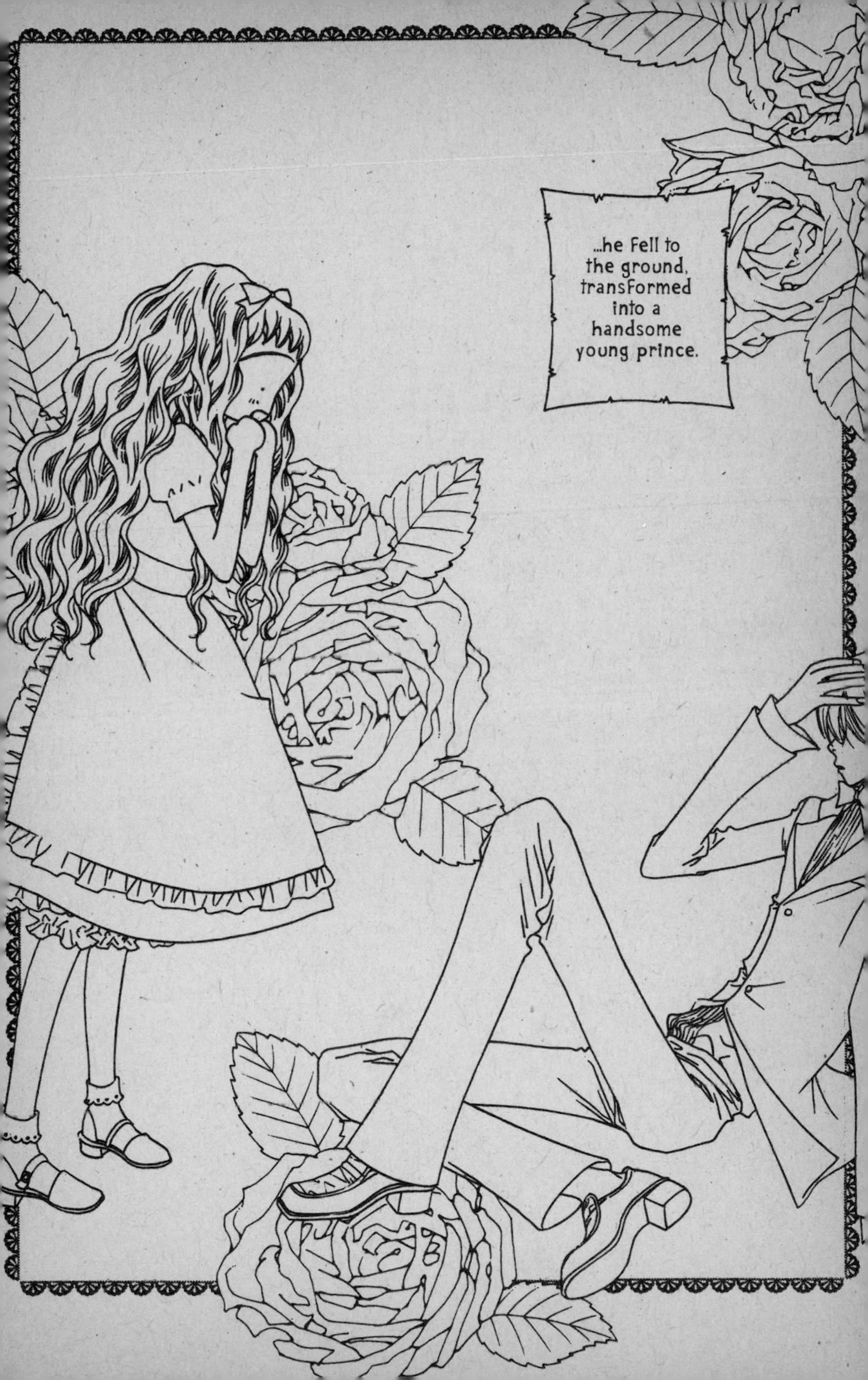
...he fell to the ground, transformed into a handsome young prince.

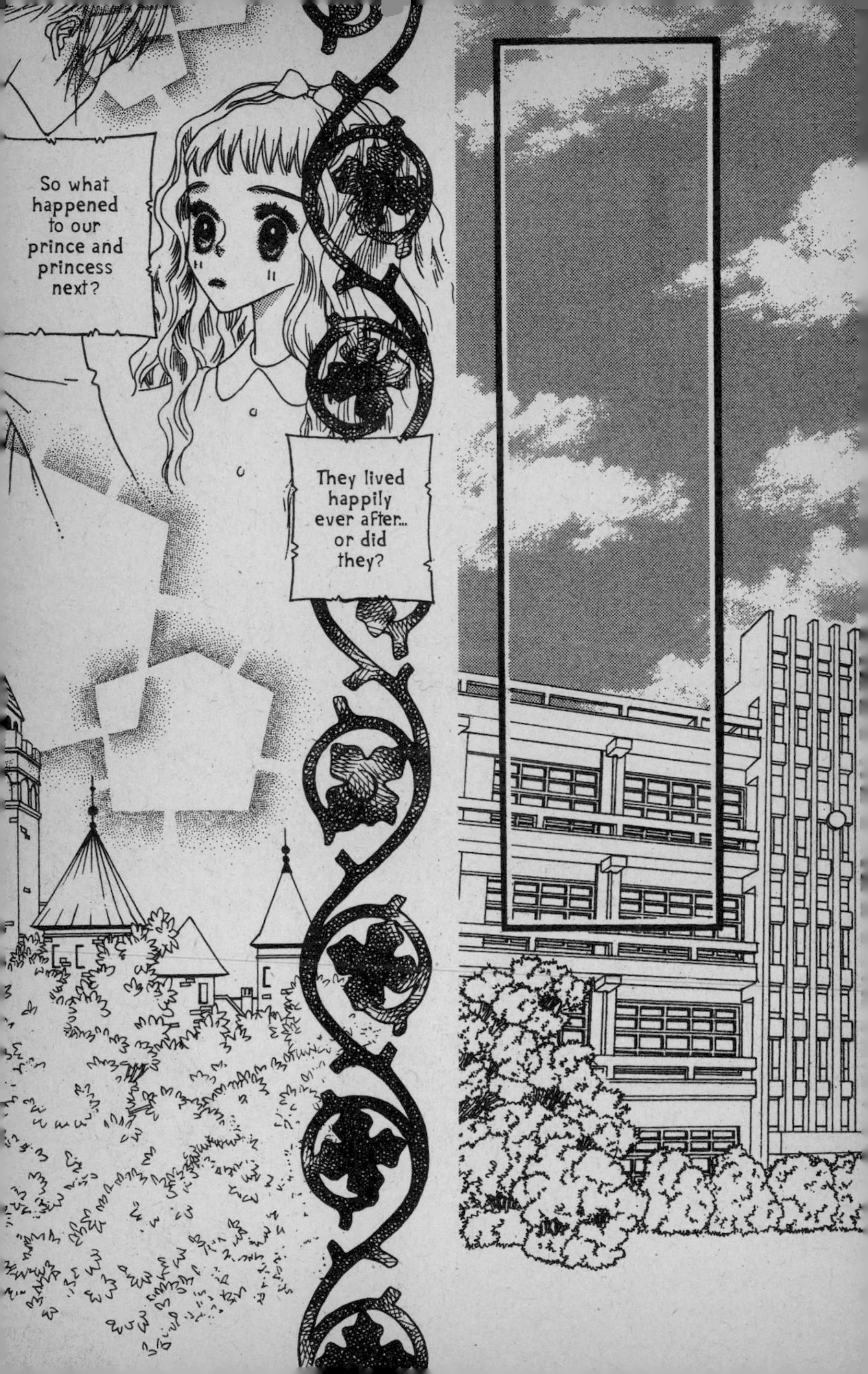
So what happened to our prince and princess next?
They lived happily ever after... or did they?

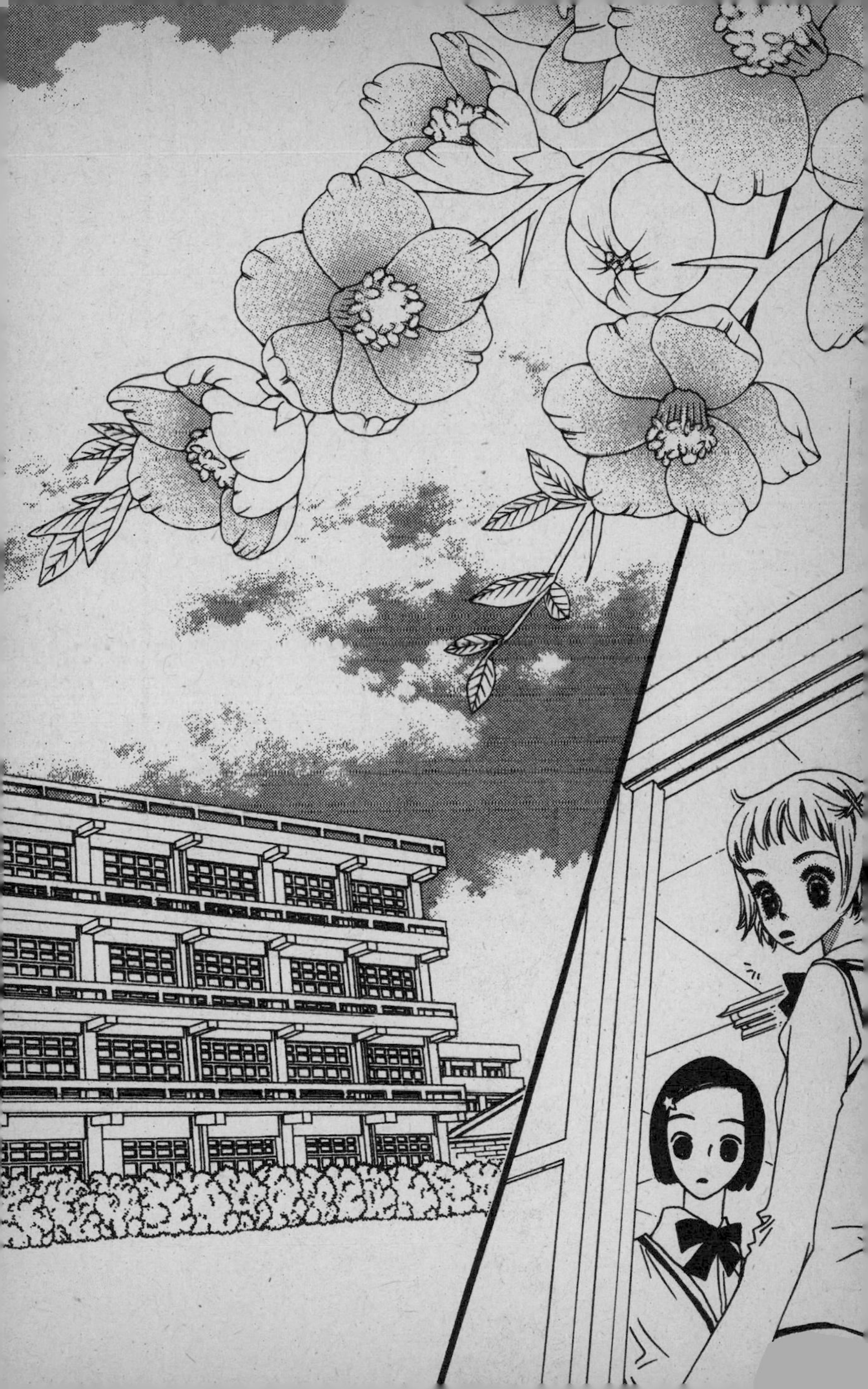

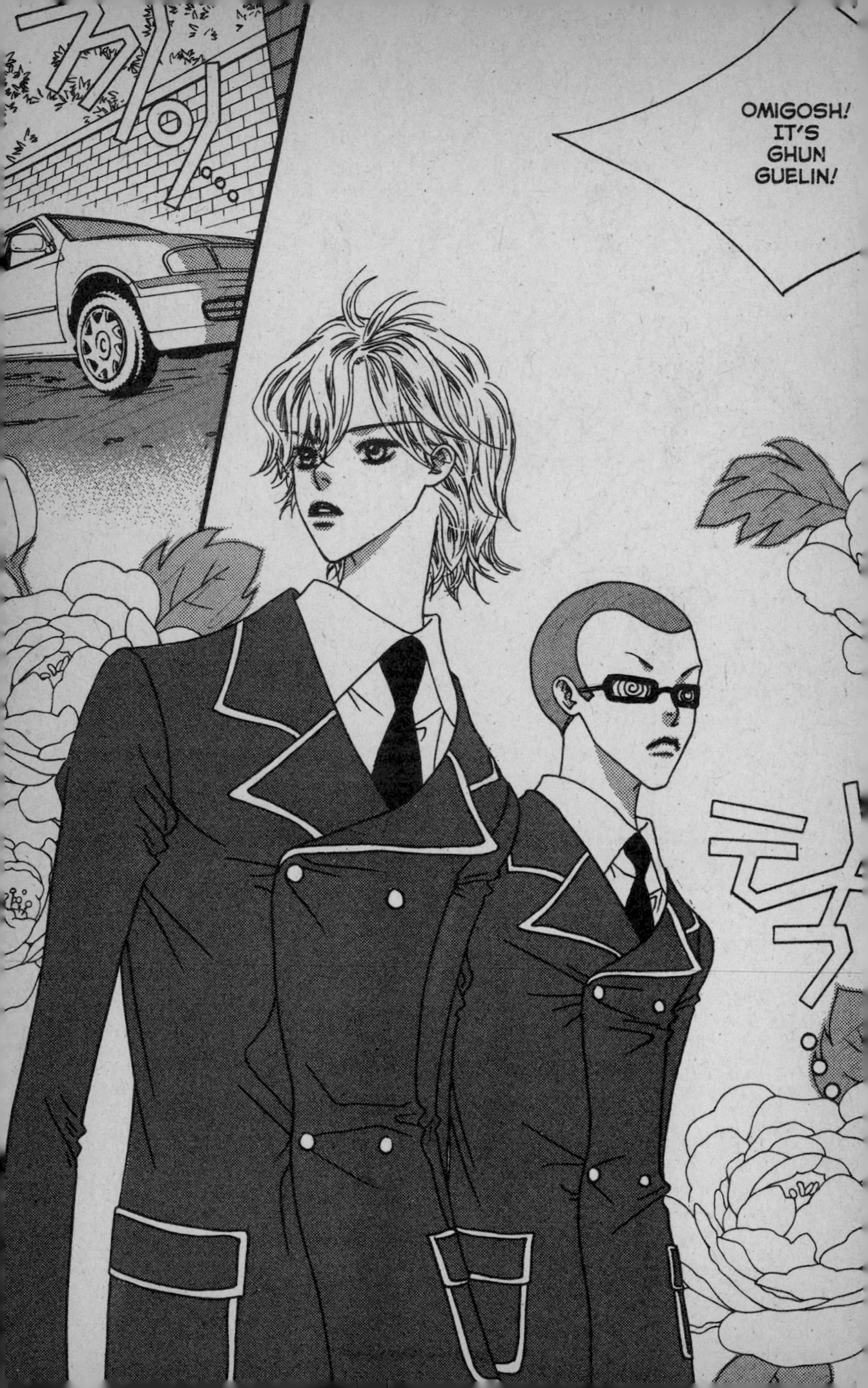
OMIGOSH! IT'S GHUN GUELIN!

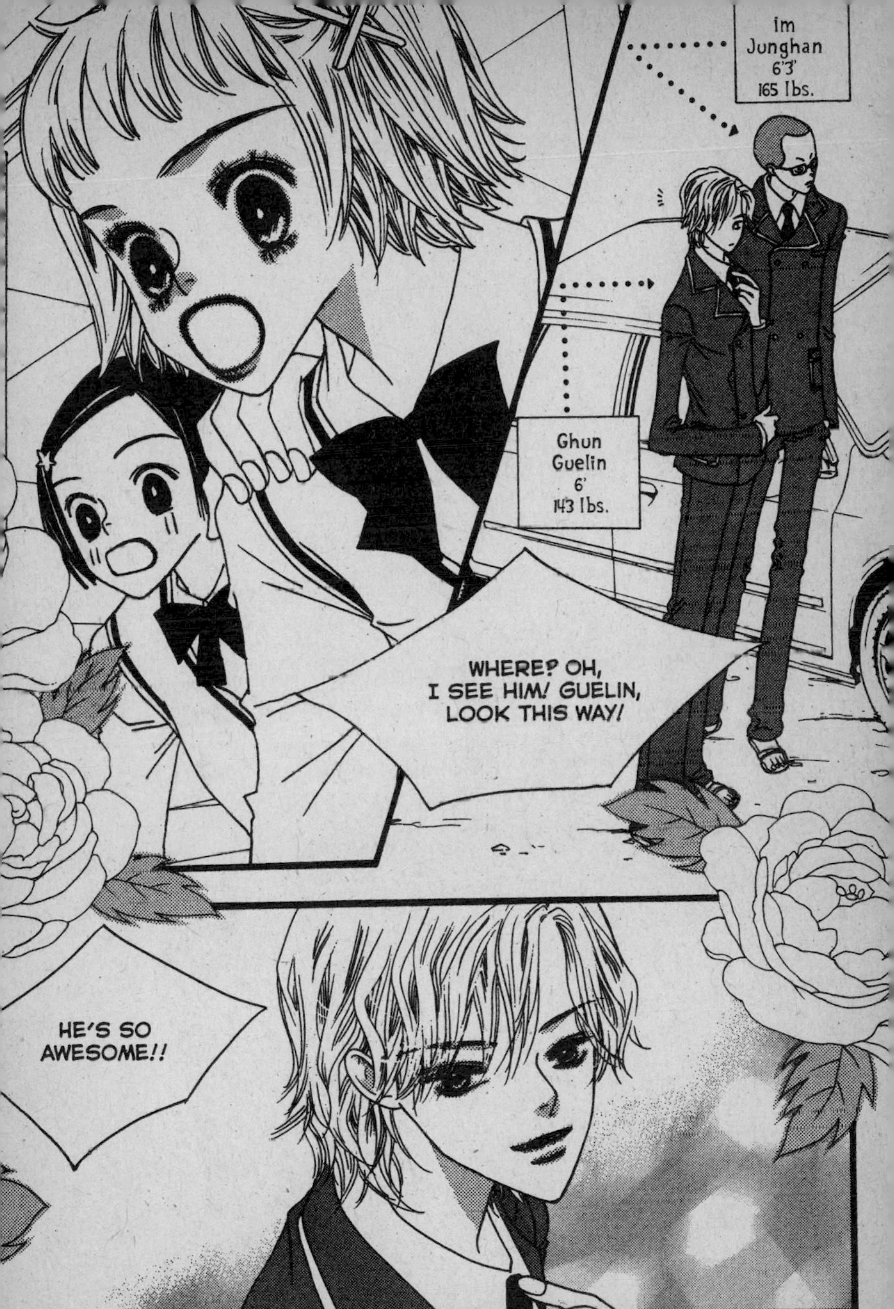
im
Junghan
6'3'
165 lbs.
Ghun
Guelin
6'
143 lbs.
WHERE? OH, I SEE HIM! GUELIN, LOOK THIS WAY!
HE'S SO AWESOME!!

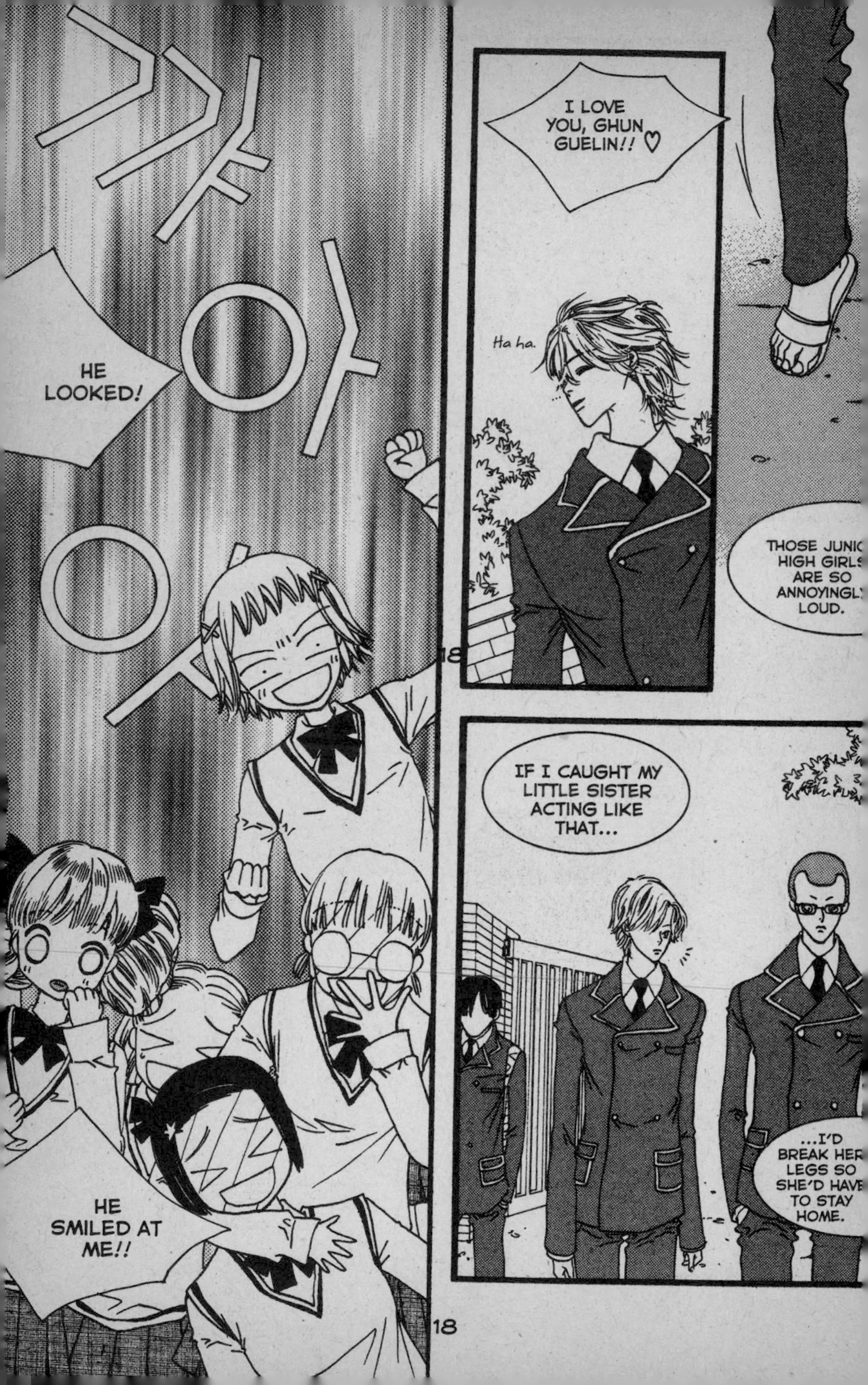

HE LOOKED!
HE SMILED AT ME!!
I LOVE YOU, GHUN GUELIN!! ♡
Ha ha.
THOSE JUNIO HIGH GIRLS ARE SO ANNOYINGLY LOUD.
IF I CAUGHT MY LITTLE SISTER ACTING LIKE THAT...
...I'D BREAK HER LEGS SO SHE'D HAVE TO STAY HOME.

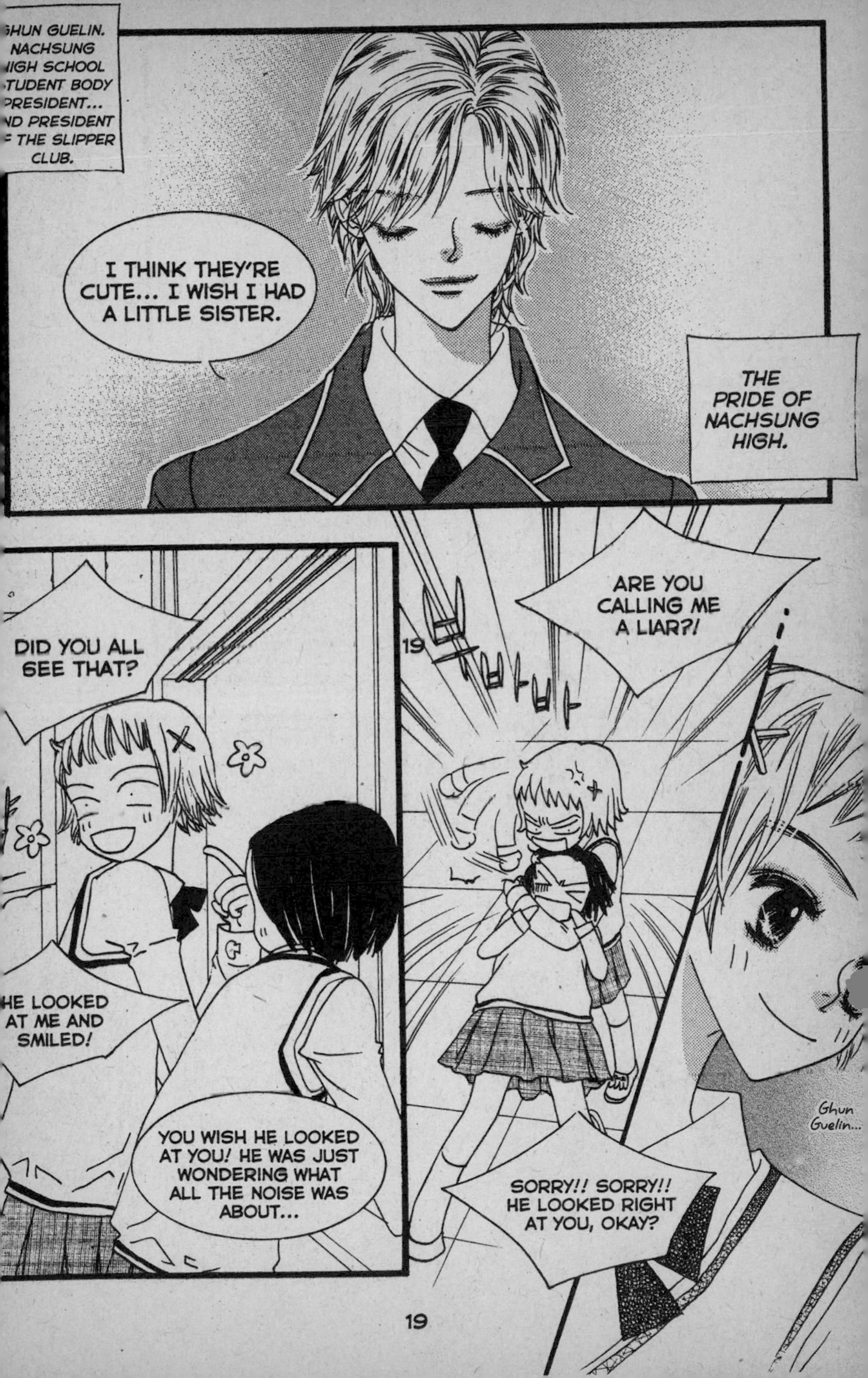
HUN GUELIN. NACHSUNG IGH SCHOOL TUDENT BODY PRESIDENT... ND PRESIDENT THE SLIPPER CLUB.
I THINK THEY'RE CUTE... I WISH I HAD A LITTLE SISTER.
THE PRIDE OF NACHSUNG HIGH.
DID YOU ALL SEE THAT?
HE LOOKED AT ME AND SMILED!
YOU WISH HE LOOKED AT YOU! HE WAS JUST WONDERING WHAT ALL THE NOISE WAS ABOUT...
ARE YOU CALLING ME A LIAR?!
SORRY!! SORRY!! HE LOOKED RIGHT AT YOU, OKAY?
Ghun Guelin...

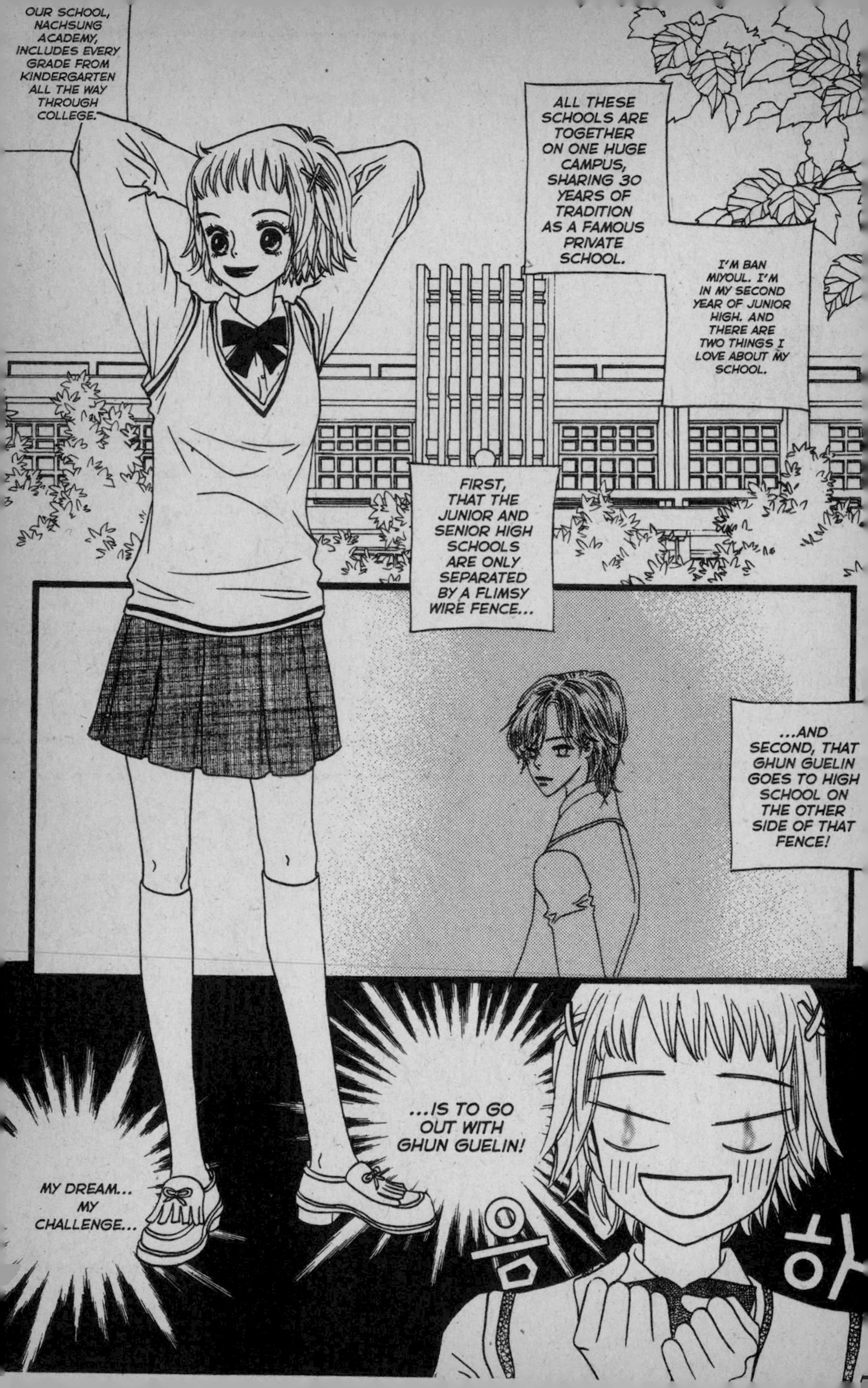
OUR SCHOOL, NACHSUNG ACADEMY, INCLUDES EVERY GRADE FROM KINDERGARTEN ALL THE WAY THROUGH COLLEGE.
ALL THESE SCHOOLS ARE TOGETHER ON ONE HUGE CAMPUS, SHARING 30 YEARS OF TRADITION AS A FAMOUS PRIVATE SCHOOL.
I'M BAN MIYOUL. I'M IN MY SECOND YEAR OF JUNIOR HIGH. AND THERE ARE TWO THINGS I LOVE ABOUT MY SCHOOL.
FIRST, THAT THE JUNIOR AND SENIOR HIGH SCHOOLS ARE ONLY SEPARATED BY A FLIMSY WIRE FENCE...
...AND SECOND, THAT GHUN GUELIN GOES TO HIGH SCHOOL ON THE OTHER SIDE OF THAT FENCE!
MY DREAM... MY CHALLENGE...
...IS TO GO OUT WITH GHUN GUELIN!

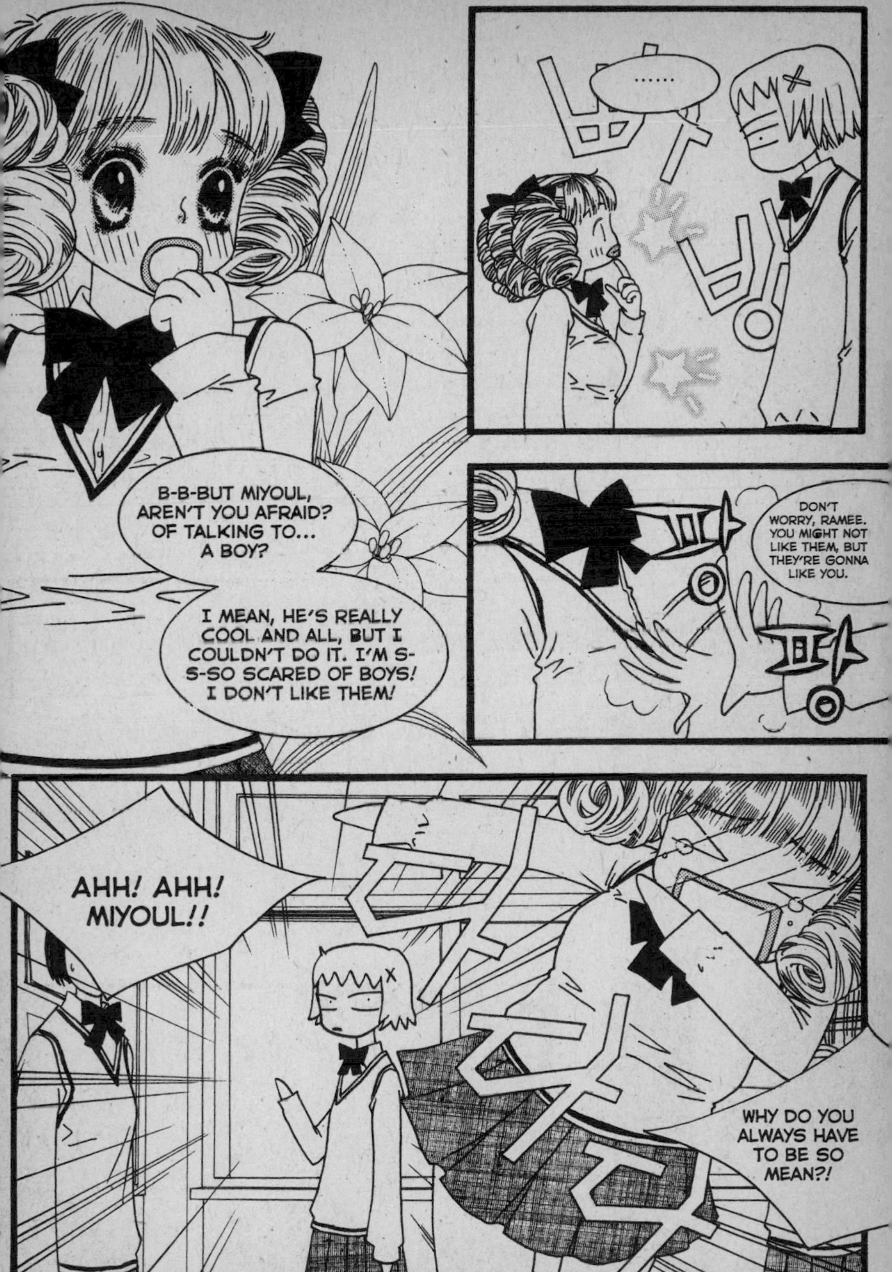
B-B-BUT MIYOUL, AREN'T YOU AFRAID? OF TALKING TO... A BOY?
I MEAN, HE'S REALLY COOL AND ALL, BUT I COULDN'T DO IT. I'M S-S-SO SCARED OF BOYS! I DON'T LIKE THEM!
......
DON'T WORRY, RAMEE. YOU MIGHT NOT LIKE THEM, BUT THEY'RE GONNA LIKE YOU.
AHH! AHH! MIYOUL!!
WHY DO YOU ALWAYS HAVE TO BE SO MEAN?!

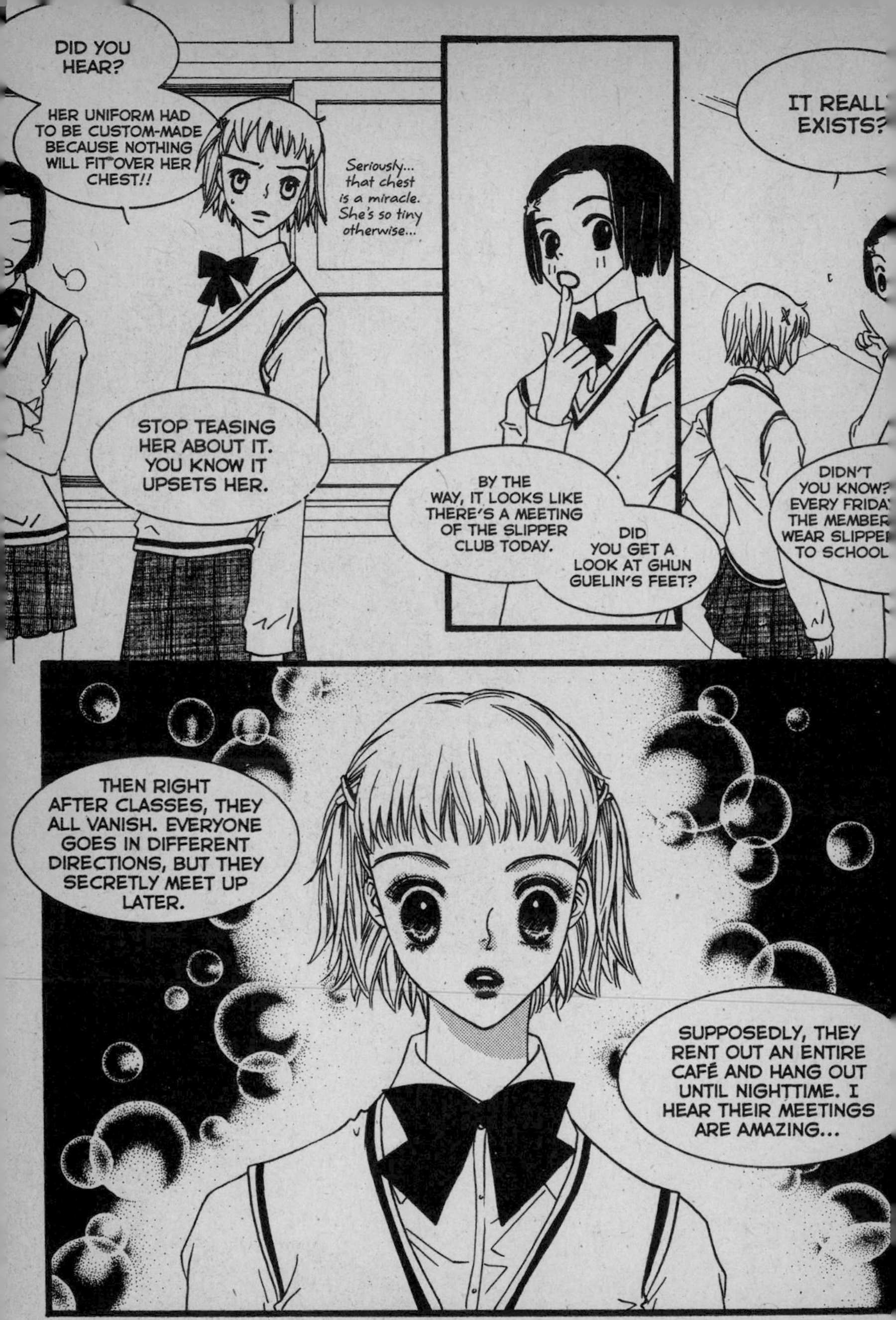
DID YOU HEAR?
HER UNIFORM HAD TO BE CUSTOM-MADE BECAUSE NOTHING WILL FIT OVER HER CHEST!!
Seriously... that chest is a miracle. She's so tiny otherwise...
STOP TEASING HER ABOUT IT. YOU KNOW IT UPSETS HER.
BY THE WAY, IT LOOKS LIKE THERE'S A MEETING OF THE SLIPPER CLUB TODAY.
DID YOU GET A LOOK AT GHUN GUELIN'S FEET?
IT REALL EXISTS?
DIDN'T YOU KNOW? EVERY FRIDA THE MEMBER WEAR SLIPPE TO SCHOOL
THEN RIGHT AFTER CLASSES, THEY ALL VANISH. EVERYONE GOES IN DIFFERENT DIRECTIONS, BUT THEY SECRETLY MEET UP LATER.
SUPPOSEDLY, THEY RENT OUT AN ENTIRE CAFÉ AND HANG OUT UNTIL NIGHTTIME. I HEAR THEIR MEETINGS ARE AMAZING...

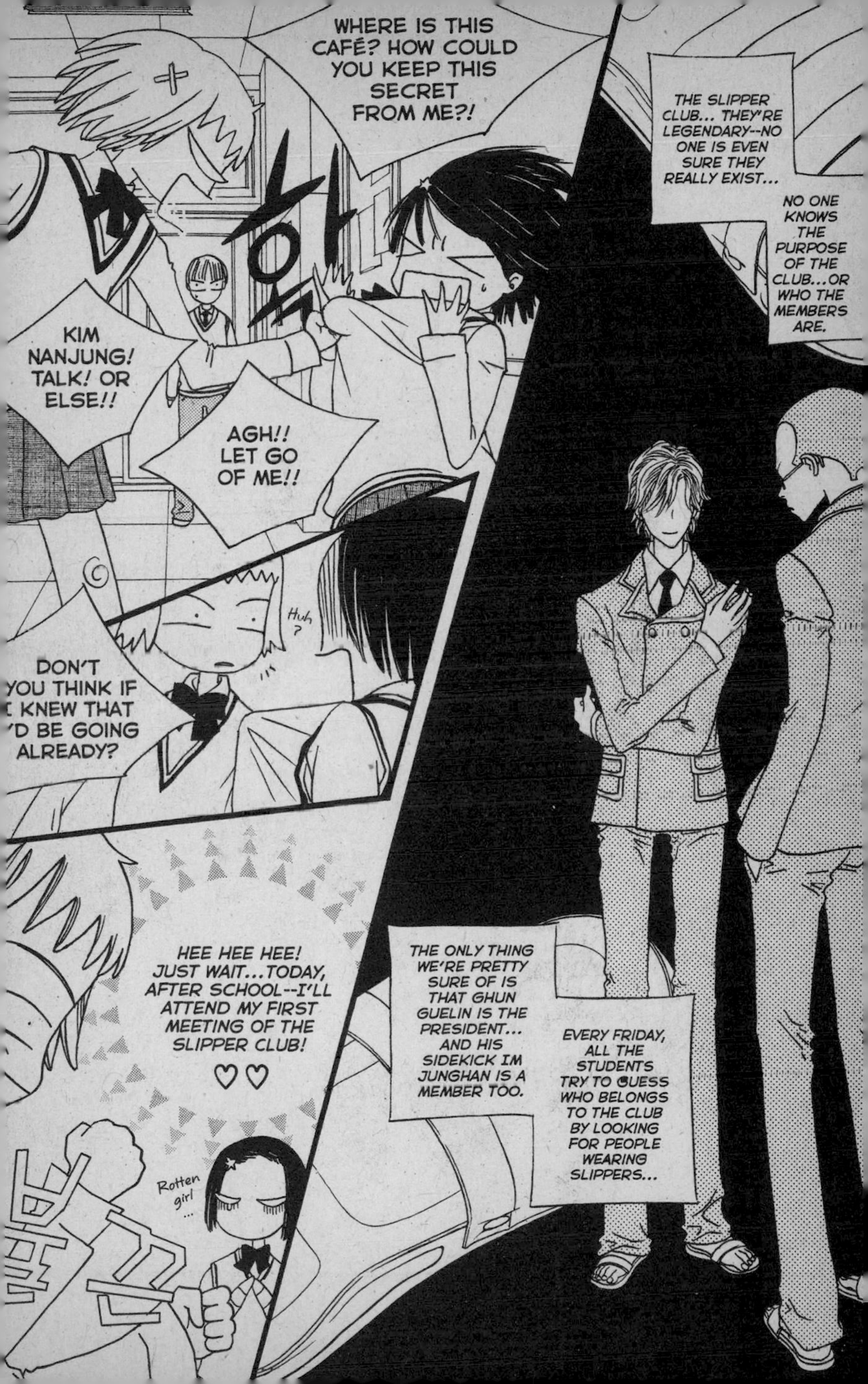
WHERE IS THIS CAFÉ? HOW COULD YOU KEEP THIS SECRET FROM ME?!
KIM NANJUNG! TALK! OR ELSE!!
AGH!! LET GO OF ME!!
Huh ?
DON'T YOU THINK IF I KNEW THAT I'D BE GOING ALREADY?
HEE HEE HEE! JUST WAIT...TODAY, AFTER SCHOOL--I'LL ATTEND MY FIRST MEETING OF THE SLIPPER CLUB! ♡♡
Rotten girl ...
THE SLIPPER CLUB... THEY'RE LEGENDARY--NO ONE IS EVEN SURE THEY REALLY EXIST...
NO ONE KNOWS THE PURPOSE OF THE CLUB...OR WHO THE MEMBERS ARE.
THE ONLY THING WE'RE PRETTY SURE OF IS THAT GHUN GUELIN IS THE PRESIDENT... AND HIS SIDEKICK IM JUNGHAN IS A MEMBER TOO.
EVERY FRIDAY, ALL THE STUDENTS TRY TO GUESS WHO BELONGS TO THE CLUB BY LOOKING FOR PEOPLE WEARING SLIPPERS...

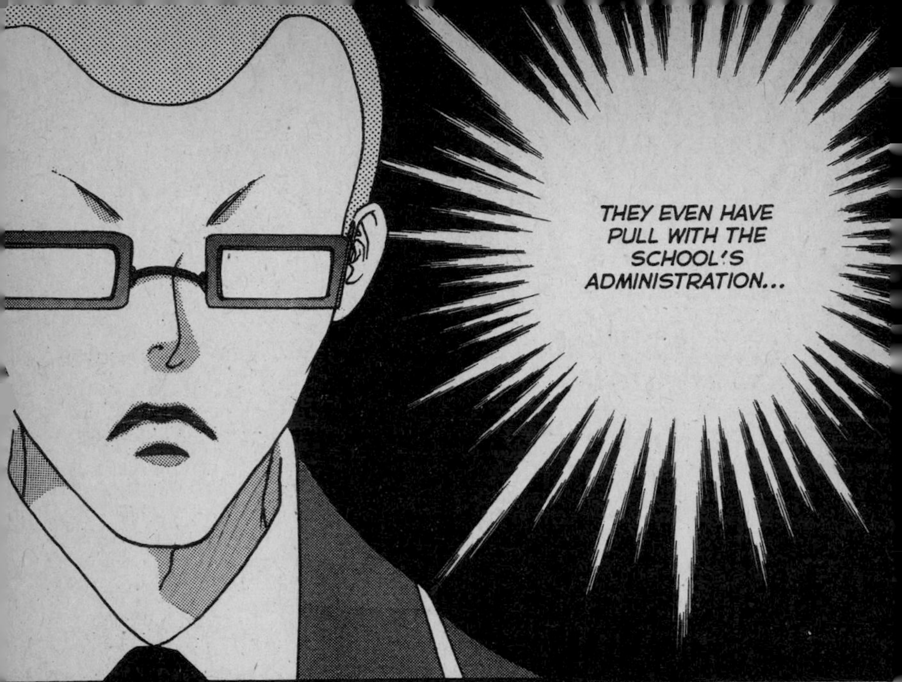
THEY EVEN HAVE PULL WITH THE SCHOOL'S ADMINISTRATION...

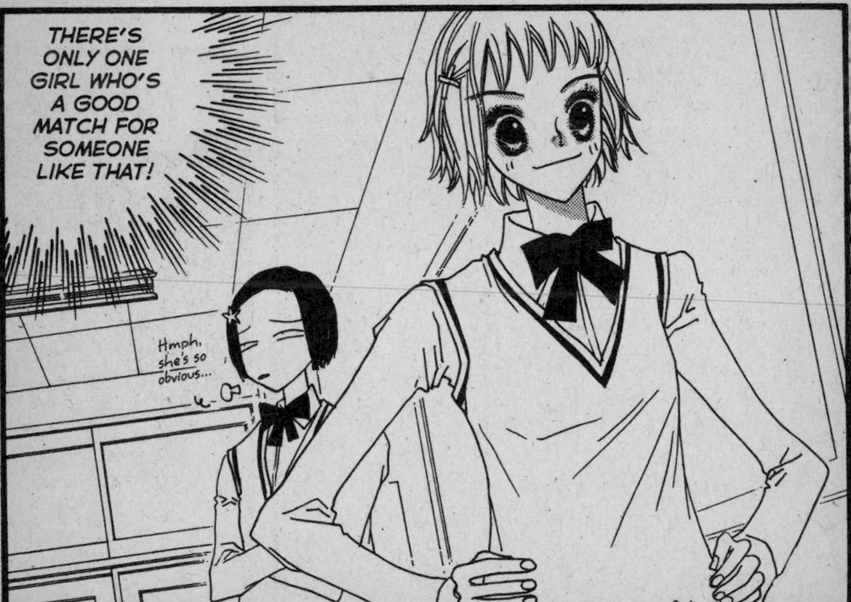
THERE'S ONLY ONE GIRL WHO'S A GOOD MATCH FOR SOMEONE LIKE THAT!
Hmph, she's so obvious...

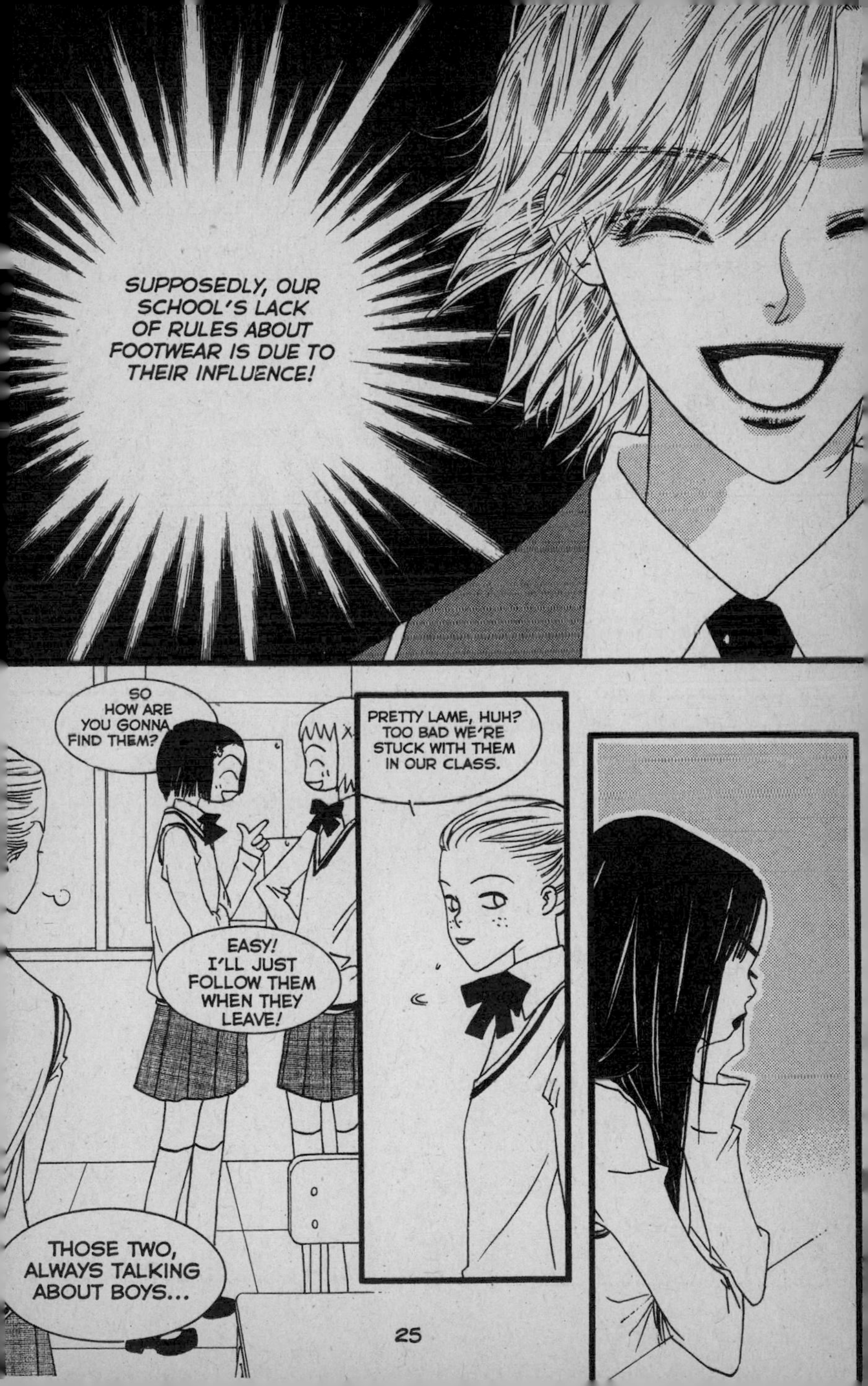
SUPPOSEDLY, OUR SCHOOL'S LACK OF RULES ABOUT FOOTWEAR IS DUE TO THEIR INFLUENCE!
SO HOW ARE YOU GONNA FIND THEM?
EASY! I'LL JUST FOLLOW THEM WHEN THEY LEAVE!
THOSE TWO, ALWAYS TALKING ABOUT BOYS...
PRETTY LAME, HUH? TOO BAD WE'RE STUCK WITH THEM IN OUR CLASS.

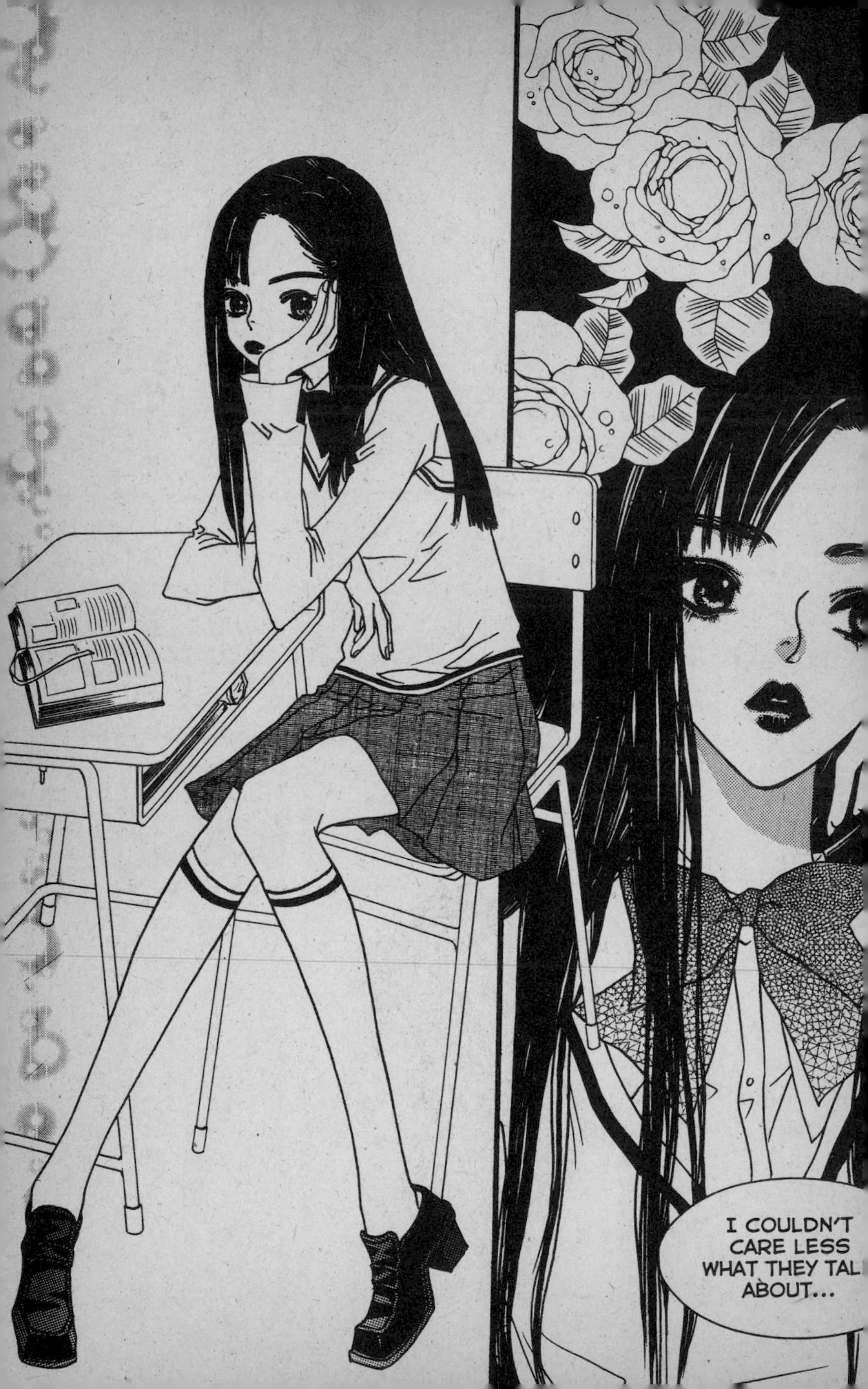
I COULDN'T CARE LESS WHAT THEY TAL ABOUT...

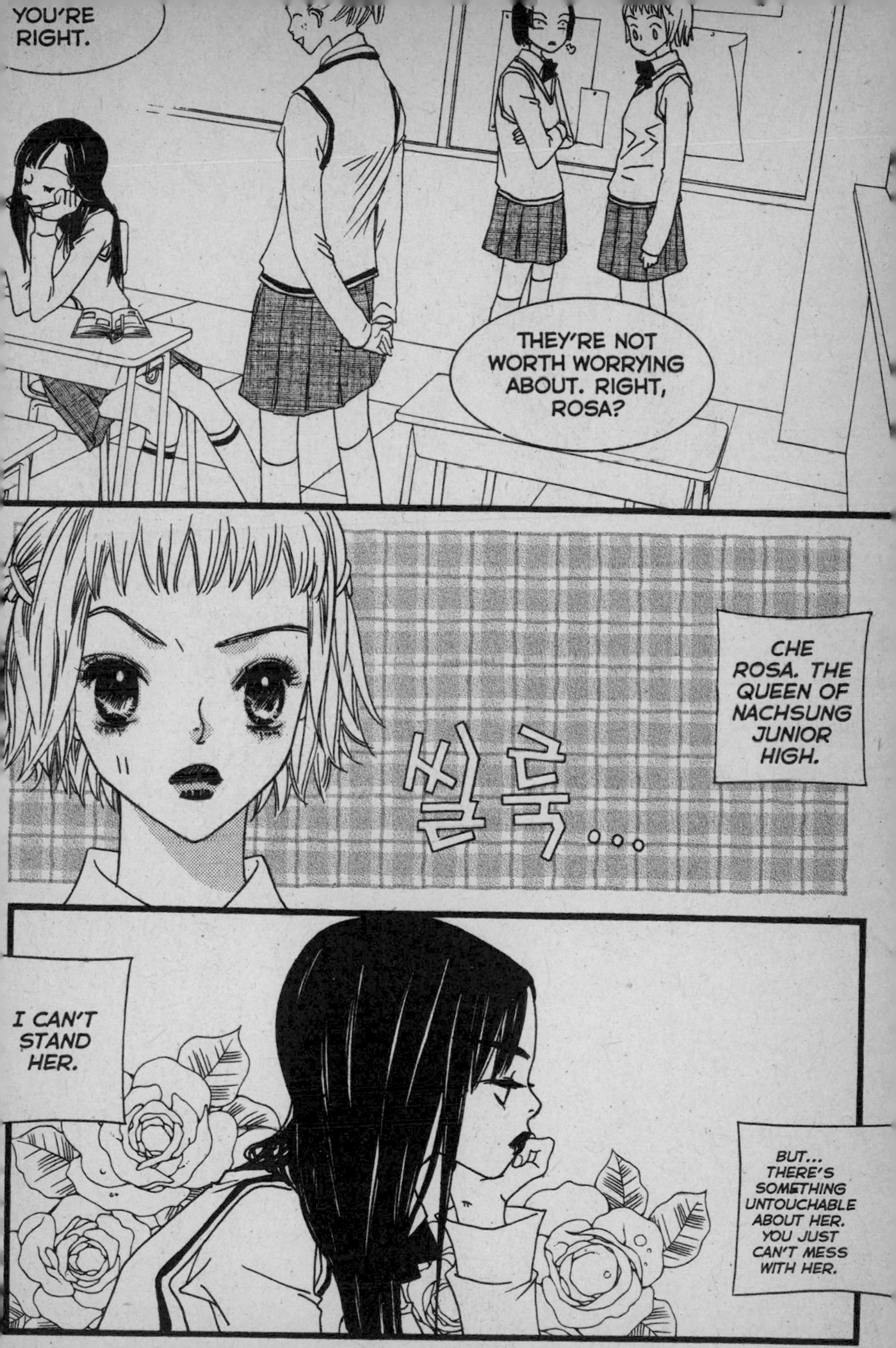
YOU'RE RIGHT.
THEY'RE NOT WORTH WORRYING ABOUT. RIGHT, ROSA?
CHE ROSA. THE QUEEN OF NACHSUNG JUNIOR HIGH.
I CAN'T STAND HER.
BUT... THERE'S SOMETHING UNTOUCHABLE ABOUT HER. YOU JUST CAN'T MESS WITH HER.

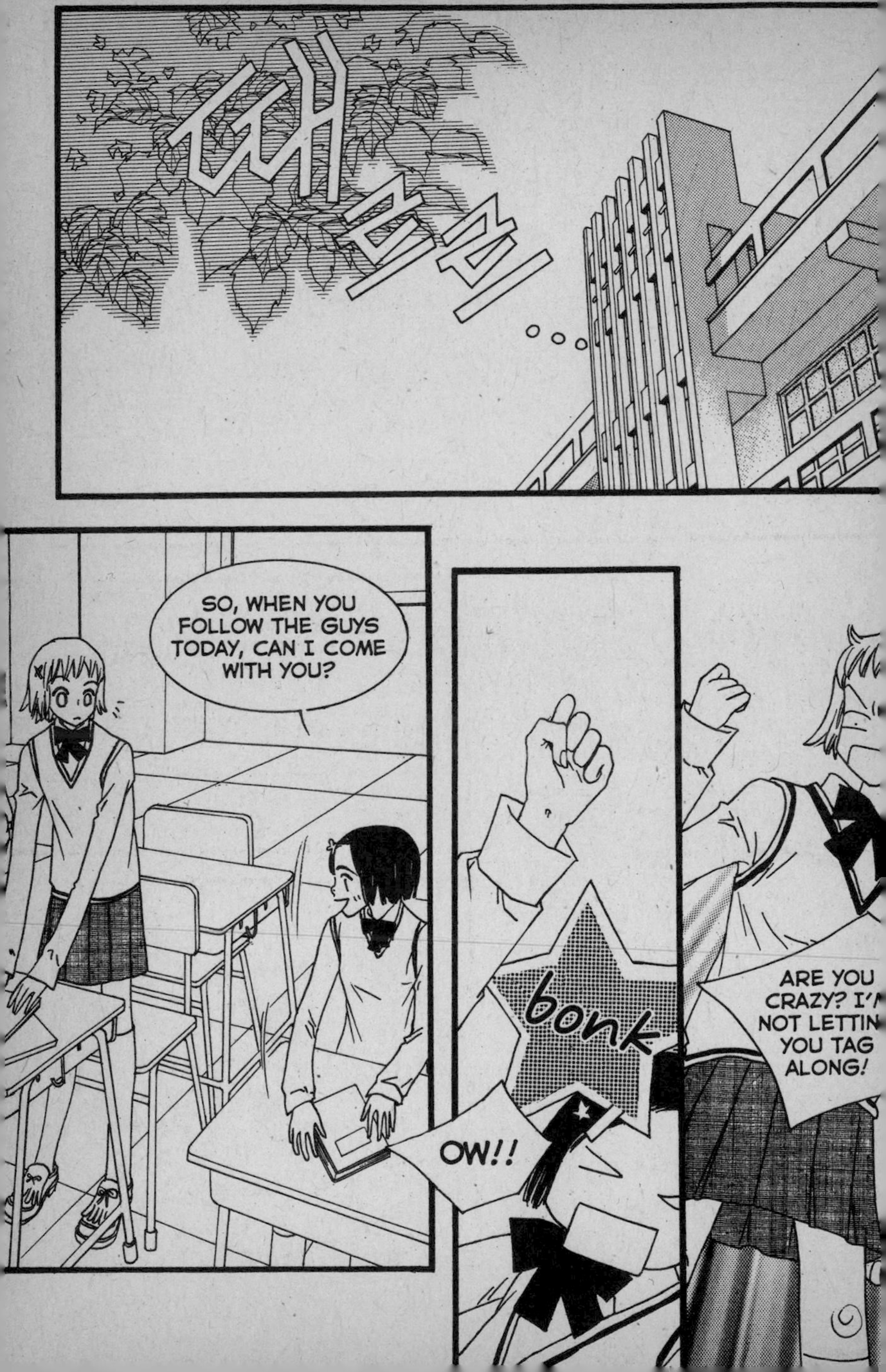
SO, WHEN YOU FOLLOW THE GUYS TODAY, CAN I COME WITH YOU?
bonk
OW!!
ARE YOU CRAZY? I'M NOT LETTIN YOU TAG ALONG!

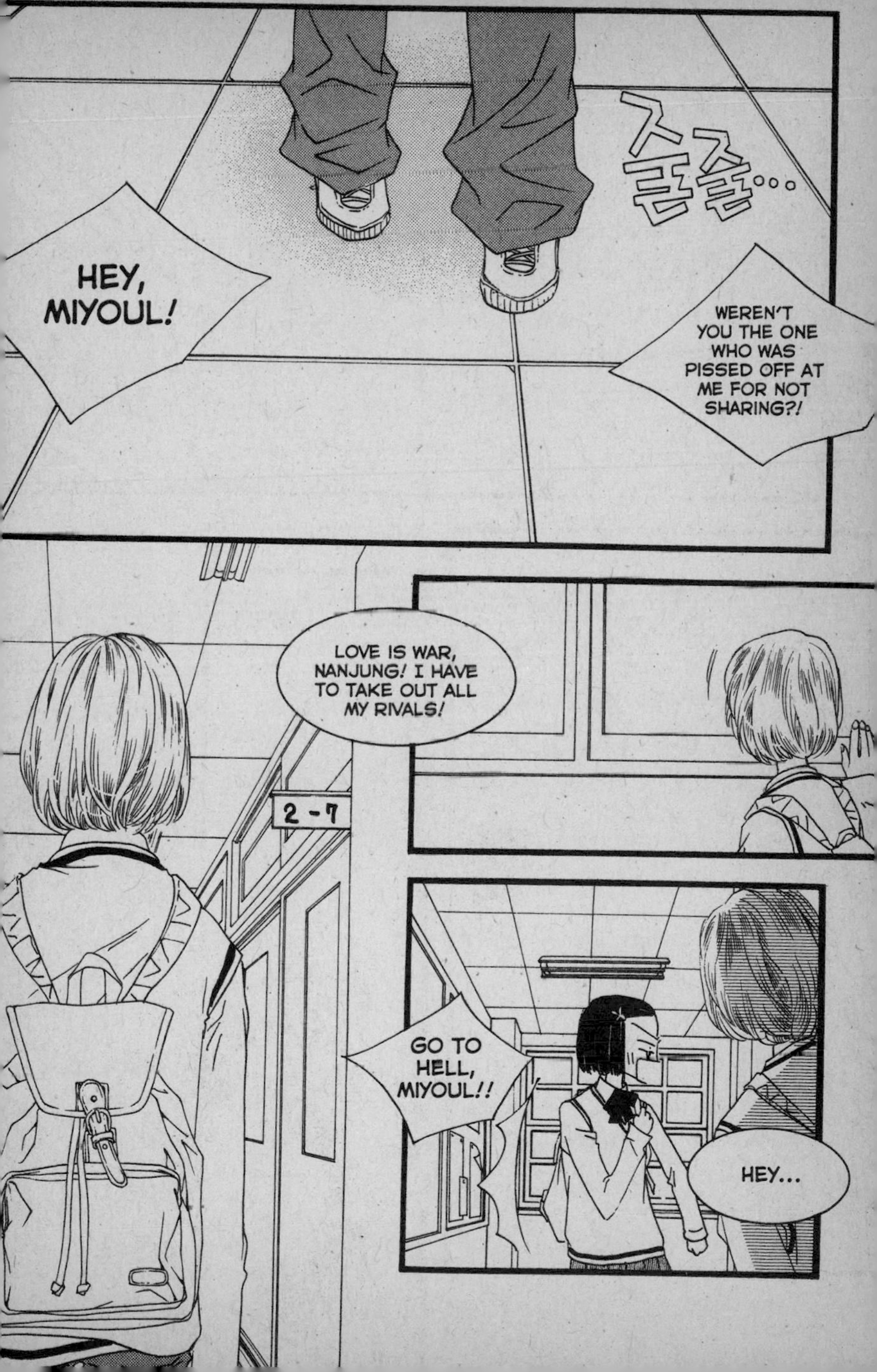
HEY, MIYOUL!
졸졸...
WEREN'T YOU THE ONE WHO WAS PISSED OFF AT ME FOR NOT SHARING?!
LOVE IS WAR, NANJUNG! I HAVE TO TAKE OUT ALL MY RIVALS!
2 - 7
GO TO HELL, MIYOUL!!
HEY...

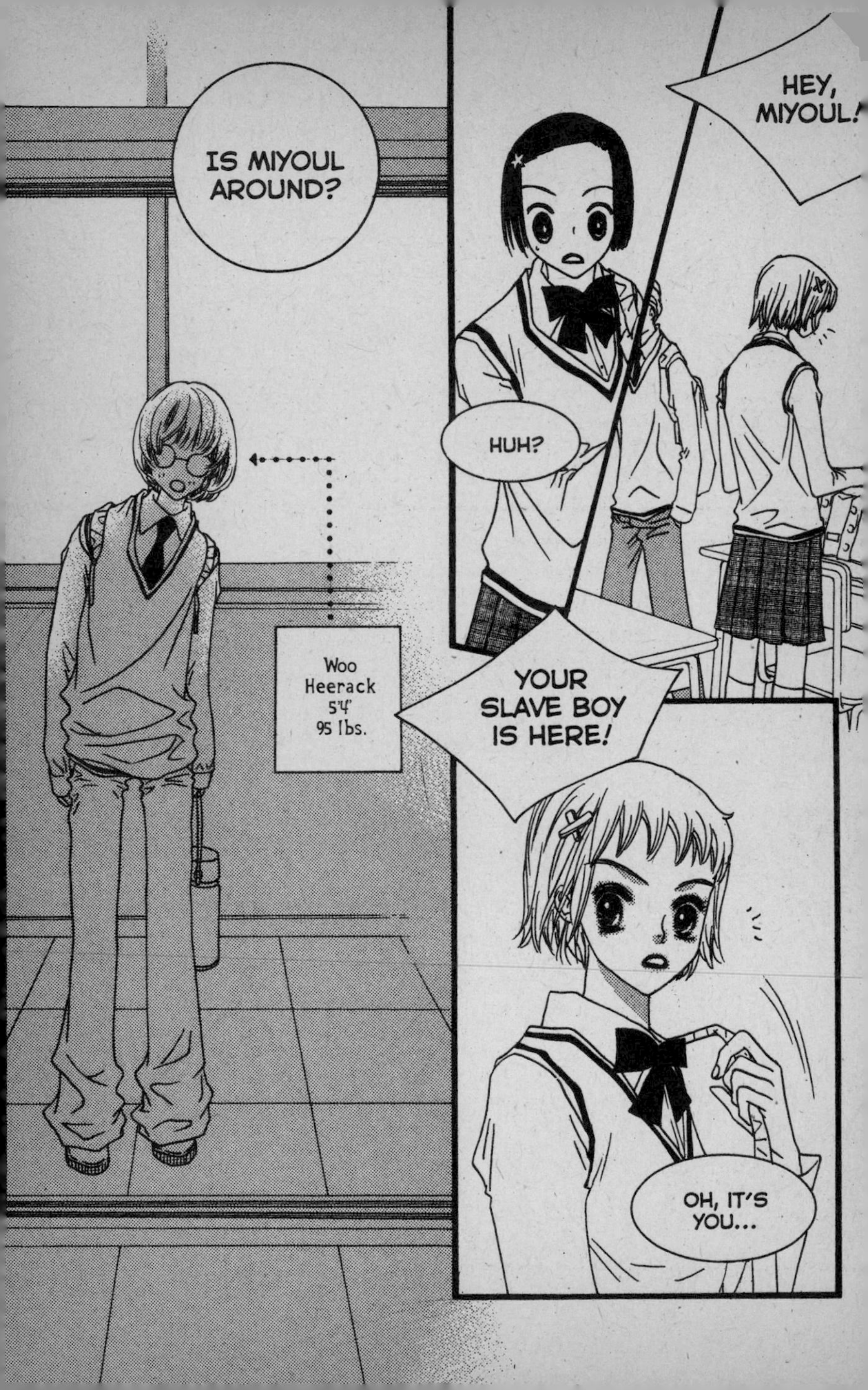
IS MIYOUL AROUND?
Woo Heerack 5'4" 95 lbs.
HEY, MIYOUL!
HUH?
YOUR SLAVE BOY IS HERE!
OH, IT'S YOU...

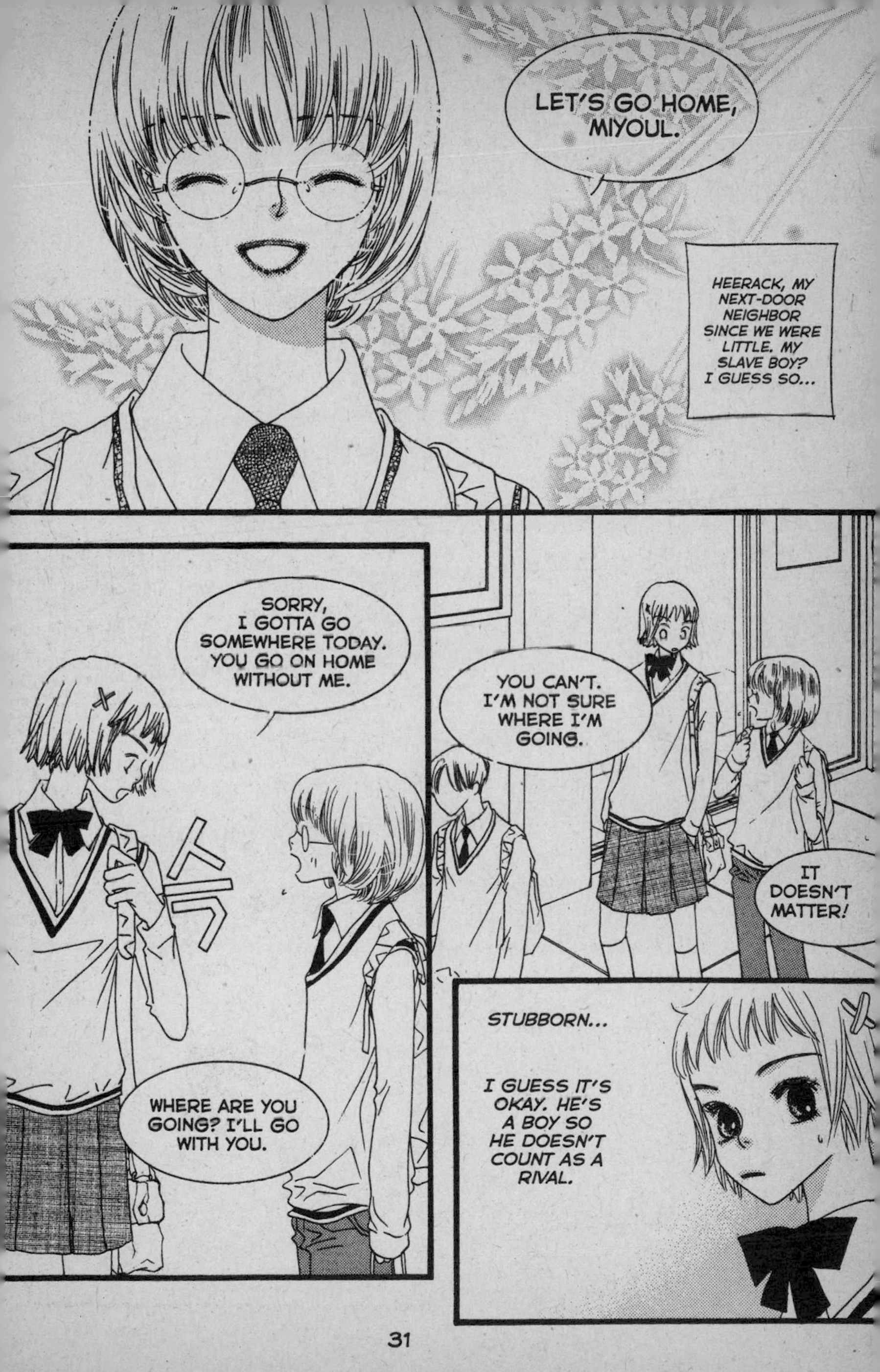
LET'S GO HOME, MIYOUL.
HEERACK, MY NEXT-DOOR NEIGHBOR SINCE WE WERE LITTLE. MY SLAVE BOY? I GUESS SO...
SORRY, I GOTTA GO SOMEWHERE TODAY. YOU GO ON HOME WITHOUT ME.
WHERE ARE YOU GOING? I'LL GO WITH YOU.
YOU CAN'T. I'M NOT SURE WHERE I'M GOING.
IT DOESN'T MATTER!
STUBBORN...
I GUESS IT'S OKAY. HE'S A BOY SO HE DOESN'T COUNT AS A RIVAL.

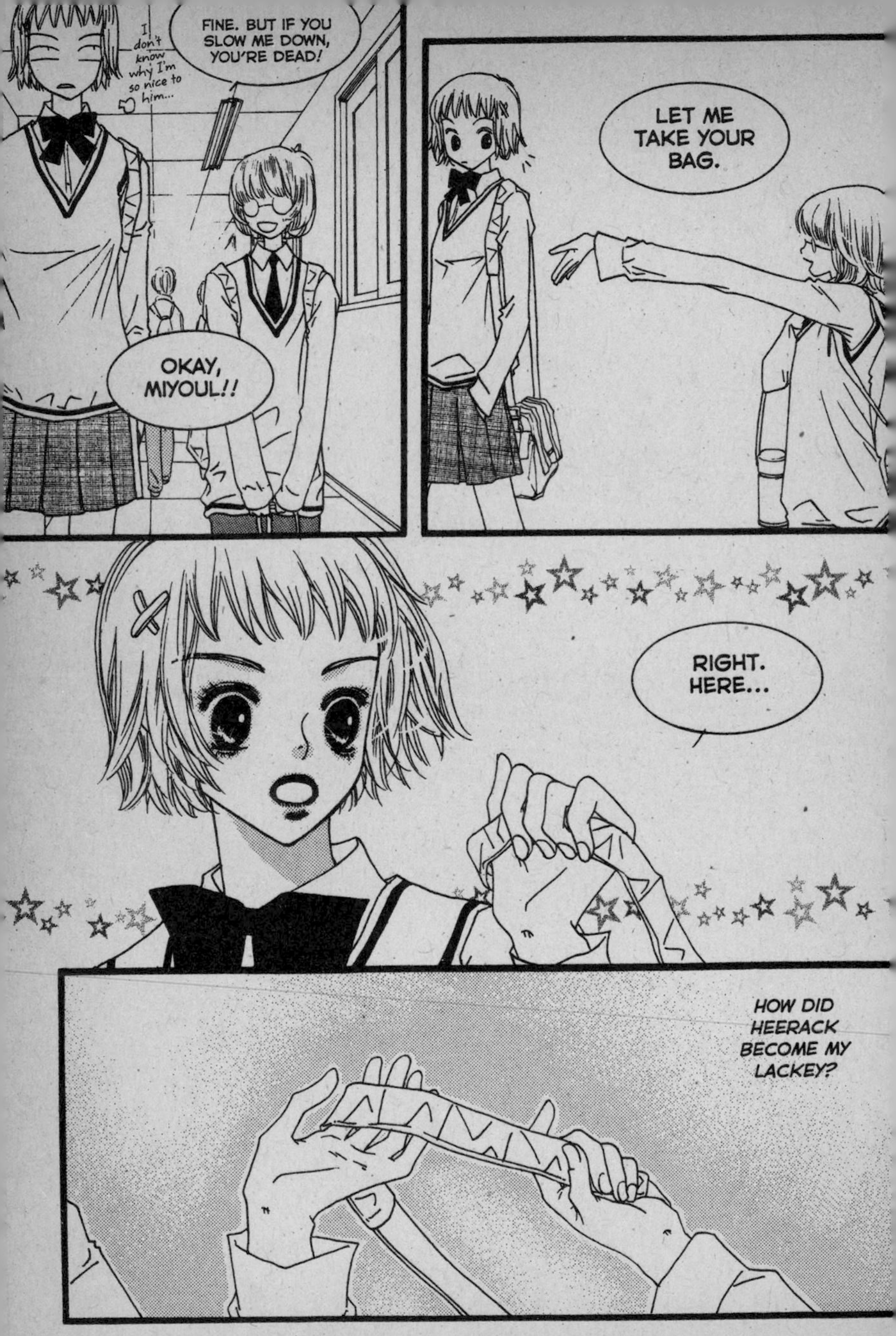
I don't know why I'm so nice to him...
FINE. BUT IF YOU SLOW ME DOWN, YOU'RE DEAD!
OKAY, MIYOUL!!
LET ME TAKE YOUR BAG.
RIGHT. HERE...
HOW DID HEERACK BECOME MY LACKEY?

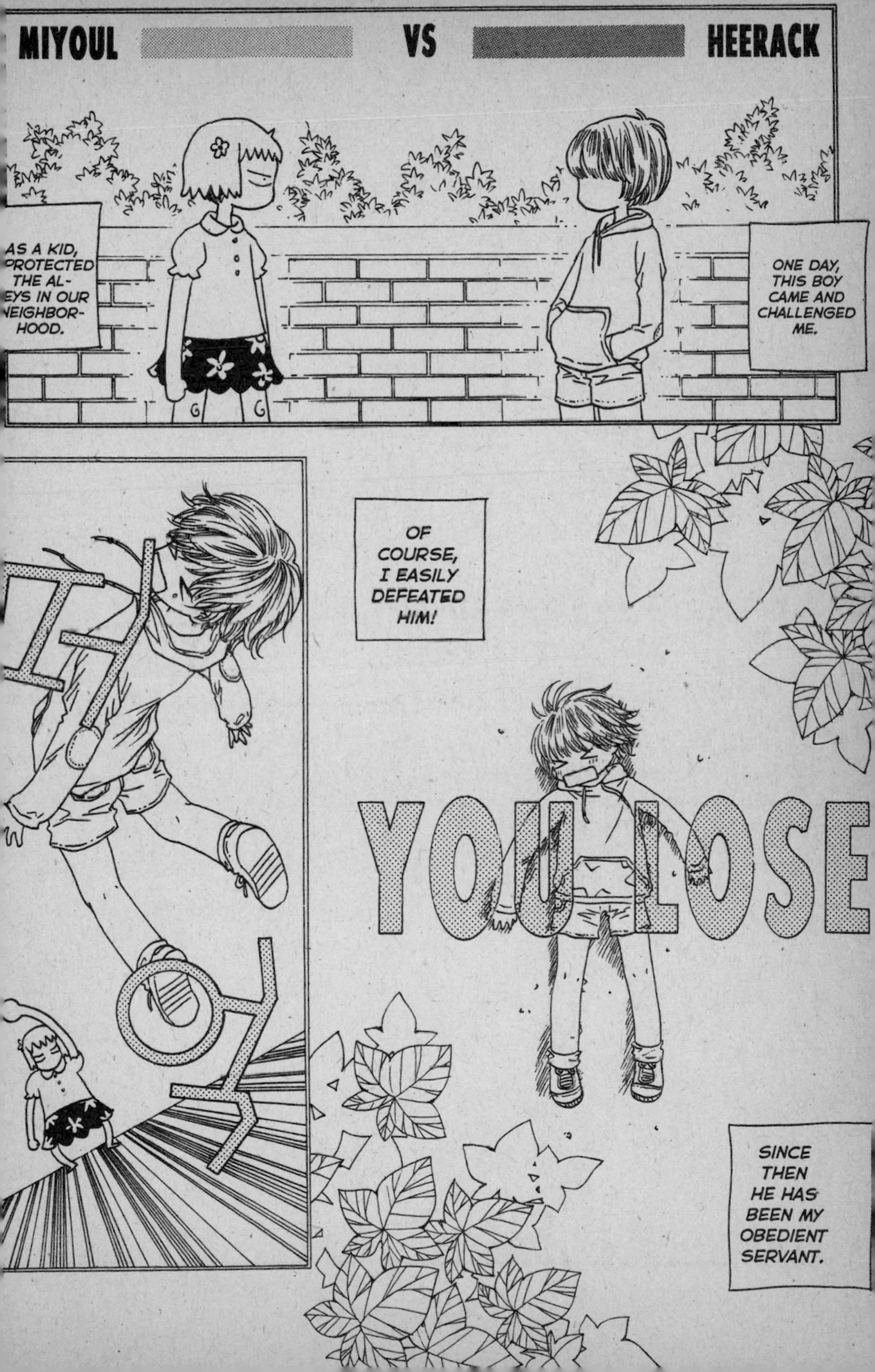
MIYOUL VS HEERACK
AS A KID, PROTECTED THE AL- EYS IN OUR NEIGHBOR- HOOD.
ONE DAY, THIS BOY CAME AND CHALLENGED ME.
OF COURSE, I EASILY DEFEATED HIM!
YOU LOSE
SINCE THEN HE HAS BEEN MY OBEDIENT SERVANT.

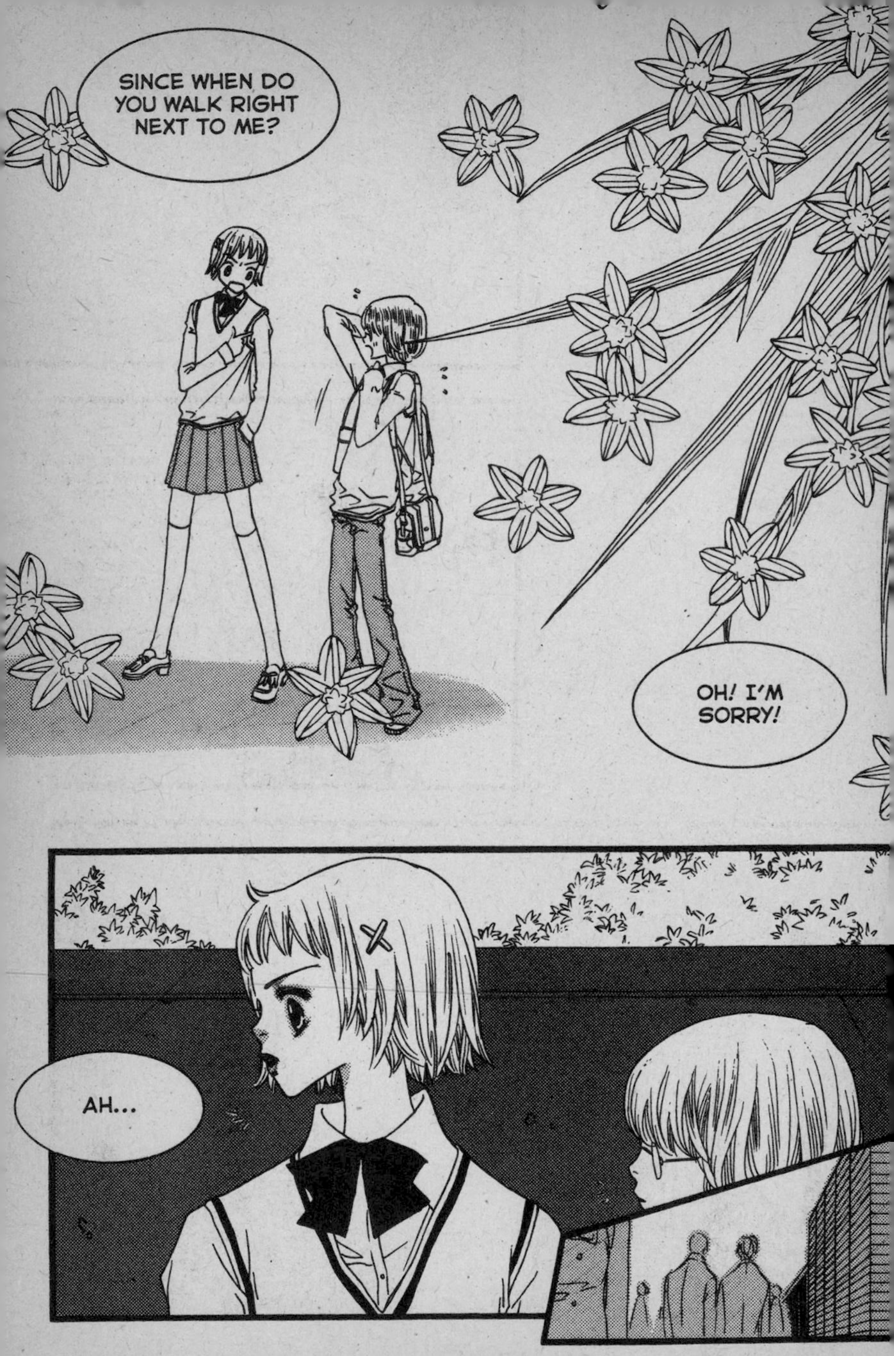
SINCE WHEN DO YOU WALK RIGHT NEXT TO ME?
OH! I'M SORRY!
AH...

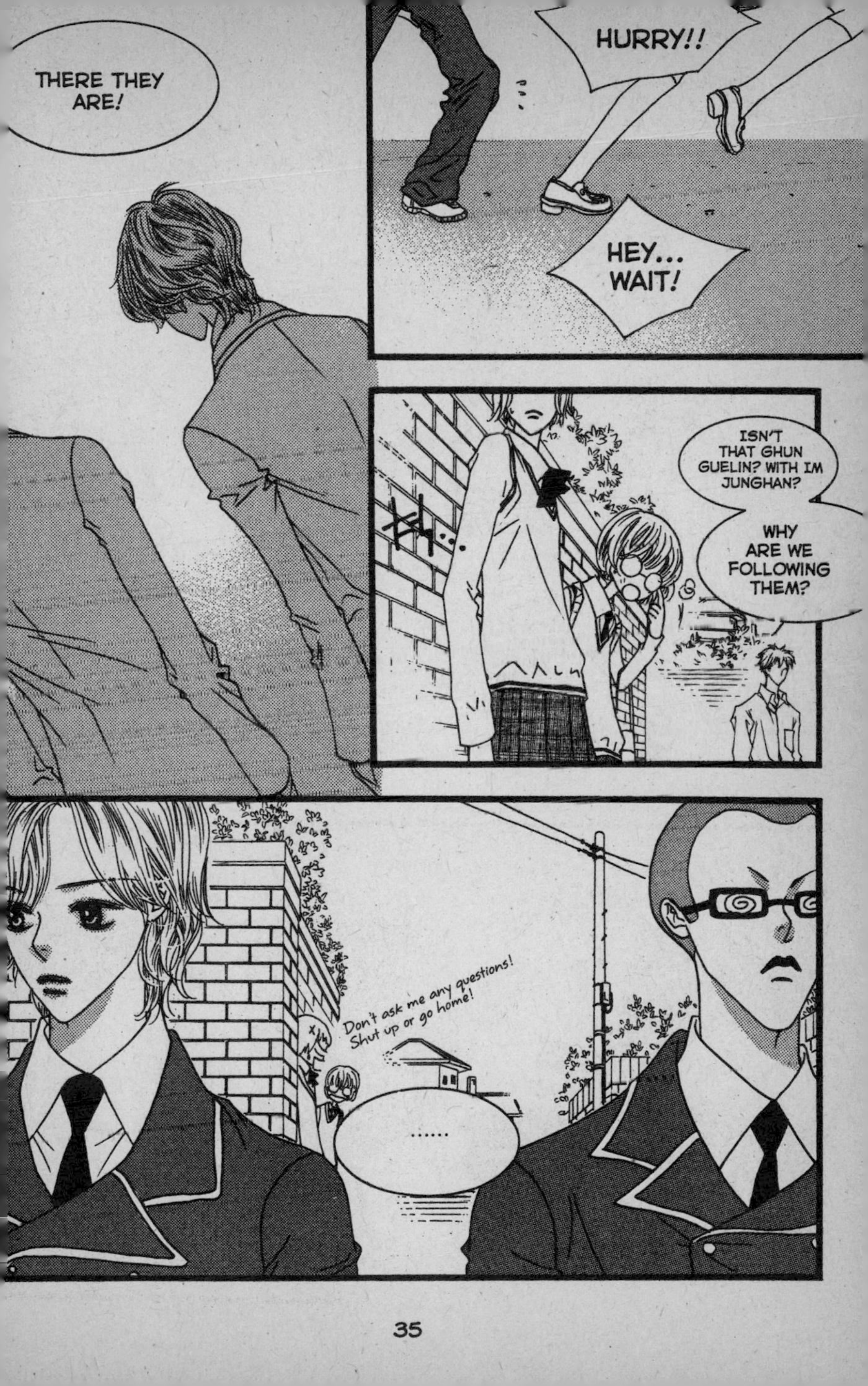
THERE THEY ARE!
HURRY!!
HEY... WAIT!
ISN'T THAT GHUN GUELIN? WITH IM JUNGHAN?
WHY ARE WE FOLLOWING THEM?
Don't ask me any questions! Shut up or go home!
......

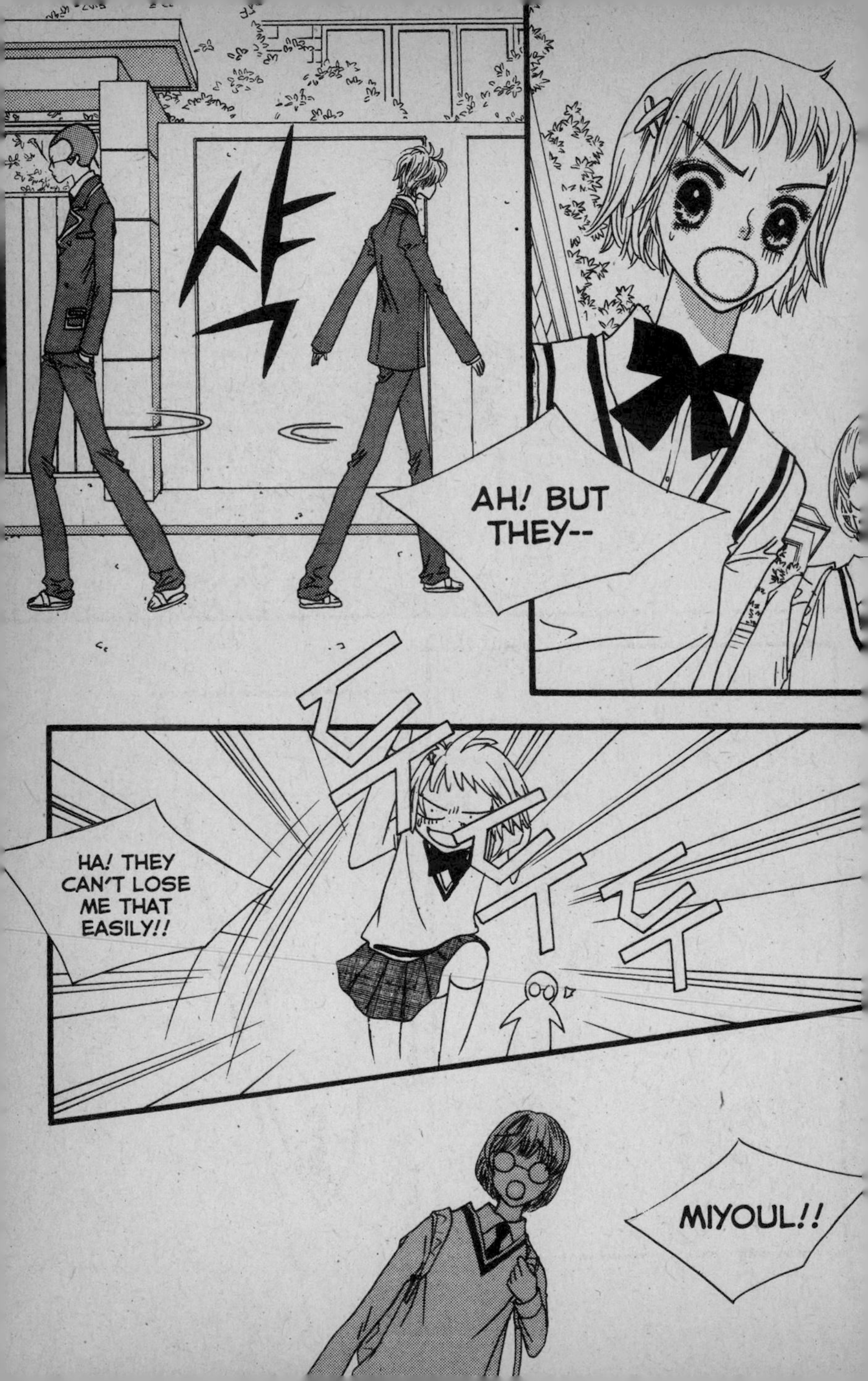
AH! BUT THEY--
HA! THEY CAN'T LOSE ME THAT EASILY!!
MIYOUL!!

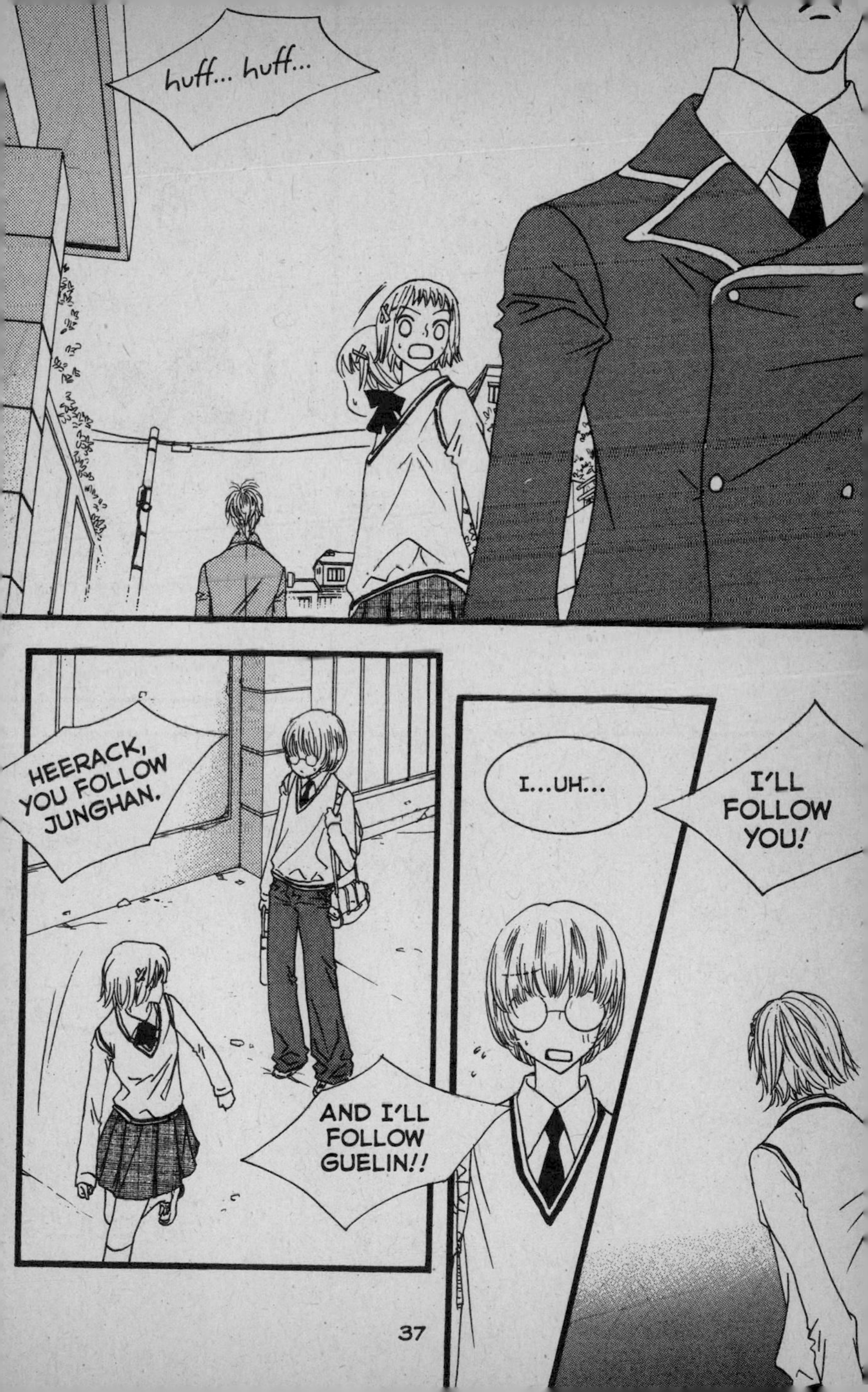
huff... huff...
HEERACK, YOU FOLLOW JUNGHAN.
AND I'LL FOLLOW GUELIN!!
I...UH...
I'LL FOLLOW YOU!

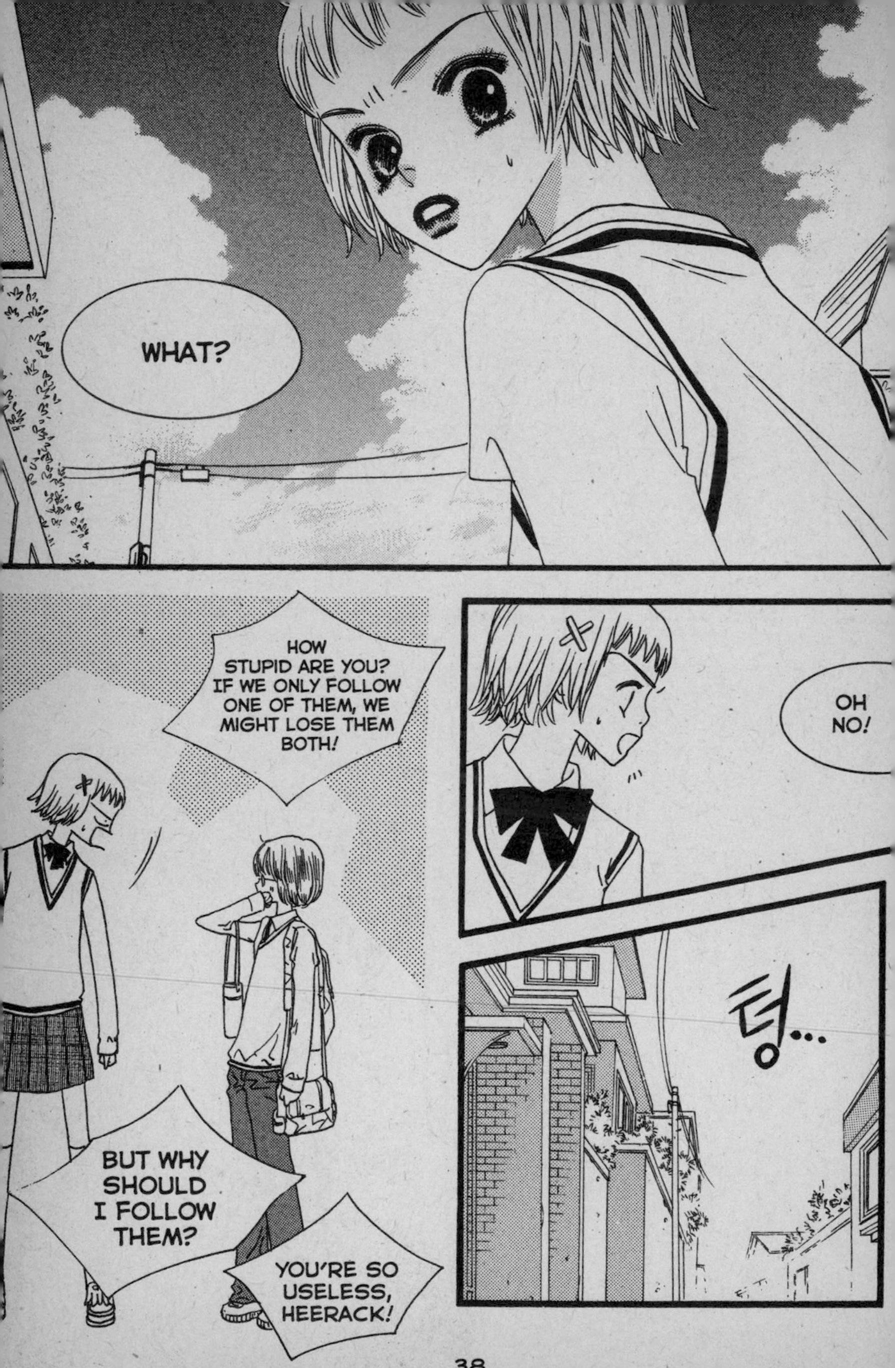
WHAT?
HOW STUPID ARE YOU? IF WE ONLY FOLLOW ONE OF THEM, WE MIGHT LOSE THEM BOTH!
BUT WHY SHOULD I FOLLOW THEM?
YOU'RE SO USELESS, HEERACK!
OH NO!
텅...

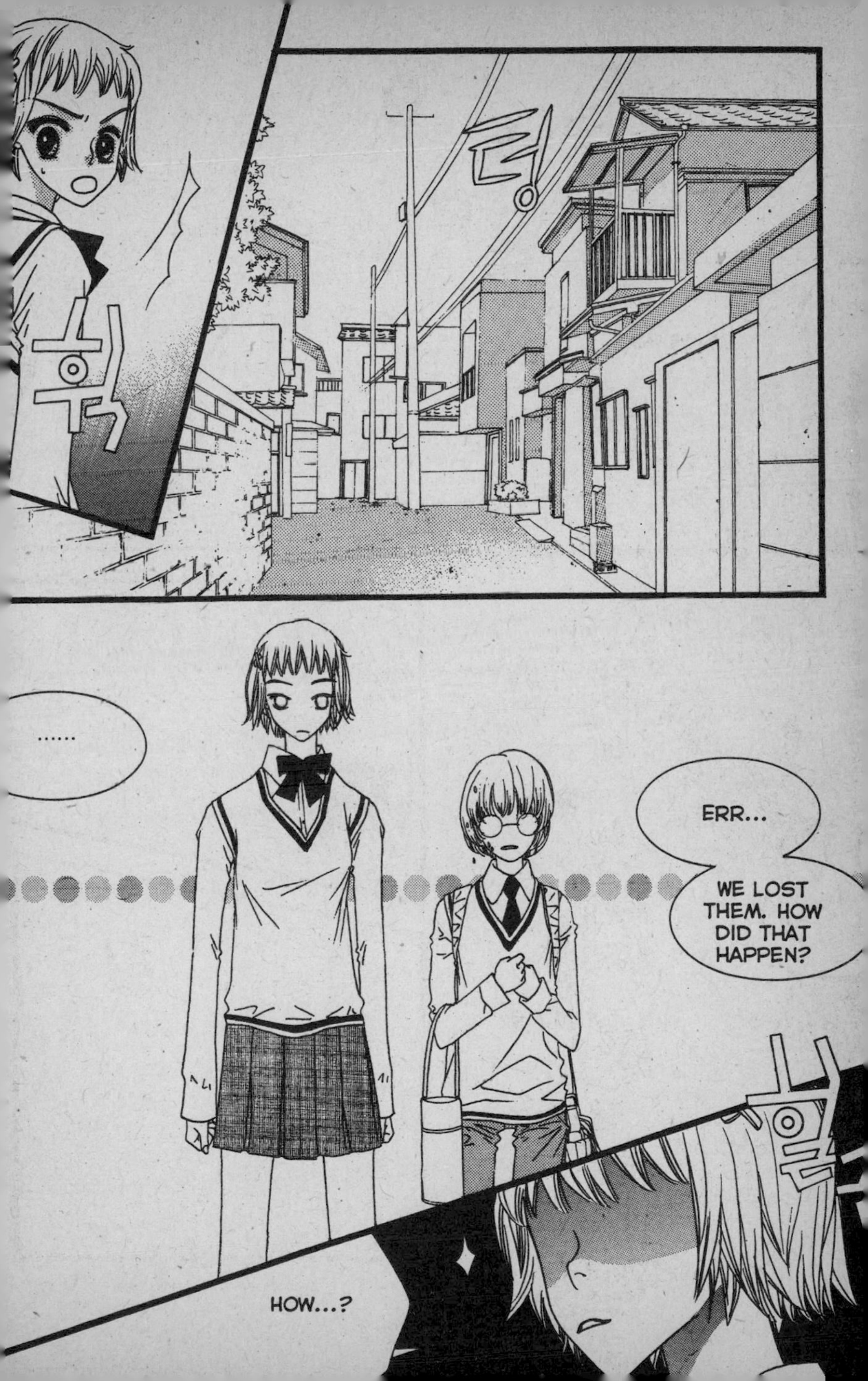
......
ERR...
WE LOST THEM. HOW DID THAT HAPPEN?
HOW...?

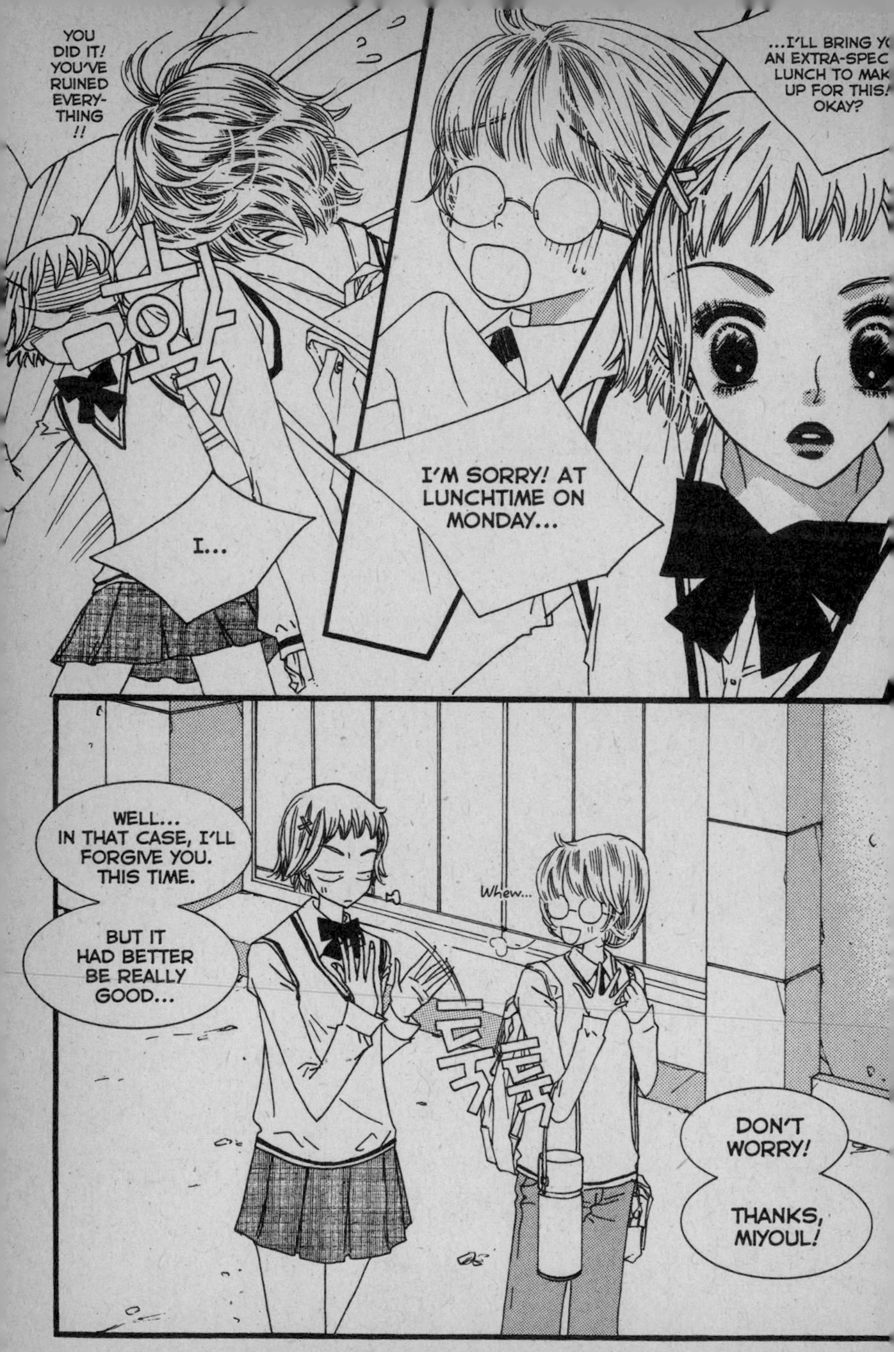
YOU DID IT! YOU'VE RUINED EVERY-THING!!
I...
I'M SORRY! AT LUNCHTIME ON MONDAY...
...I'LL BRING YO AN EXTRA-SPEC LUNCH TO MAK UP FOR THIS! OKAY?
WELL... IN THAT CASE, I'LL FORGIVE YOU. THIS TIME.
BUT IT HAD BETTER BE REALLY GOOD...
Whew...
DON'T WORRY!
THANKS, MIYOUL!

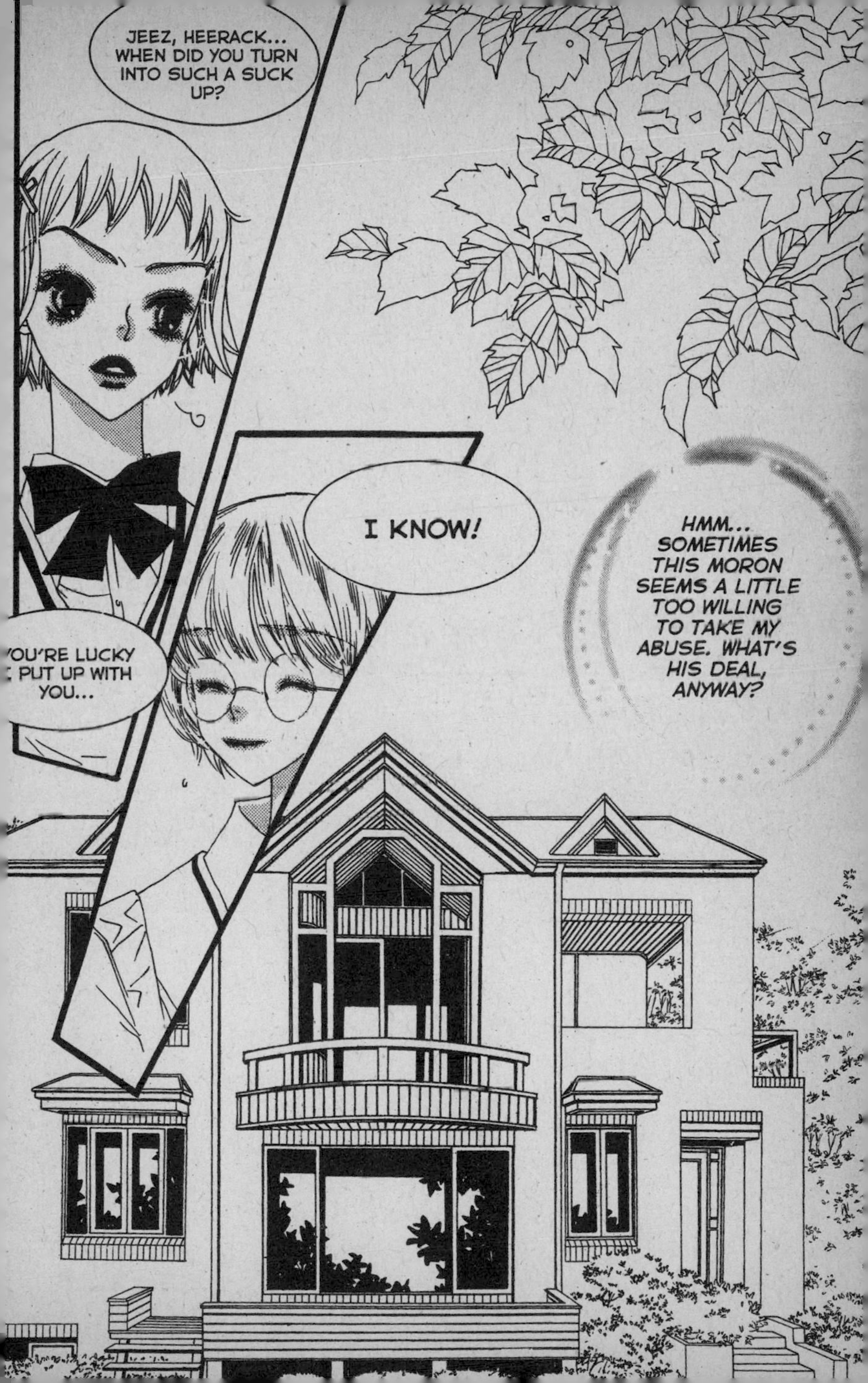
JEEZ, HEERACK... WHEN DID YOU TURN INTO SUCH A SUCK UP?
I KNOW!
YOU'RE LUCKY I PUT UP WITH YOU...
HMM... SOMETIMES THIS MORON SEEMS A LITTLE TOO WILLING TO TAKE MY ABUSE. WHAT'S HIS DEAL, ANYWAY?

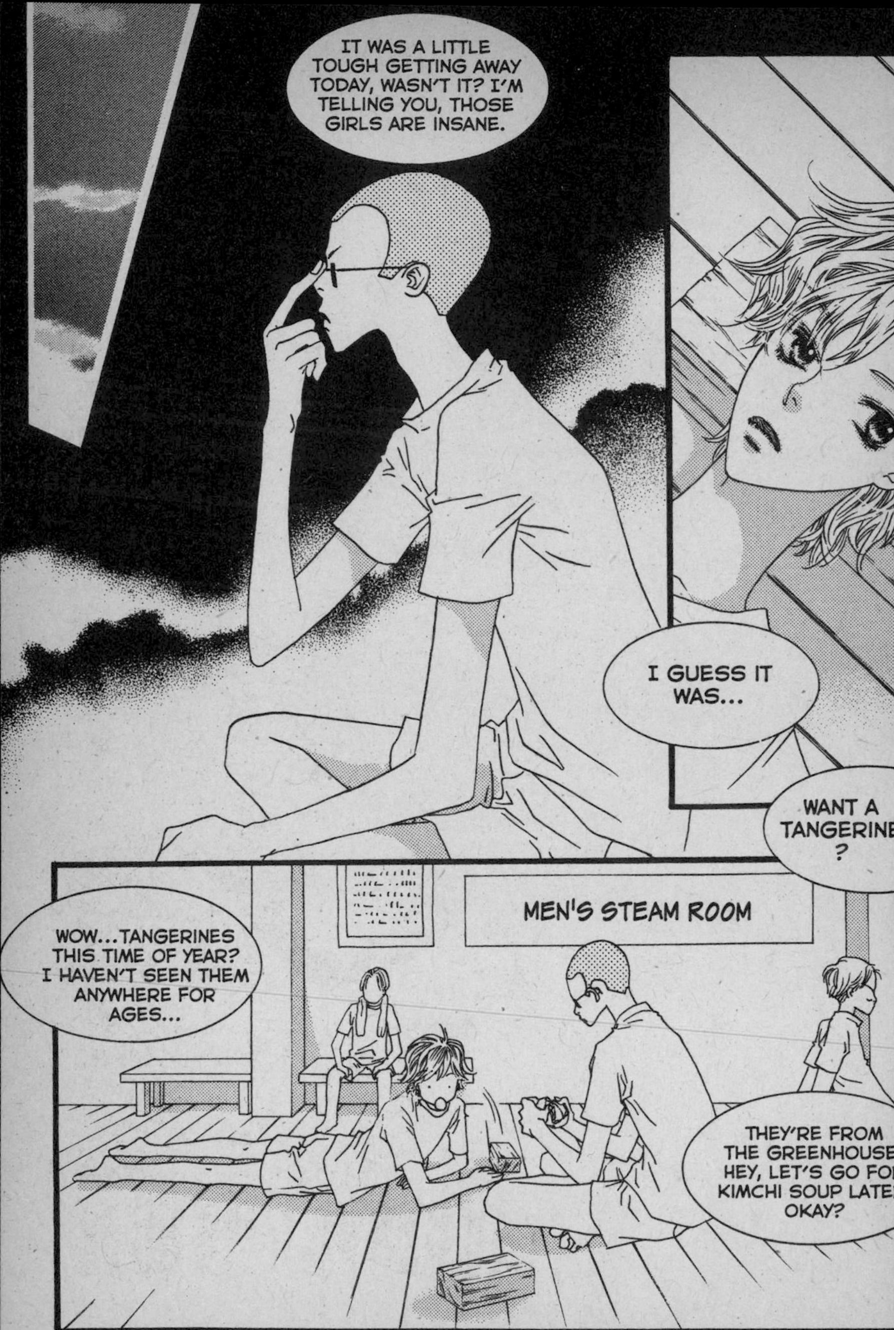
IT WAS A LITTLE TOUGH GETTING AWAY TODAY, WASN'T IT? I'M TELLING YOU, THOSE GIRLS ARE INSANE.
I GUESS IT WAS...
WANT A TANGERINE?
MEN'S STEAM ROOM
WOW...TANGERINES THIS TIME OF YEAR? I HAVEN'T SEEN THEM ANYWHERE FOR AGES...
THEY'RE FROM THE GREENHOUSE. HEY, LET'S GO FOR KIMCHI SOUP LATER, OKAY?

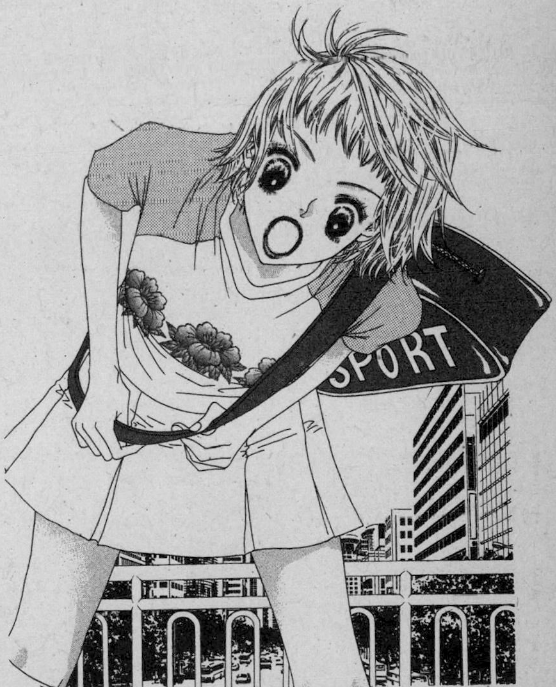
SPORT

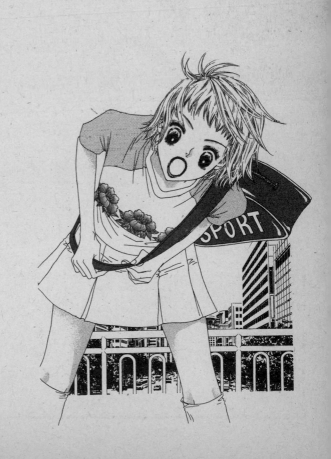

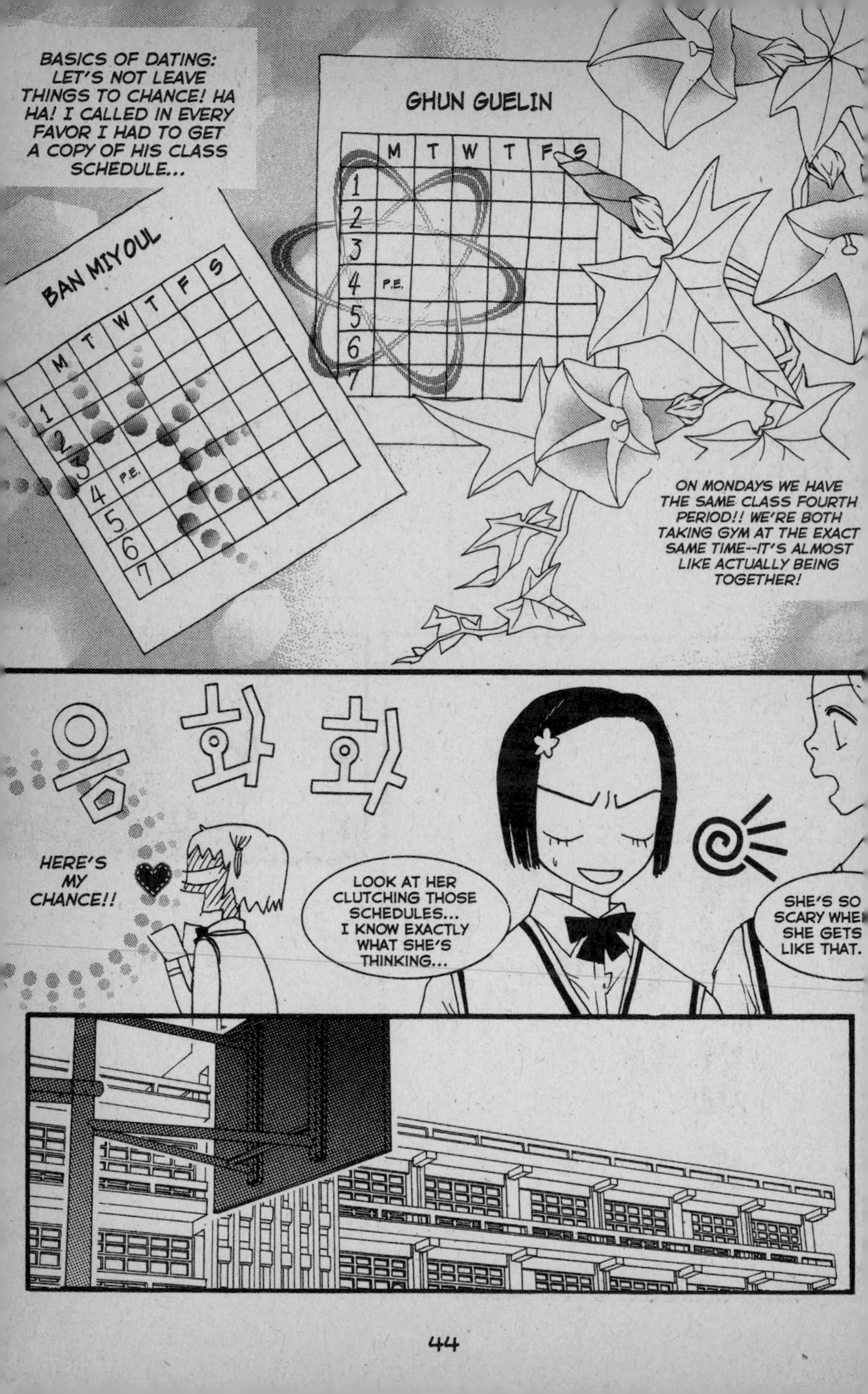
BASICS OF DATING: LET'S NOT LEAVE THINGS TO CHANCE! HA HA! I CALLED IN EVERY FAVOR I HAD TO GET A COPY OF HIS CLASS SCHEDULE...
BAN MIYOUL
P.E.
GHUN GUELIN
P.E.
ON MONDAYS WE HAVE THE SAME CLASS FOURTH PERIOD!! WE'RE BOTH TAKING GYM AT THE EXACT SAME TIME--IT'S ALMOST LIKE ACTUALLY BEING TOGETHER!
응 화 화
HERE'S MY CHANCE!!
LOOK AT HER CLUTCHING THOSE SCHEDULES... I KNOW EXACTLY WHAT SHE'S THINKING...
SHE'S SO SCARY WHE SHE GETS LIKE THAT.

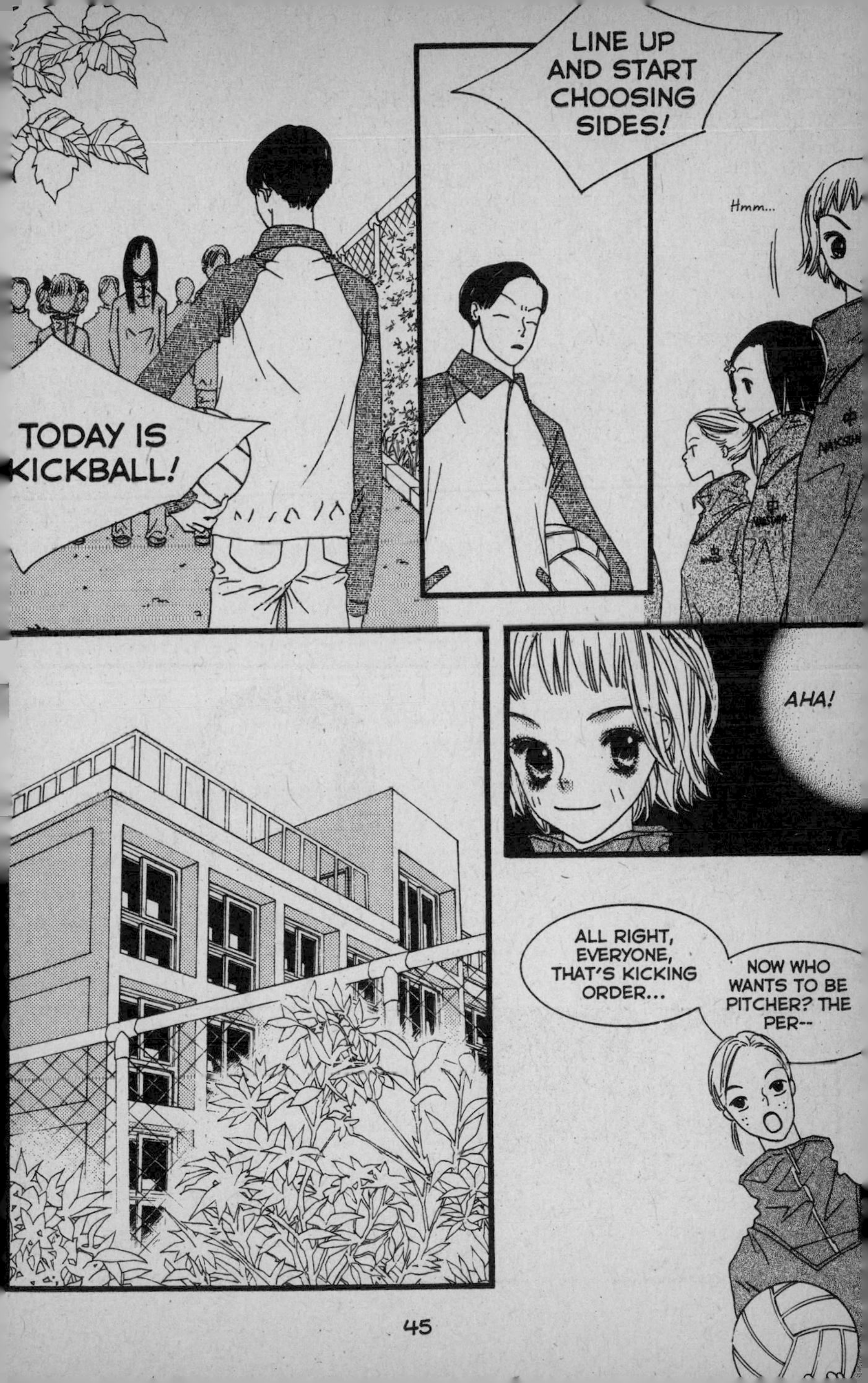
TODAY IS KICKBALL!
LINE UP AND START CHOOSING SIDES!
Hmm...
AHA!
ALL RIGHT, EVERYONE, THAT'S KICKING ORDER...
NOW WHO WANTS TO BE PITCHER? THE PER--

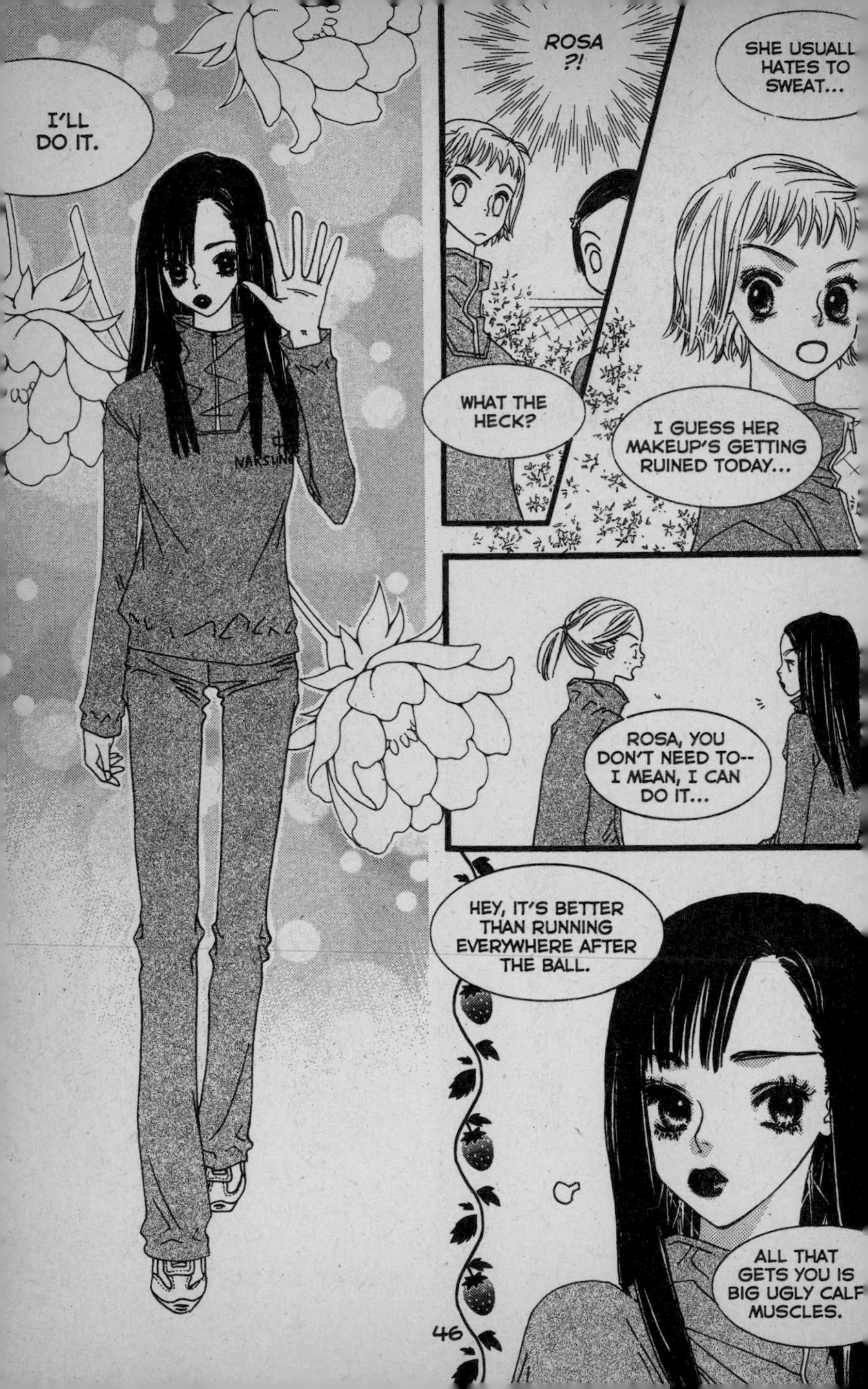
I'LL DO IT.
ROSA ?!
SHE USUALL HATES TO SWEAT...
WHAT THE HECK?
I GUESS HER MAKEUP'S GETTING RUINED TODAY...
ROSA, YOU DON'T NEED TO-- I MEAN, I CAN DO IT...
HEY, IT'S BETTER THAN RUNNING EVERYWHERE AFTER THE BALL.
ALL THAT GETS YOU IS BIG UGLY CALF MUSCLES.

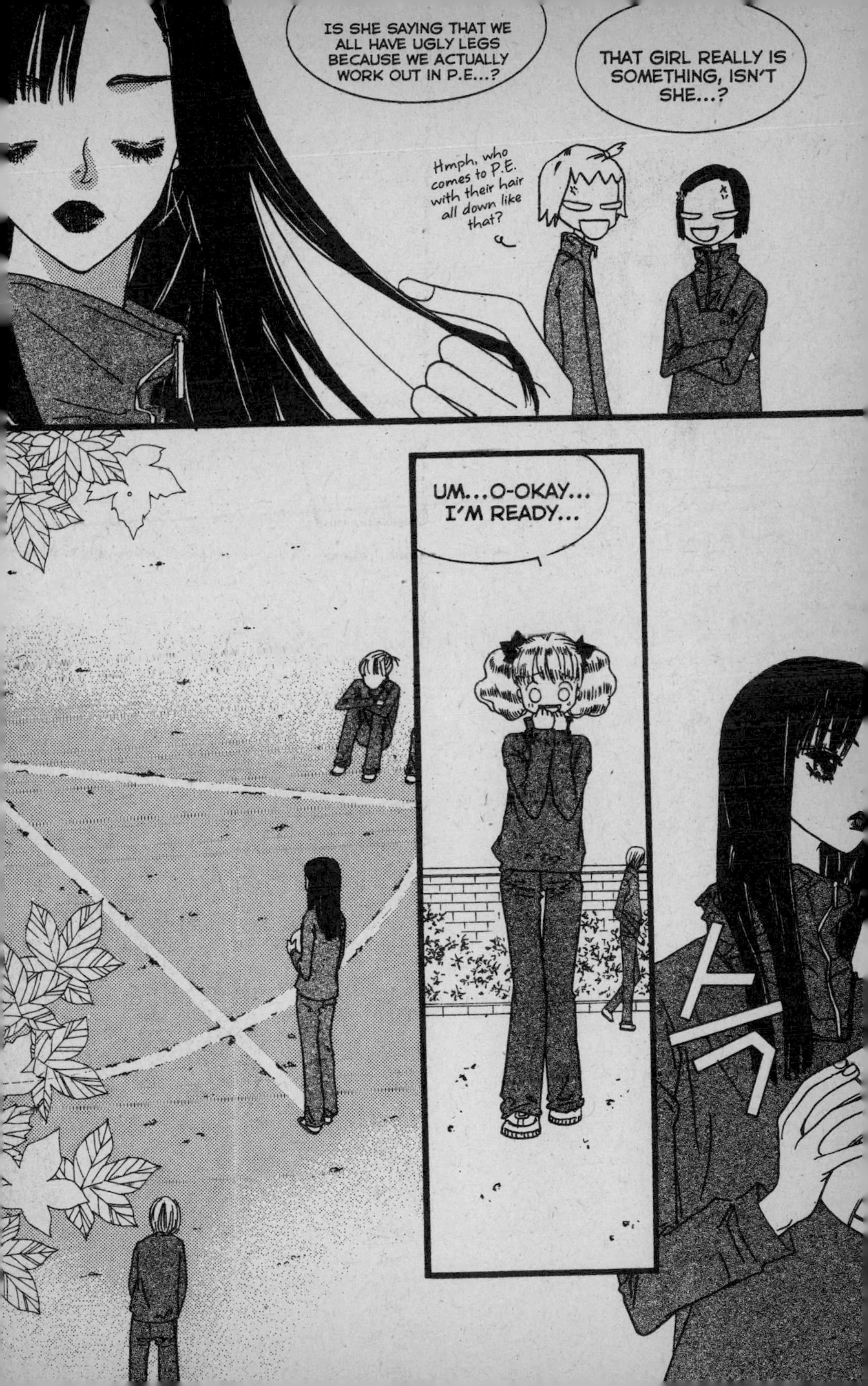
IS SHE SAYING THAT WE ALL HAVE UGLY LEGS BECAUSE WE ACTUALLY WORK OUT IN P.E...?
THAT GIRL REALLY IS SOMETHING, ISN'T SHE...?
Hmph, who comes to P.E. with their hair all down like that?
UM...O-OKAY... I'M READY...

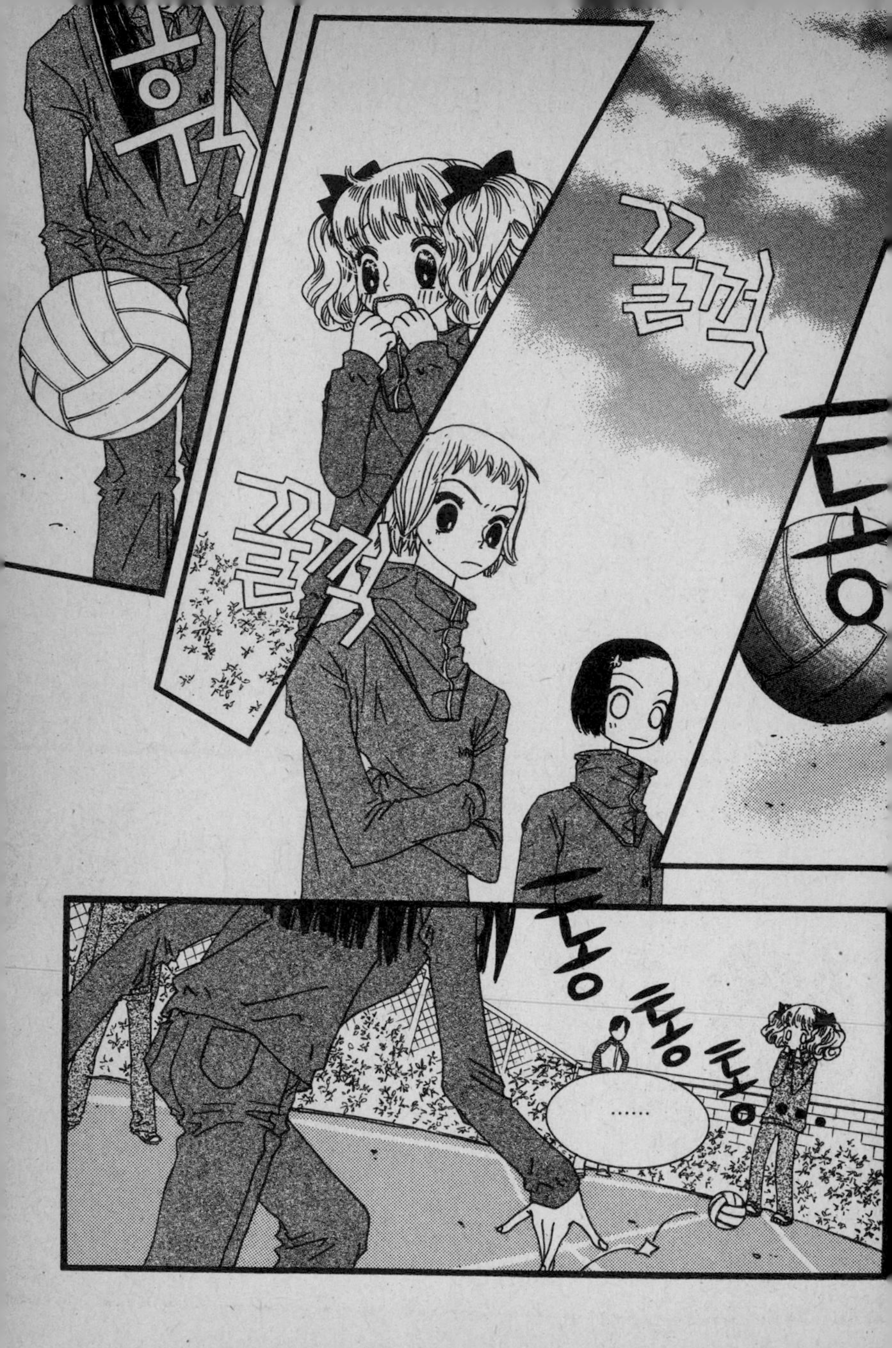
꿀꺽
꿀꺽
통
통 통 통
......

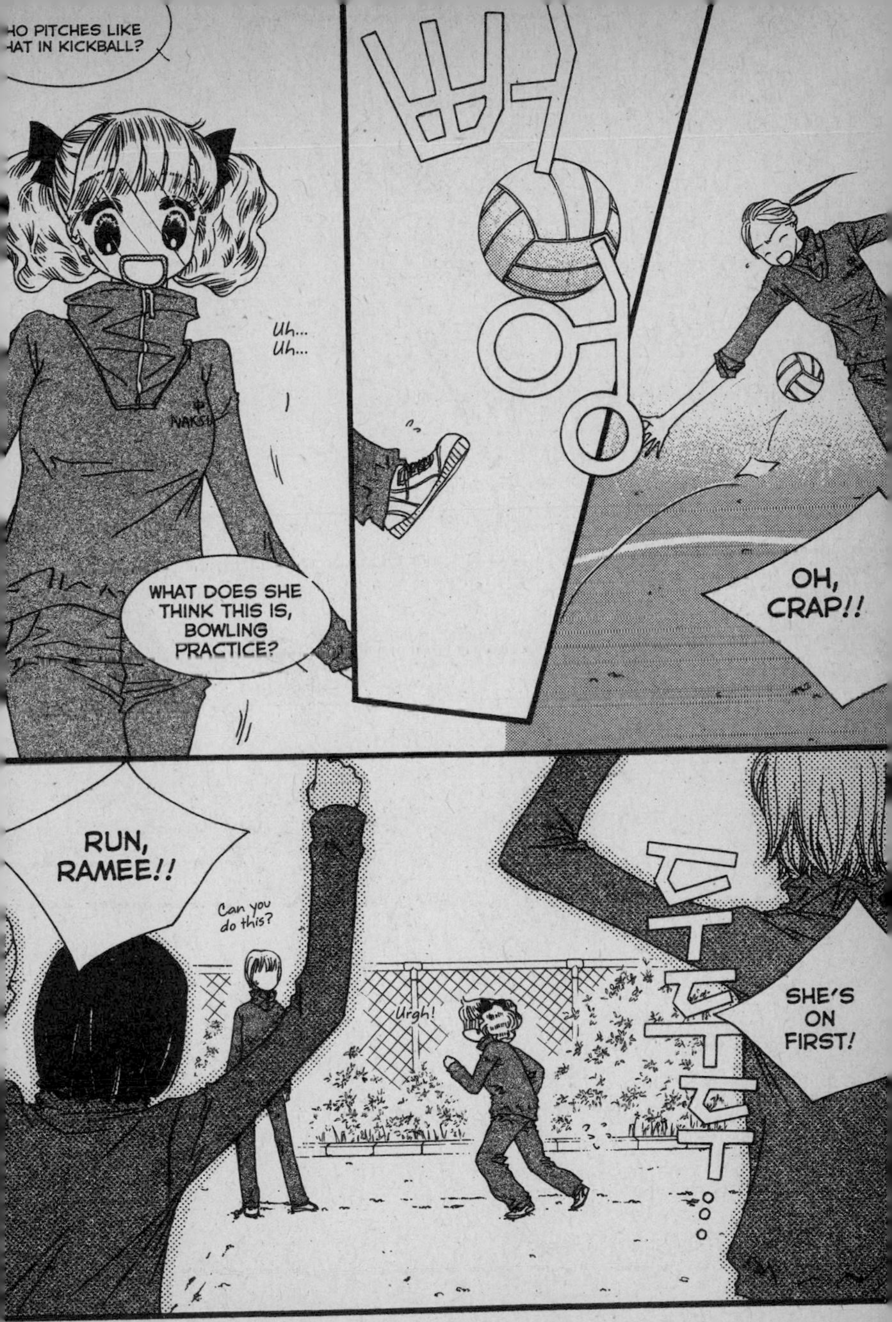
HO PITCHES LIKE HAT IN KICKBALL?
Uh... Uh...
WHAT DOES SHE THINK THIS IS, BOWLING PRACTICE?
OH, CRAP!!
RUN, RAMEE!!
Can you do this?
Urgh!
SHE'S ON FIRST!

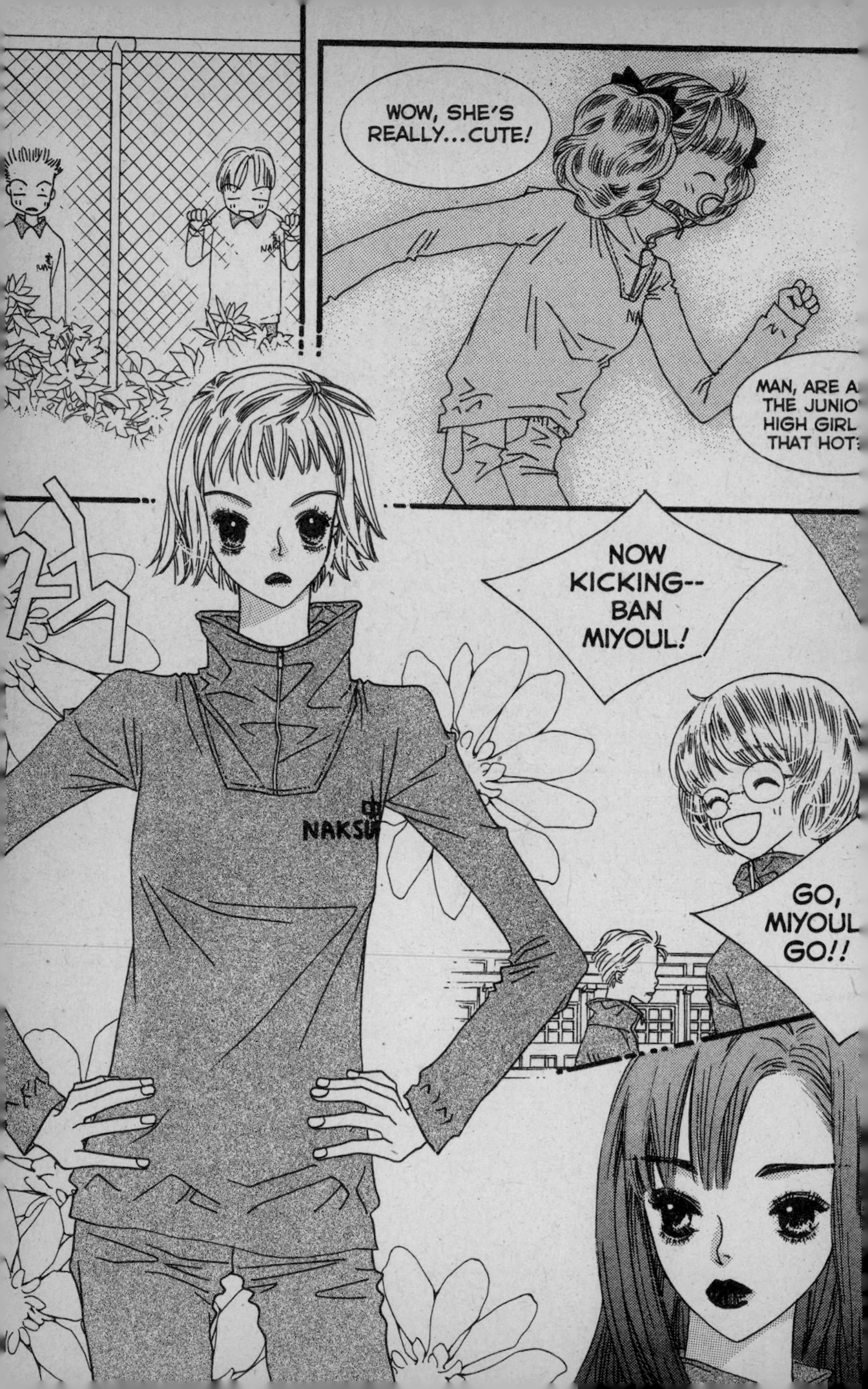
WOW, SHE'S REALLY...CUTE!
MAN, ARE A
THE JUNIO
HIGH GIRL
THAT HOT
NAKSU
NOW KICKING-- BAN MIYOUL!
GO, MIYOUL GO!!

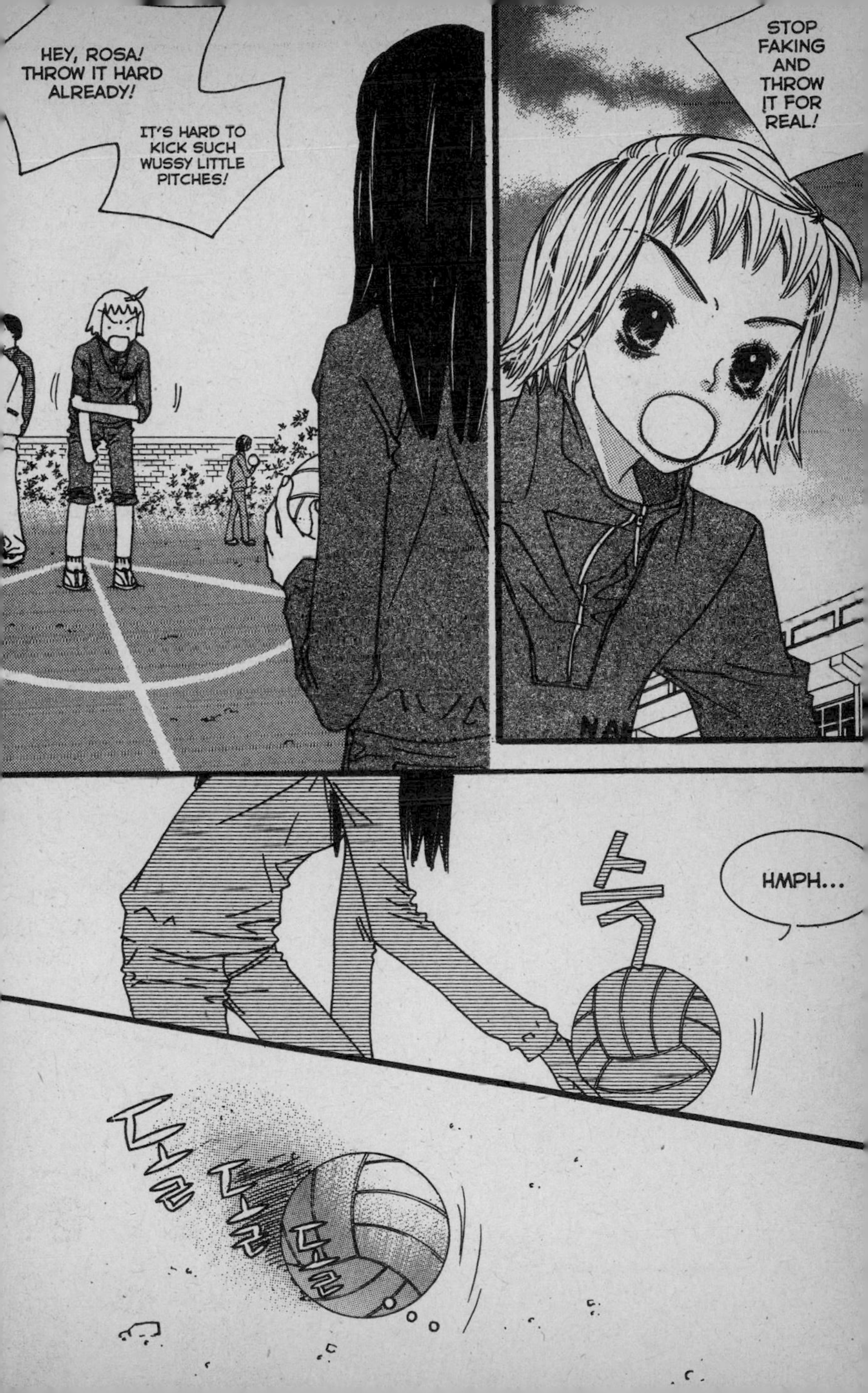
HEY, ROSA! THROW IT HARD ALREADY!
IT'S HARD TO KICK SUCH WUSSY LITTLE PITCHES!
STOP FAKING AND THROW IT FOR REAL!
슥
HMPH...
돌 돌 돌

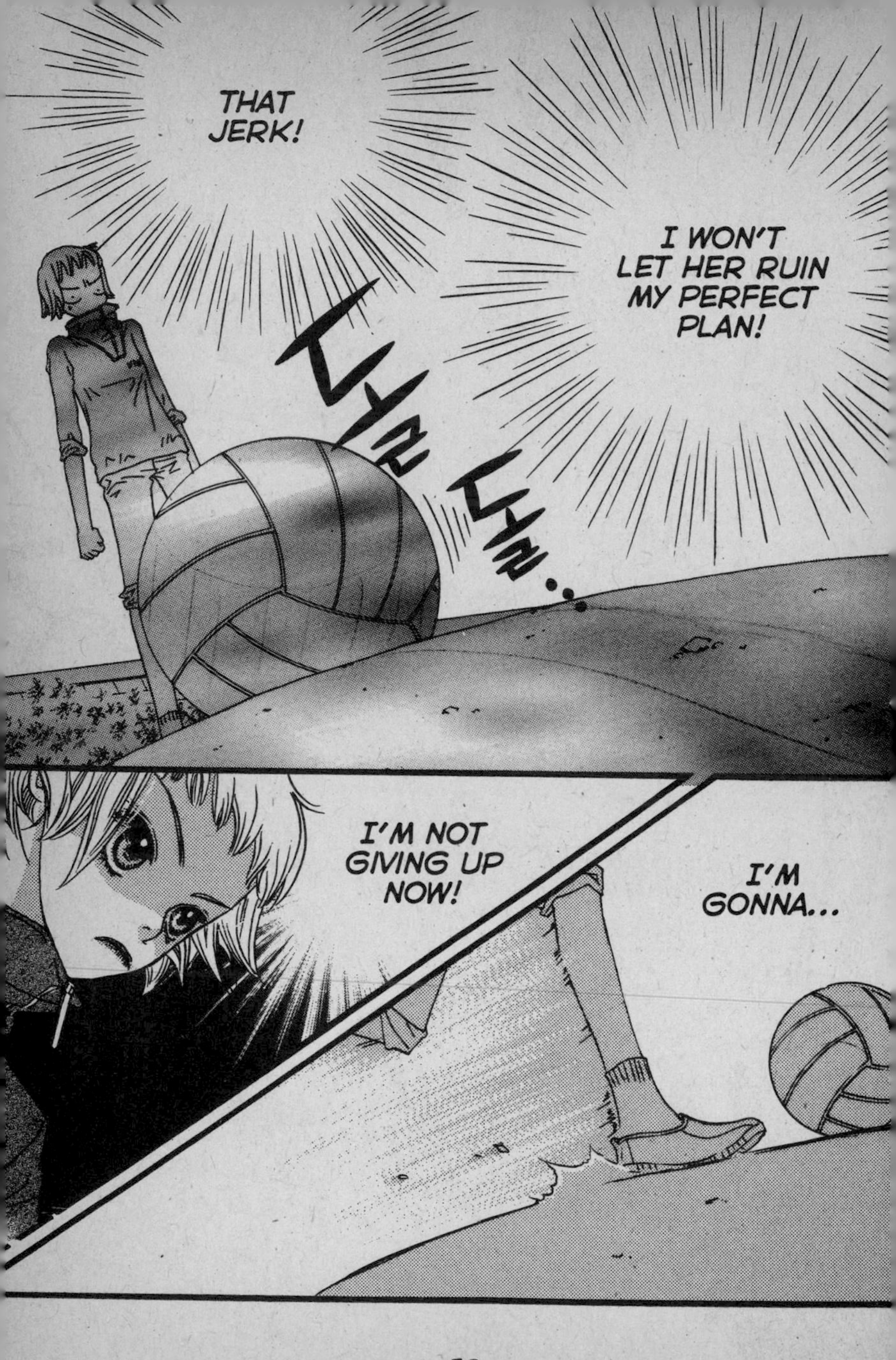
THAT JERK!
I WON'T LET HER RUIN MY PERFECT PLAN!
데굴 데굴...
I'M NOT GIVING UP NOW!
I'M GONNA...

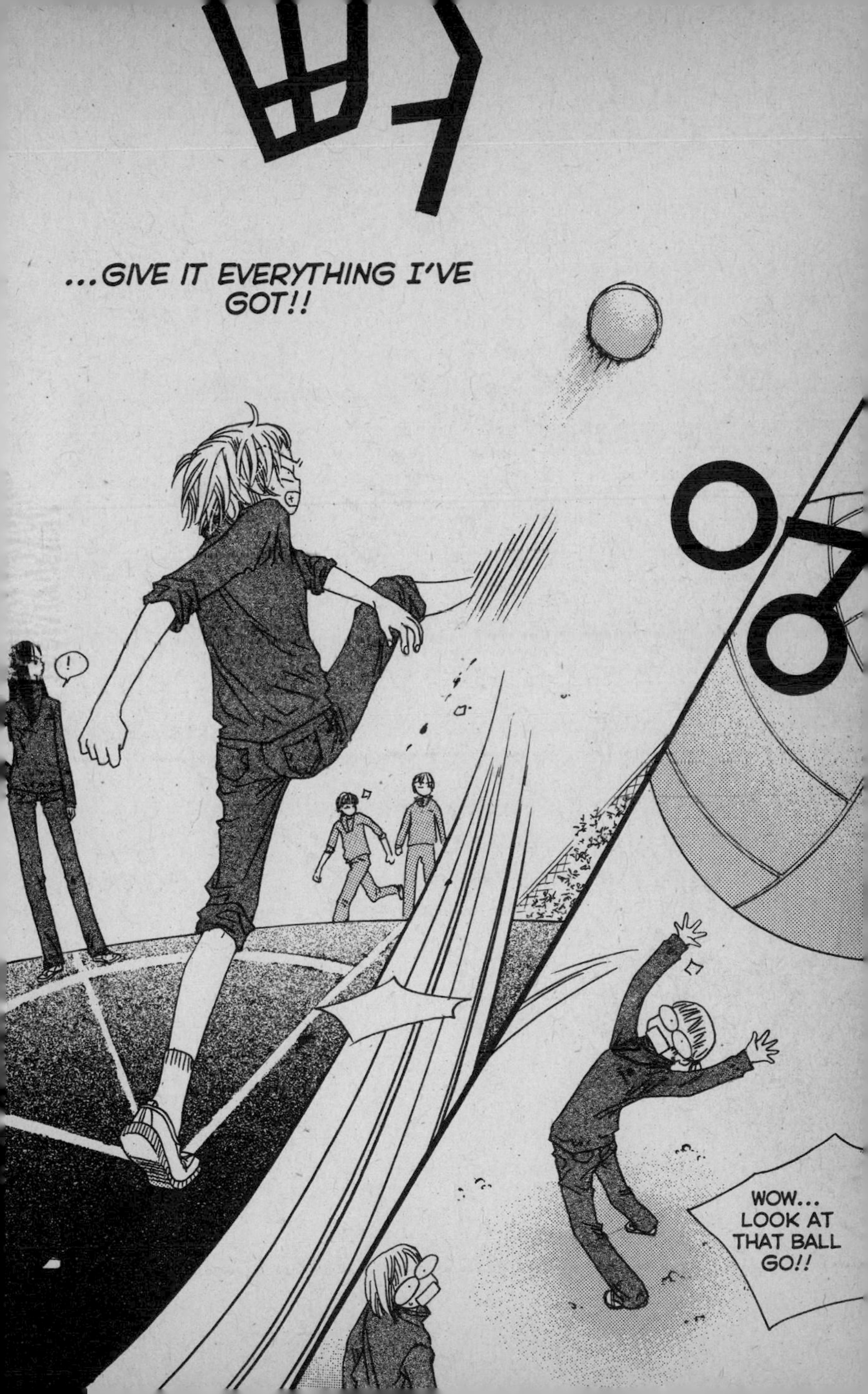
...GIVE IT EVERYTHING I'VE GOT!!
!
WOW... LOOK AT THAT BALL GO!!

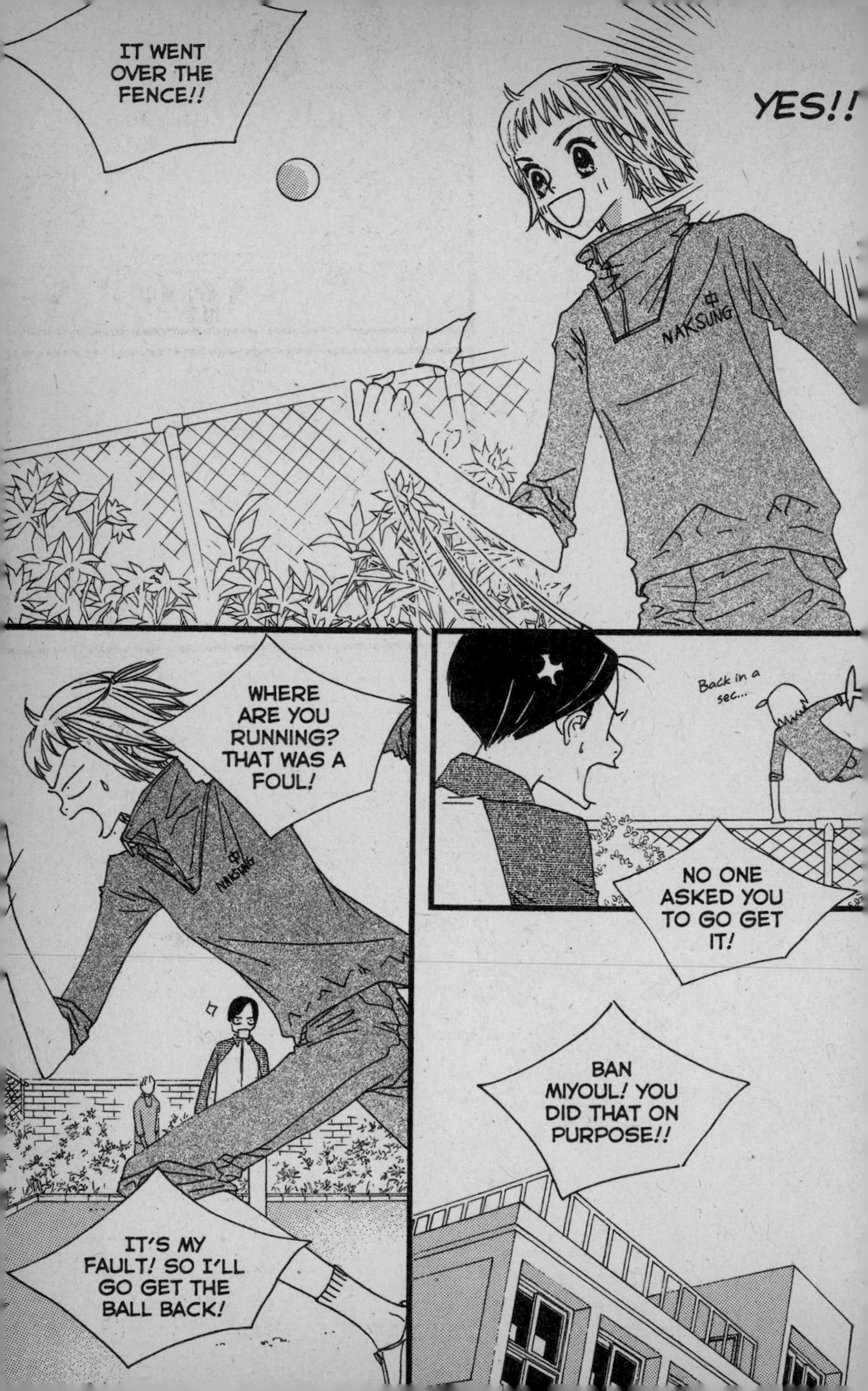
IT WENT OVER THE FENCE!!
YES!!
NAKSUNG
WHERE ARE YOU RUNNING? THAT WAS A FOUL!
NAKSUNG
IT'S MY FAULT! SO I'LL GO GET THE BALL BACK!
Back in a sec...
NO ONE ASKED YOU TO GO GET IT!
BAN MIYOUL! YOU DID THAT ON PURPOSE!!

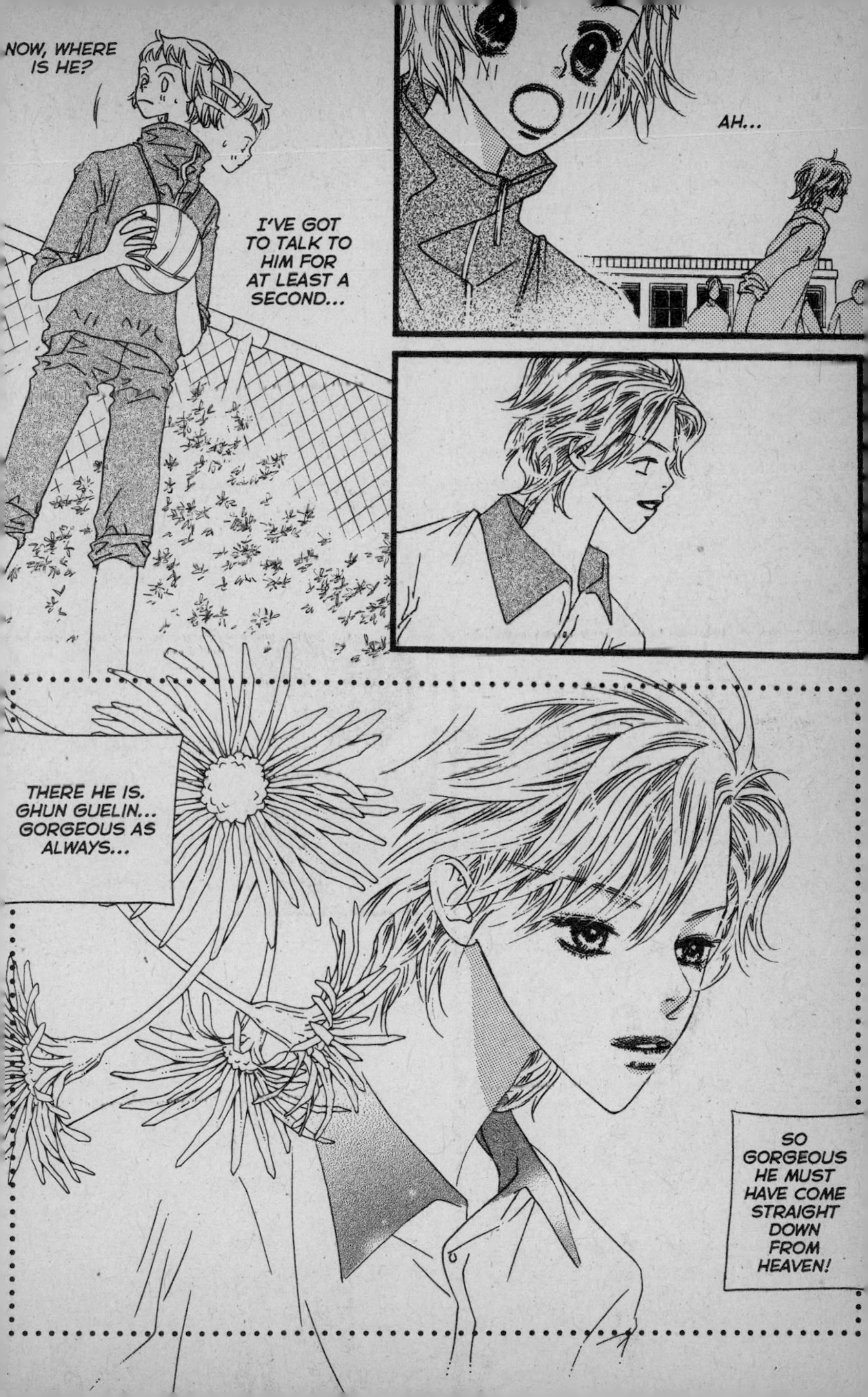
NOW, WHERE IS HE?
I'VE GOT TO TALK TO HIM FOR AT LEAST A SECOND...
AH...
THERE HE IS. GHUN GUELIN... GORGEOUS AS ALWAYS...
SO GORGEOUS HE MUST HAVE COME STRAIGHT DOWN FROM HEAVEN!

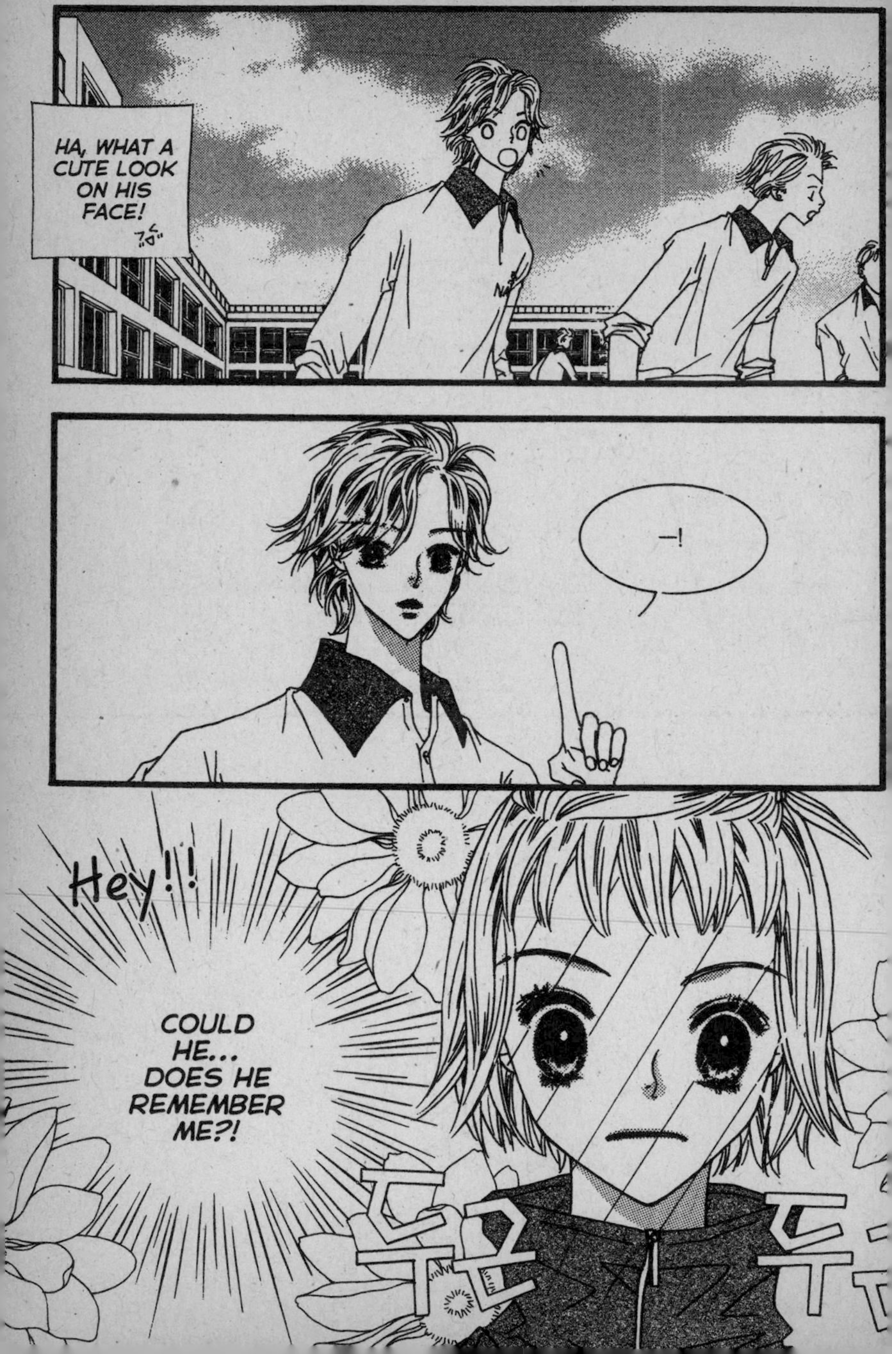
HA, WHAT A CUTE LOOK ON HIS FACE!
—!
Hey!!
COULD HE... DOES HE REMEMBER ME?!

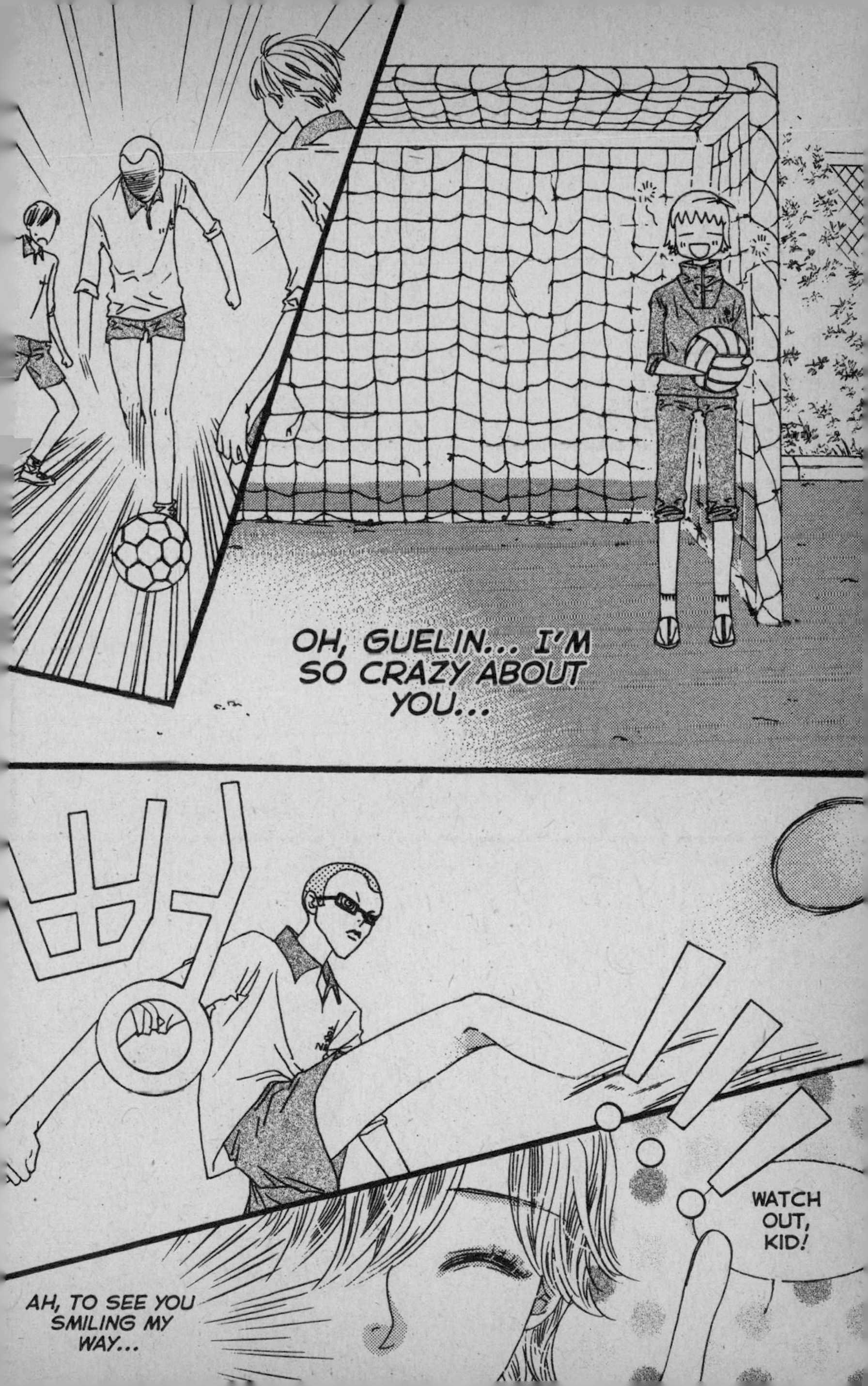
OH, GUELIN... I'M SO CRAZY ABOUT YOU...
AH, TO SEE YOU SMILING MY WAY...
WATCH OUT, KID!

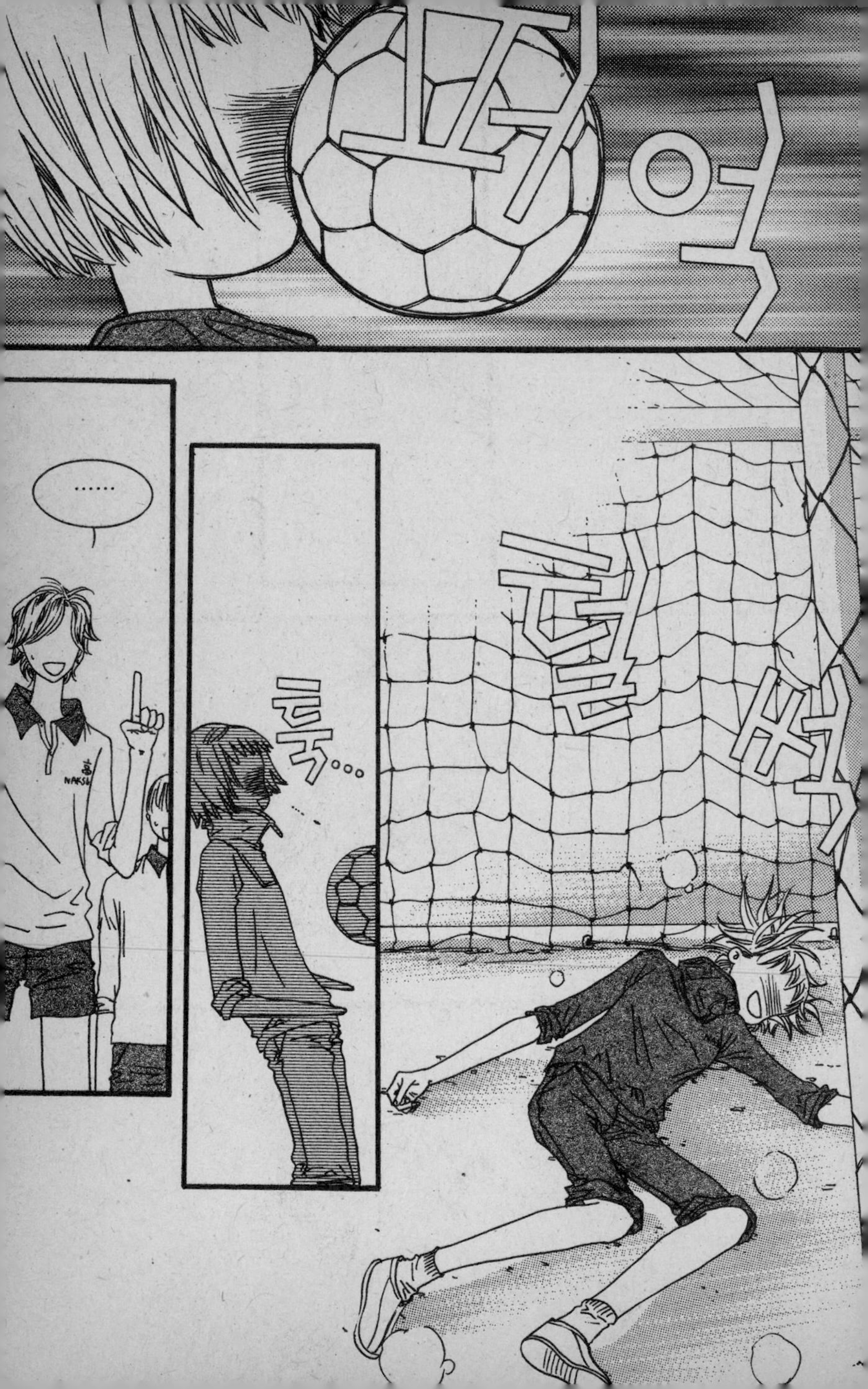

퍼억
……
툭…
털썩

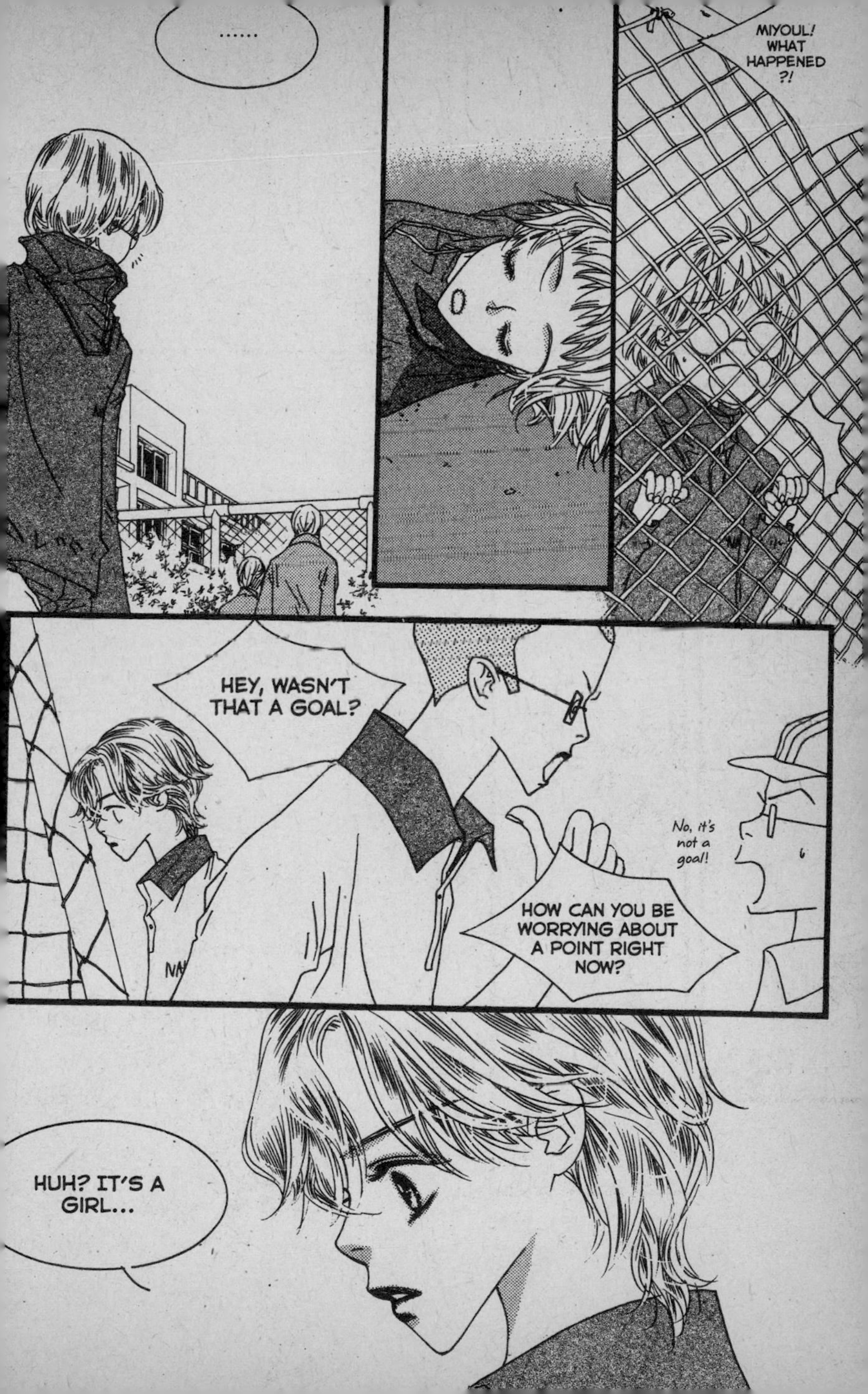
......
MIYOUL! WHAT HAPPENED ?!
HEY, WASN'T THAT A GOAL?
No, it's not a goal!
HOW CAN YOU BE WORRYING ABOUT A POINT RIGHT NOW?
HUH? IT'S A GIRL...

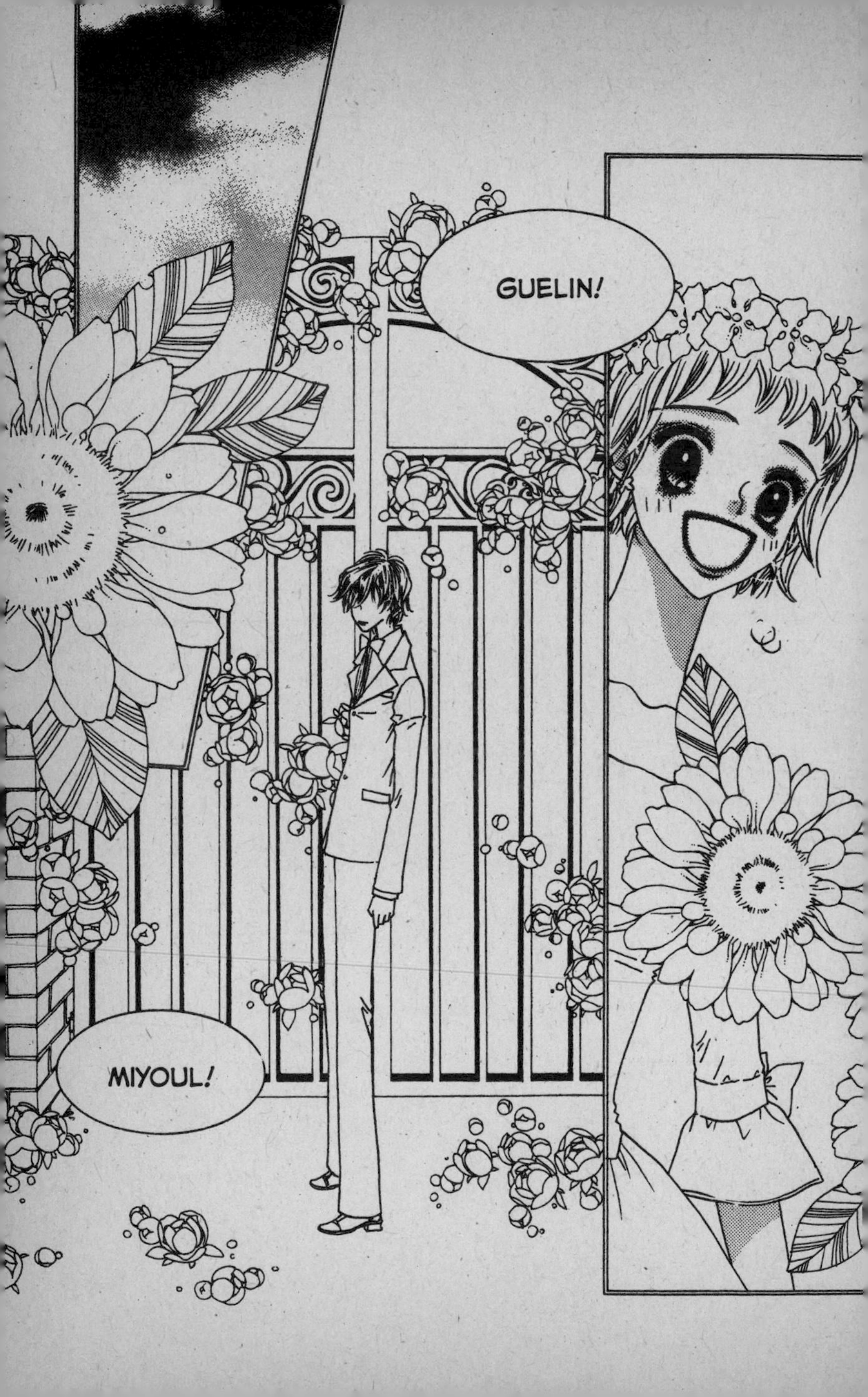
MIYOUL!
GUELIN!

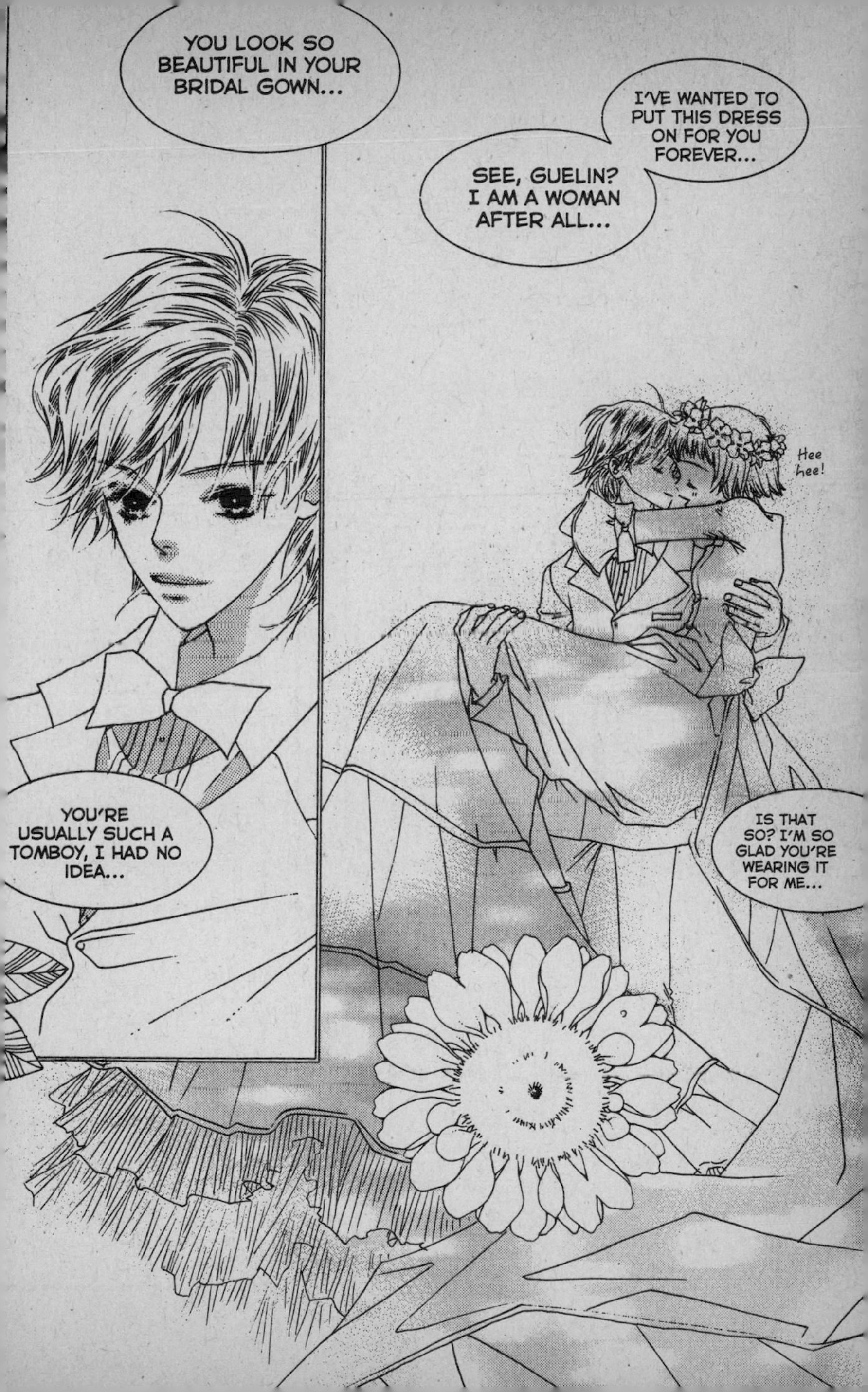
YOU LOOK SO BEAUTIFUL IN YOUR BRIDAL GOWN...
YOU'RE USUALLY SUCH A TOMBOY, I HAD NO IDEA...
SEE, GUELIN? I AM A WOMAN AFTER ALL...
I'VE WANTED TO PUT THIS DRESS ON FOR YOU FOREVER...
Hee hee!
IS THAT SO? I'M SO GLAD YOU'RE WEARING IT FOR ME...

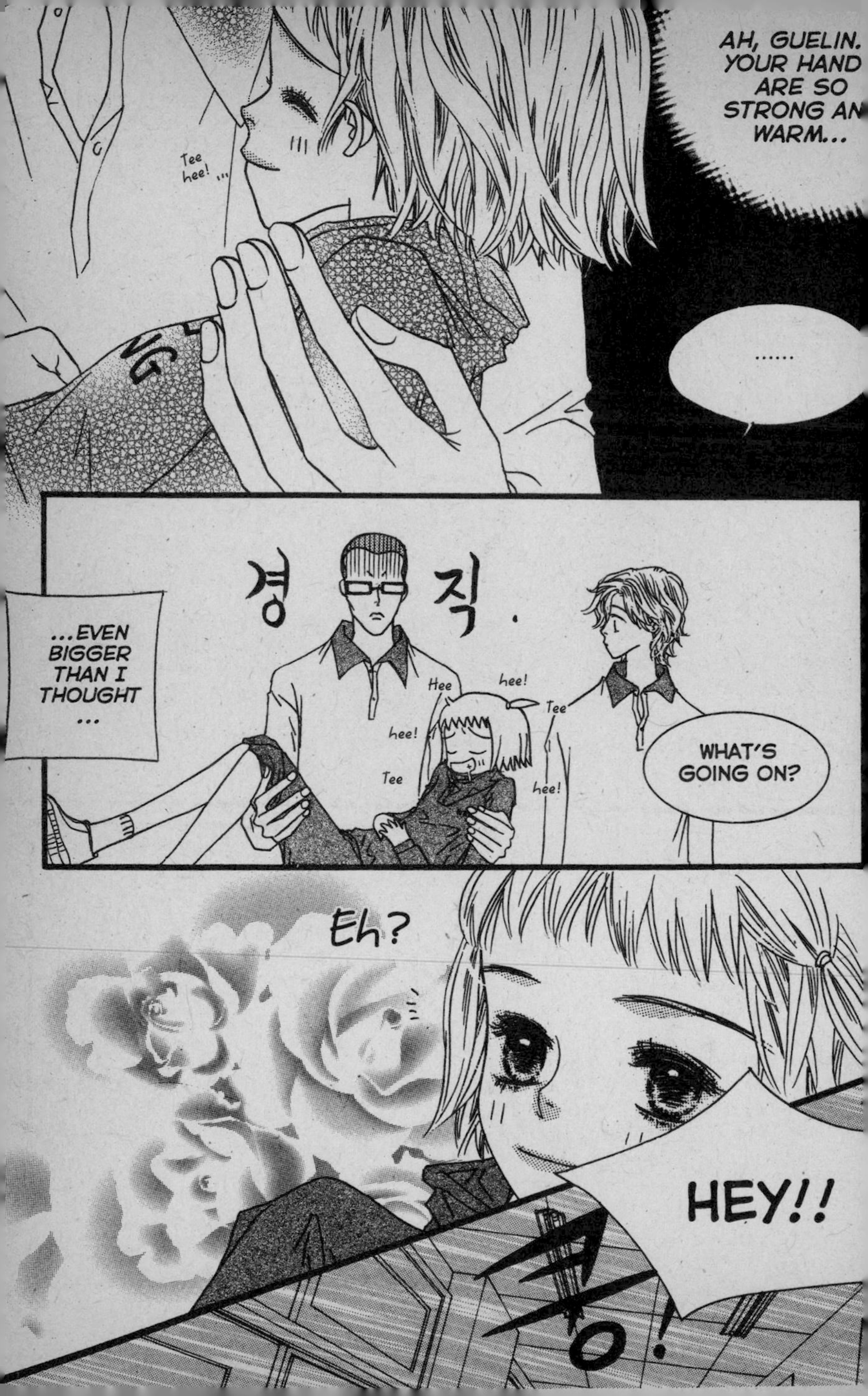
Tee hee! ...
AH, GUELIN. YOUR HAND ARE SO STRONG AN WARM...
......
...EVEN BIGGER THAN I THOUGHT ...
경 직 .
Hee hee!
Tee hee!
Tee hee!
WHAT'S GOING ON?
Eh?
HEY!!

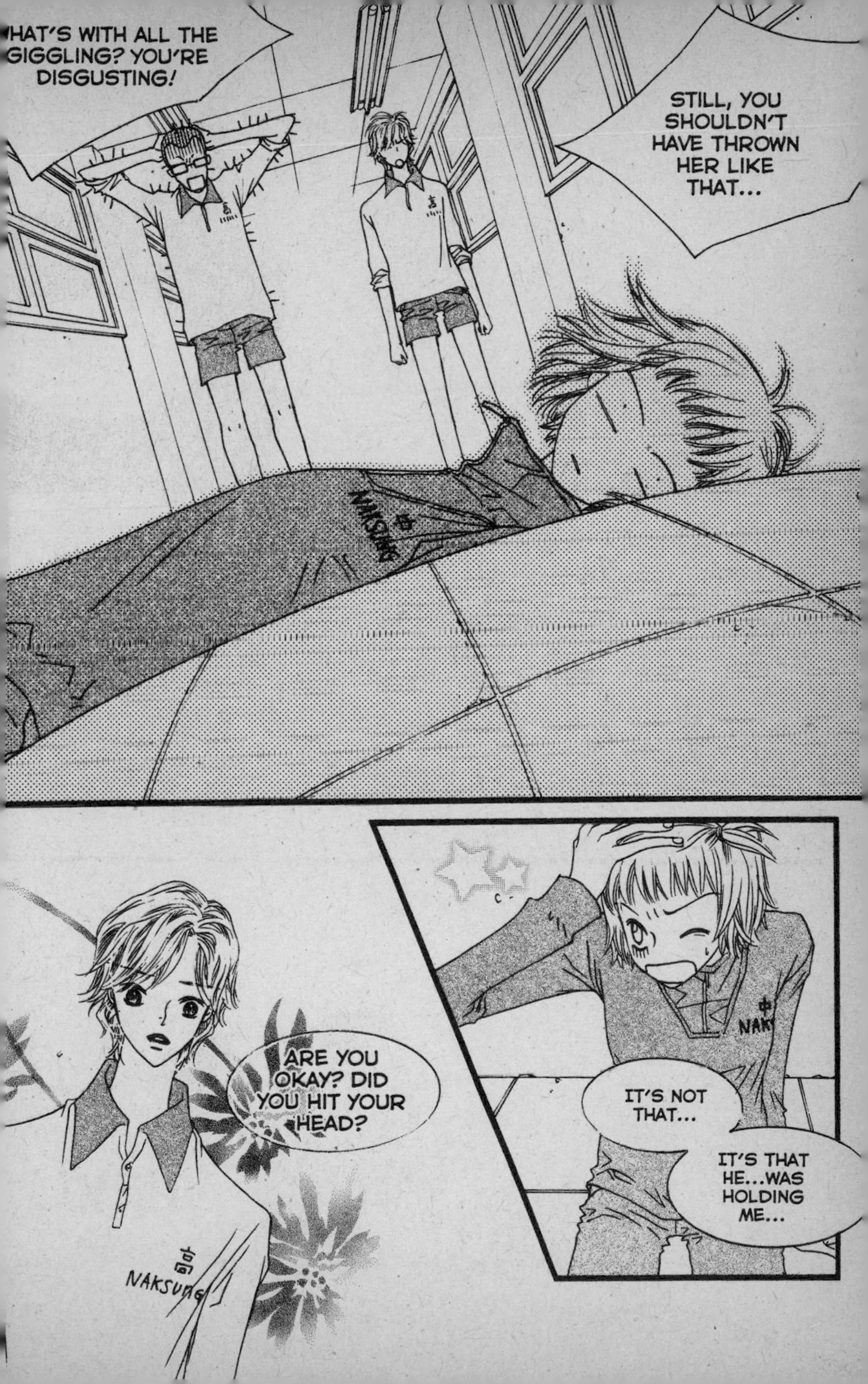
HAT'S WITH ALL THE GIGGLING? YOU'RE DISGUSTING!
STILL, YOU SHOULDN'T HAVE THROWN HER LIKE THAT...
NAKSUNG
ARE YOU OKAY? DID YOU HIT YOUR HEAD?
NAKSUNG
NAK
IT'S NOT THAT...
IT'S THAT HE...WAS HOLDING ME...

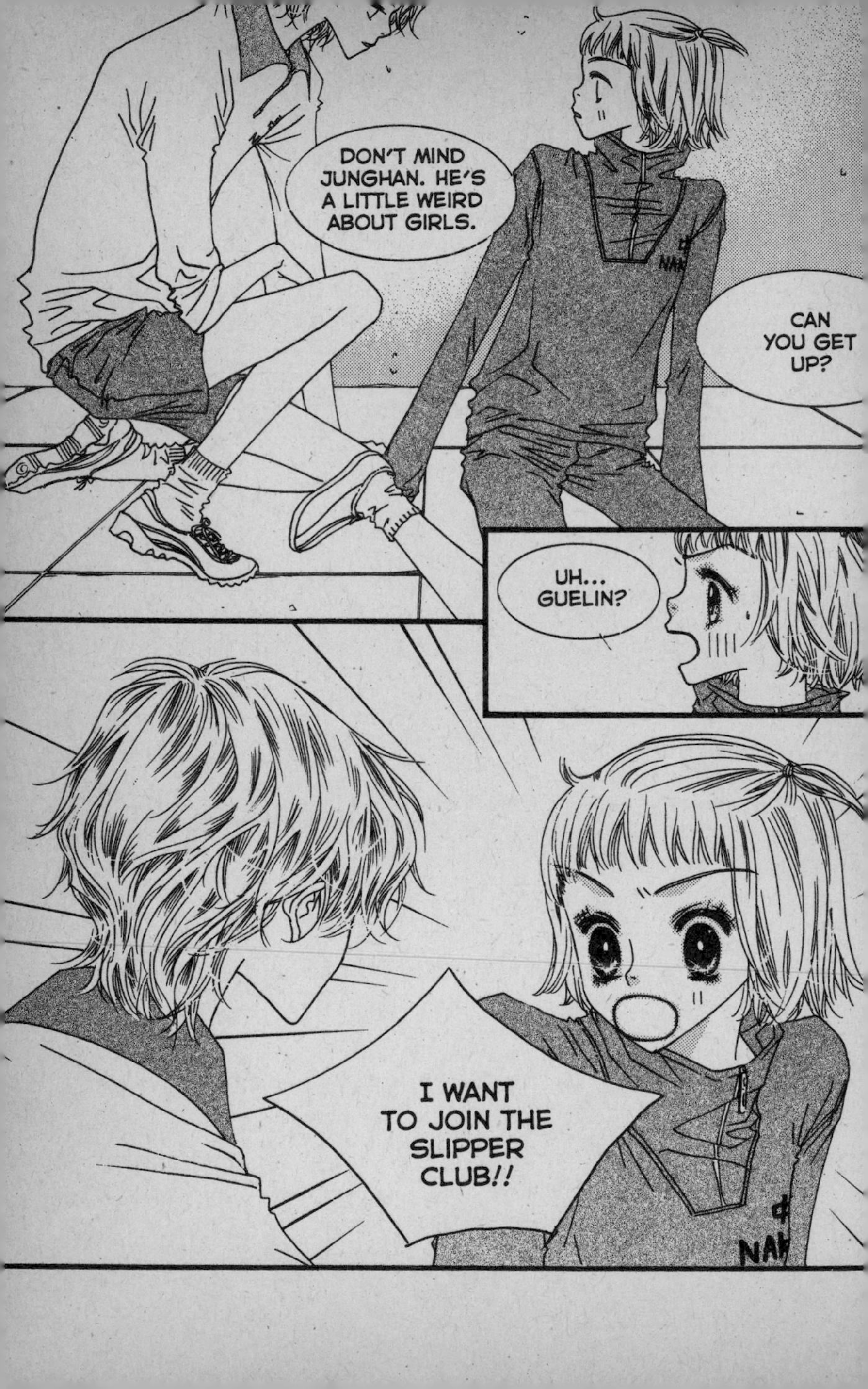
DON'T MIND JUNGHAN. HE'S A LITTLE WEIRD ABOUT GIRLS.
CAN YOU GET UP?
UH... GUELIN?
I WANT TO JOIN THE SLIPPER CLUB!!

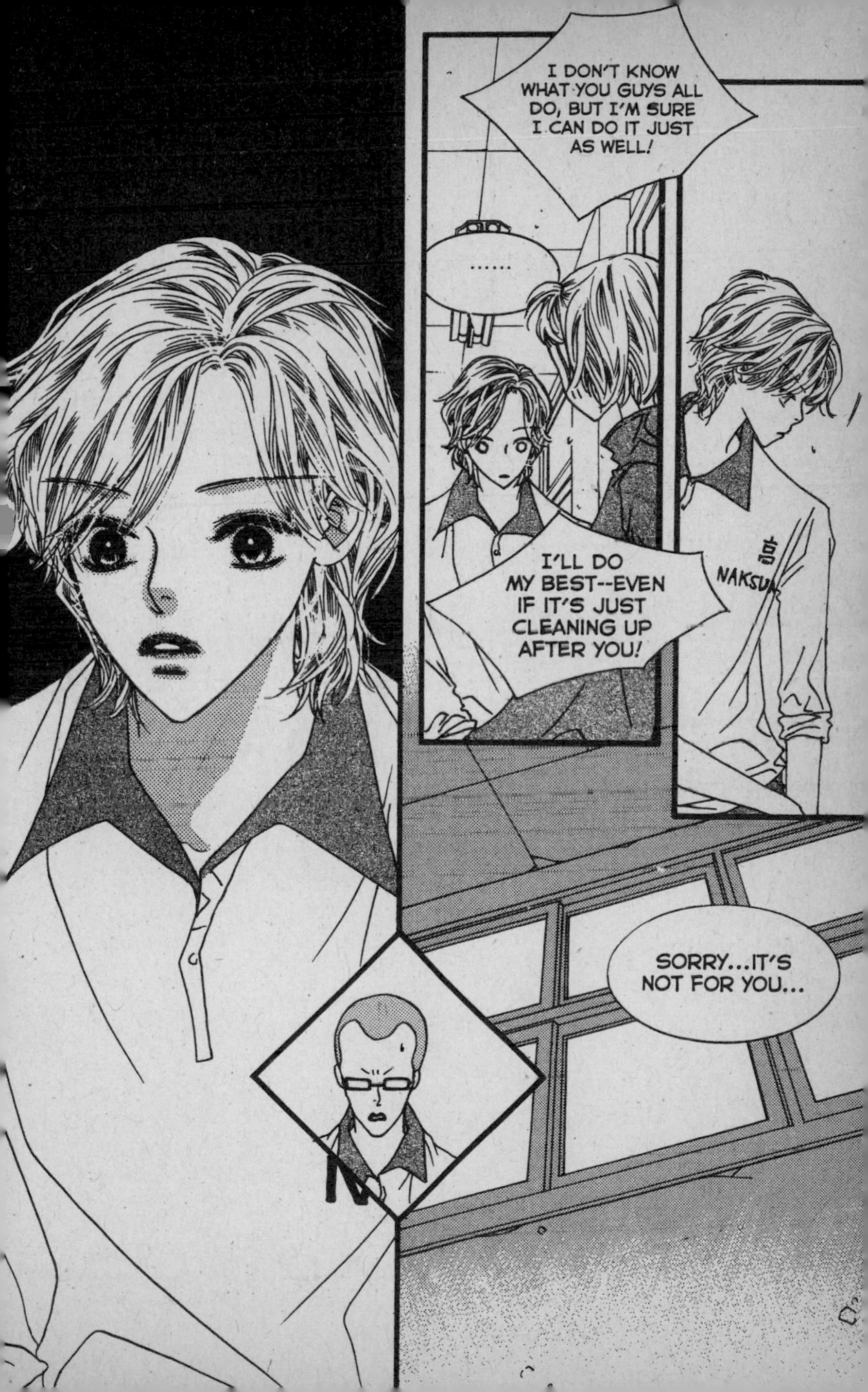
I DON'T KNOW WHAT YOU GUYS ALL DO, BUT I'M SURE I CAN DO IT JUST AS WELL!
......
I'LL DO MY BEST--EVEN IF IT'S JUST CLEANING UP AFTER YOU!
SORRY...IT'S NOT FOR YOU...

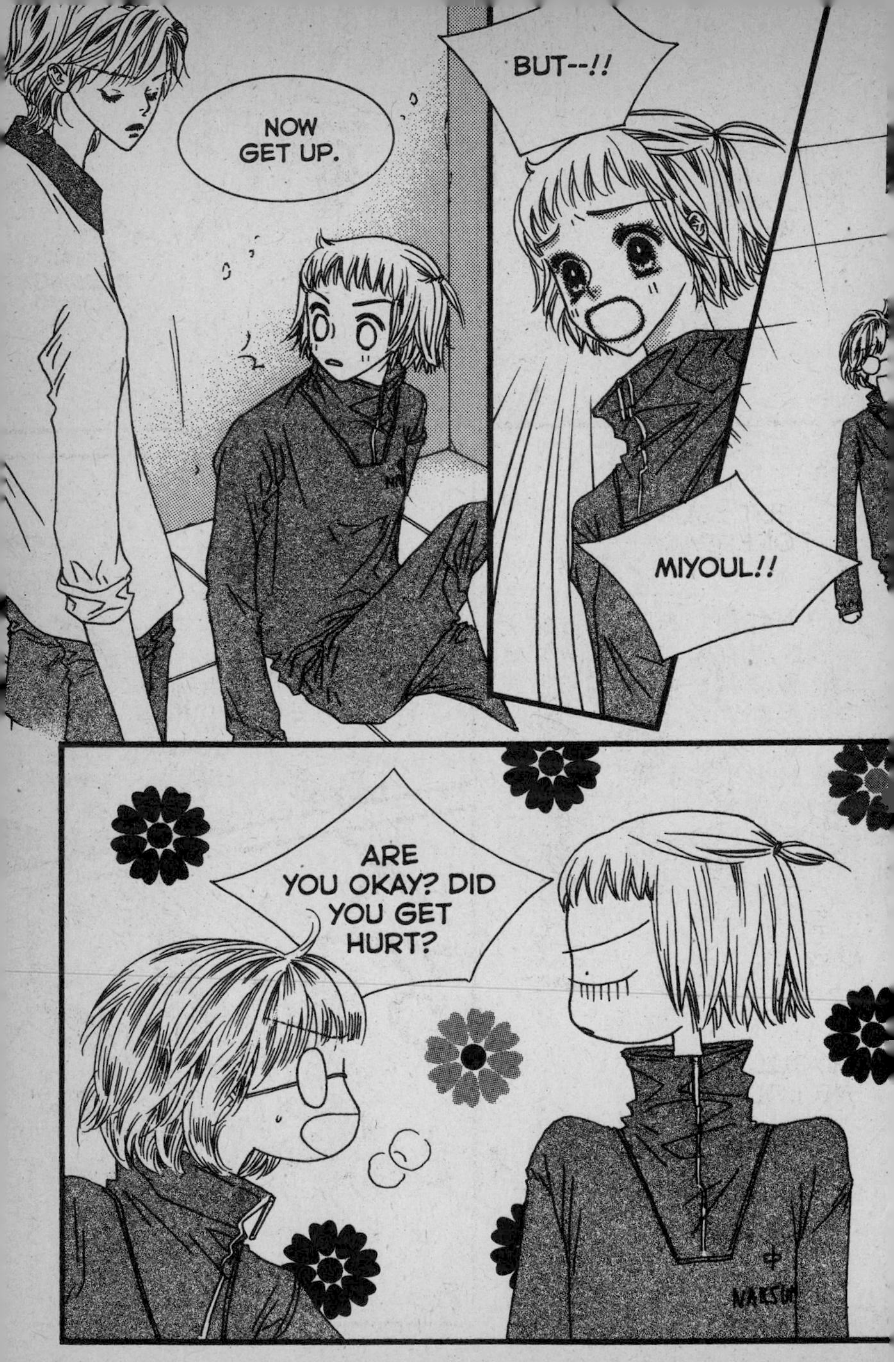
NOW GET UP.
BUT--!!
MIYOUL!!
ARE YOU OKAY? DID YOU GET HURT?

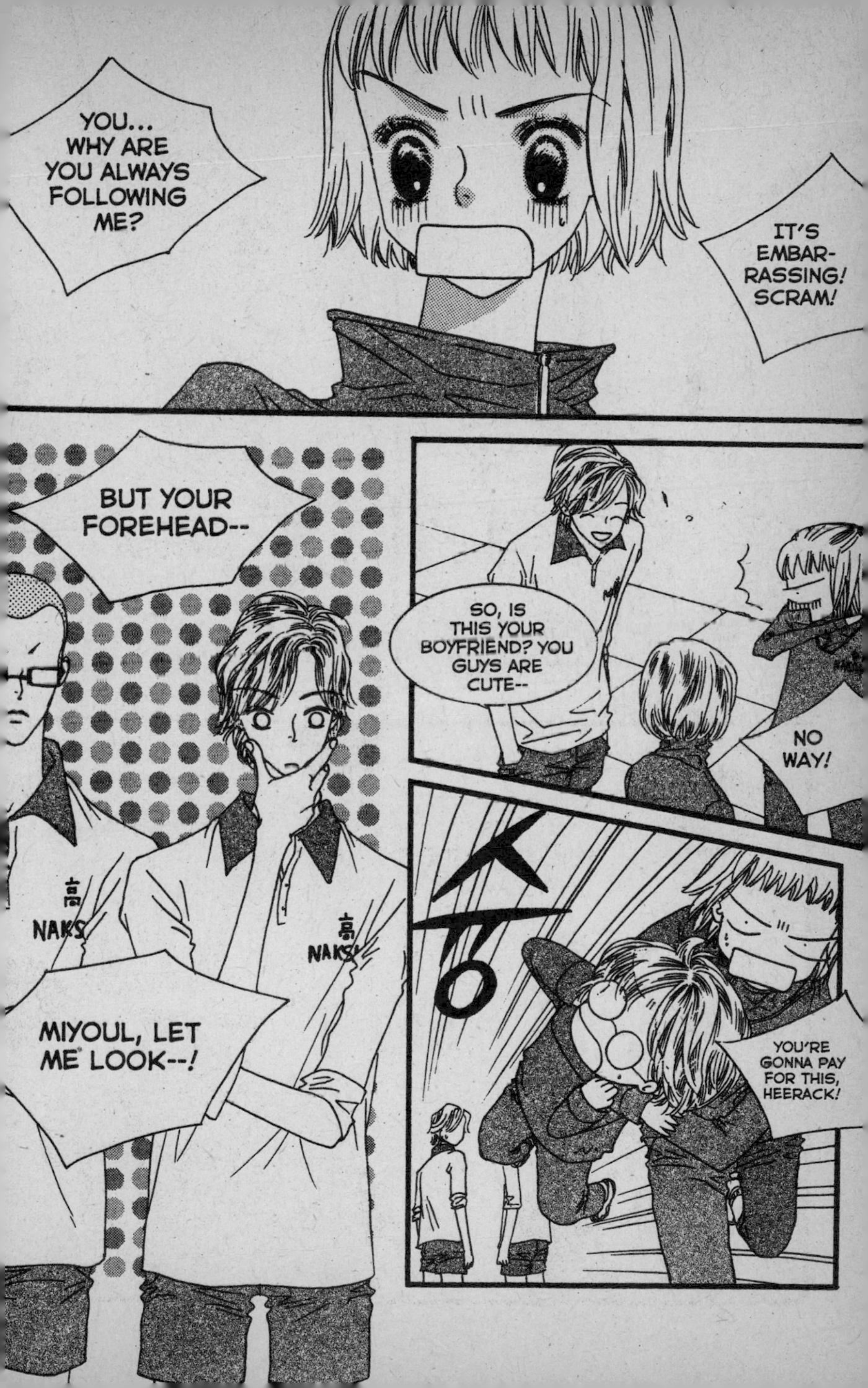
YOU... WHY ARE YOU ALWAYS FOLLOWING ME?
IT'S EMBAR-RASSING! SCRAM!
BUT YOUR FOREHEAD--
MIYOUL, LET ME LOOK--!
SO, IS THIS YOUR BOYFRIEND? YOU GUYS ARE CUTE--
NO WAY!
YOU'RE GONNA PAY FOR THIS, HEERACK!

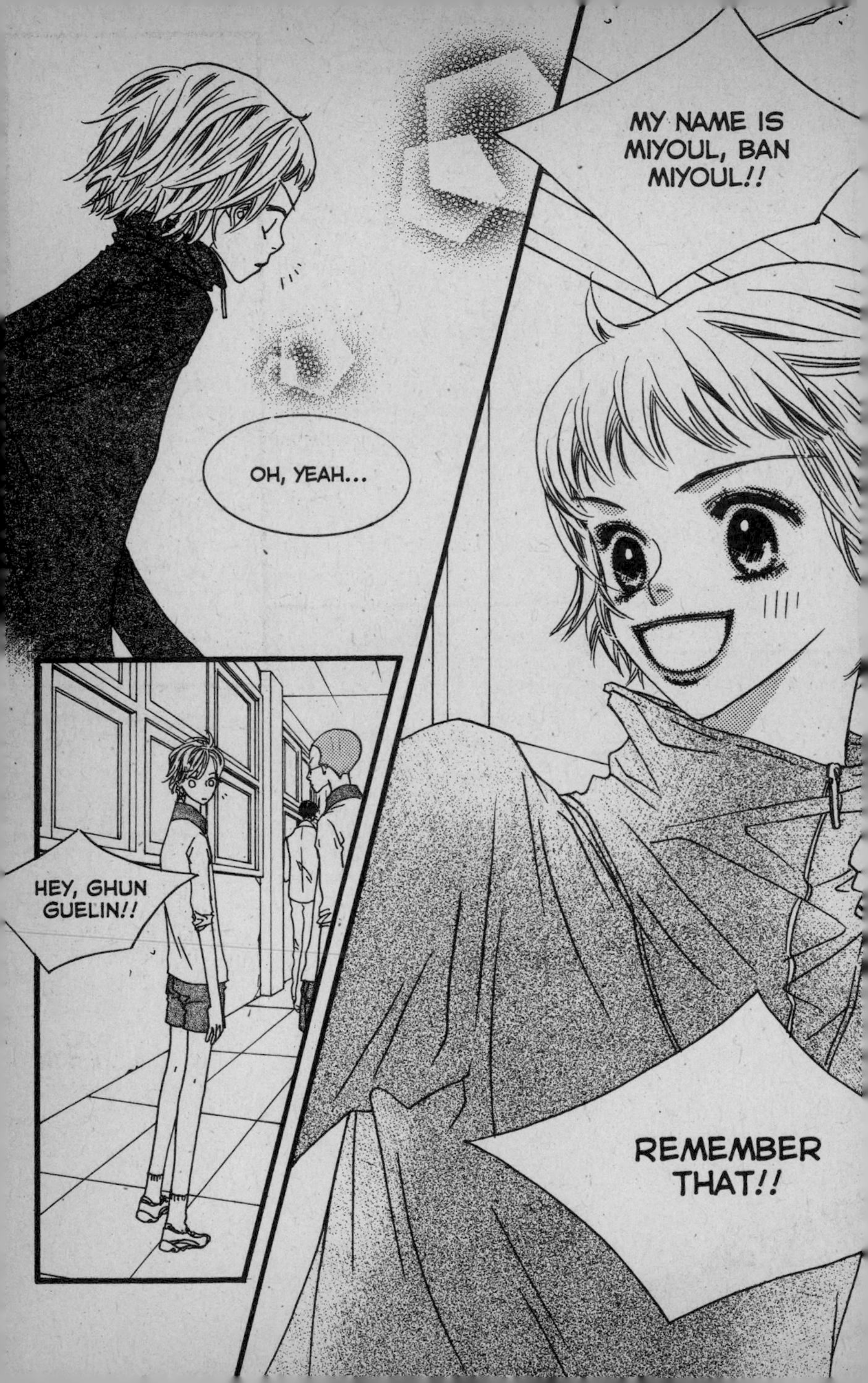
OH, YEAH...
HEY, GHUN GUELIN!!
MY NAME IS MIYOUL, BAN MIYOUL!!
REMEMBER THAT!!

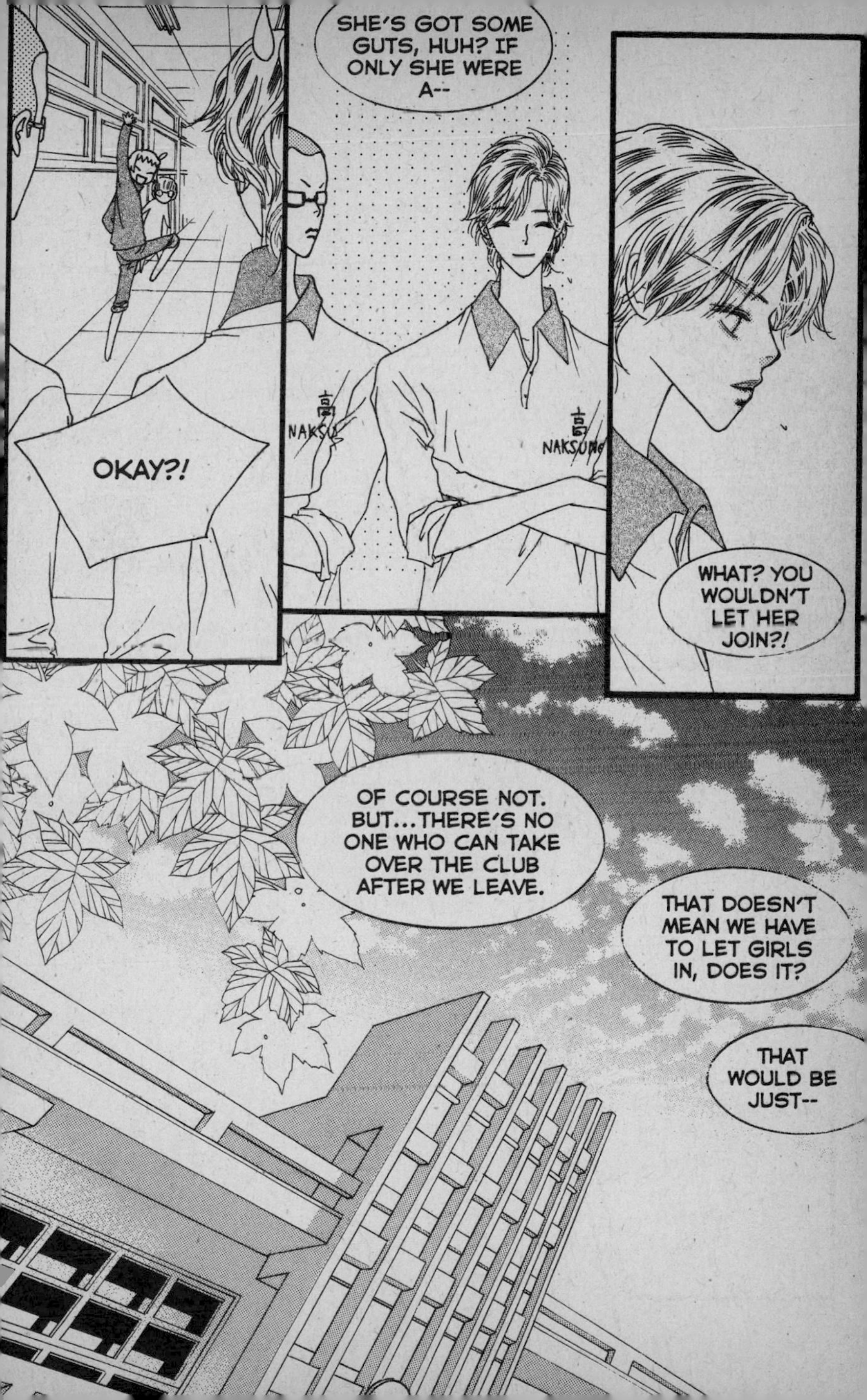
OKAY?!
SHE'S GOT SOME GUTS, HUH? IF ONLY SHE WERE A--
NAKSU
NAKSU
WHAT? YOU WOULDN'T LET HER JOIN?!
OF COURSE NOT. BUT...THERE'S NO ONE WHO CAN TAKE OVER THE CLUB AFTER WE LEAVE.
THAT DOESN'T MEAN WE HAVE TO LET GIRLS IN, DOES IT?
THAT WOULD BE JUST--

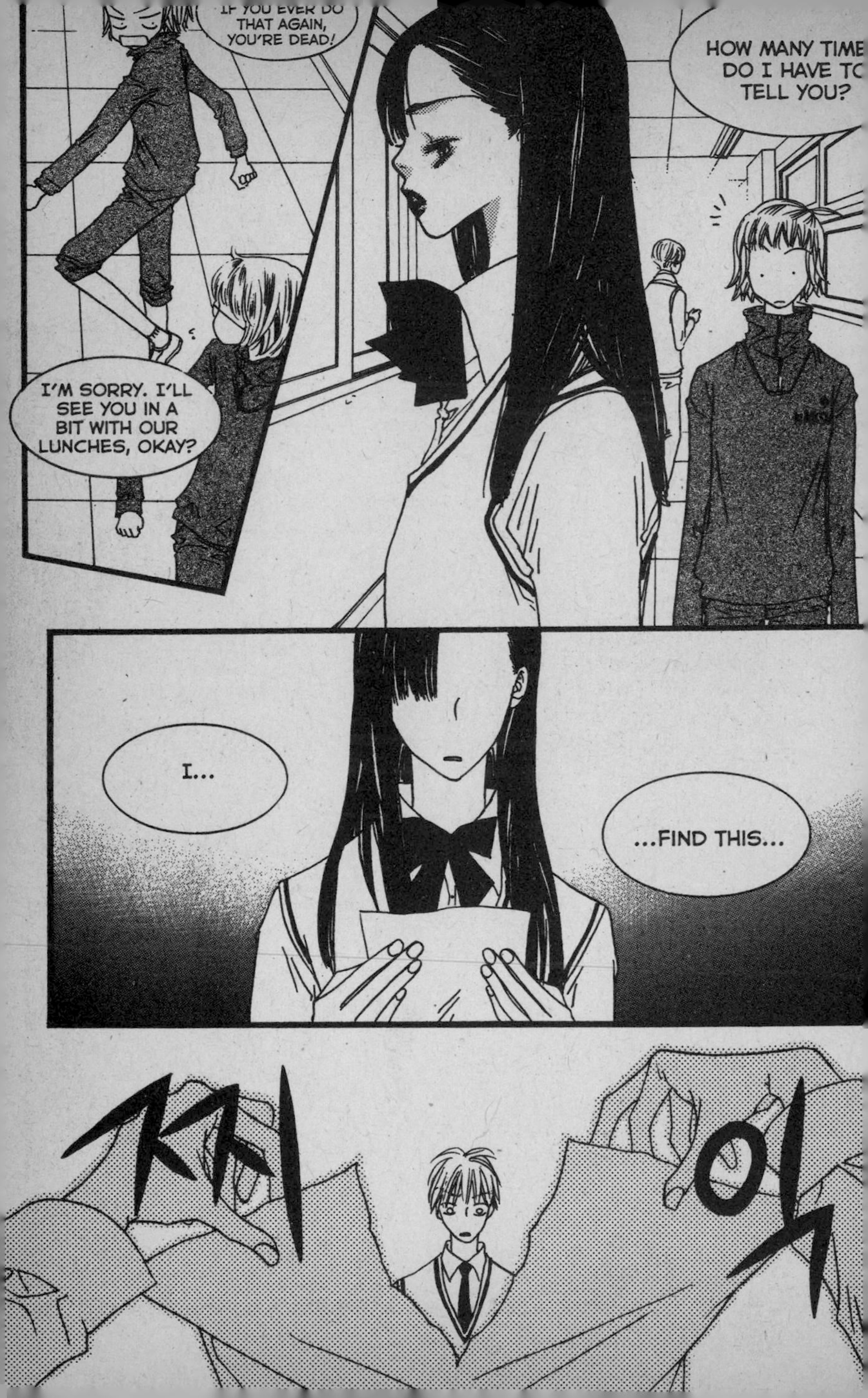
IF YOU EVER DO THAT AGAIN, YOU'RE DEAD!
I'M SORRY. I'LL SEE YOU IN A BIT WITH OUR LUNCHES, OKAY?
HOW MANY TIME DO I HAVE TO TELL YOU?
I...
...FIND THIS...

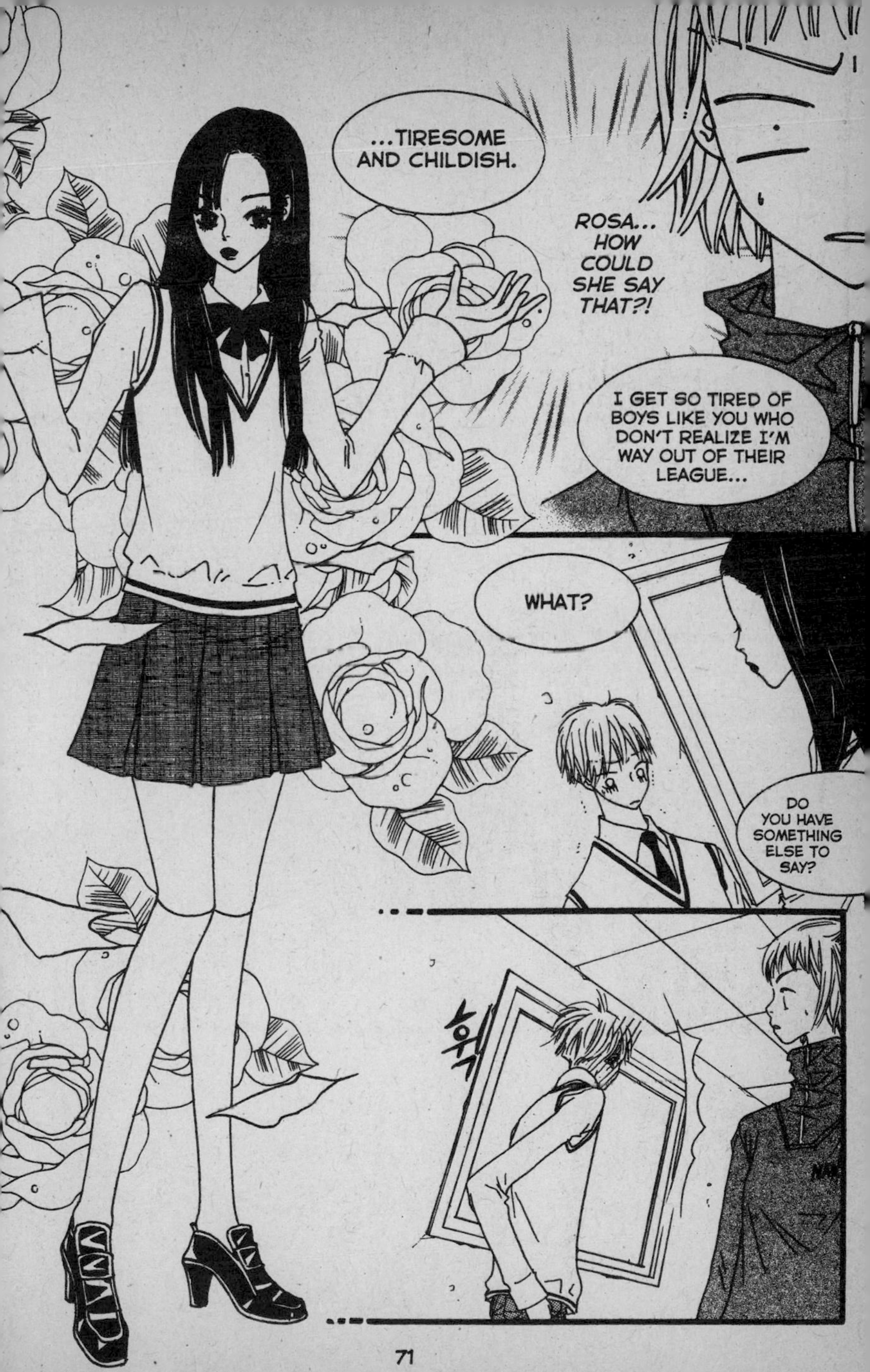
...TIRESOME AND CHILDISH.
ROSA... HOW COULD SHE SAY THAT?!
I GET SO TIRED OF BOYS LIKE YOU WHO DON'T REALIZE I'M WAY OUT OF THEIR LEAGUE...
WHAT?
DO YOU HAVE SOMETHING ELSE TO SAY?

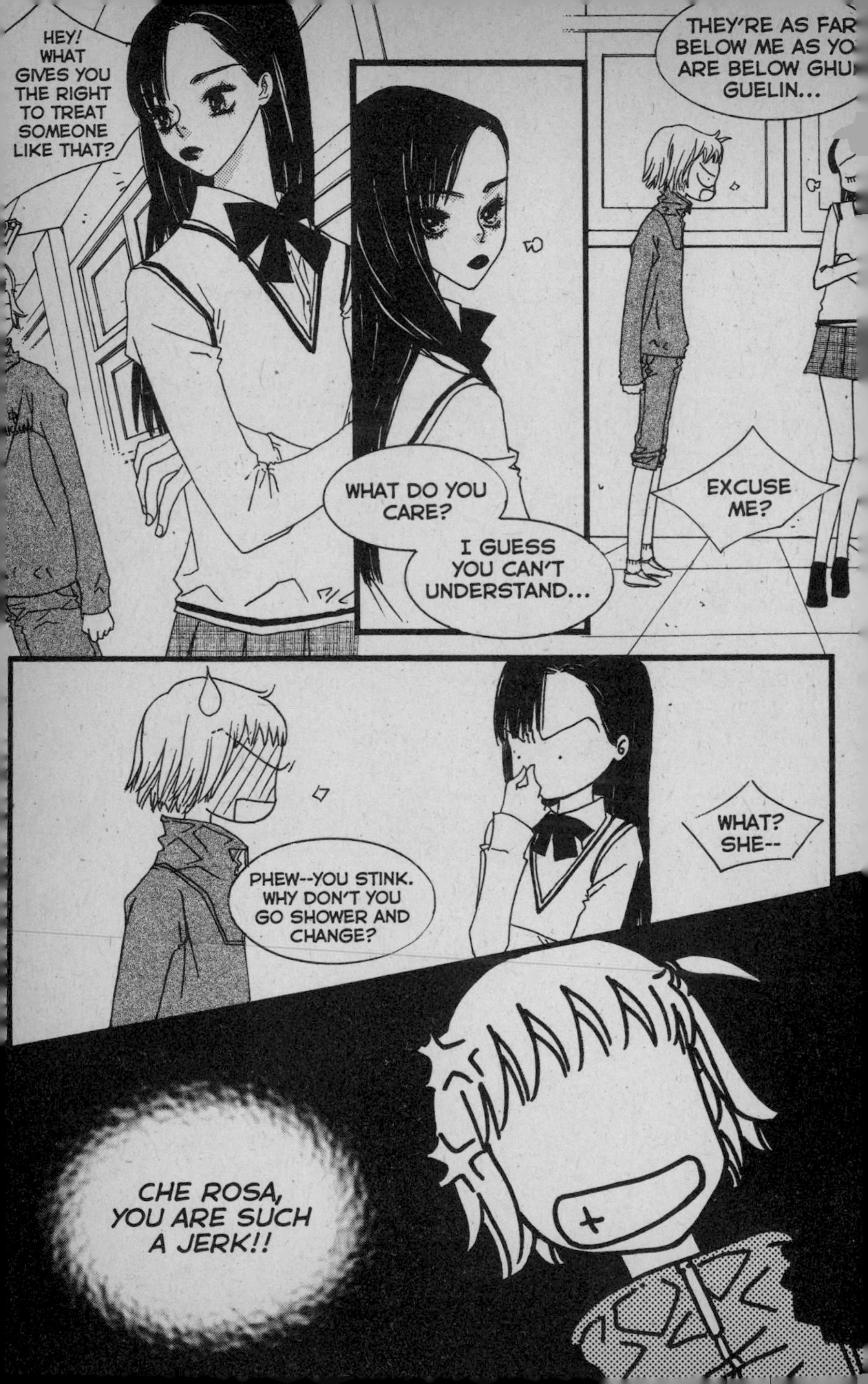
HEY! WHAT GIVES YOU THE RIGHT TO TREAT SOMEONE LIKE THAT?
WHAT DO YOU CARE?
I GUESS YOU CAN'T UNDERSTAND...
THEY'RE AS FAR BELOW ME AS YO ARE BELOW GHU GUELIN...
EXCUSE ME?
PHEW--YOU STINK. WHY DON'T YOU GO SHOWER AND CHANGE?
WHAT? SHE--
CHE ROSA, YOU ARE SUCH A JERK!!

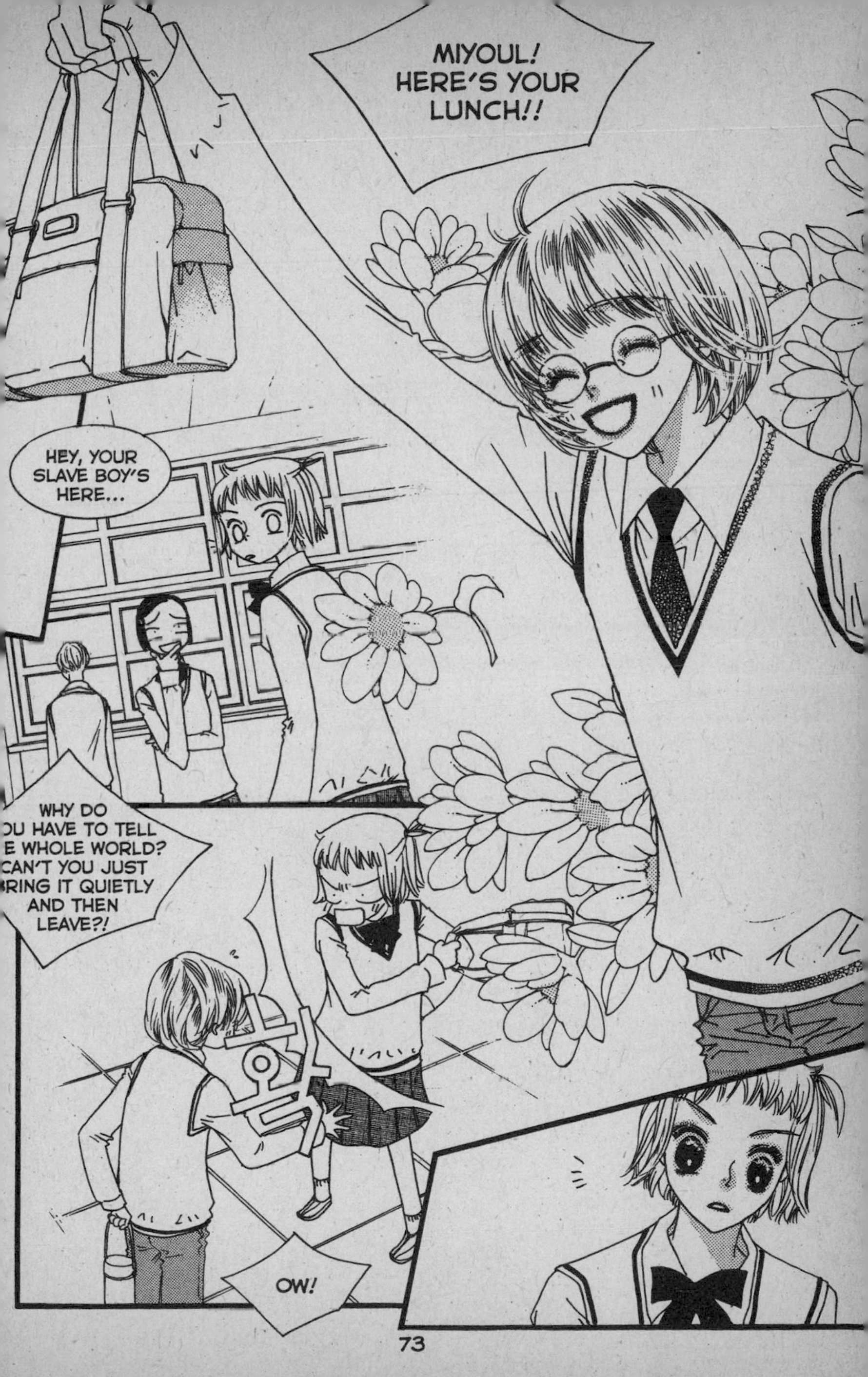
MIYOUL! HERE'S YOUR LUNCH!!
HEY, YOUR SLAVE BOY'S HERE...
WHY DO
OU HAVE TO TELL
E WHOLE WORLD?
CAN'T YOU JUST
RING IT QUIETLY
AND THEN
LEAVE?!
OW!

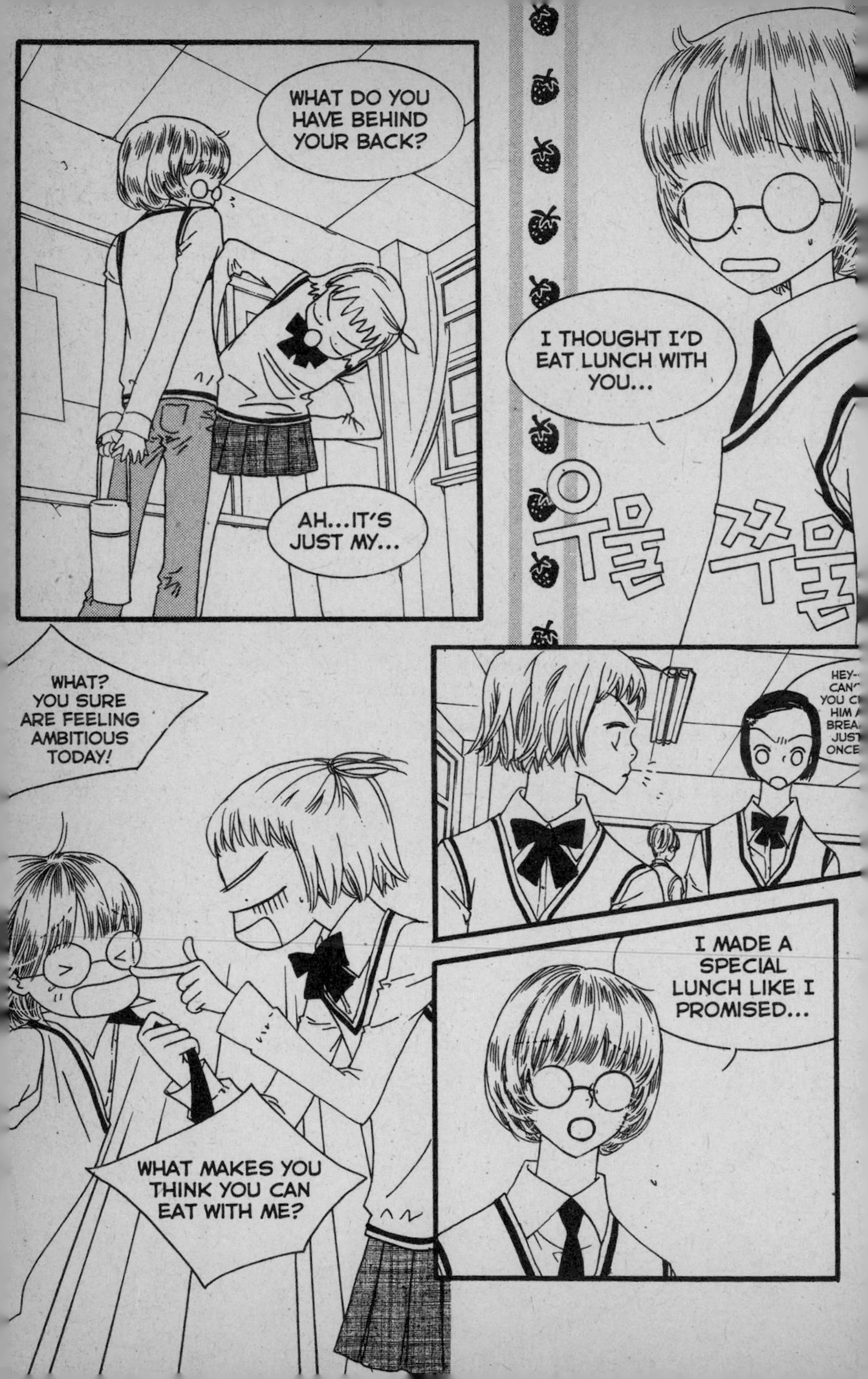
WHAT DO YOU HAVE BEHIND YOUR BACK?
AH...IT'S JUST MY...
I THOUGHT I'D EAT LUNCH WITH YOU...
우물
쭈물
WHAT? YOU SURE ARE FEELING AMBITIOUS TODAY!
WHAT MAKES YOU THINK YOU CAN EAT WITH ME?
HEY--
I MADE A SPECIAL LUNCH LIKE I PROMISED...

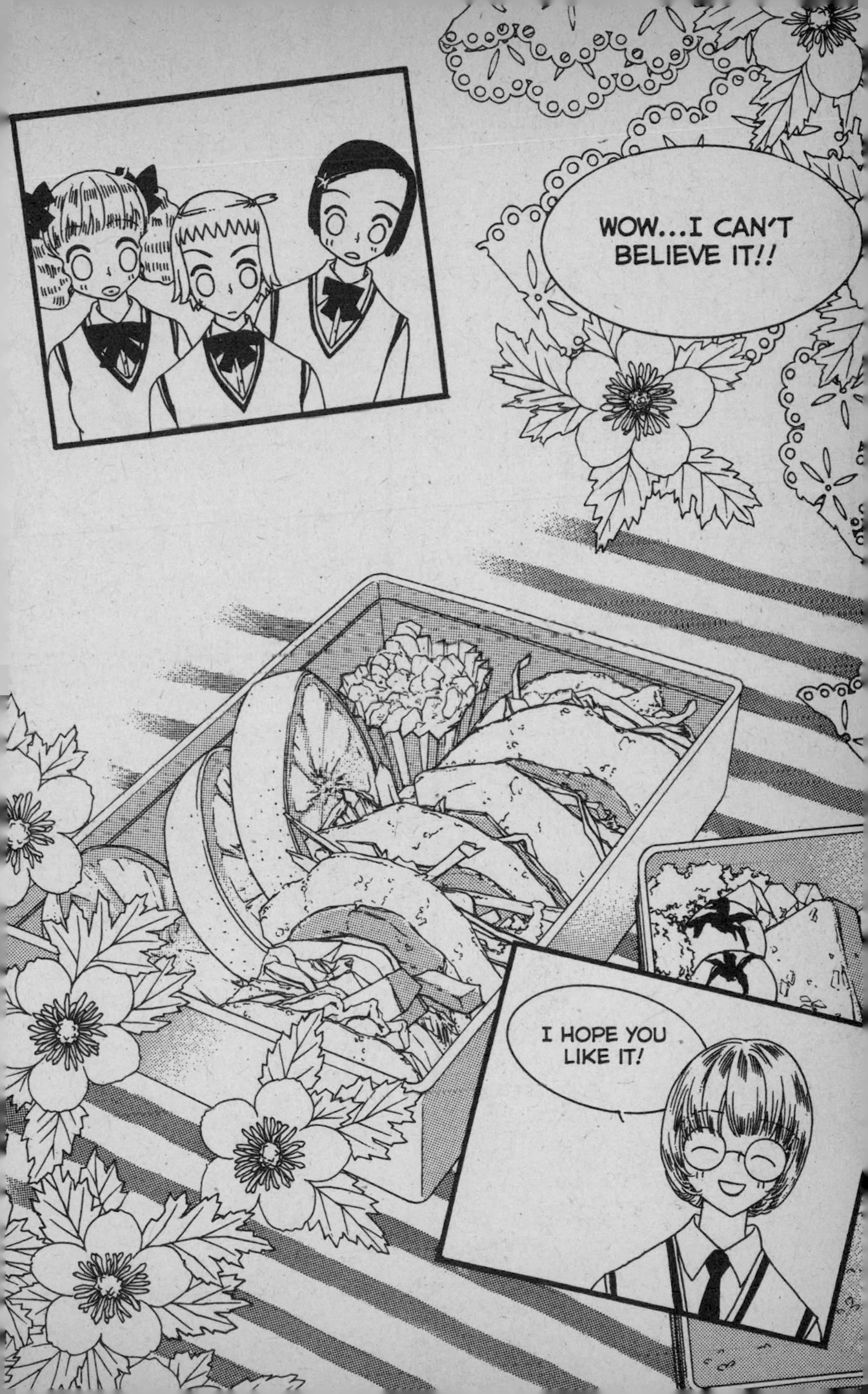
WOW...I CAN'T BELIEVE IT!!
I HOPE YOU LIKE IT!

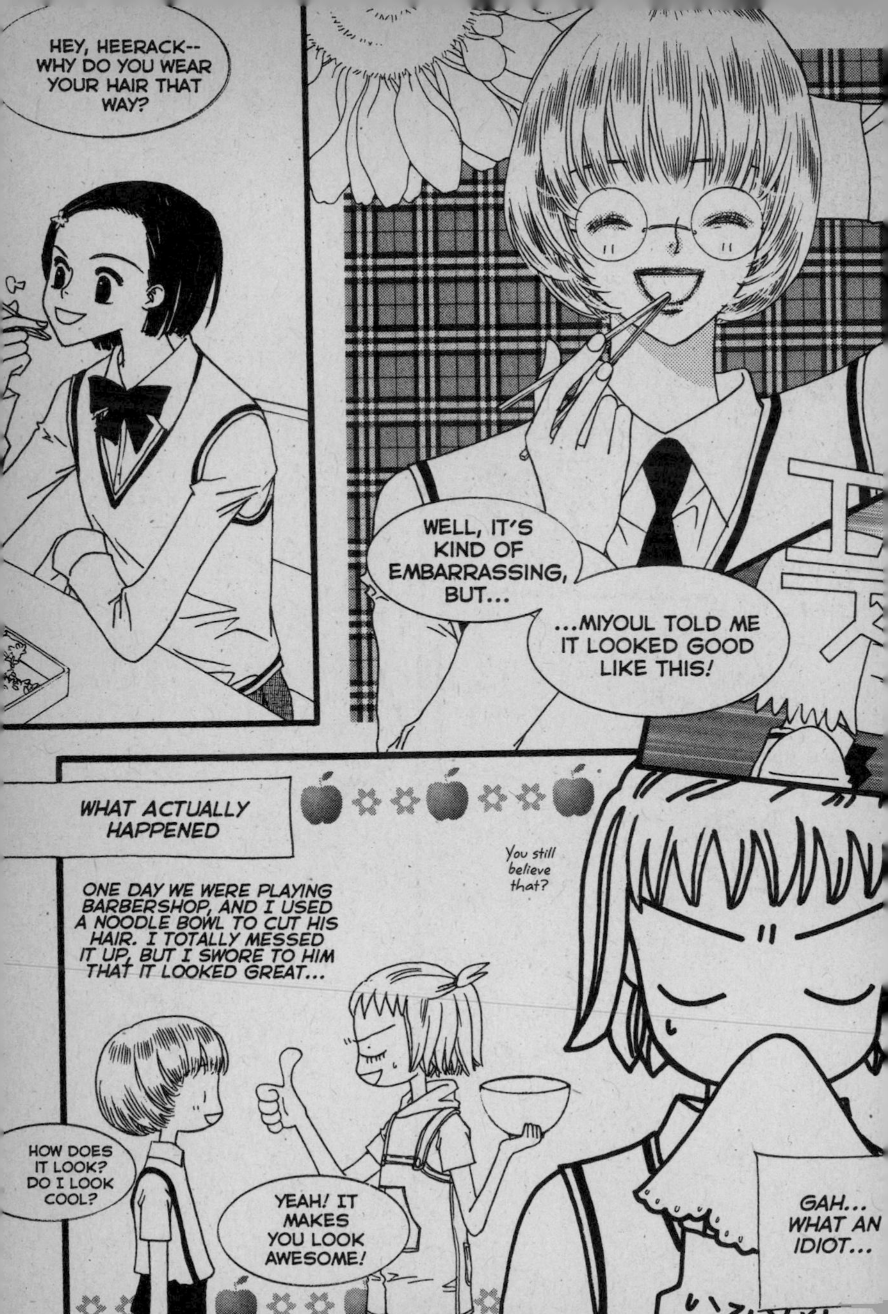
HEY, HEERACK-- WHY DO YOU WEAR YOUR HAIR THAT WAY?
WELL, IT'S KIND OF EMBARRASSING, BUT...
...MIYOUL TOLD ME IT LOOKED GOOD LIKE THIS!
WHAT ACTUALLY HAPPENED
ONE DAY WE WERE PLAYING BARBERSHOP, AND I USED A NOODLE BOWL TO CUT HIS HAIR. I TOTALLY MESSED IT UP, BUT I SWORE TO HIM THAT IT LOOKED GREAT...
HOW DOES IT LOOK? DO I LOOK COOL?
YEAH! IT MAKES YOU LOOK AWESOME!
You still believe that?
GAH... WHAT AN IDIOT...

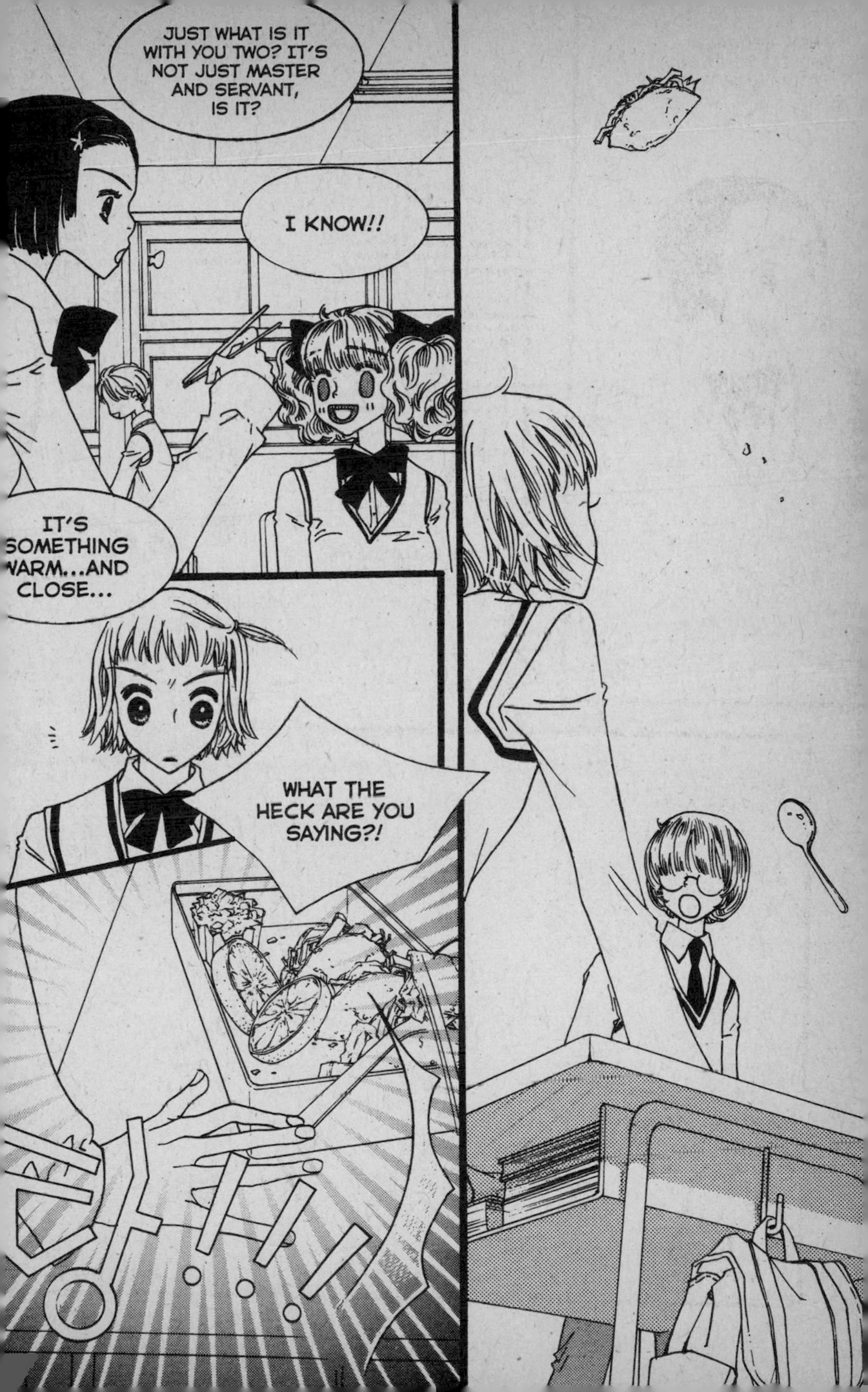
JUST WHAT IS IT WITH YOU TWO? IT'S NOT JUST MASTER AND SERVANT, IS IT?
I KNOW!!
IT'S SOMETHING WARM...AND CLOSE...
WHAT THE HECK ARE YOU SAYING?!

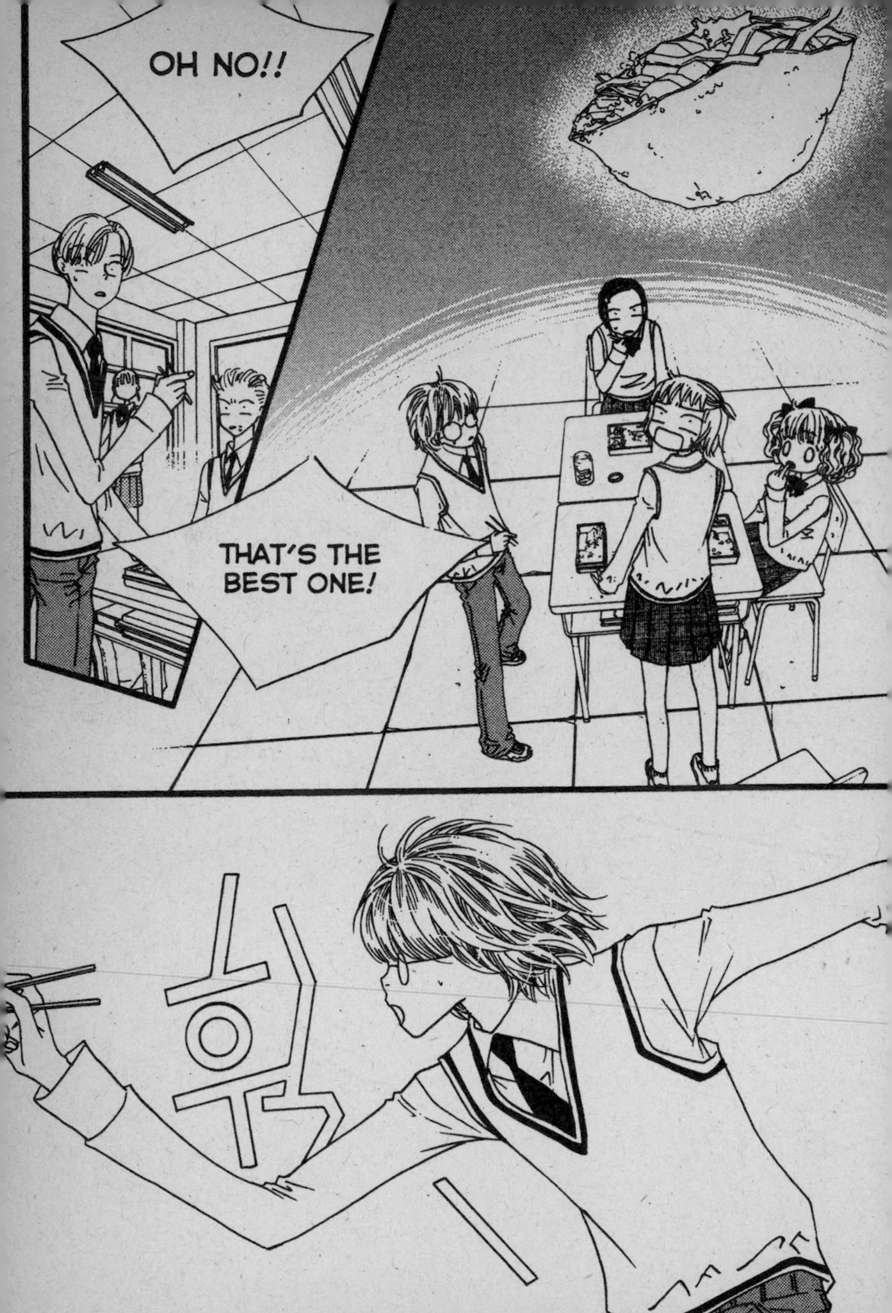
OH NO!!
THAT'S THE BEST ONE!

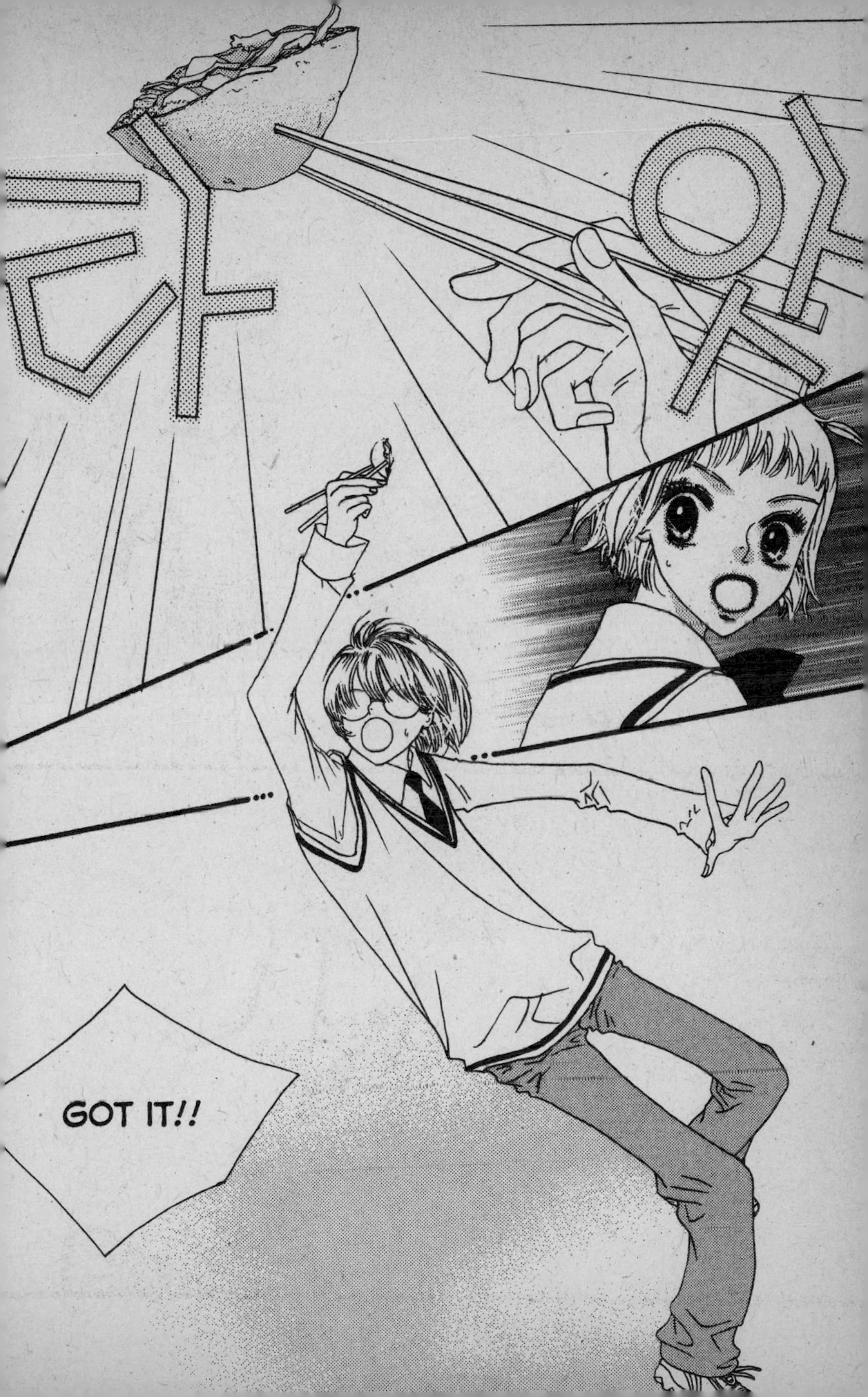
GOT IT!!

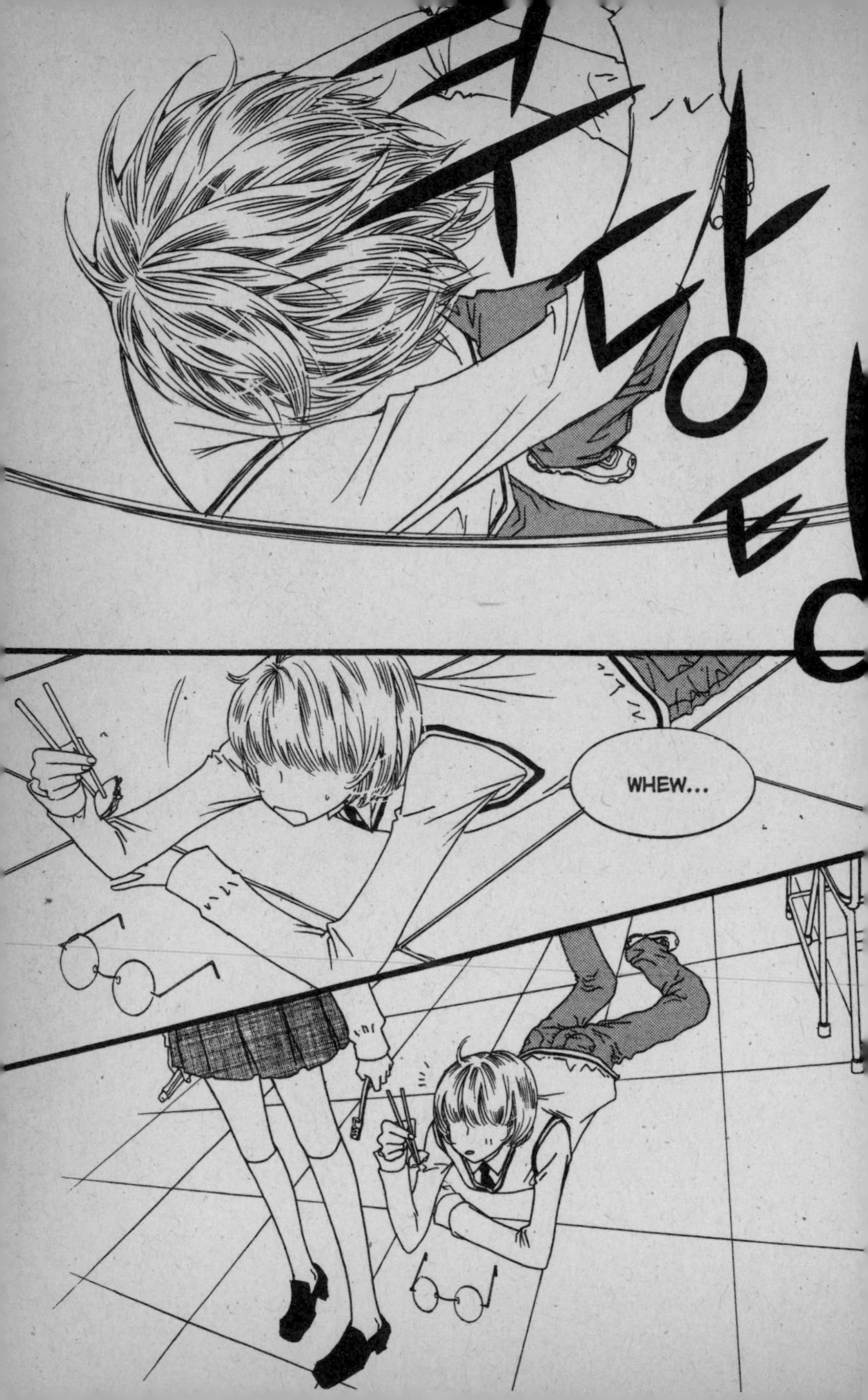
WHEW...

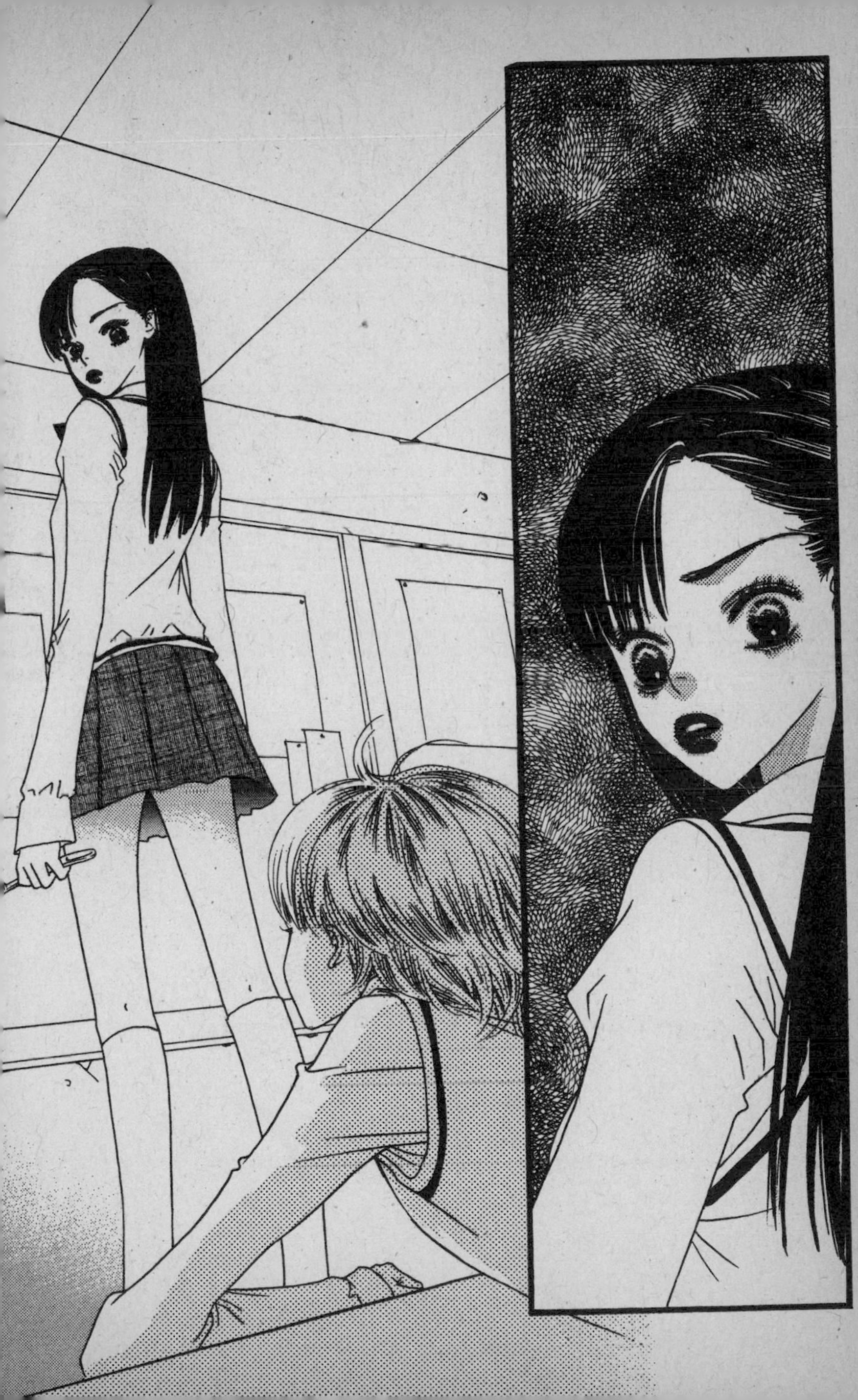

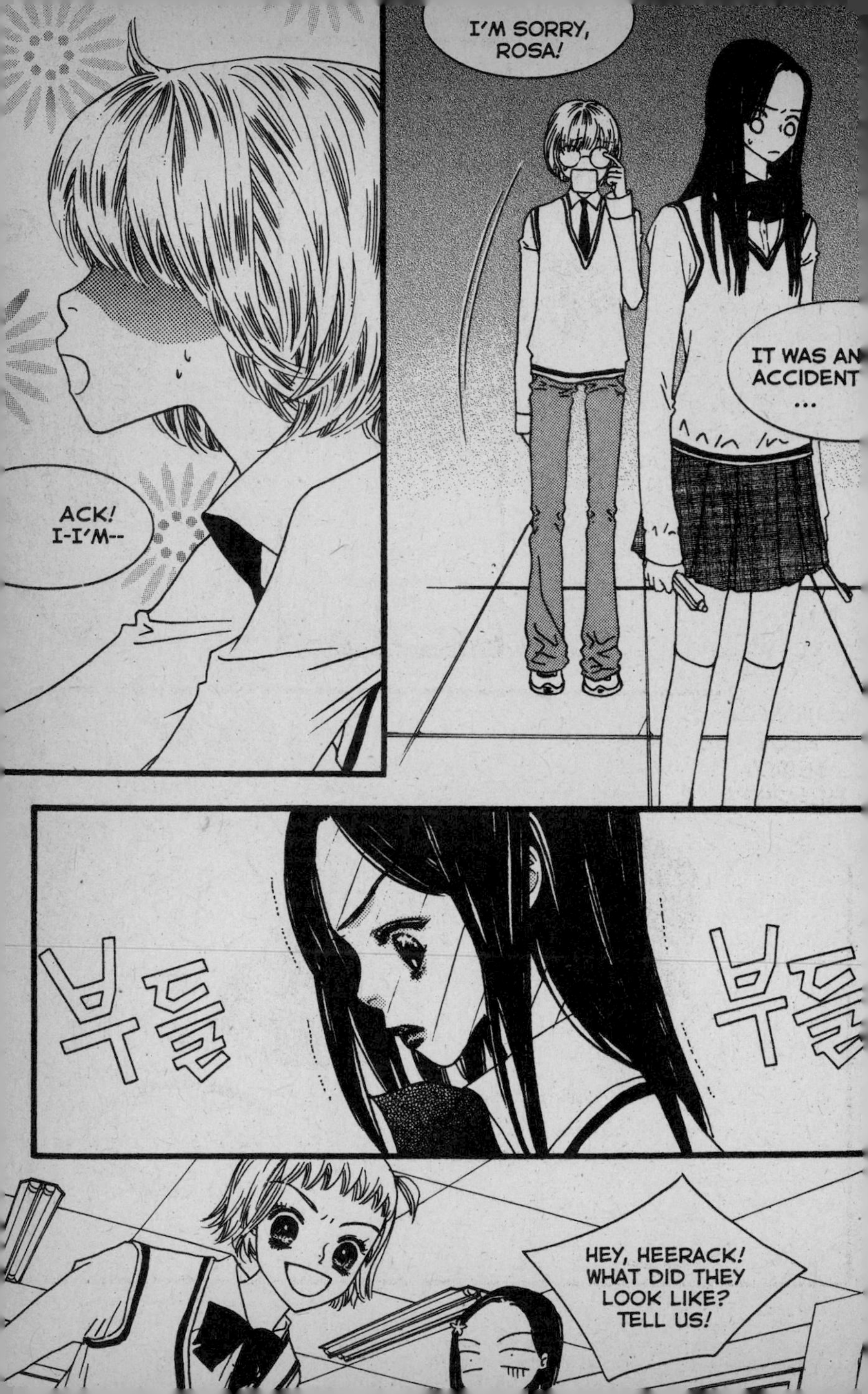
ACK! I-I'M--
I'M SORRY, ROSA!
IT WAS AN ACCIDENT ...
부들
부들
HEY, HEERACK! WHAT DID THEY LOOK LIKE? TELL US!

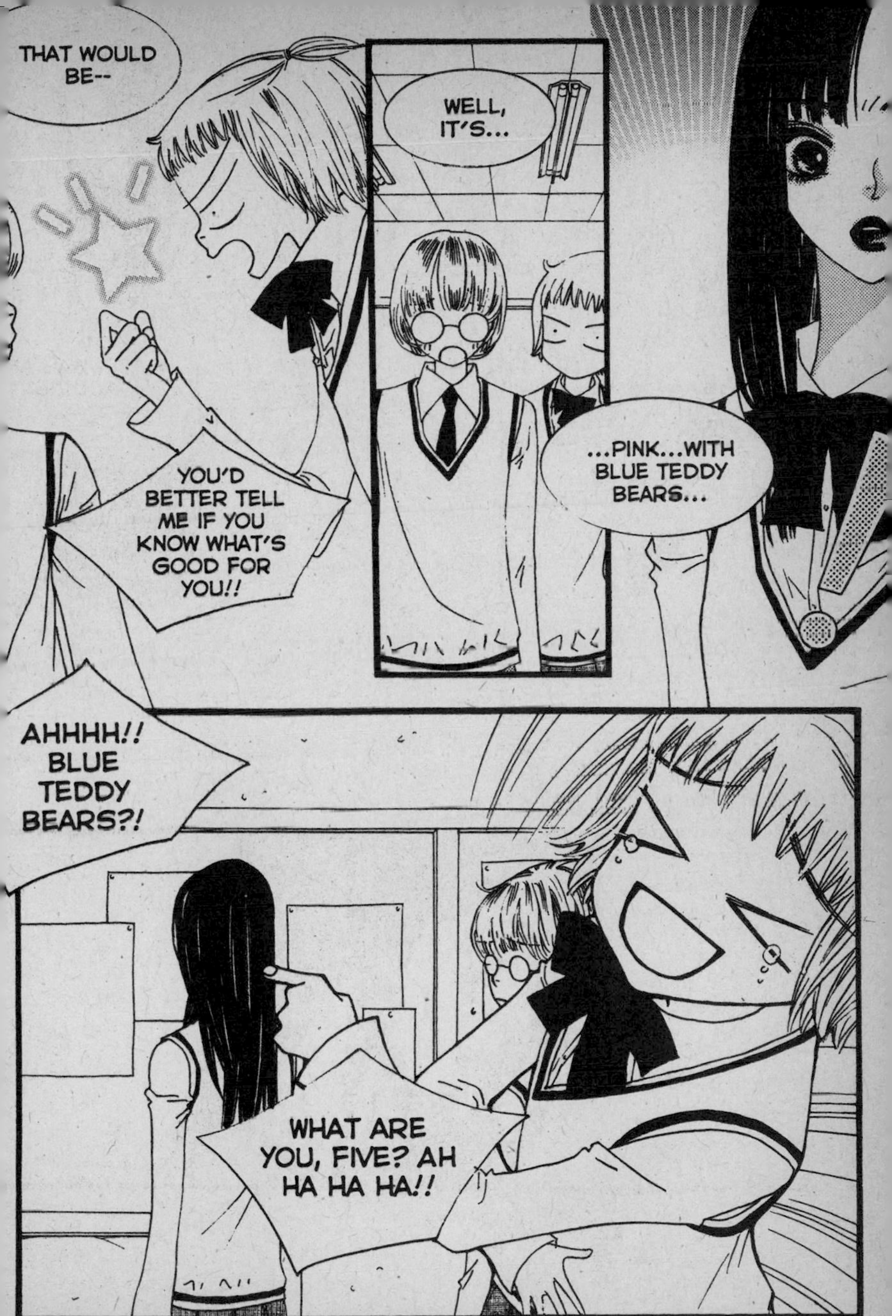
THAT WOULD BE--
YOU'D BETTER TELL ME IF YOU KNOW WHAT'S GOOD FOR YOU!!
WELL, IT'S...
...PINK...WITH BLUE TEDDY BEARS...
AHHHH!! BLUE TEDDY BEARS?!
WHAT ARE YOU, FIVE? AH HA HA HA!!

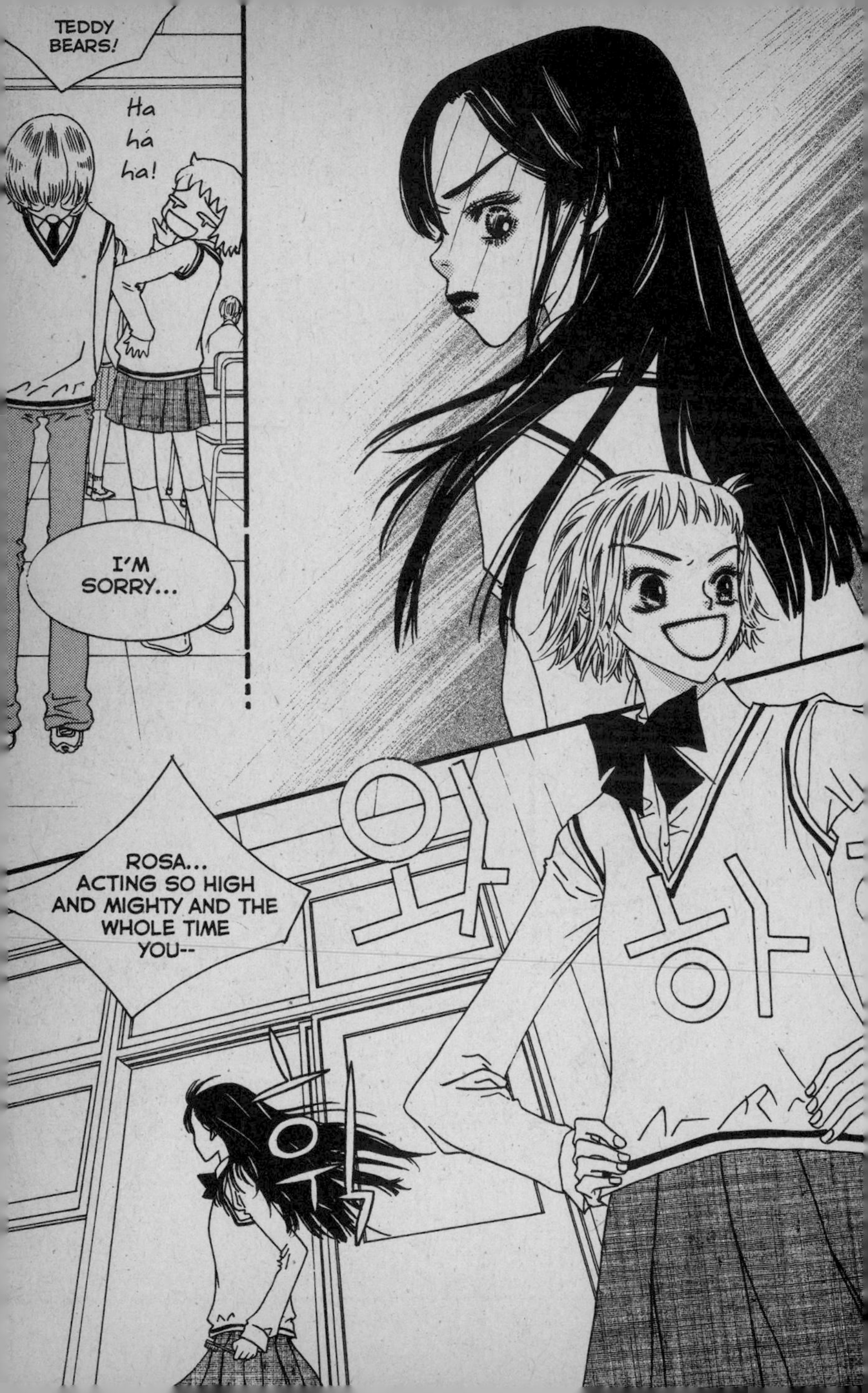
TEDDY BEARS!
Ha ha ha!
I'M SORRY...
ROSA... ACTING SO HIGH AND MIGHTY AND THE WHOLE TIME YOU--

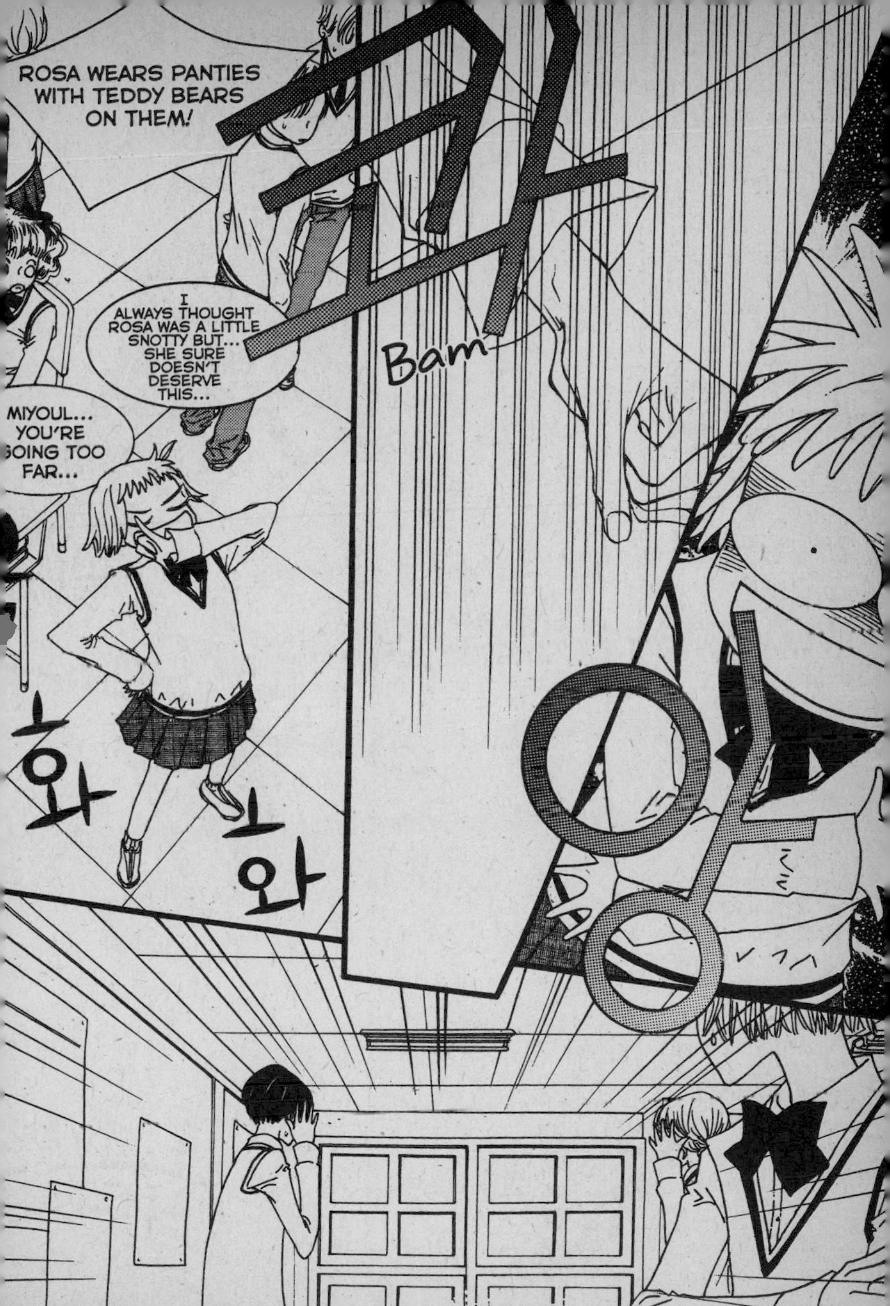
ROSA WEARS PANTIES WITH TEDDY BEARS ON THEM!
I ALWAYS THOUGHT ROSA WAS A LITTLE SNOTTY BUT... SHE SURE DOESN'T DESERVE THIS...
MIYOUL... YOU'RE GOING TOO FAR...
Bam

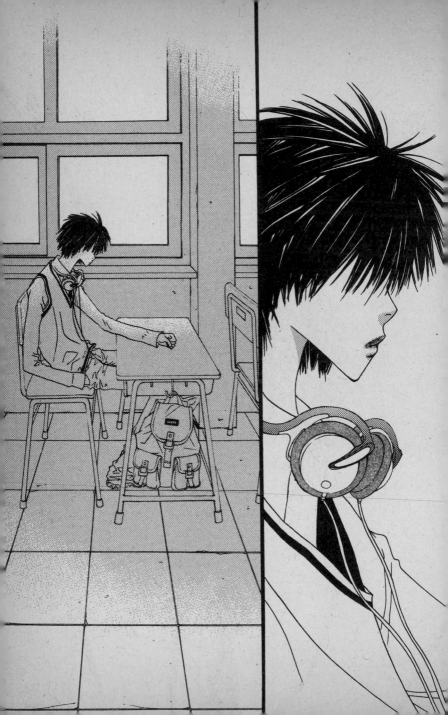

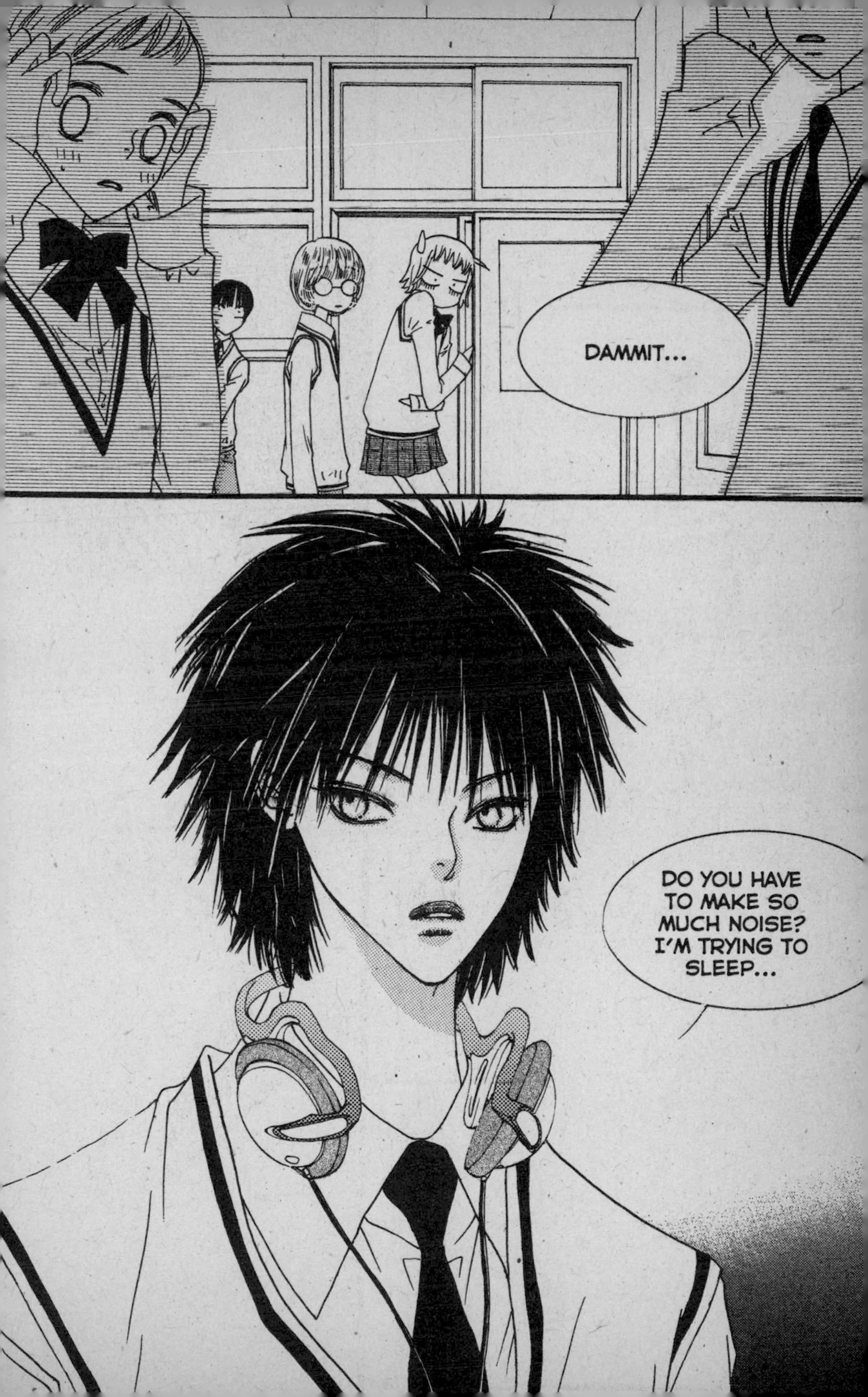
DAMMIT...
DO YOU HAVE TO MAKE SO MUCH NOISE? I'M TRYING TO SLEEP...

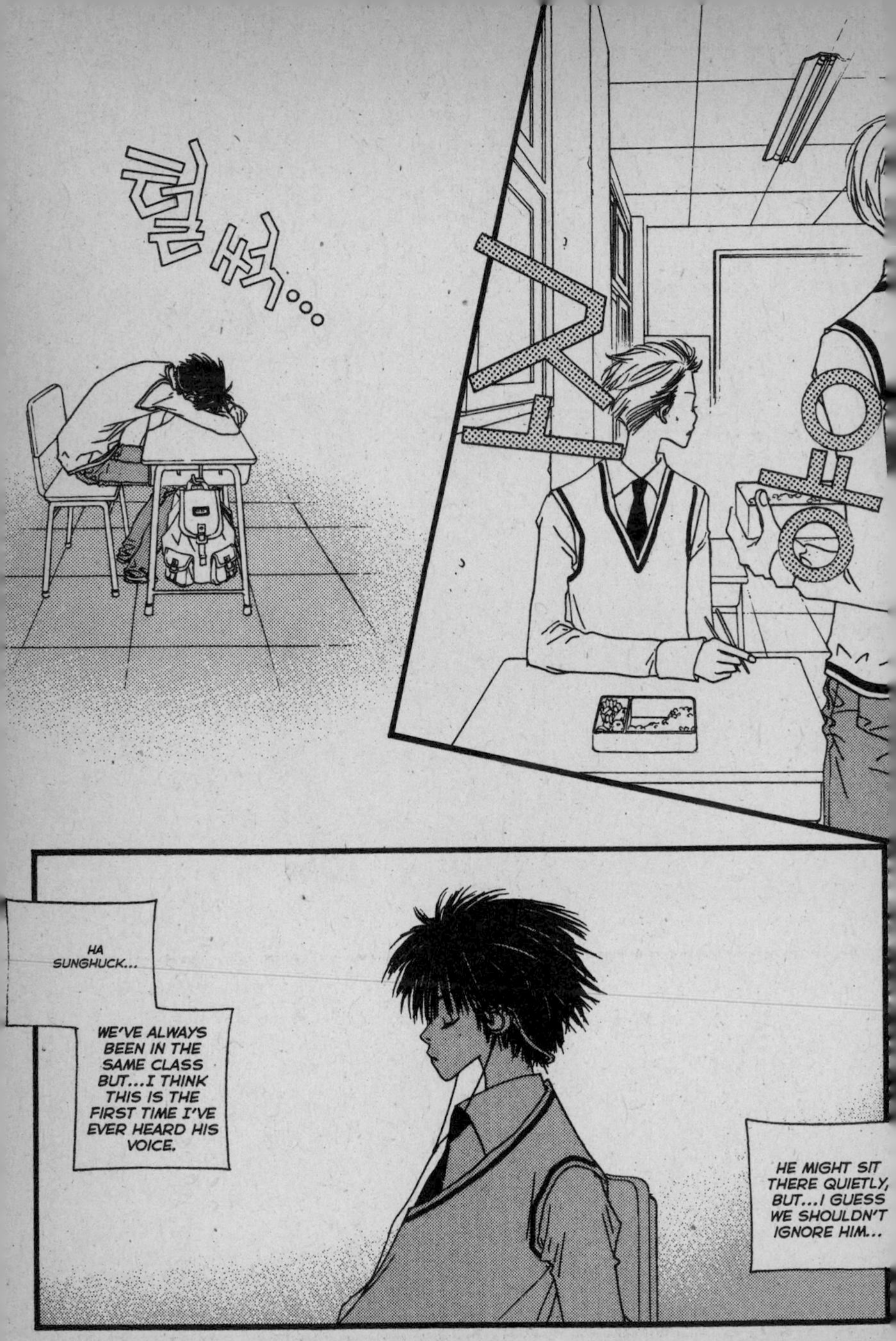
털썩...
HA SUNGHUCK...
WE'VE ALWAYS BEEN IN THE SAME CLASS BUT...I THINK THIS IS THE FIRST TIME I'VE EVER HEARD HIS VOICE.
HE MIGHT SIT THERE QUIETLY, BUT...I GUESS WE SHOULDN'T IGNORE HIM...

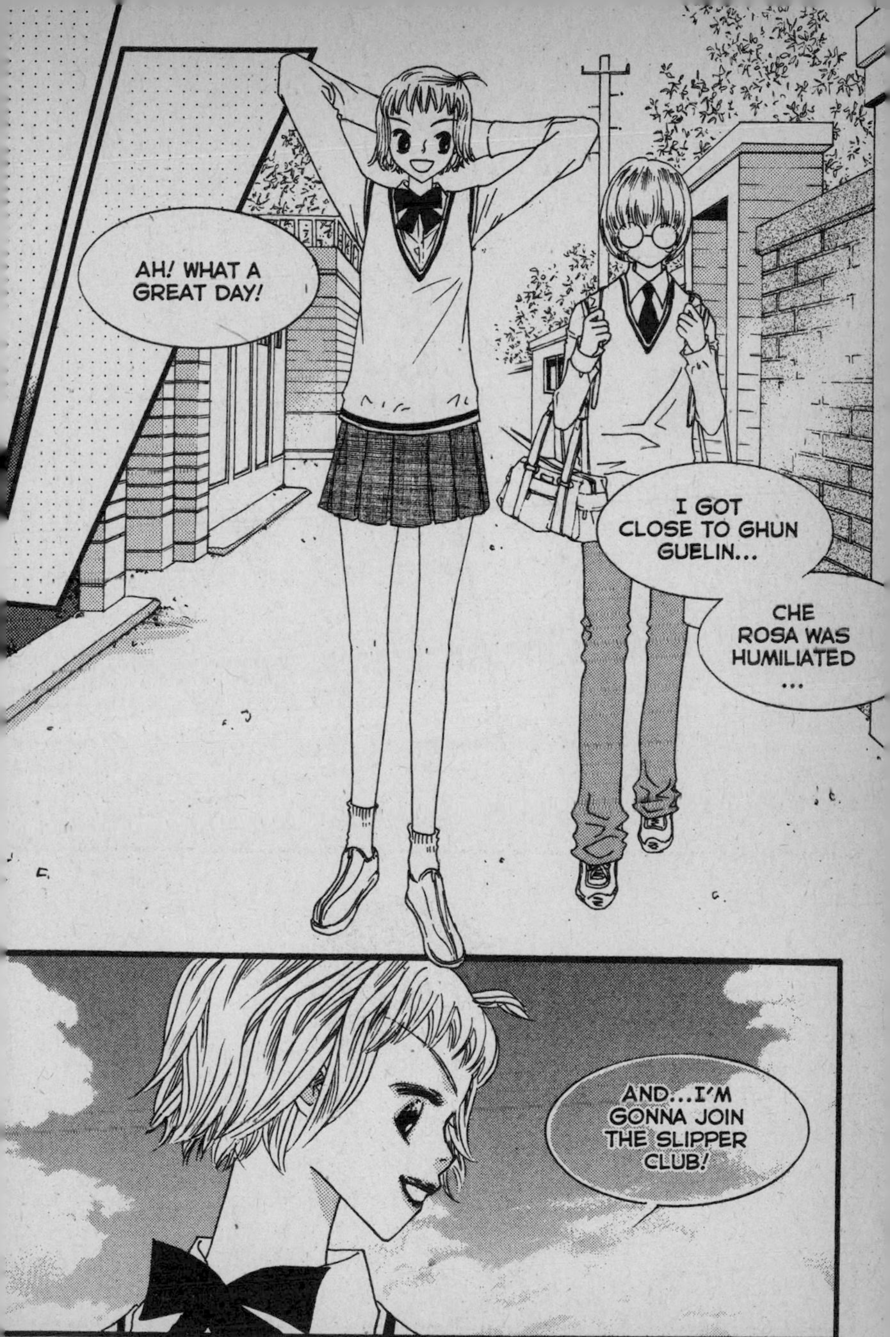
AH! WHAT A GREAT DAY!
I GOT CLOSE TO GHUN GUELIN...
CHE ROSA WAS HUMILIATED ...
AND...I'M GONNA JOIN THE SLIPPER CLUB!

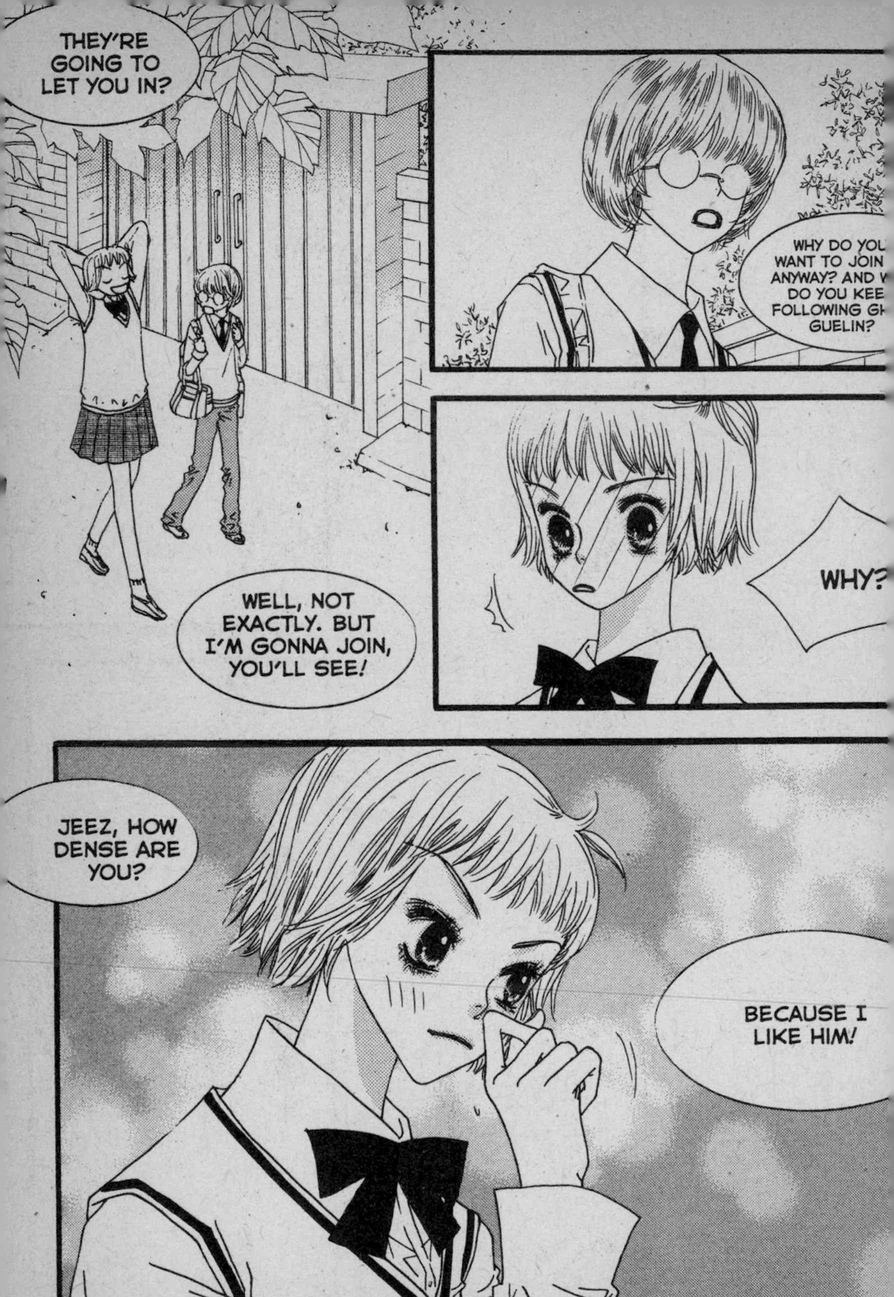
THEY'RE GOING TO LET YOU IN?
WELL, NOT EXACTLY. BUT I'M GONNA JOIN, YOU'LL SEE!
WHY DO YOU WANT TO JOIN ANYWAY? AND W DO YOU KEE FOLLOWING GH GUELIN?
WHY?
JEEZ, HOW DENSE ARE YOU?
BECAUSE I LIKE HIM!

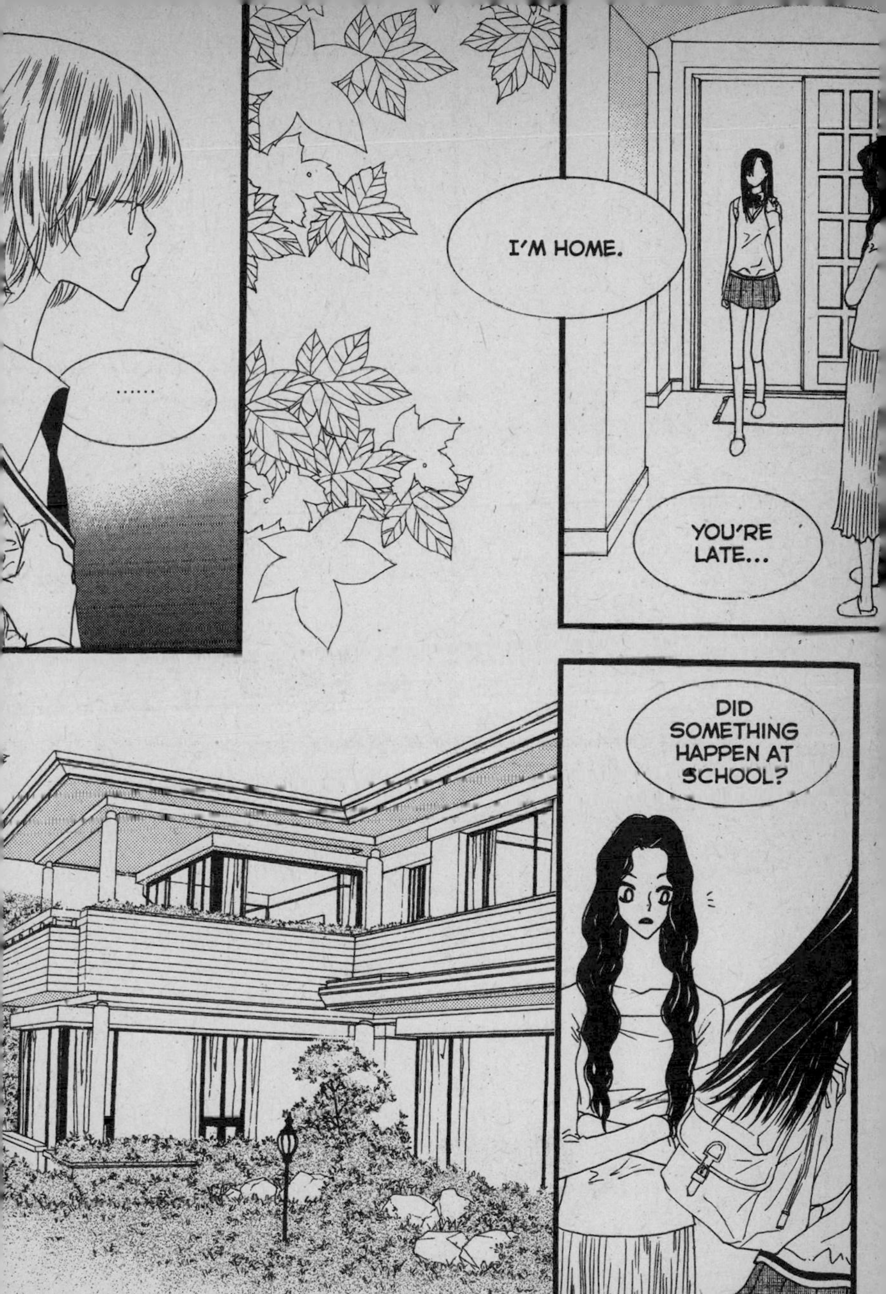
......
I'M HOME.
YOU'RE LATE...
DID SOMETHING HAPPEN AT SCHOOL?

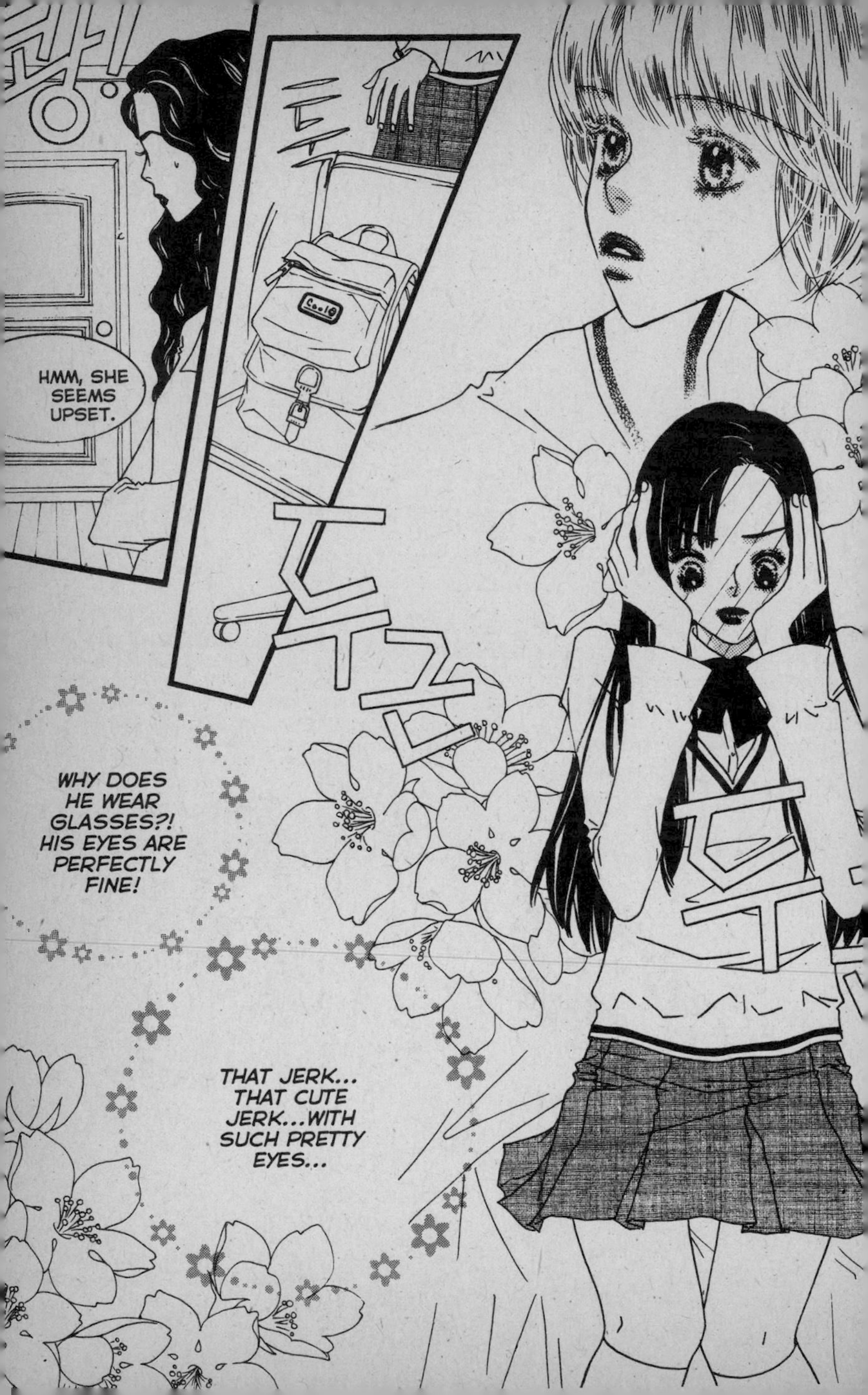
HMM, SHE SEEMS UPSET.
WHY DOES HE WEAR GLASSES?! HIS EYES ARE PERFECTLY FINE!
THAT JERK... THAT CUTE JERK...WITH SUCH PRETTY EYES...

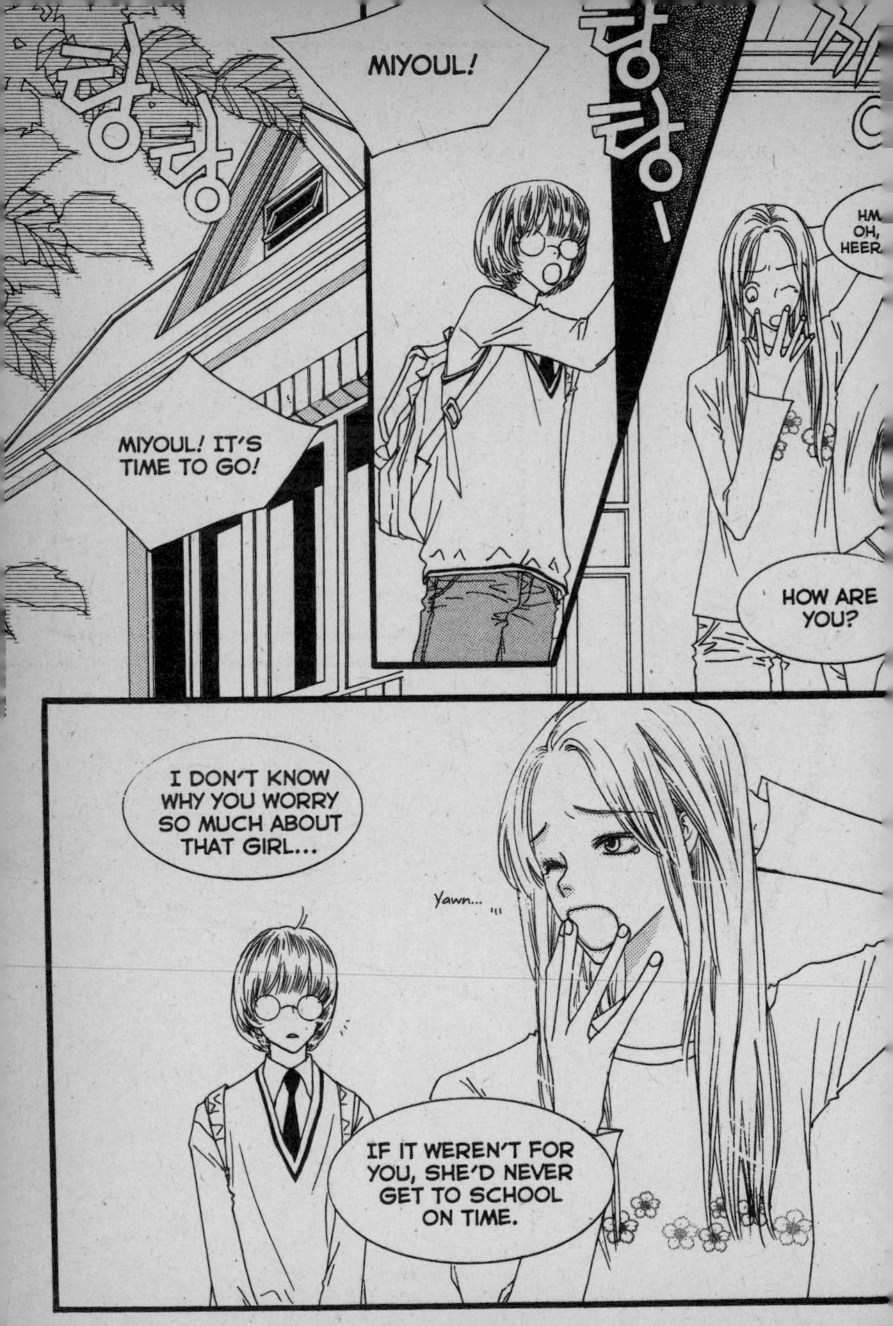
MIYOUL! IT'S TIME TO GO!
MIYOUL!
HOW ARE YOU?
I DON'T KNOW WHY YOU WORRY SO MUCH ABOUT THAT GIRL...
Yawn...
IF IT WEREN'T FOR YOU, SHE'D NEVER GET TO SCHOOL ON TIME.

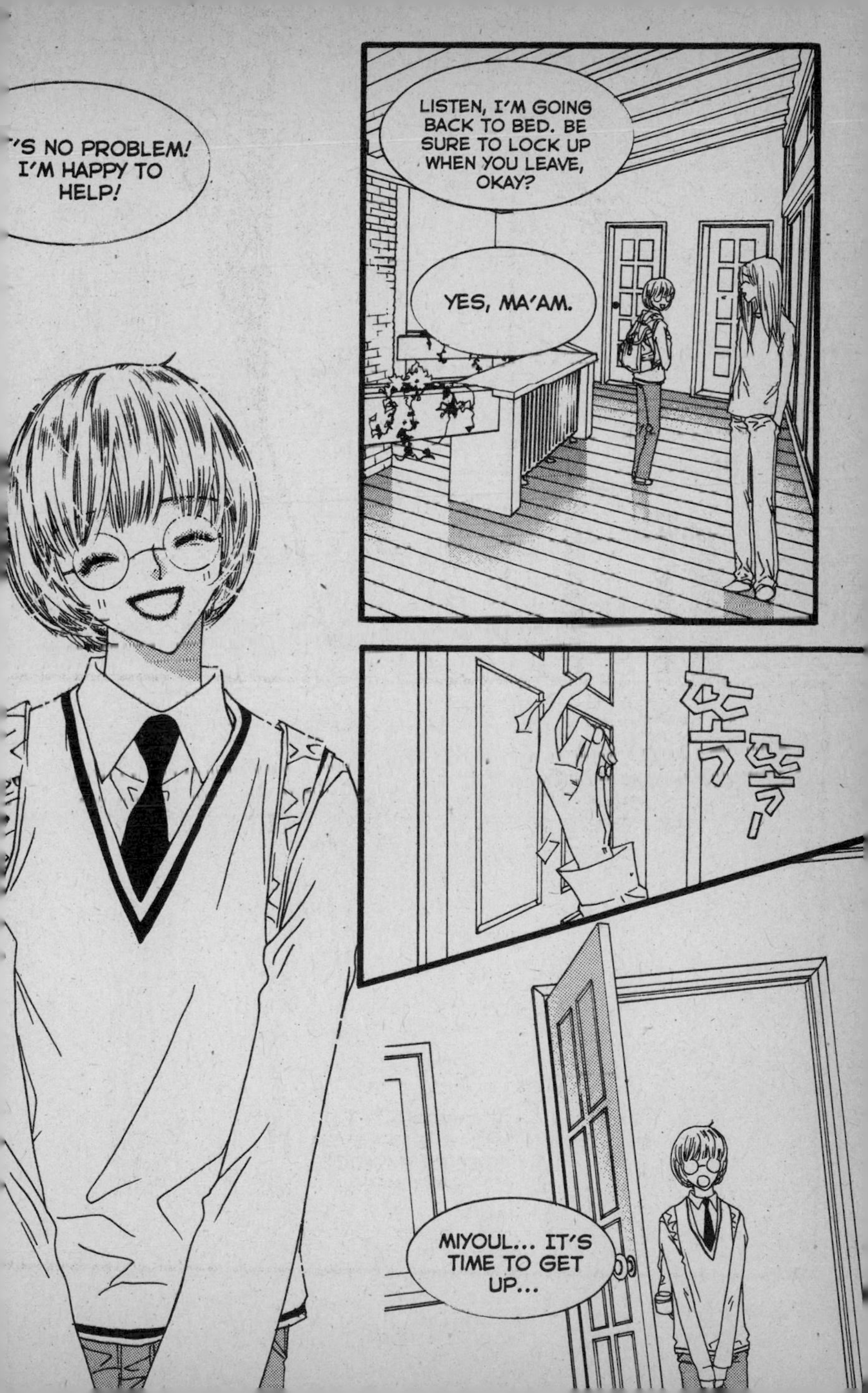
’S NO PROBLEM! I’M HAPPY TO HELP!
LISTEN, I’M GOING BACK TO BED. BE SURE TO LOCK UP WHEN YOU LEAVE, OKAY?
YES, MA’AM.
똑 똑
MIYOUL... IT’S TIME TO GET UP...

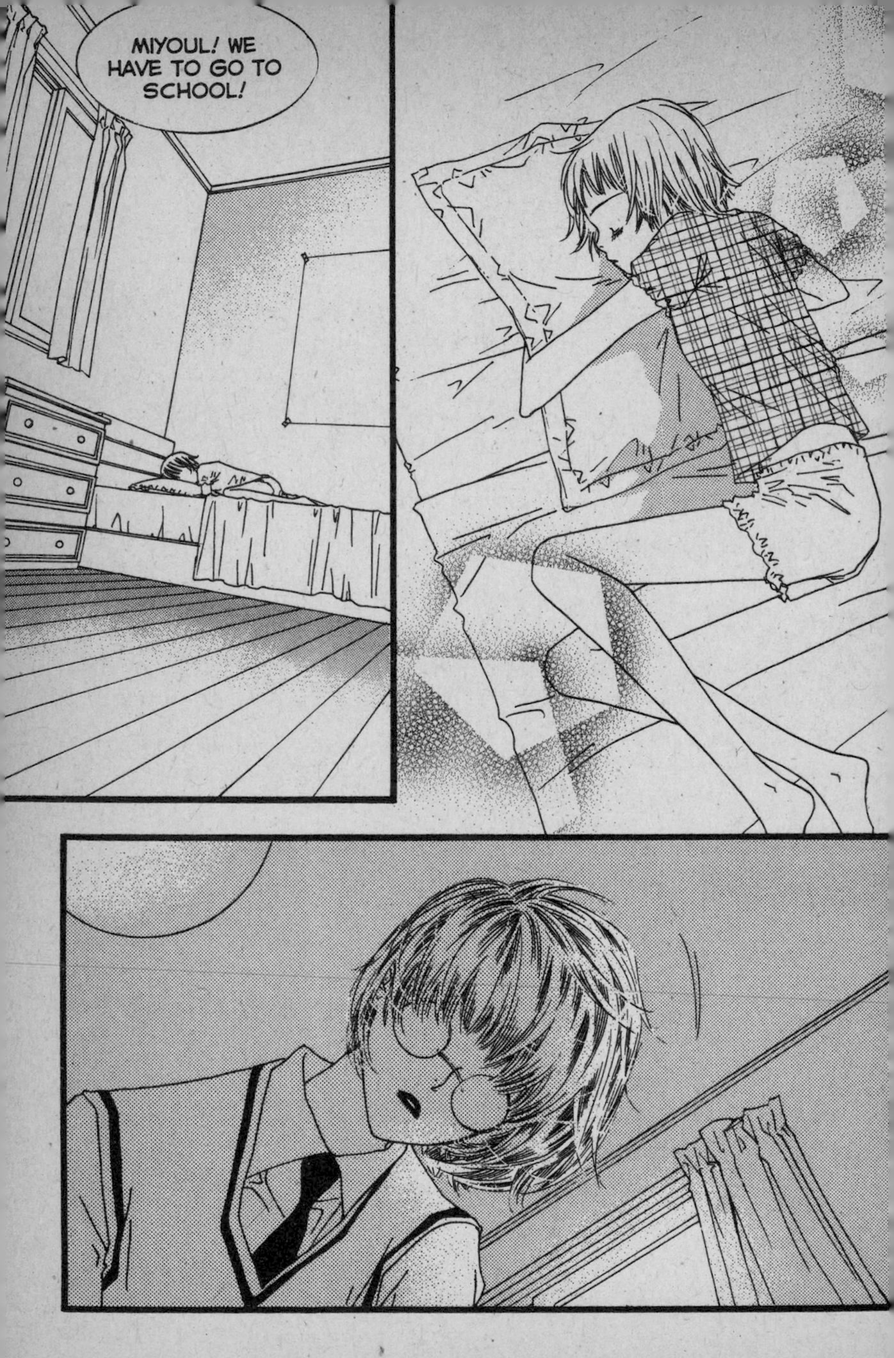
MIYOUL! WE HAVE TO GO TO SCHOOL!

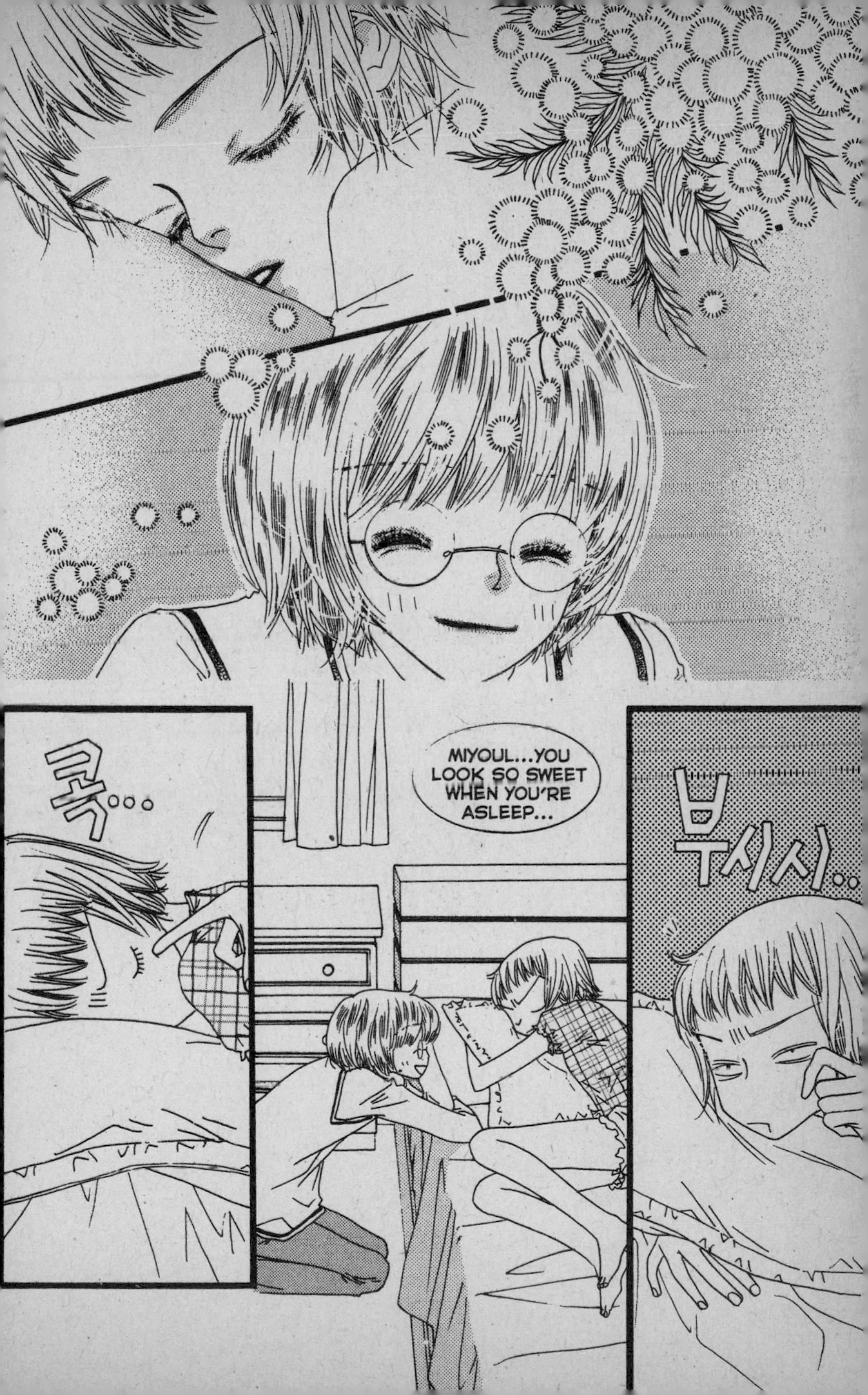
쿡...
MIYOUL...YOU LOOK SO SWEET WHEN YOU'RE ASLEEP...
부시시...

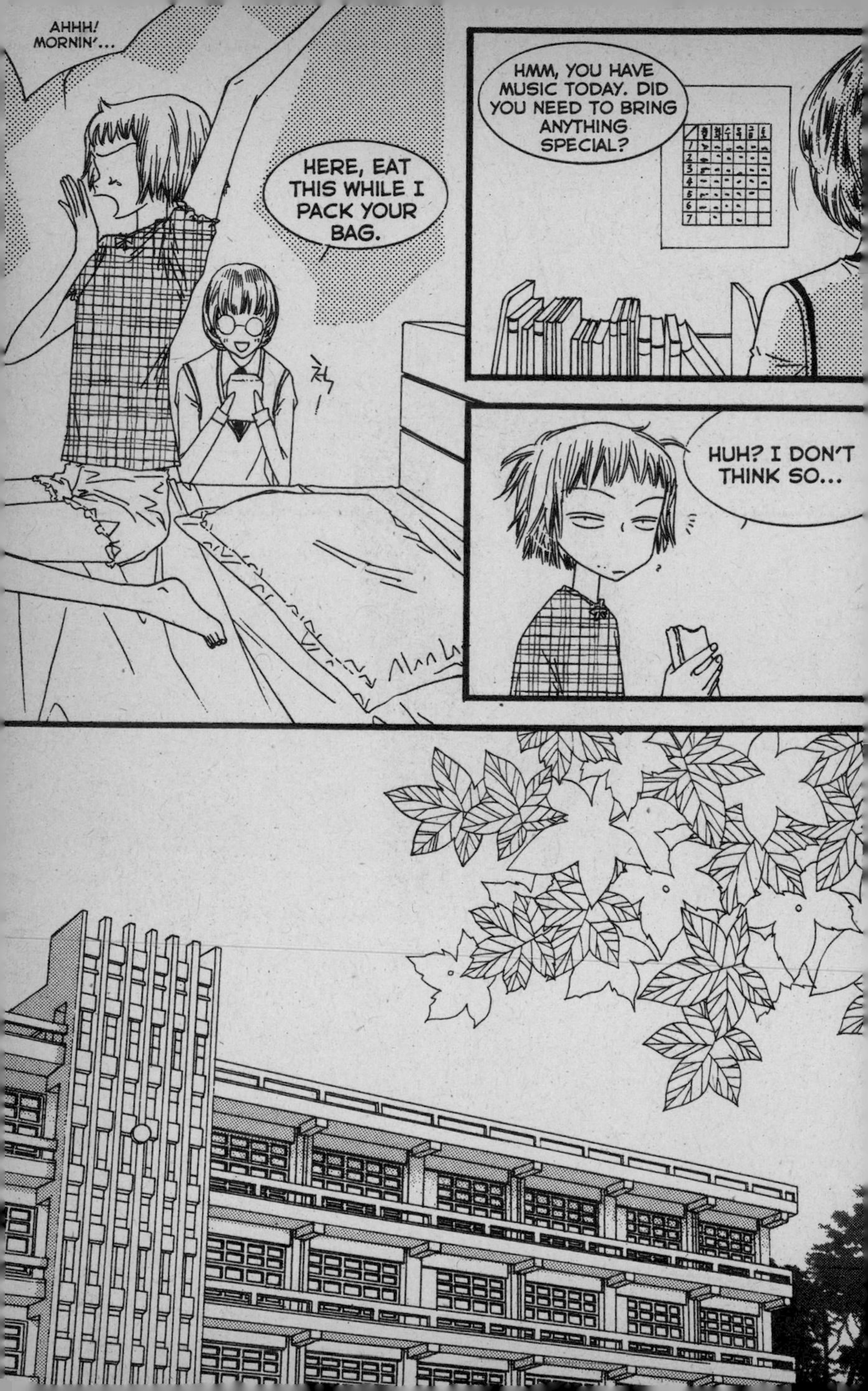
AHHH! MORNIN'...
HERE, EAT THIS WHILE I PACK YOUR BAG.
HMM, YOU HAVE MUSIC TODAY. DID YOU NEED TO BRING ANYTHING SPECIAL?
HUH? I DON'T THINK SO...

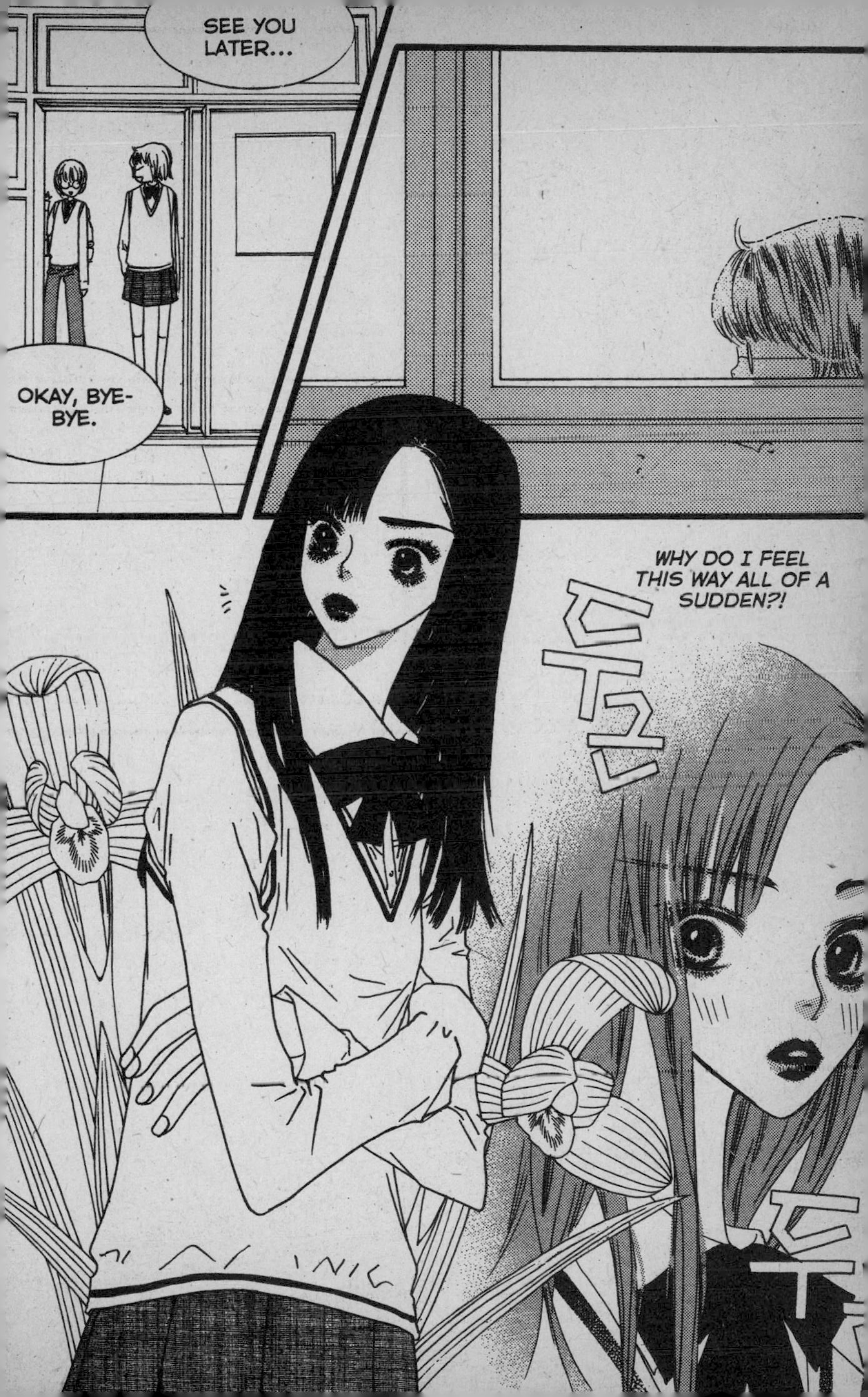

SEE YOU LATER...
OKAY, BYE-BYE.
WHY DO I FEEL THIS WAY ALL OF A SUDDEN?!

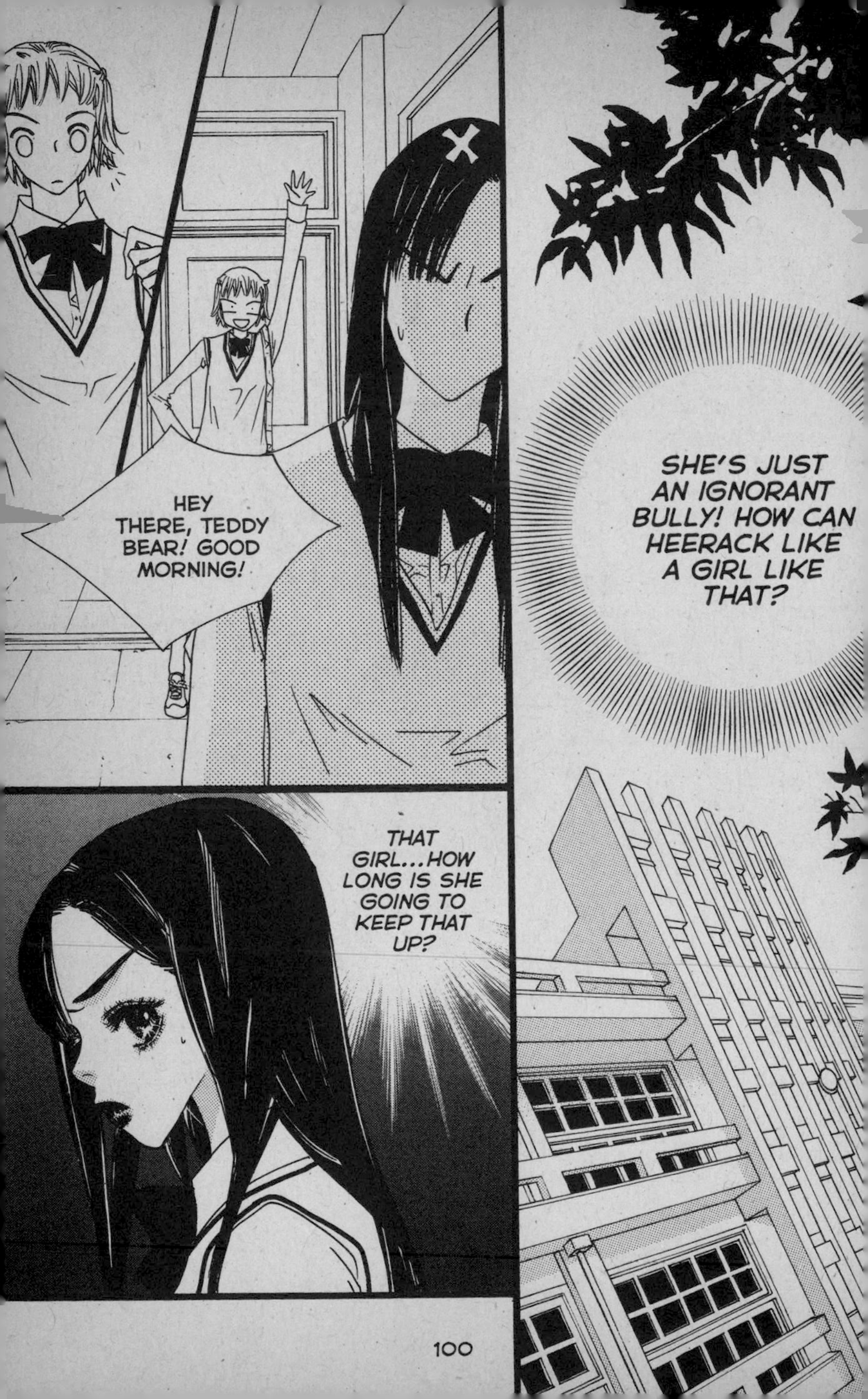
HEY THERE, TEDDY BEAR! GOOD MORNING!
THAT GIRL...HOW LONG IS SHE GOING TO KEEP THAT UP?
SHE'S JUST AN IGNORANT BULLY! HOW CAN HEERACK LIKE A GIRL LIKE THAT?

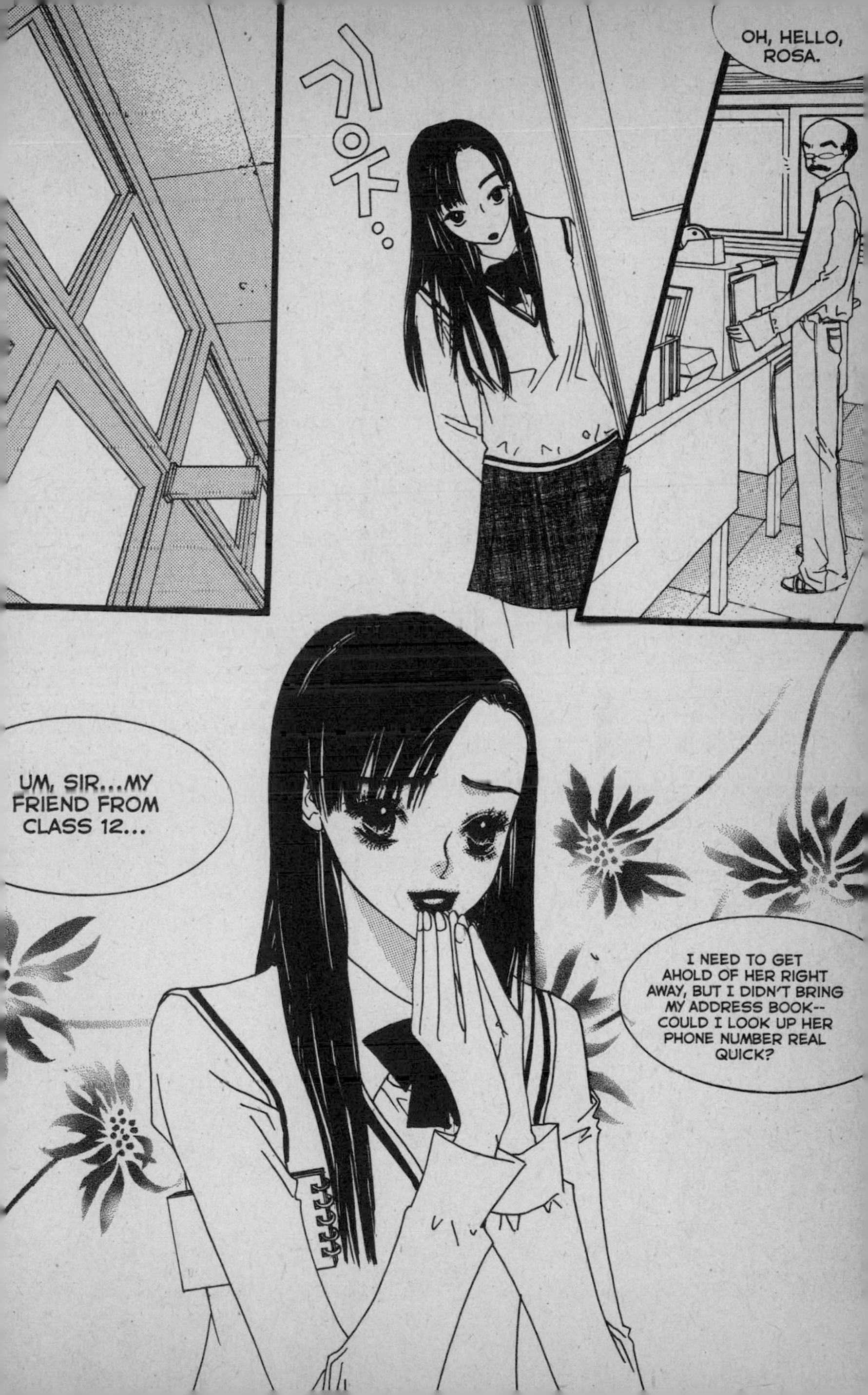
OH, HELLO, ROSA.
UM, SIR...MY FRIEND FROM CLASS 12...
I NEED TO GET AHOLD OF HER RIGHT AWAY, BUT I DIDN'T BRING MY ADDRESS BOOK--COULD I LOOK UP HER PHONE NUMBER REAL QUICK?

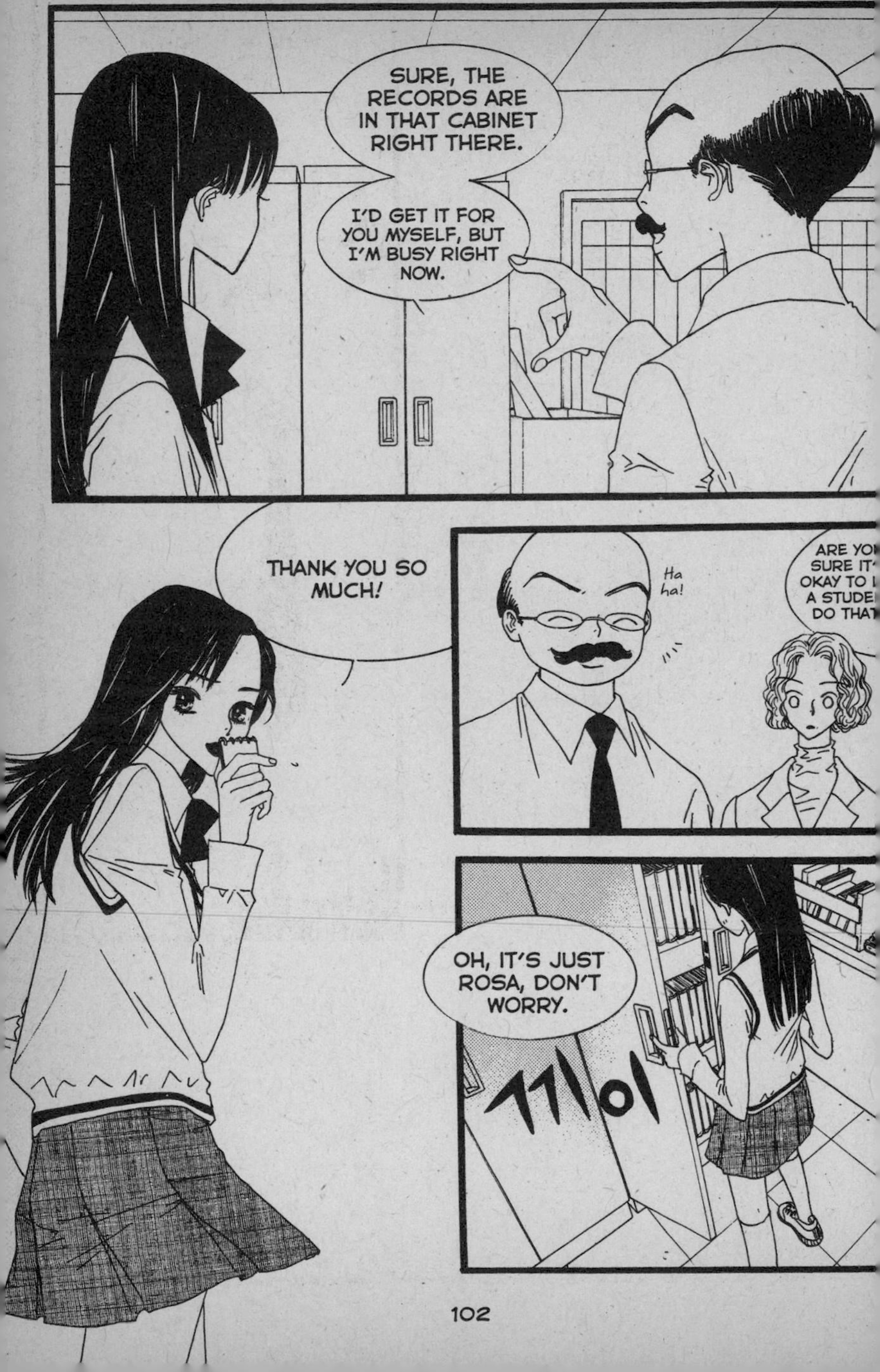
SURE, THE RECORDS ARE IN THAT CABINET RIGHT THERE.
I'D GET IT FOR YOU MYSELF, BUT I'M BUSY RIGHT NOW.
THANK YOU SO MUCH!
Ha ha!
ARE YO SURE IT OKAY TO A STUDE DO THA
OH, IT'S JUST ROSA, DON'T WORRY.

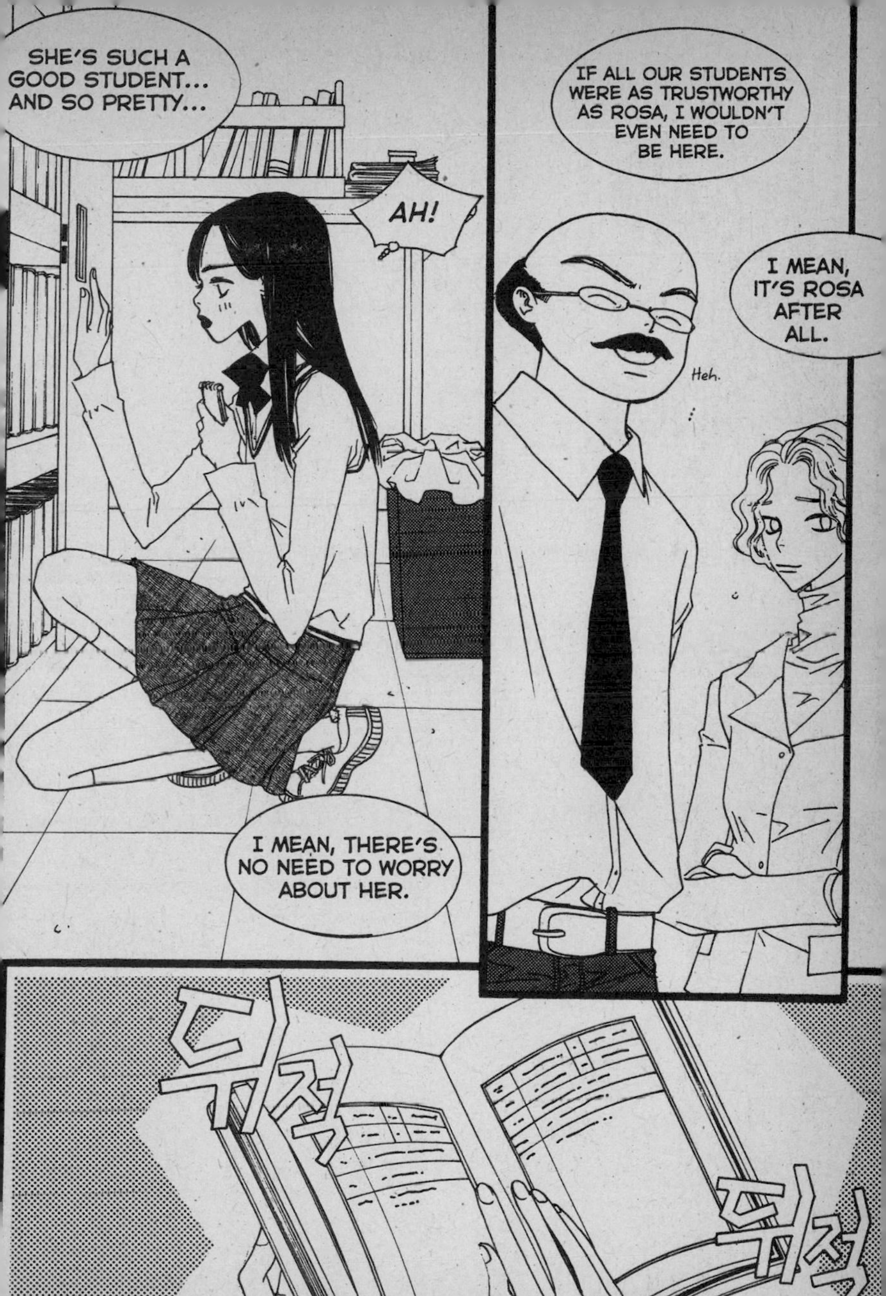
SHE'S SUCH A GOOD STUDENT... AND SO PRETTY...
AH!
I MEAN, THERE'S NO NEED TO WORRY ABOUT HER.
IF ALL OUR STUDENTS WERE AS TRUSTWORTHY AS ROSA, I WOULDN'T EVEN NEED TO BE HERE.
Heh.
I MEAN, IT'S ROSA AFTER ALL.
뒤적
뒤적

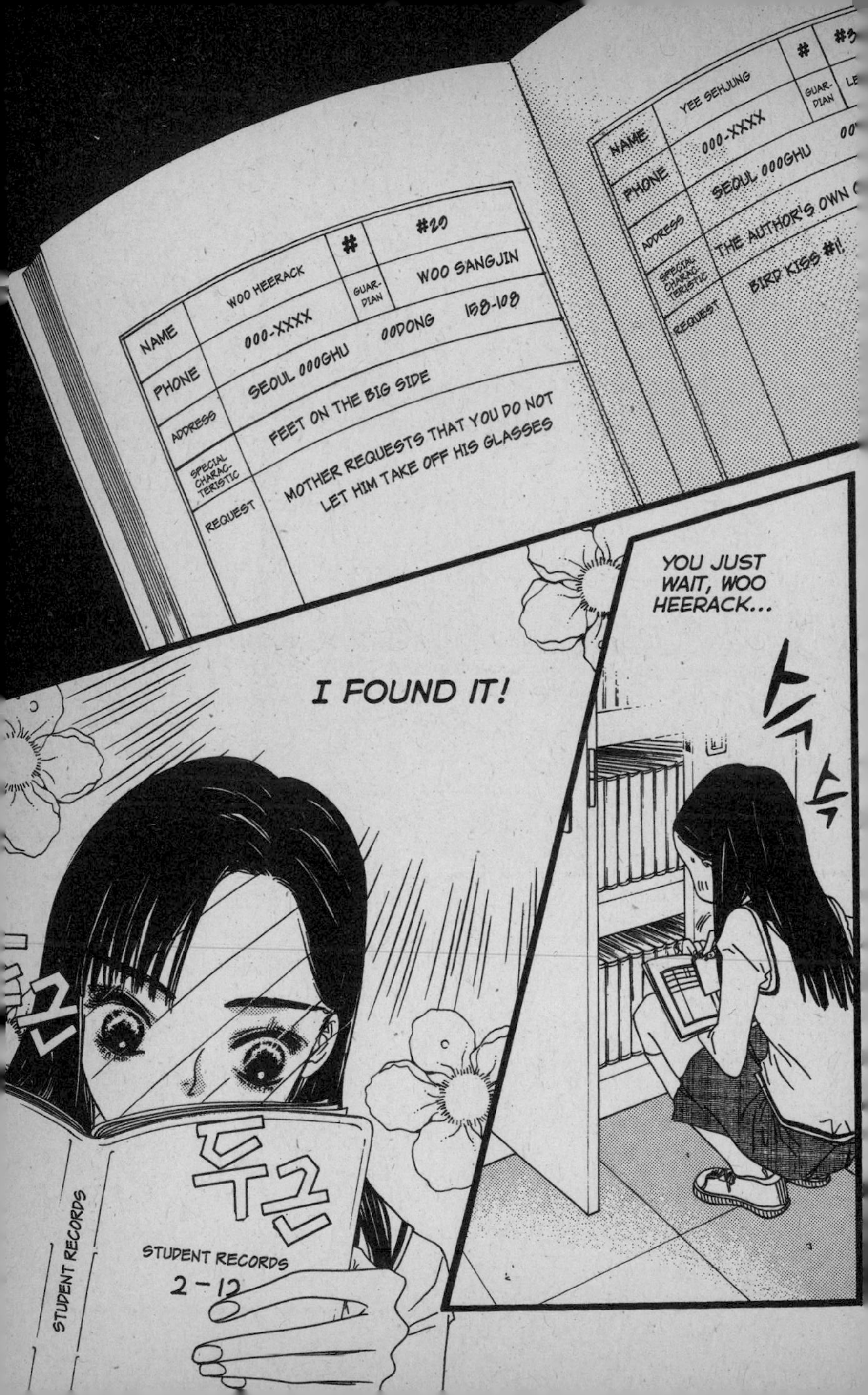
NAME
WOO HEERACK
#
#29
PHONE
000-XXXX
GUARDIAN
WOO SANGJIN
ADDRESS
SEOUL 000GHU 00DONG 158-108
SPECIAL CHARACTERISTIC
FEET ON THE BIG SIDE
REQUEST
MOTHER REQUESTS THAT YOU DO NOT LET HIM TAKE OFF HIS GLASSES
NAME
YEE SEHJUNG
#
PHONE
000-XXXX
GUARDIAN
ADDRESS
SEOUL 000GHU
SPECIAL CHARACTERISTIC
THE AUTHOR'S OWN
REQUEST
BIRD KISS #1!
I FOUND IT!
STUDENT RECORDS
STUDENT RECORDS
2-12
YOU JUST WAIT, WOO HEERACK...

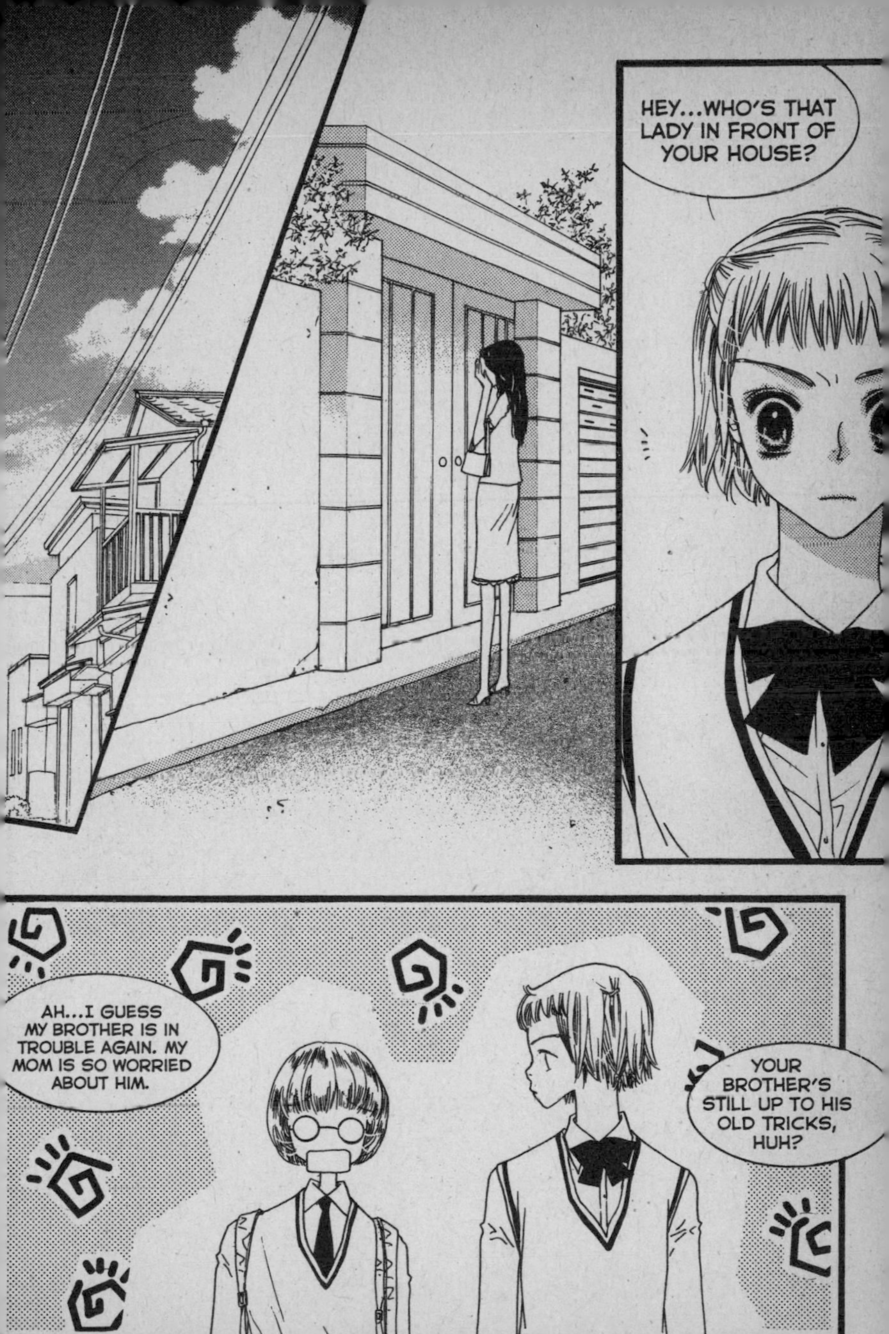
HEY...WHO'S THAT LADY IN FRONT OF YOUR HOUSE?
AH...I GUESS MY BROTHER IS IN TROUBLE AGAIN. MY MOM IS SO WORRIED ABOUT HIM.
YOUR BROTHER'S STILL UP TO HIS OLD TRICKS, HUH?

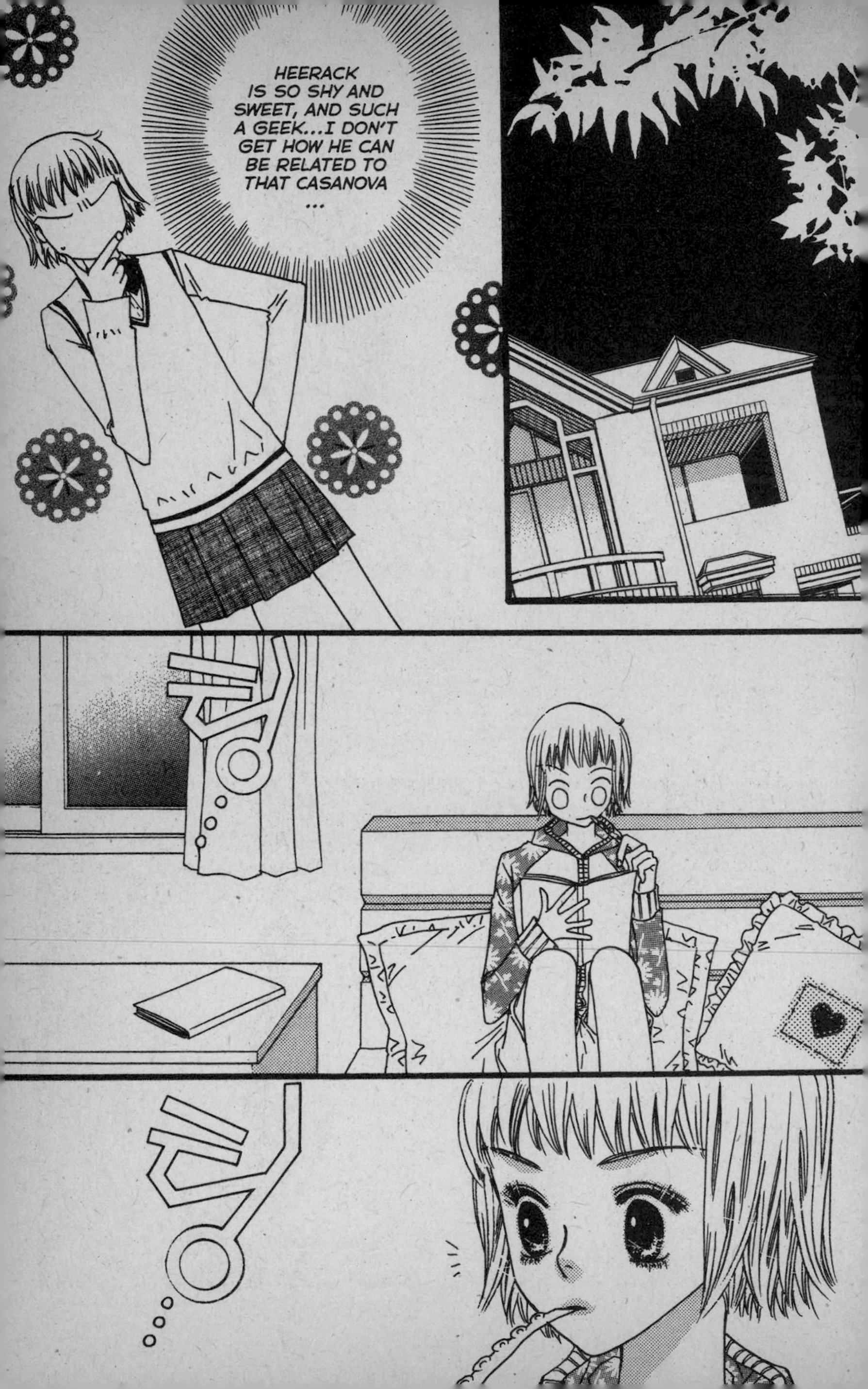
HEERACK IS SO SHY AND SWEET, AND SUCH A GEEK...I DON'T GET HOW HE CAN BE RELATED TO THAT CASANOVA ...

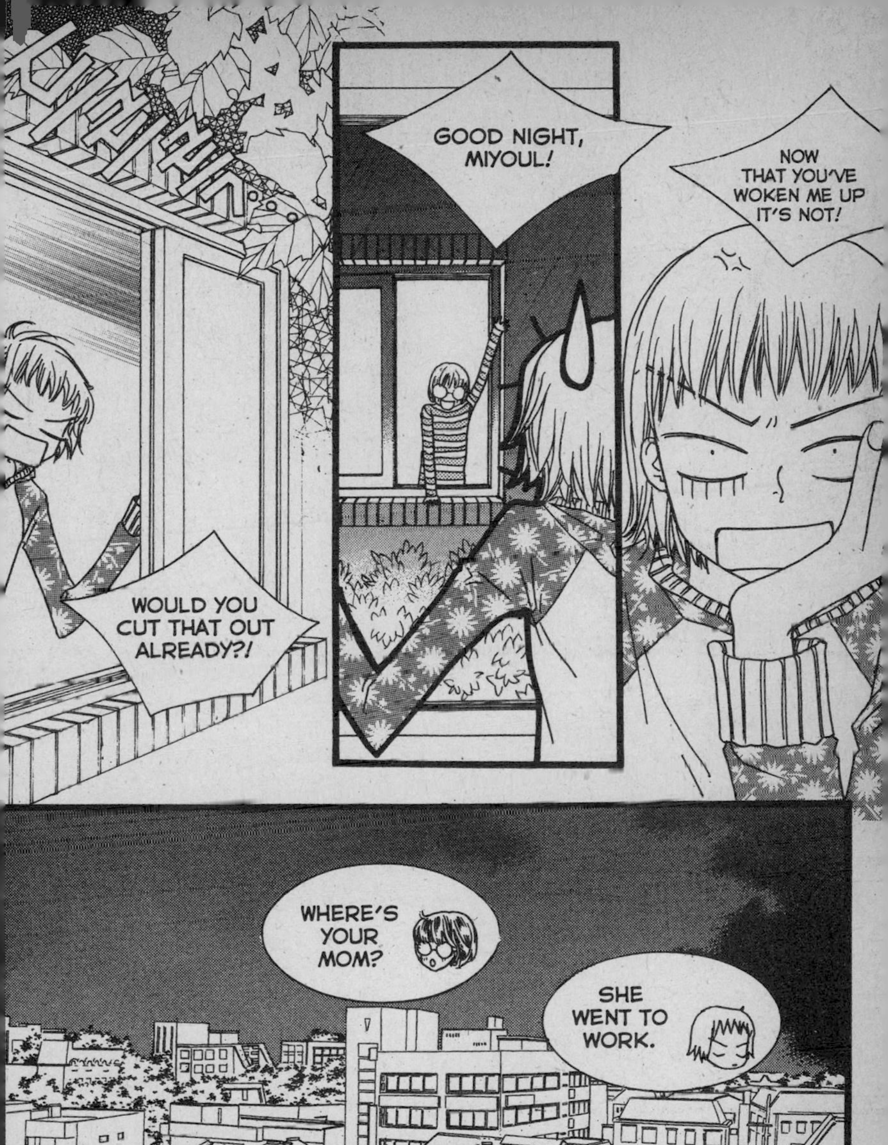
WOULD YOU CUT THAT OUT ALREADY?!
GOOD NIGHT, MIYOUL!
NOW THAT YOU'VE WOKEN ME UP IT'S NOT!
WHERE'S YOUR MOM?
SHE WENT TO WORK.

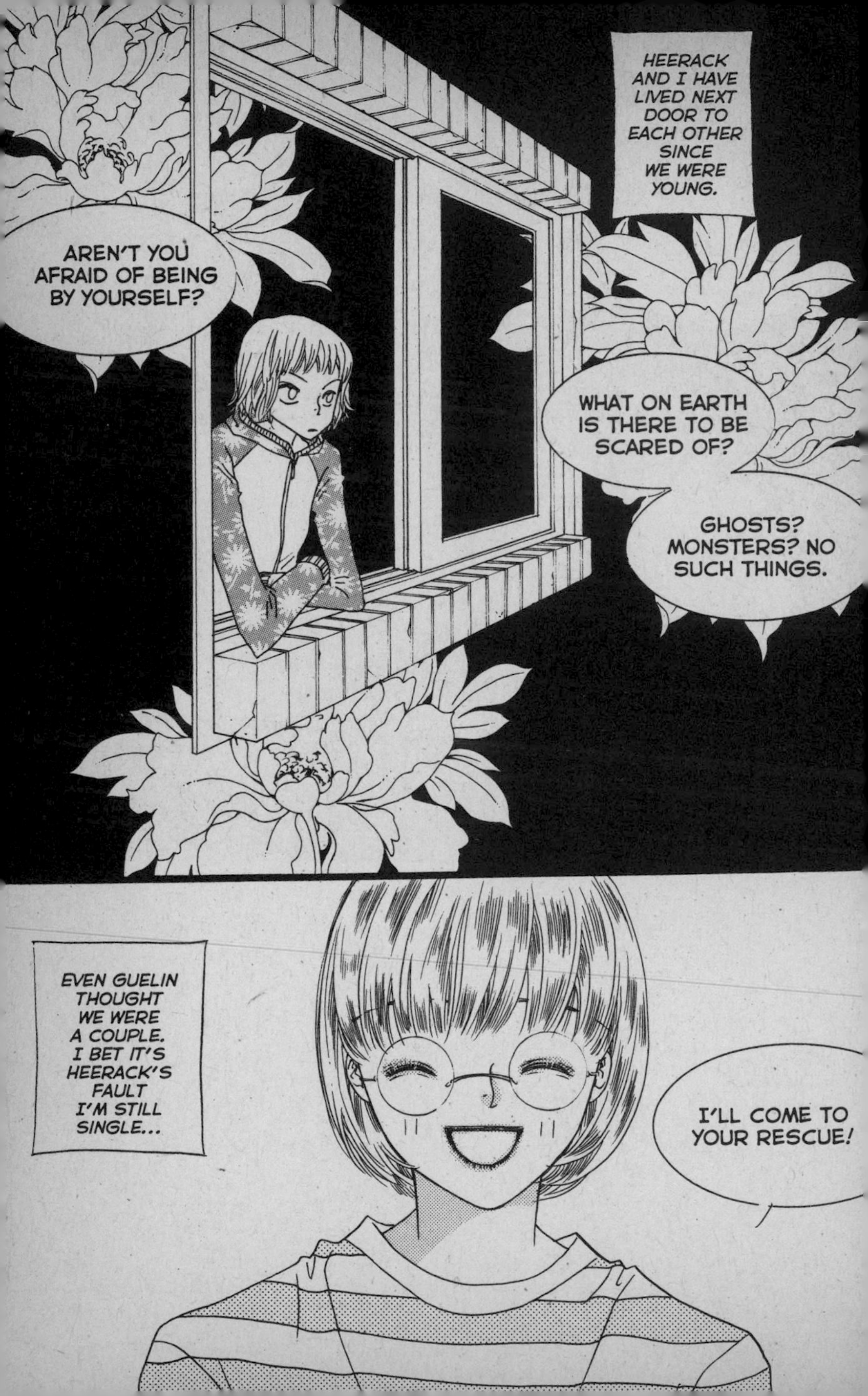
HEERACK AND I HAVE LIVED NEXT DOOR TO EACH OTHER SINCE WE WERE YOUNG.
AREN'T YOU AFRAID OF BEING BY YOURSELF?
WHAT ON EARTH IS THERE TO BE SCARED OF?
GHOSTS? MONSTERS? NO SUCH THINGS.
EVEN GUELIN THOUGHT WE WERE A COUPLE. I BET IT'S HEERACK'S FAULT I'M STILL SINGLE...
I'LL COME TO YOUR RESCUE!

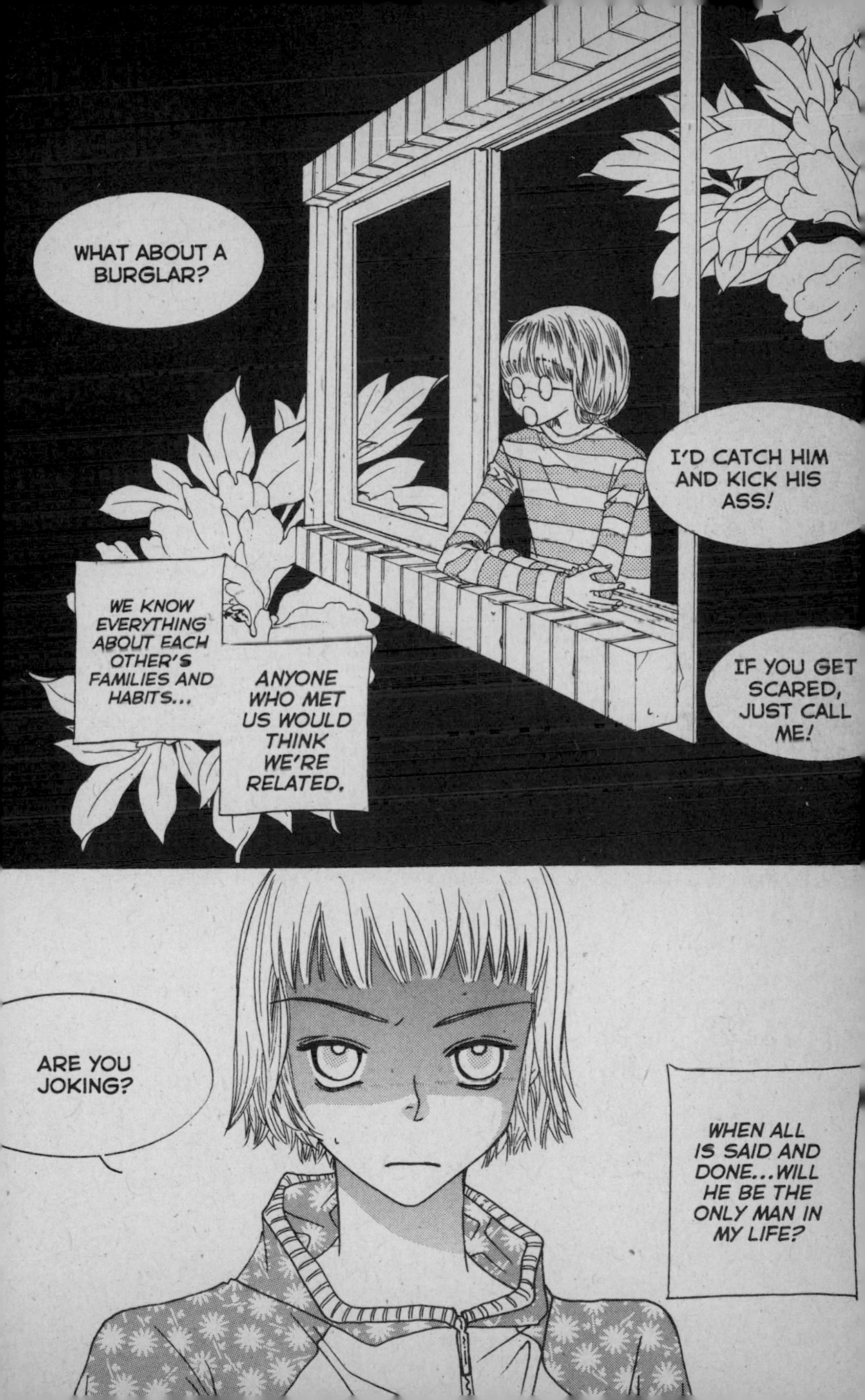
WHAT ABOUT A BURGLAR?
I'D CATCH HIM AND KICK HIS ASS!
WE KNOW EVERYTHING ABOUT EACH OTHER'S FAMILIES AND HABITS...
IF YOU GET SCARED, JUST CALL ME!
ANYONE WHO MET US WOULD THINK WE'RE RELATED.
ARE YOU JOKING?
WHEN ALL IS SAID AND DONE...WILL HE BE THE ONLY MAN IN MY LIFE?

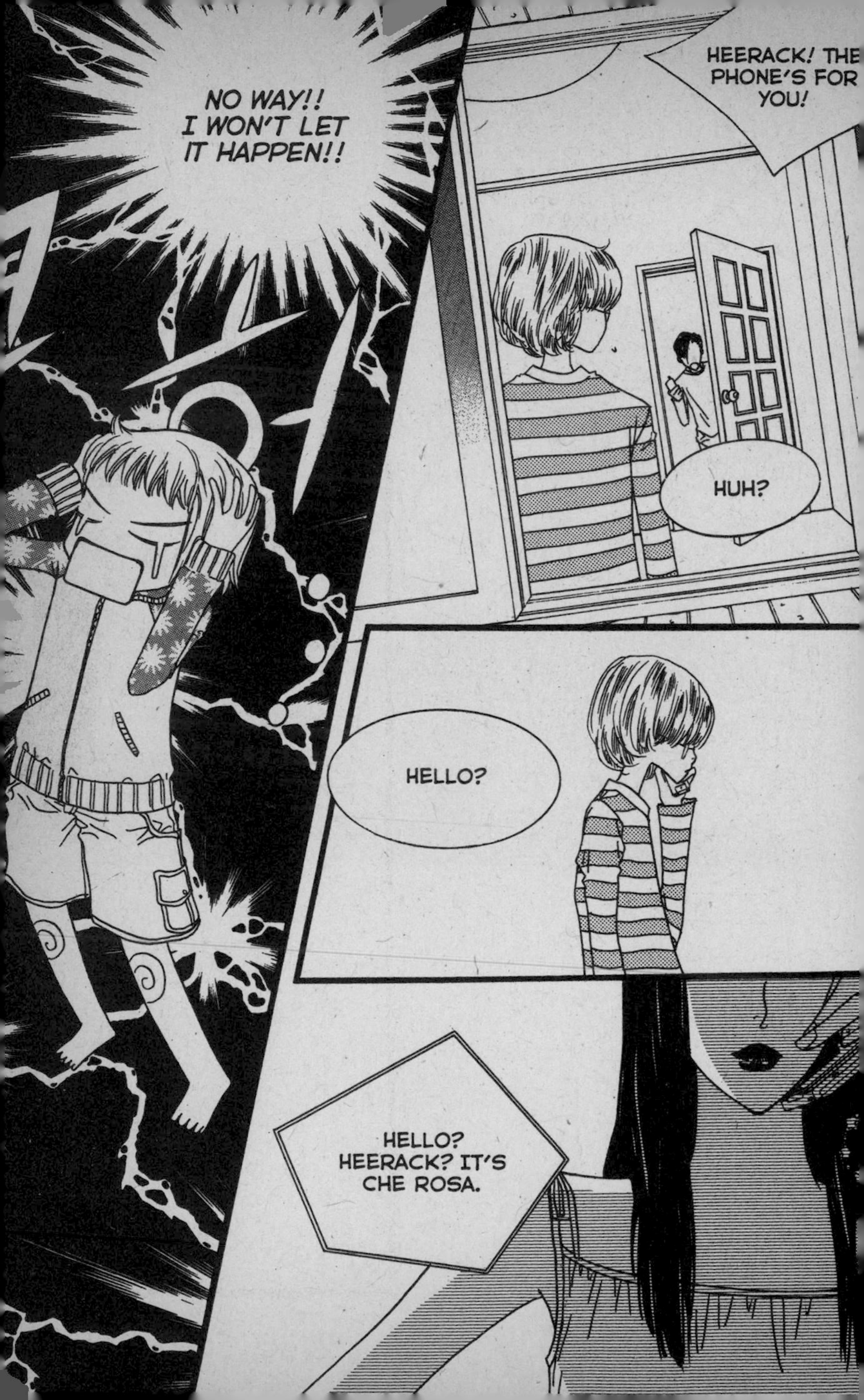
NO WAY!! I WON'T LET IT HAPPEN!!
HEERACK! THE PHONE'S FOR YOU!
HUH?
HELLO?
HELLO? HEERACK? IT'S CHE ROSA.

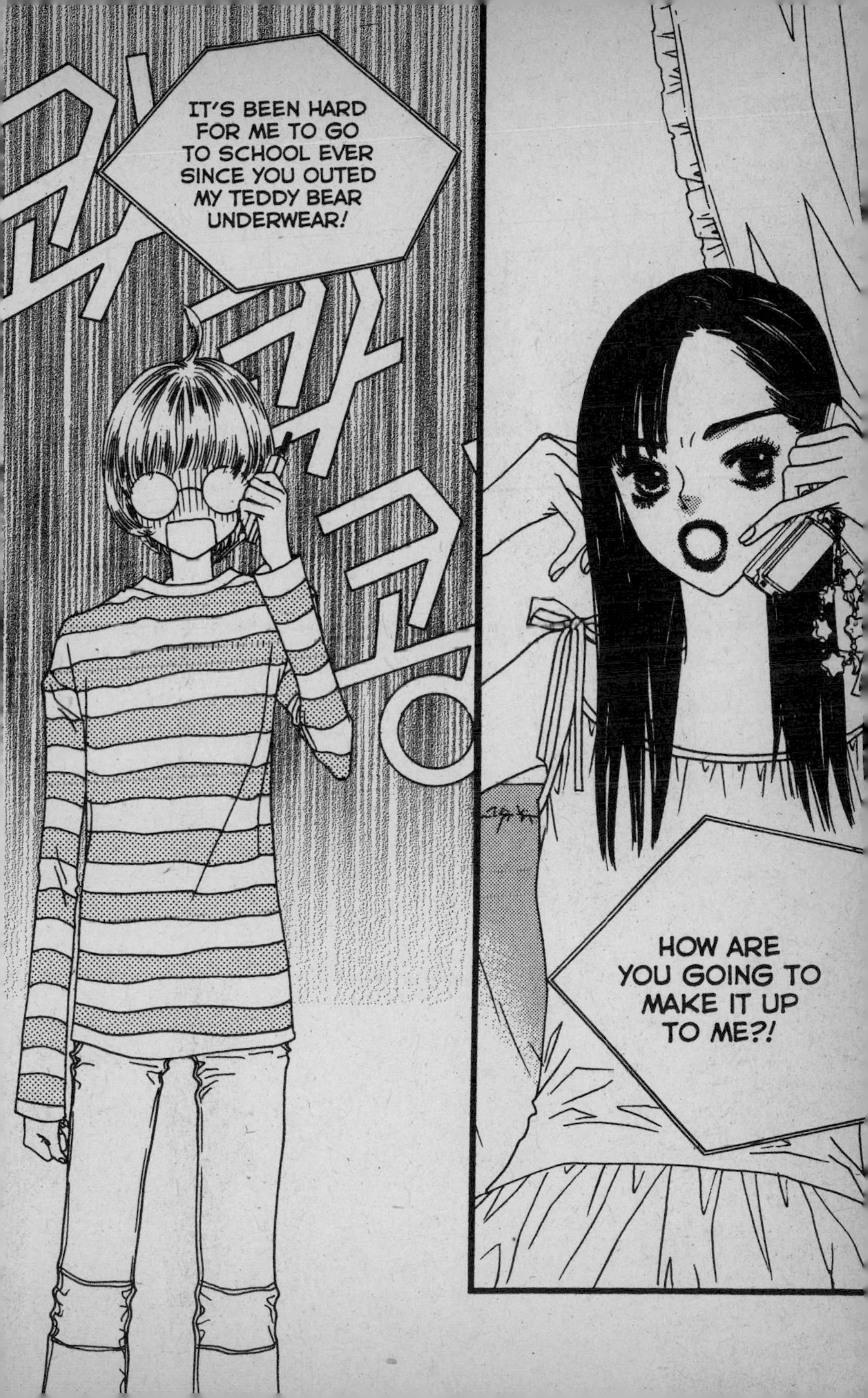
IT'S BEEN HARD FOR ME TO GO TO SCHOOL EVER SINCE YOU OUTED MY TEDDY BEAR UNDERWEAR!
HOW ARE YOU GOING TO MAKE IT UP TO ME?!

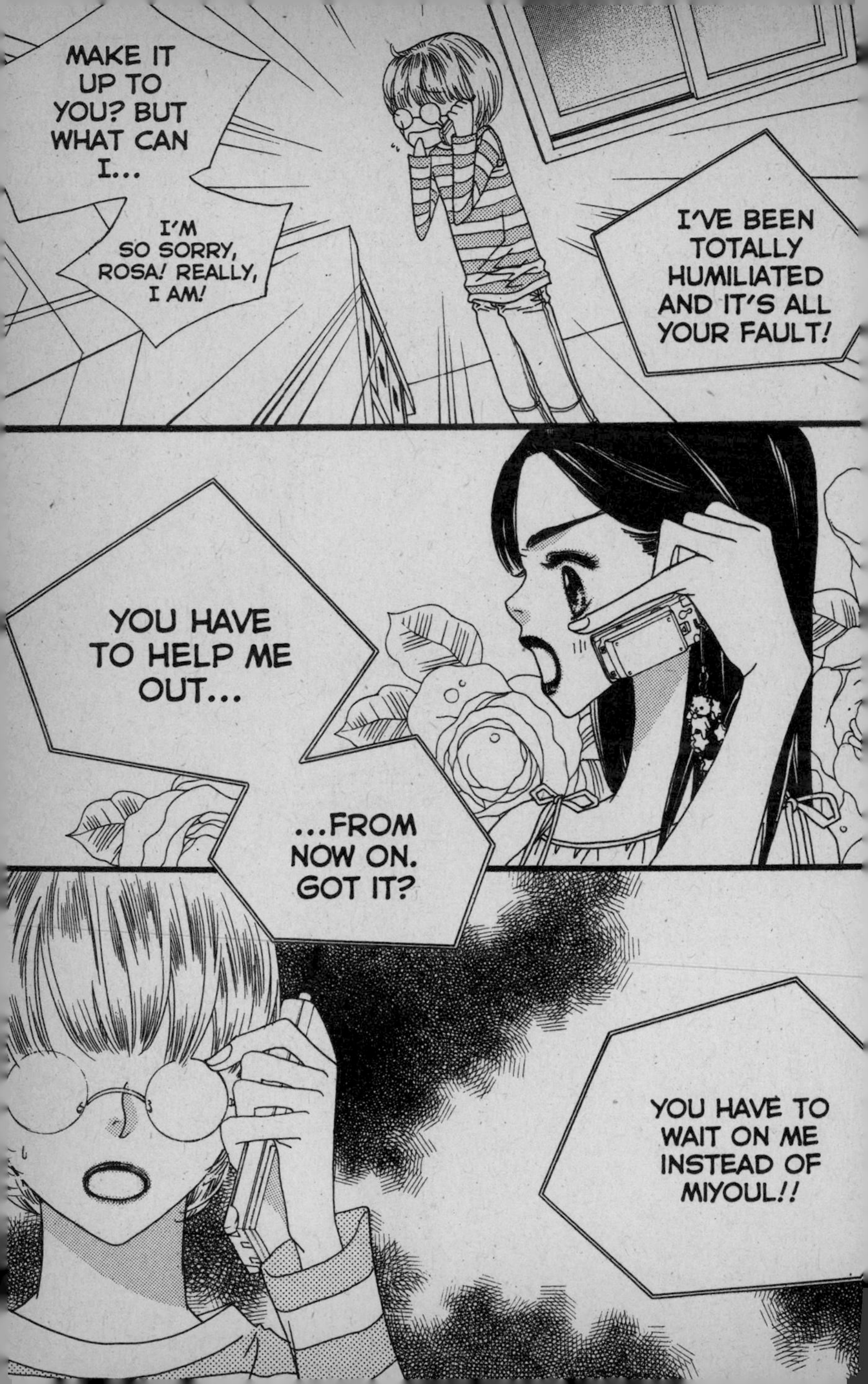
MAKE IT UP TO YOU? BUT WHAT CAN I...
I'M SO SORRY, ROSA! REALLY, I AM!
I'VE BEEN TOTALLY HUMILIATED AND IT'S ALL YOUR FAULT!
YOU HAVE TO HELP ME OUT...
...FROM NOW ON. GOT IT?
YOU HAVE TO WAIT ON ME INSTEAD OF MIYOUL!!

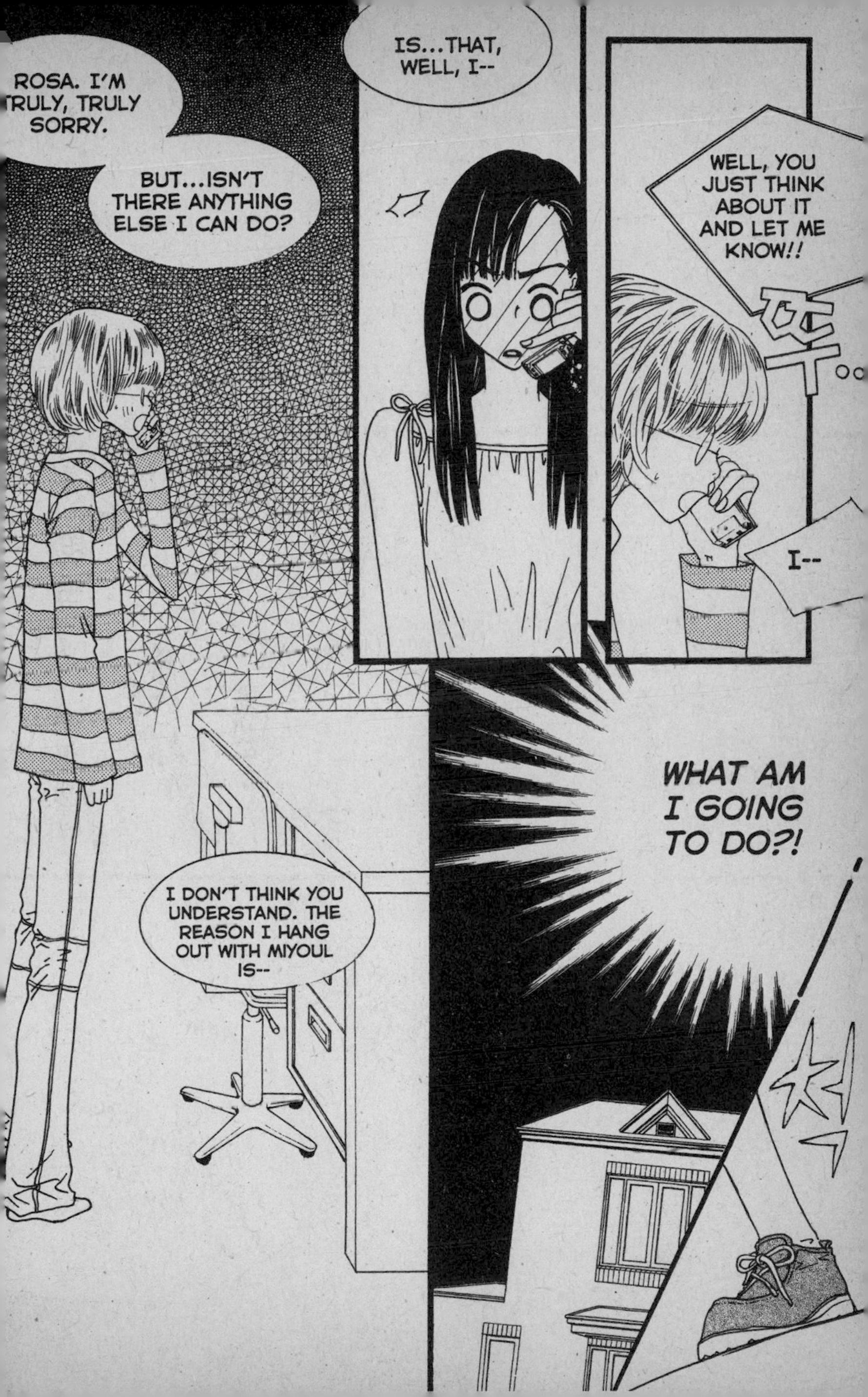
ROSA. I'M TRULY, TRULY SORRY.
BUT...ISN'T THERE ANYTHING ELSE I CAN DO?
I DON'T THINK YOU UNDERSTAND. THE REASON I HANG OUT WITH MIYOUL IS--
IS...THAT, WELL, I--
WELL, YOU JUST THINK ABOUT IT AND LET ME KNOW!!
I--
WHAT AM I GOING TO DO?!

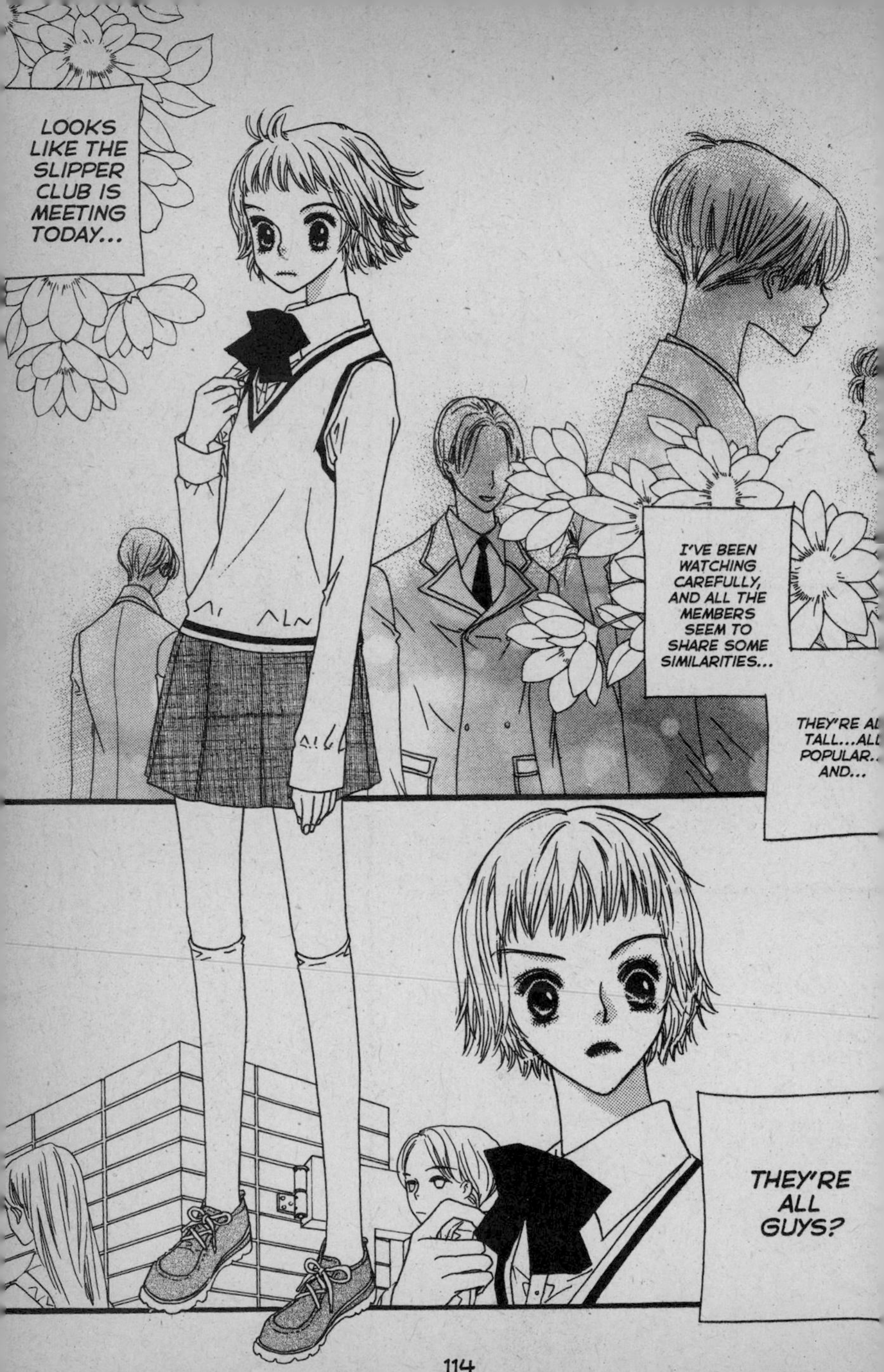
LOOKS LIKE THE SLIPPER CLUB IS MEETING TODAY...
I'VE BEEN WATCHING CAREFULLY, AND ALL THE MEMBERS SEEM TO SHARE SOME SIMILARITIES...
THEY'RE ALL TALL...ALL POPULAR... AND...
THEY'RE ALL GUYS?

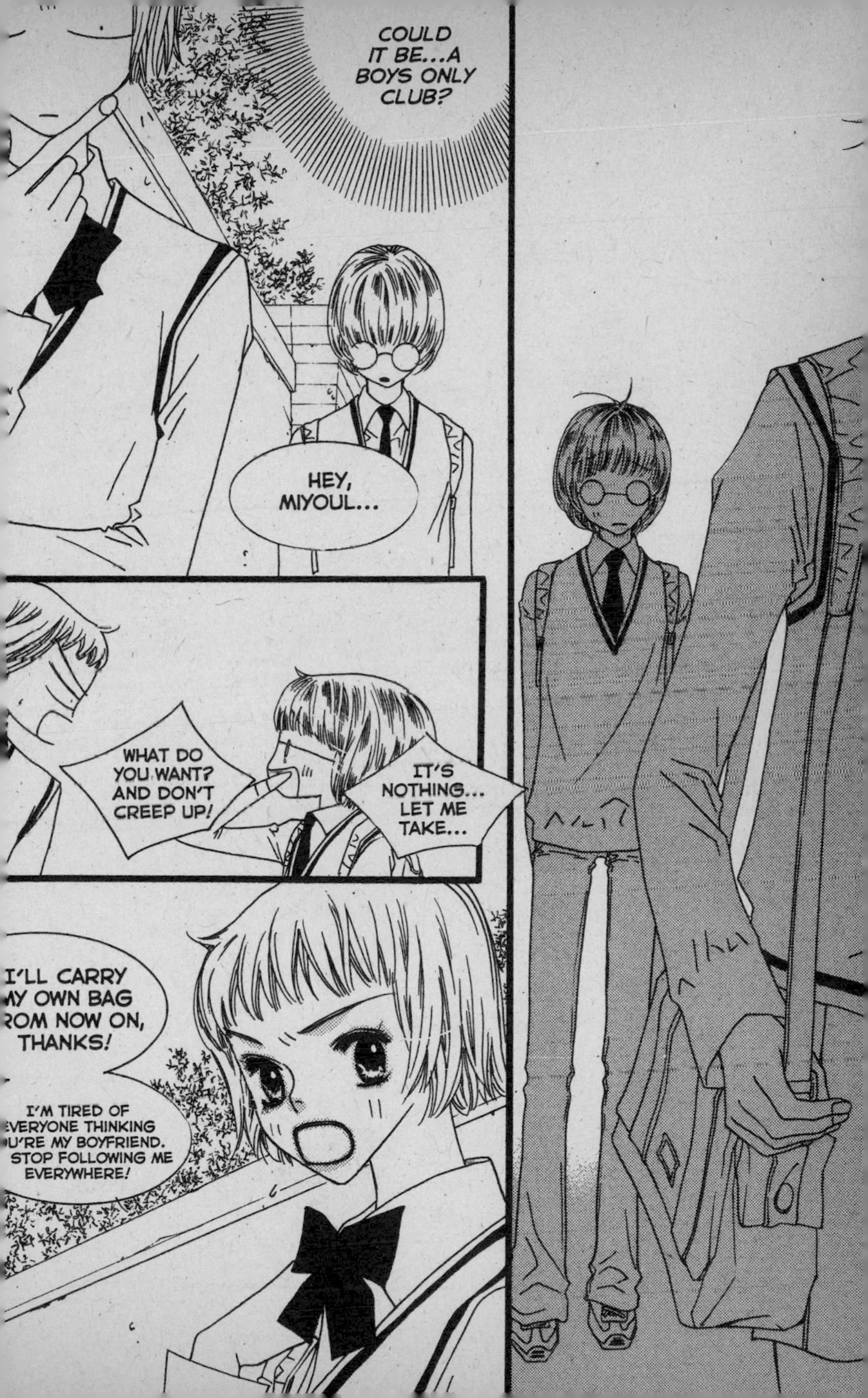
COULD IT BE...A BOYS ONLY CLUB?
HEY, MIYOUL...
WHAT DO YOU WANT? AND DON'T CREEP UP!
IT'S NOTHING... LET ME TAKE...
I'LL CARRY MY OWN BAG ROM NOW ON, THANKS!
I'M TIRED OF VERYONE THINKING U'RE MY BOYFRIEND. STOP FOLLOWING ME EVERYWHERE!

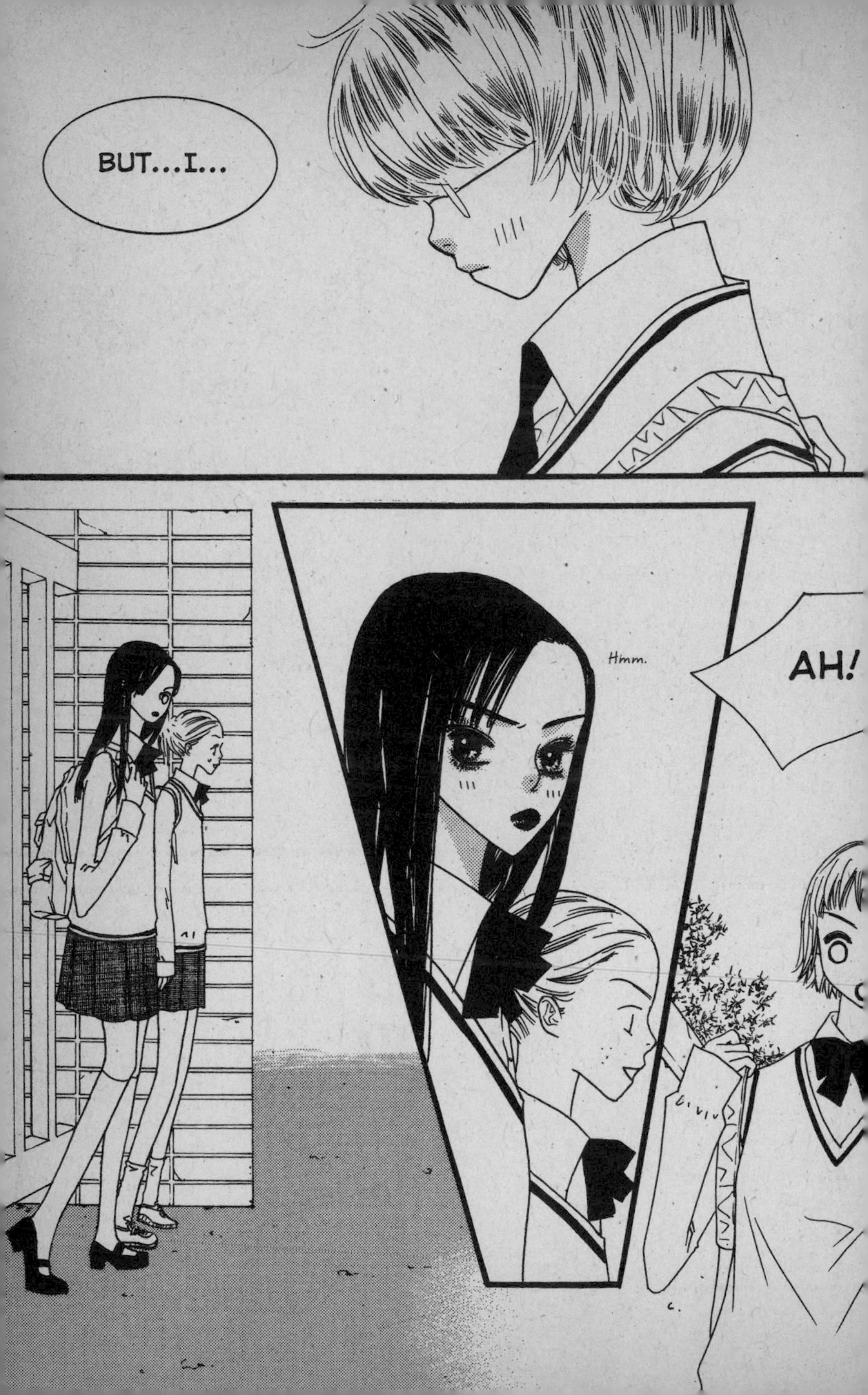
BUT...I...
Hmm.
AH!

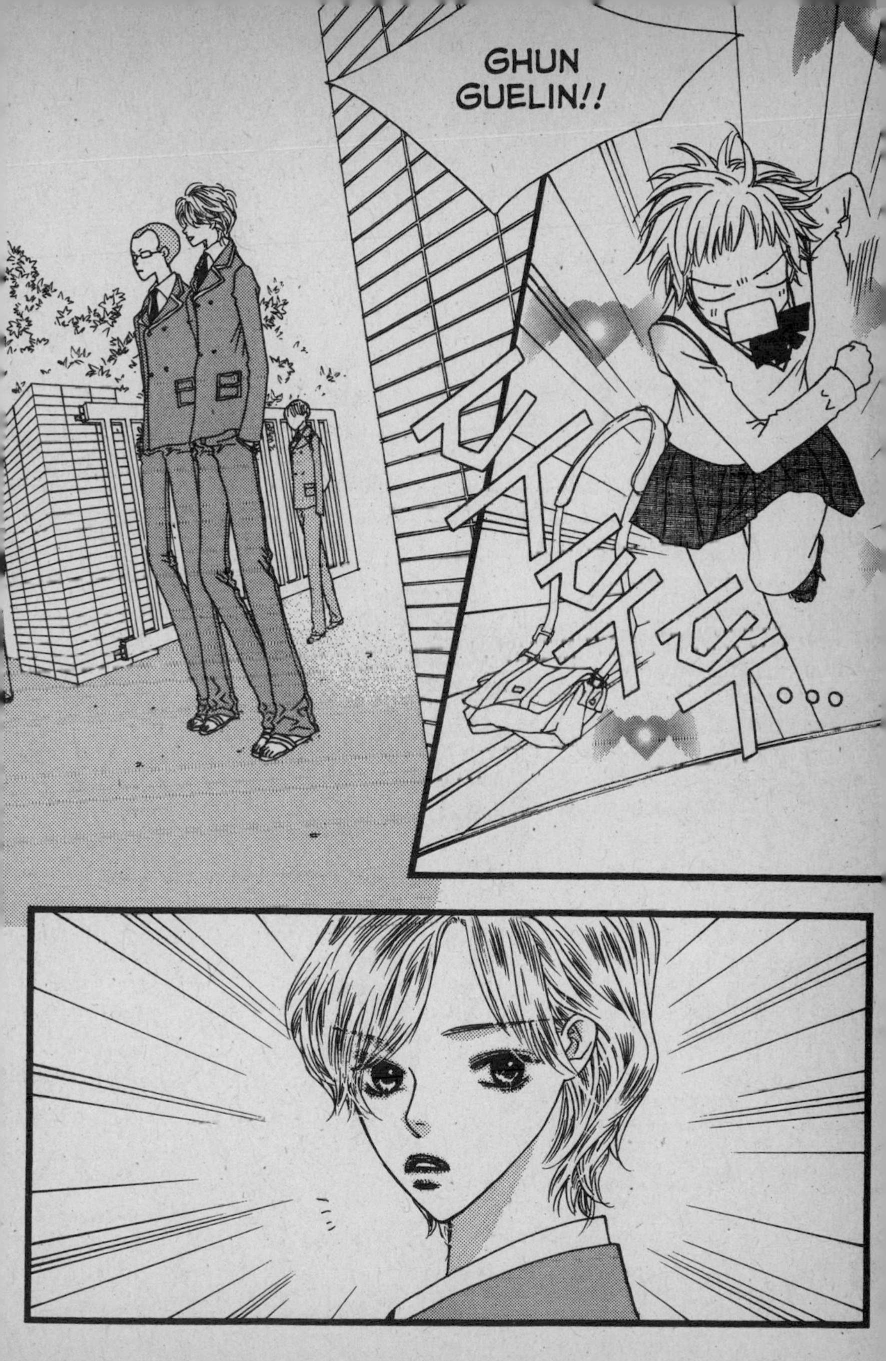
GHUN GUELIN!!
...

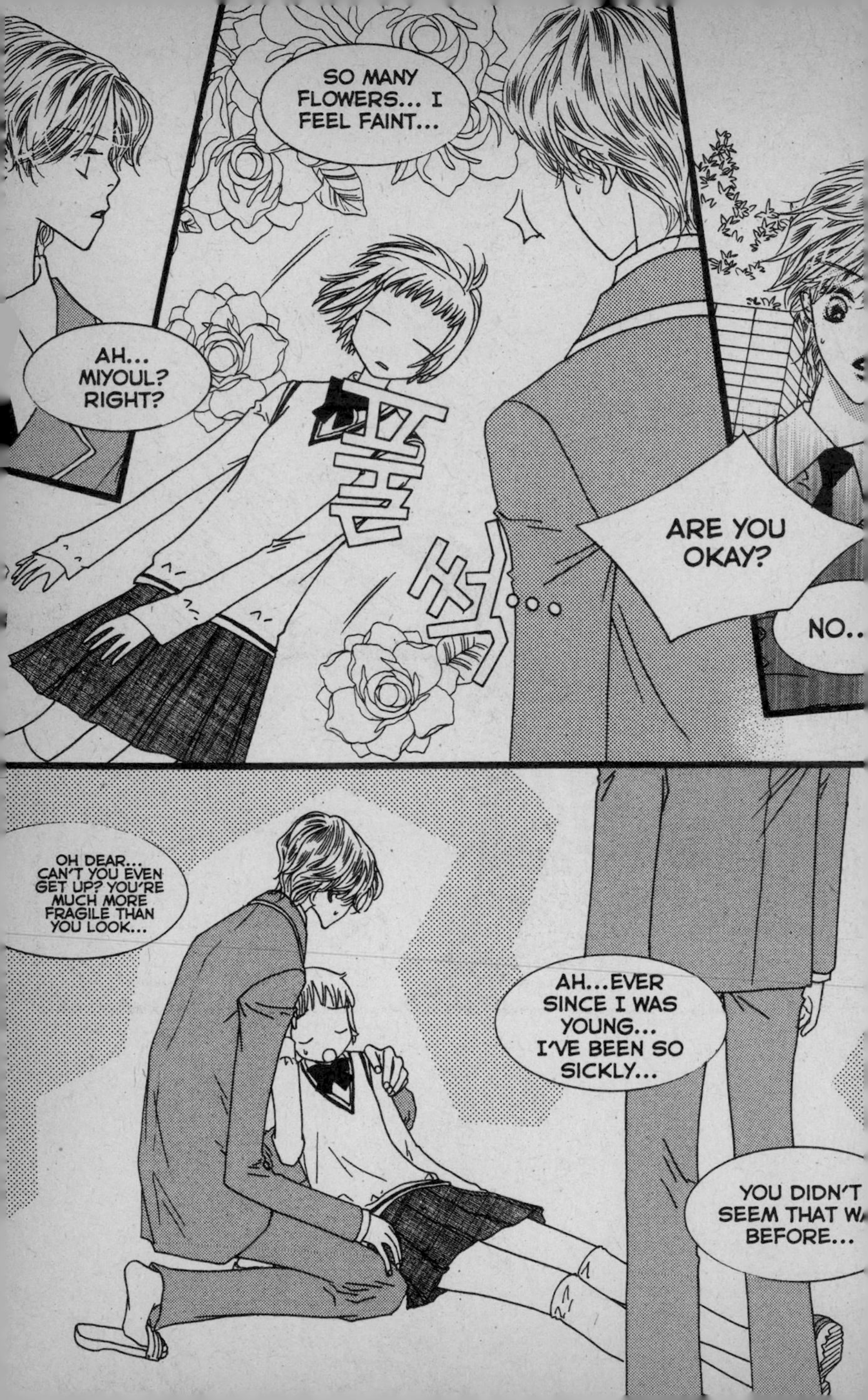
SO MANY FLOWERS... I FEEL FAINT...
AH... MIYOUL? RIGHT?
ARE YOU OKAY?
NO...
OH DEAR... CAN'T YOU EVEN GET UP? YOU'RE MUCH MORE FRAGILE THAN YOU LOOK...
AH...EVER SINCE I WAS YOUNG... I'VE BEEN SO SICKLY...
YOU DIDN'T SEEM THAT W BEFORE...

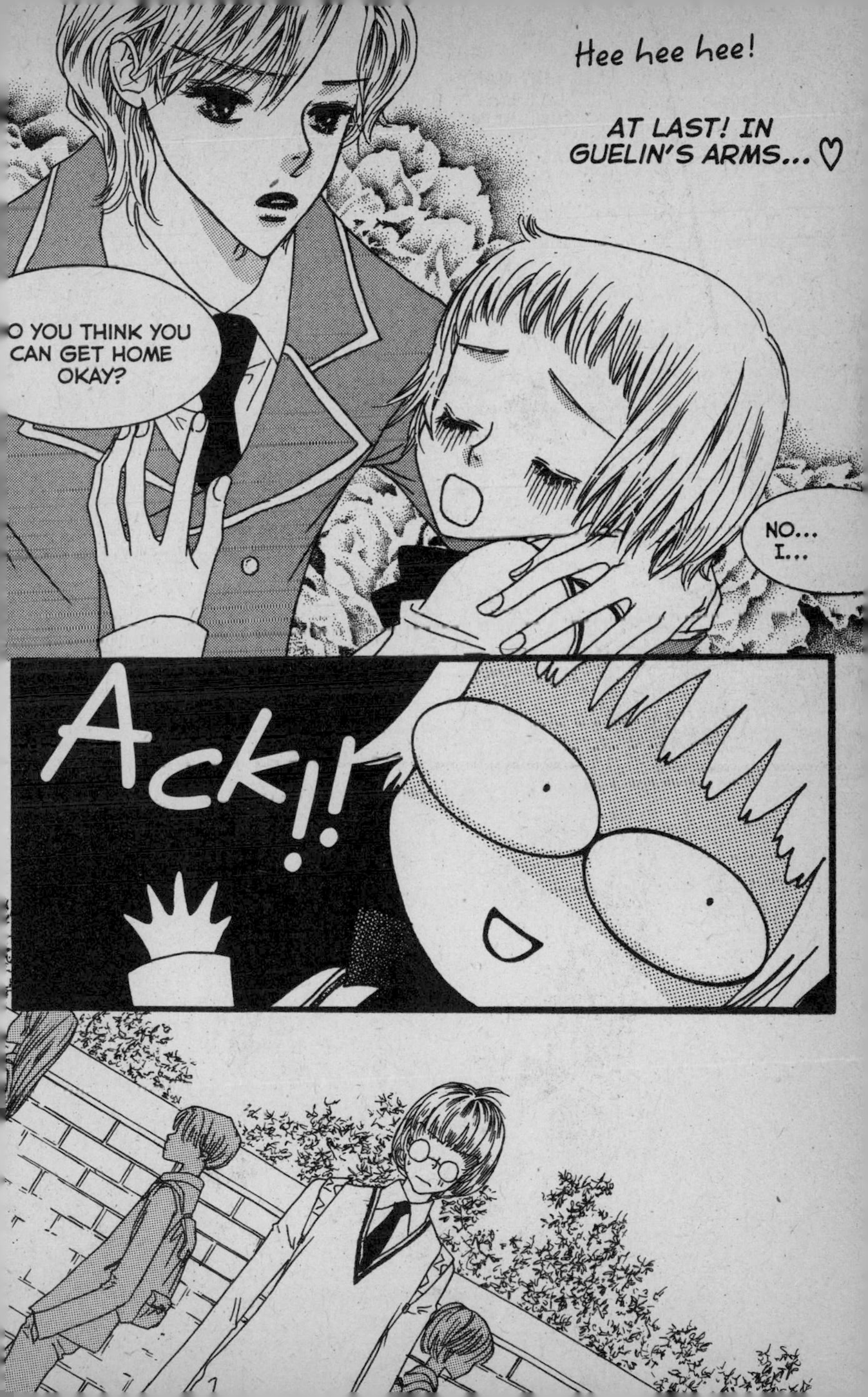
Hee hee hee!
AT LAST! IN GUELIN'S ARMS... ♡
O YOU THINK YOU CAN GET HOME OKAY?
NO... I...
Ack!!

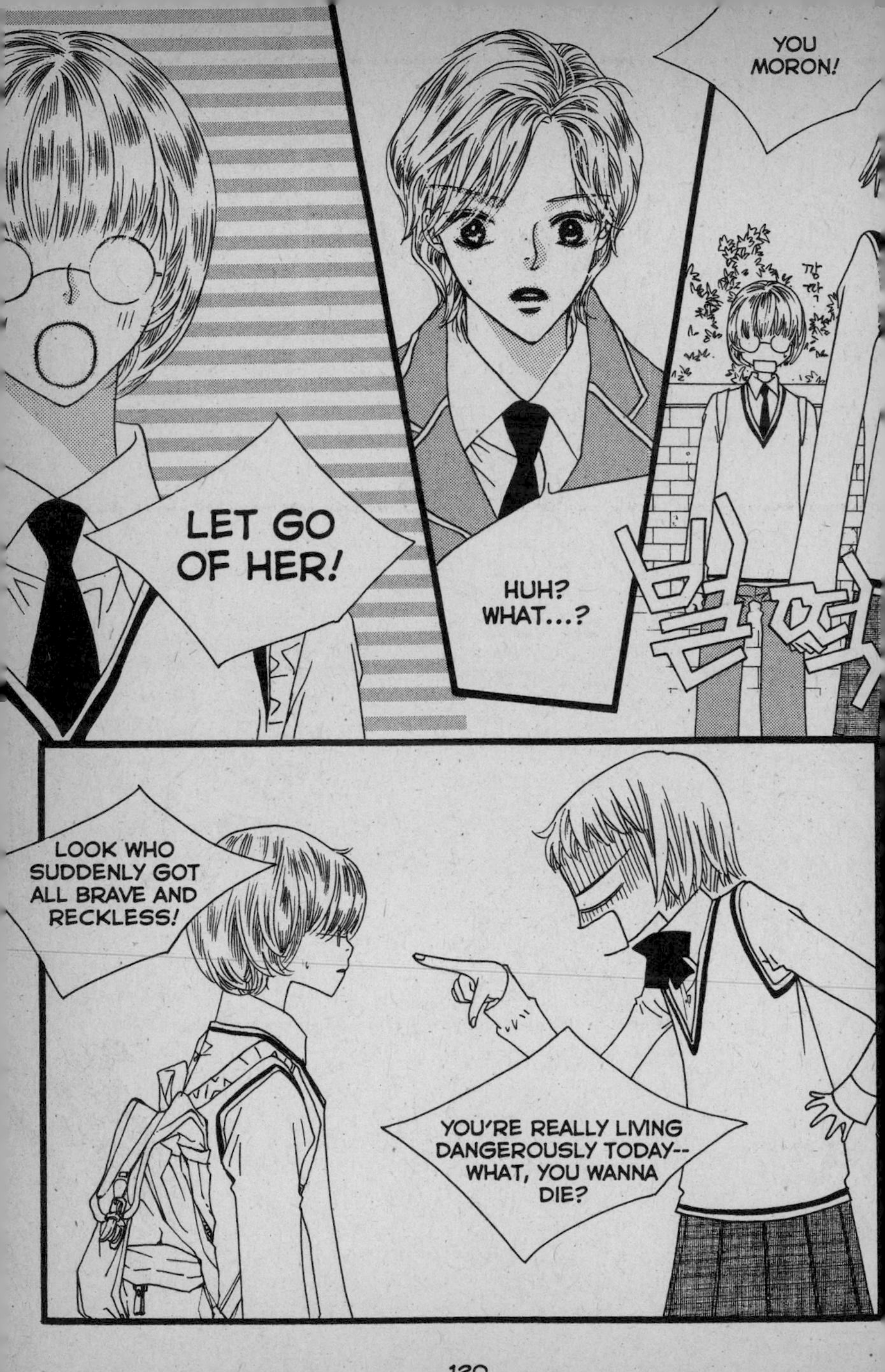
LET GO OF HER!
HUH? WHAT...?
YOU MORON!
깡딱
벌떡
LOOK WHO SUDDENLY GOT ALL BRAVE AND RECKLESS!
YOU'RE REALLY LIVING DANGEROUSLY TODAY-- WHAT, YOU WANNA DIE?

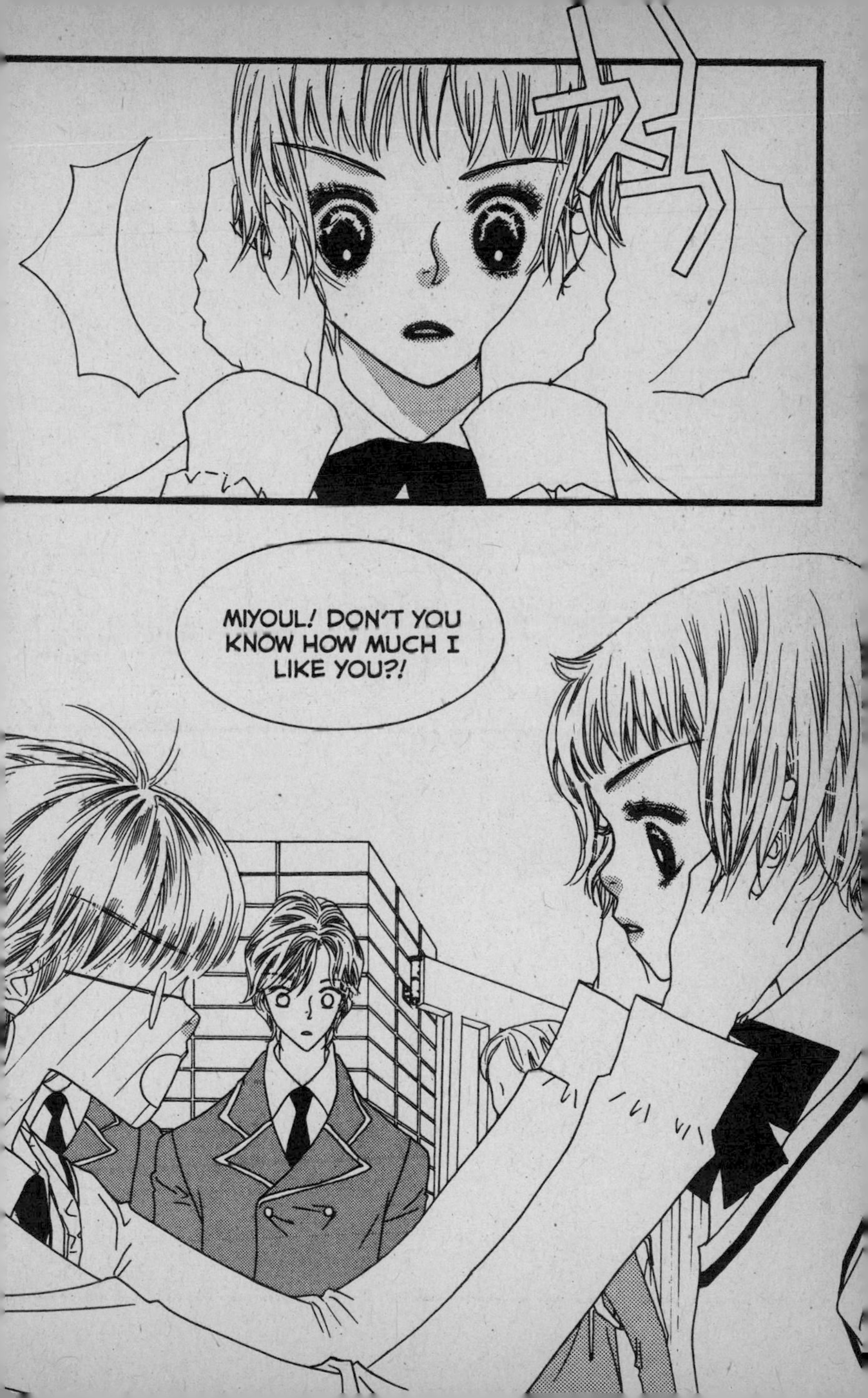
MIYOUL! DON'T YOU KNOW HOW MUCH I LIKE YOU?!

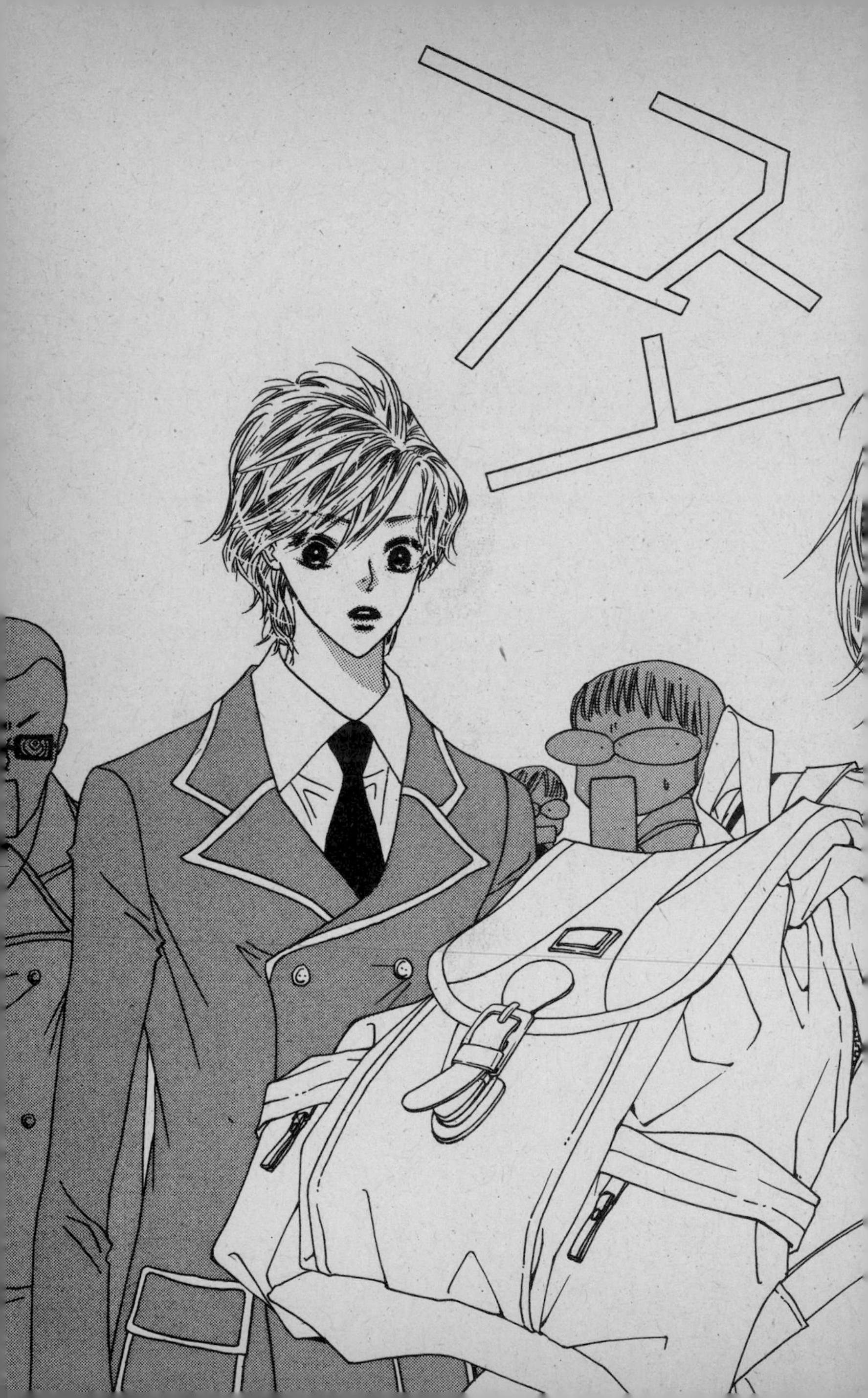
スス

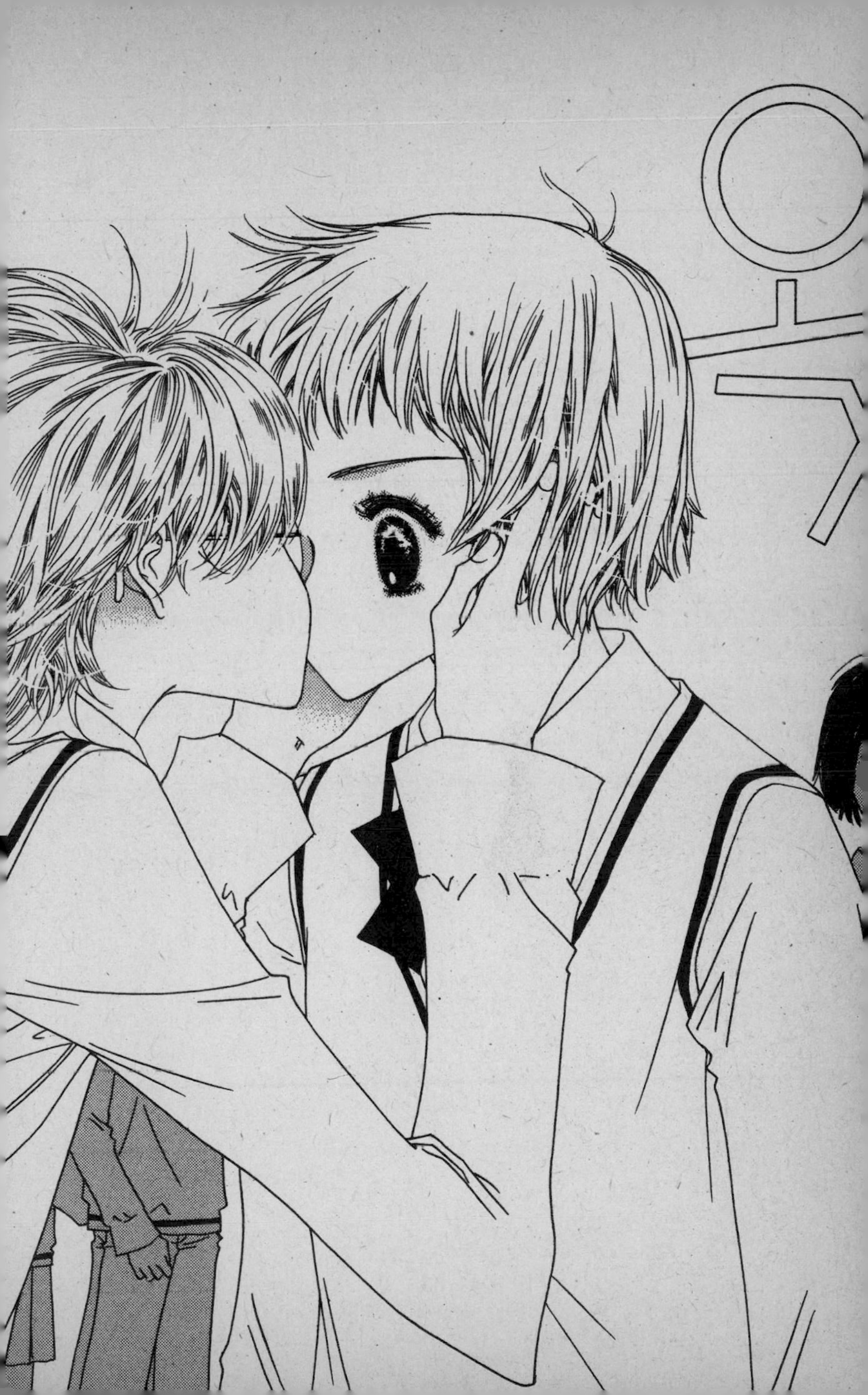

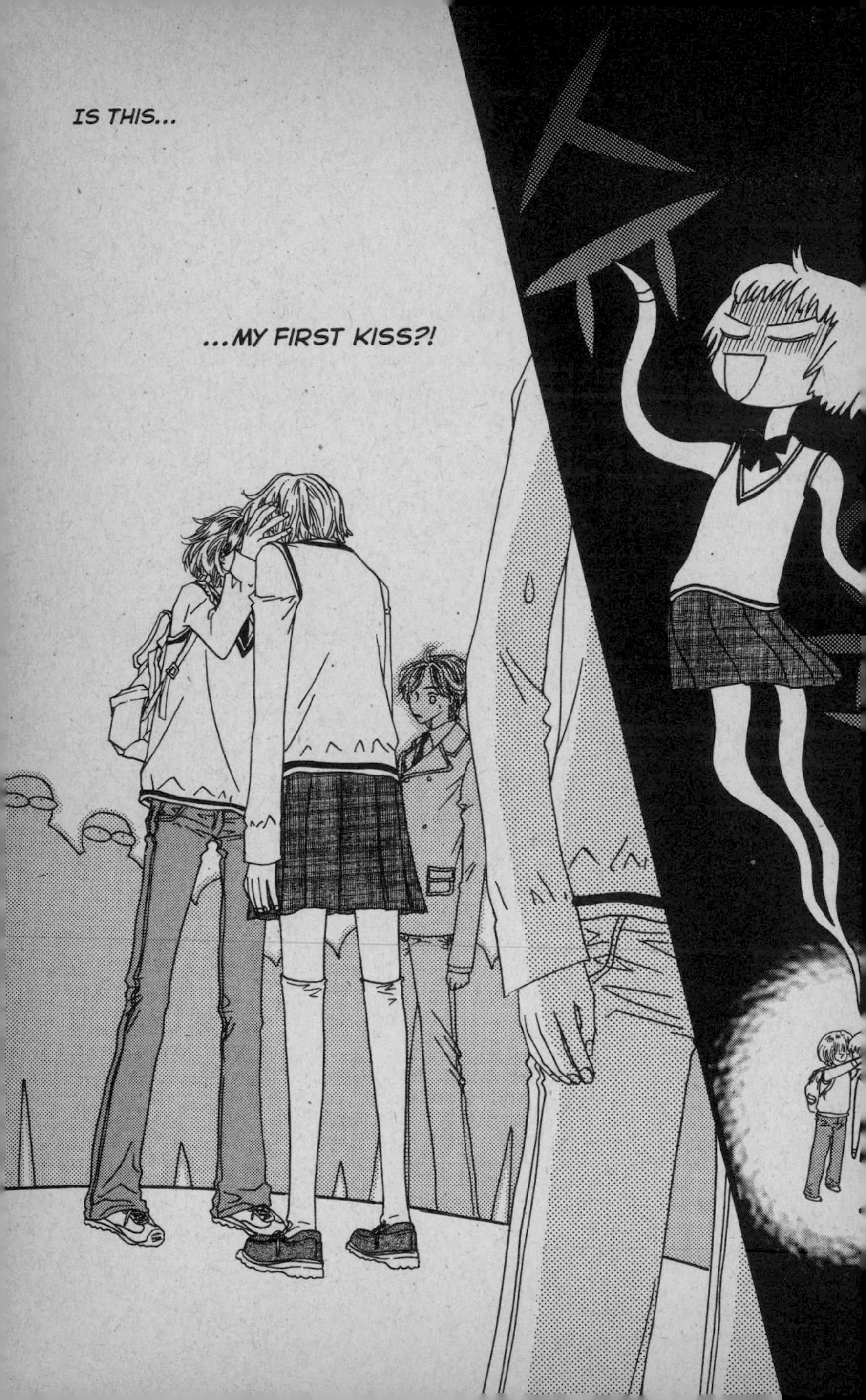
IS THIS...
...MY FIRST KISS?!

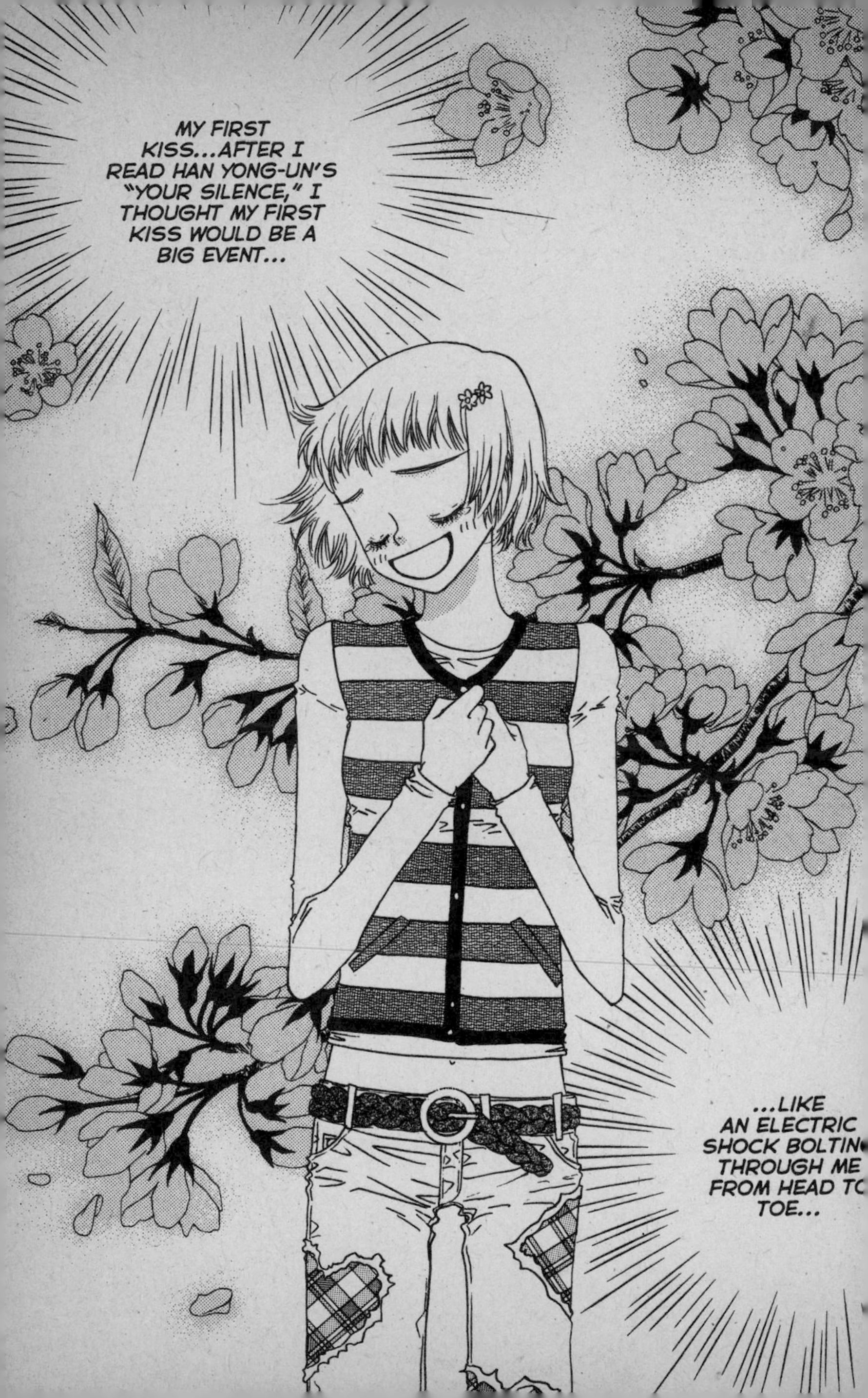
MY FIRST KISS...AFTER I READ HAN YONG-UN'S "YOUR SILENCE," I THOUGHT MY FIRST KISS WOULD BE A BIG EVENT...
...LIKE AN ELECTRIC SHOCK BOLTIN THROUGH ME FROM HEAD TO TOE...

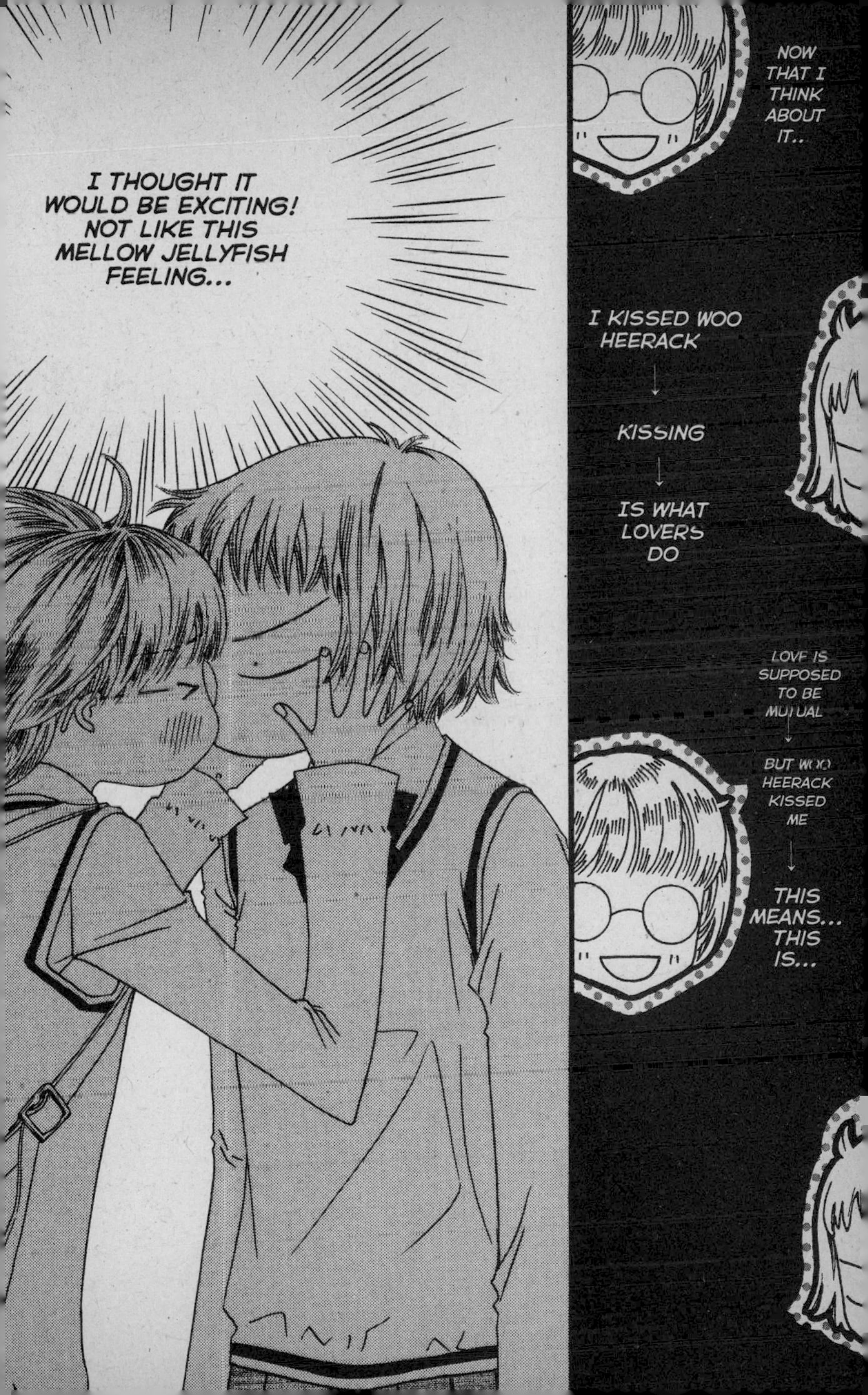
I THOUGHT IT WOULD BE EXCITING! NOT LIKE THIS MELLOW JELLYFISH FEELING...
NOW THAT I THINK ABOUT IT..
I KISSED WOO HEERACK
↓
KISSING
↓
IS WHAT LOVERS DO
LOVE IS SUPPOSED TO BE MUTUAL
↓
BUT WOO HEERACK KISSED ME
↓
THIS MEANS... THIS IS...

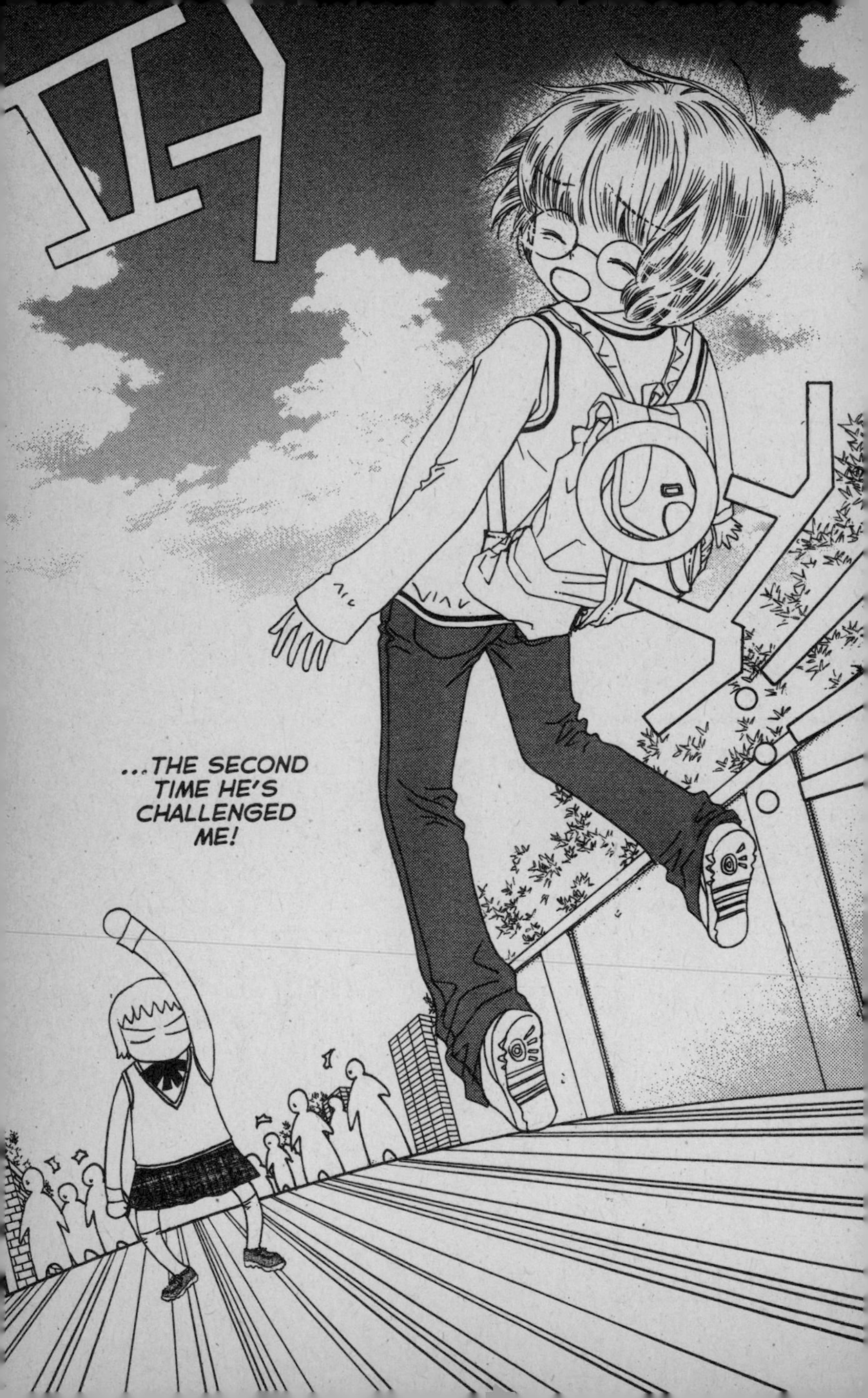
...THE SECOND TIME HE'S CHALLENGED ME!

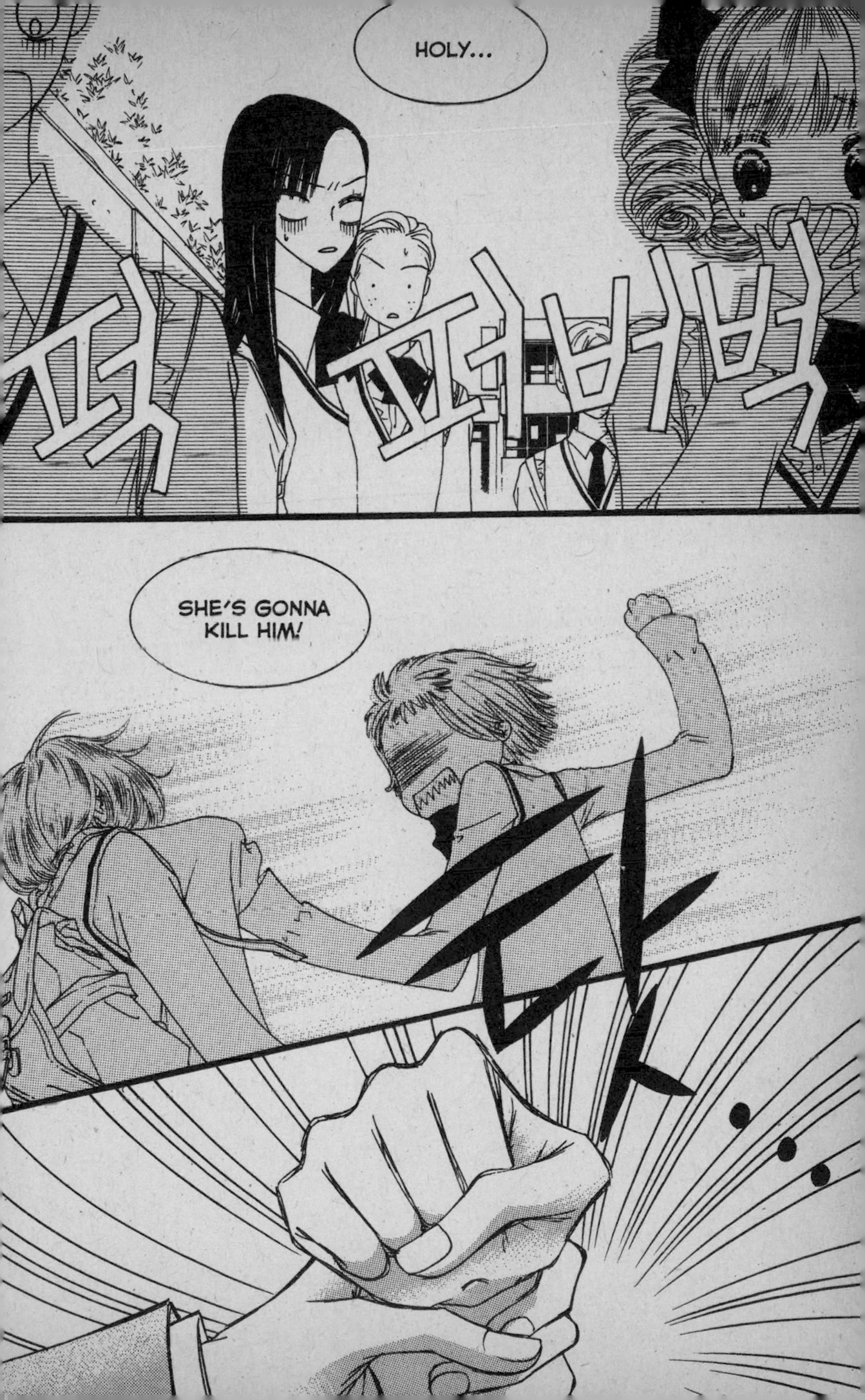
HOLY...
SHE'S GONNA KILL HIM!

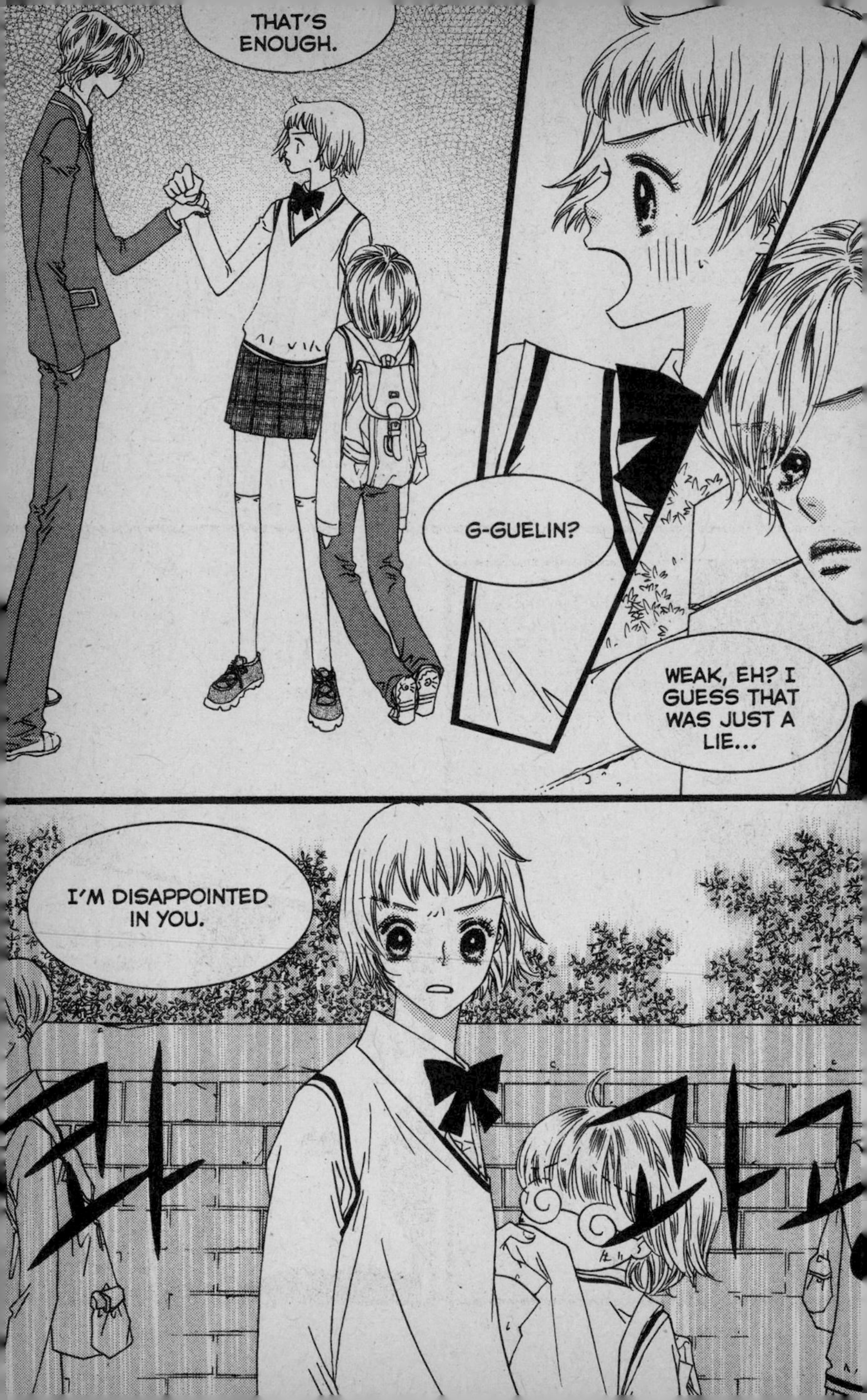
THAT'S ENOUGH.
G-GUELIN?
WEAK, EH? I GUESS THAT WAS JUST A LIE...
I'M DISAPPOINTED IN YOU.

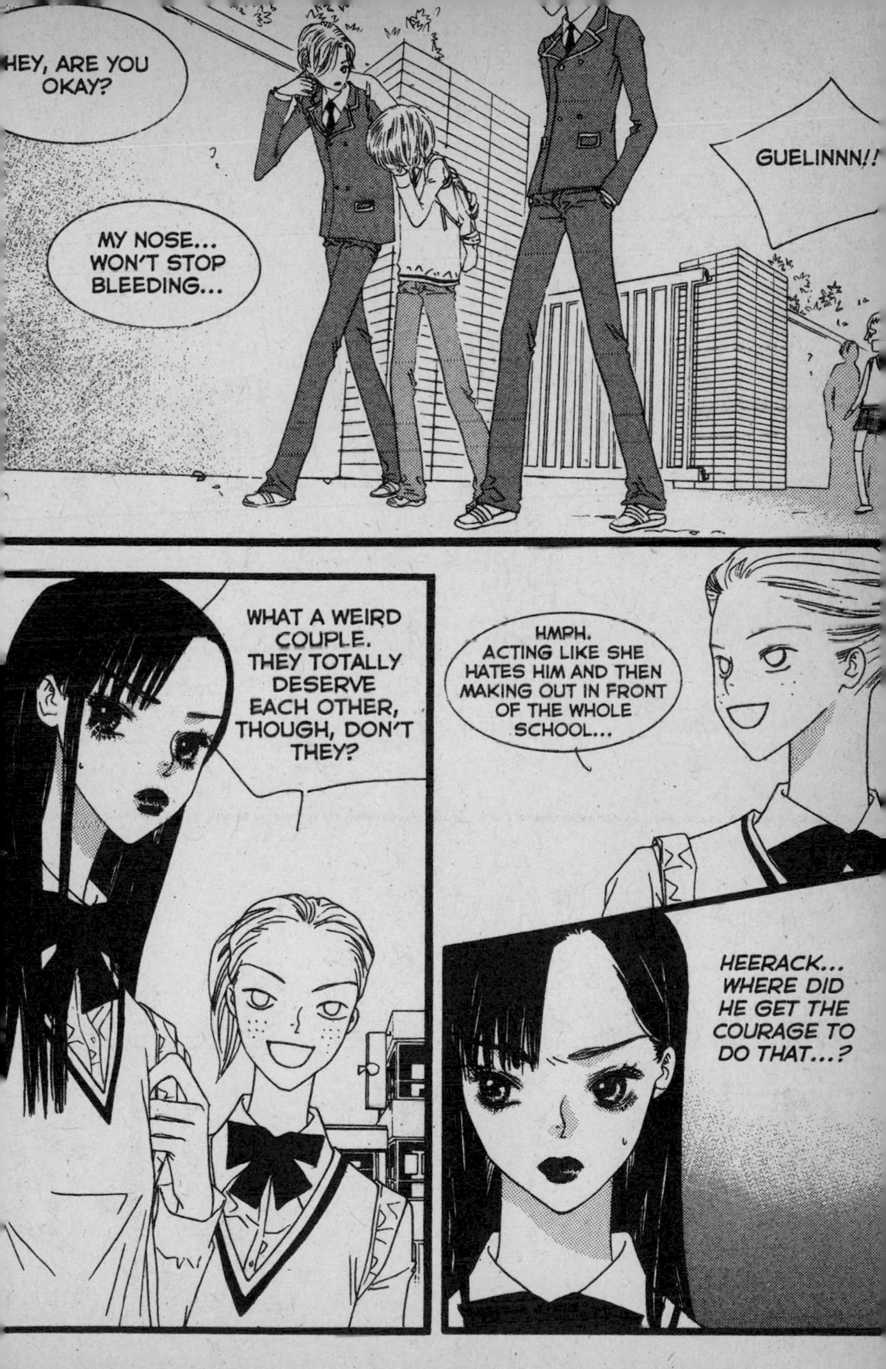
HEY, ARE YOU OKAY?
GUELINNN!!
MY NOSE... WON'T STOP BLEEDING...
WHAT A WEIRD COUPLE. THEY TOTALLY DESERVE EACH OTHER, THOUGH, DON'T THEY?
HMPH. ACTING LIKE SHE HATES HIM AND THEN MAKING OUT IN FRONT OF THE WHOLE SCHOOL...
HEERACK... WHERE DID HE GET THE COURAGE TO DO THAT...?

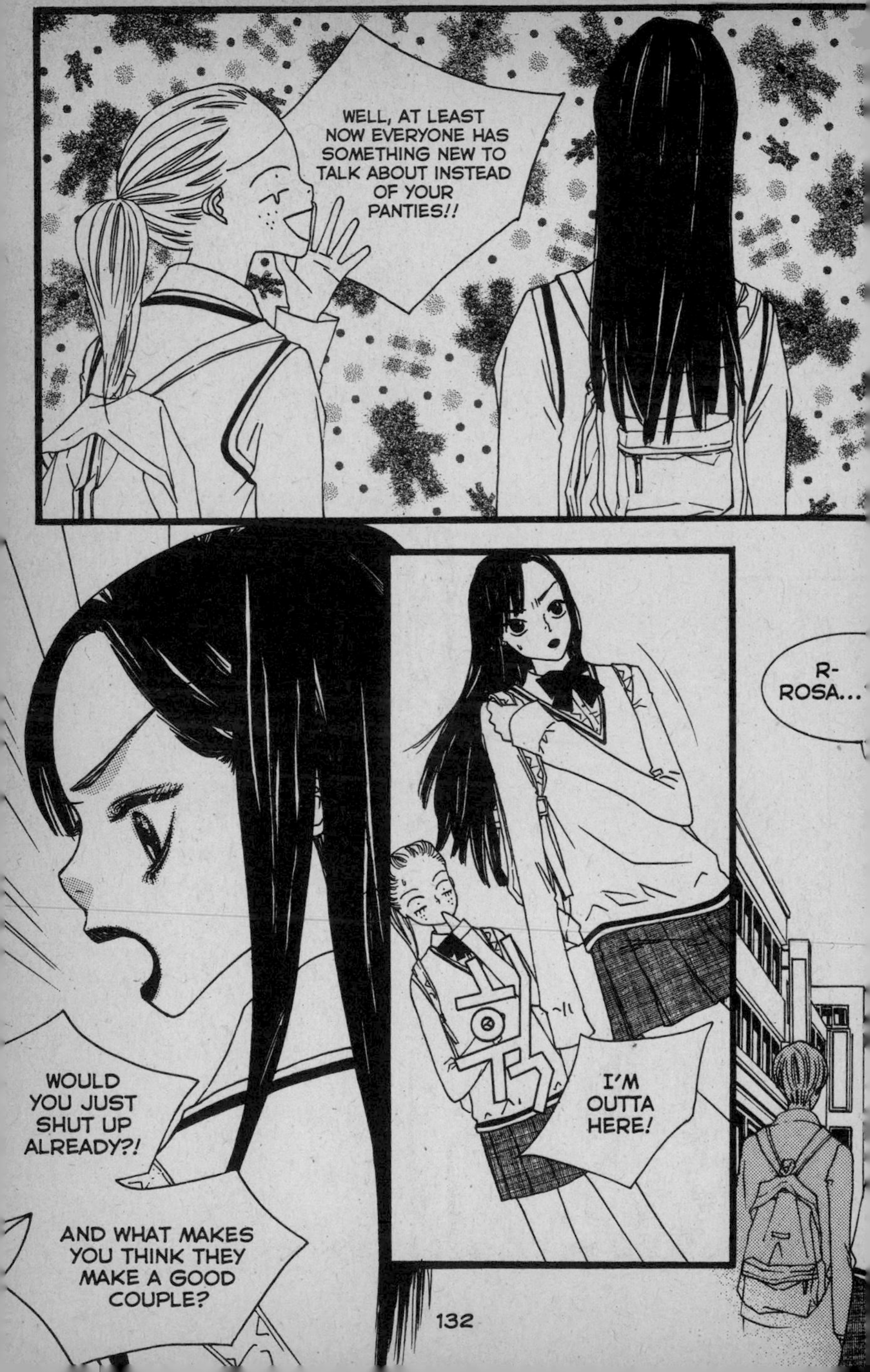

WELL, AT LEAST NOW EVERYONE HAS SOMETHING NEW TO TALK ABOUT INSTEAD OF YOUR PANTIES!!
WOULD YOU JUST SHUT UP ALREADY?!
AND WHAT MAKES YOU THINK THEY MAKE A GOOD COUPLE?
I'M OUTTA HERE!
R-ROSA...

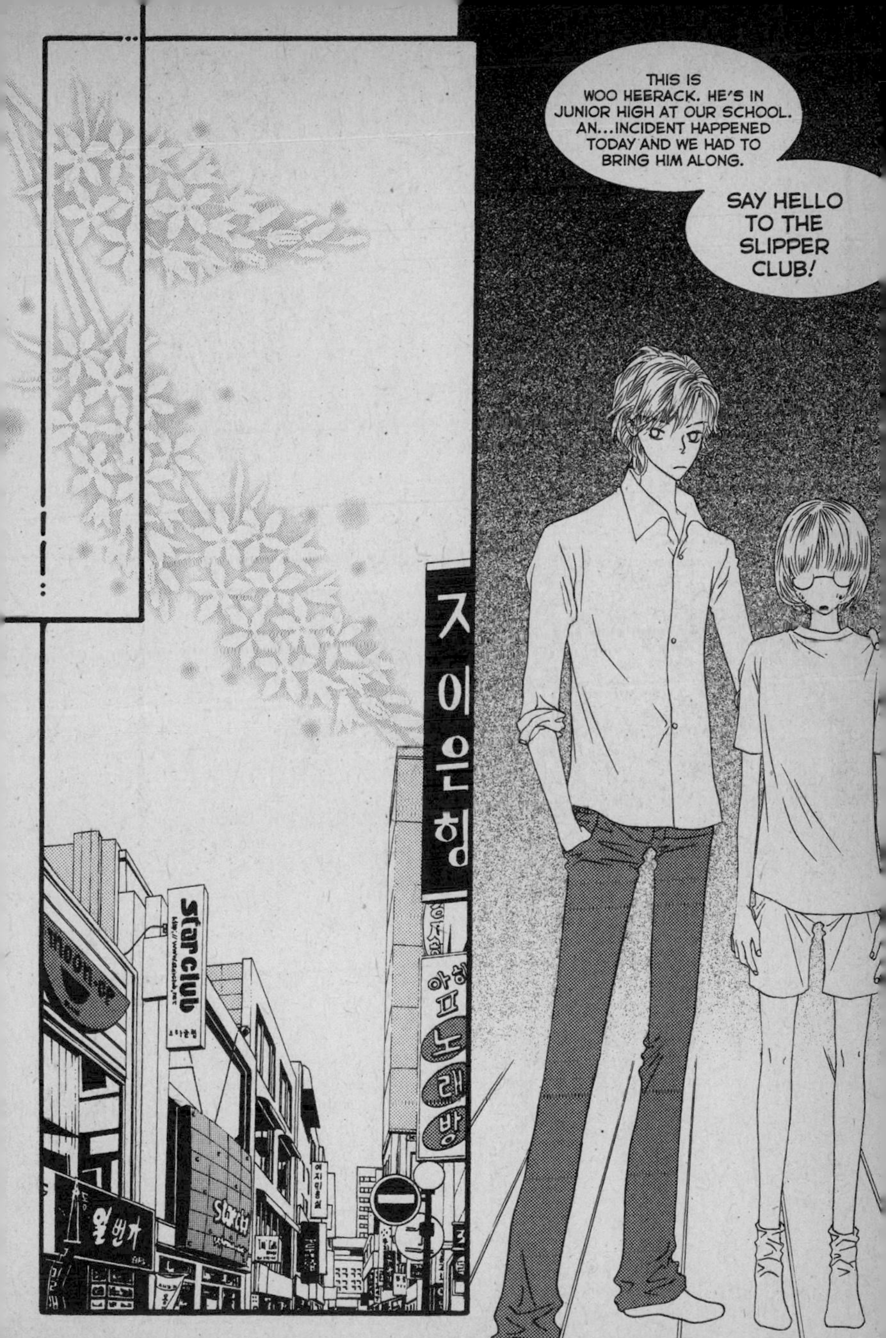
THIS IS WOO HEERACK. HE'S IN JUNIOR HIGH AT OUR SCHOOL. AN...INCIDENT HAPPENED TODAY AND WE HAD TO BRING HIM ALONG.
SAY HELLO TO THE SLIPPER CLUB!
starclub
노래방

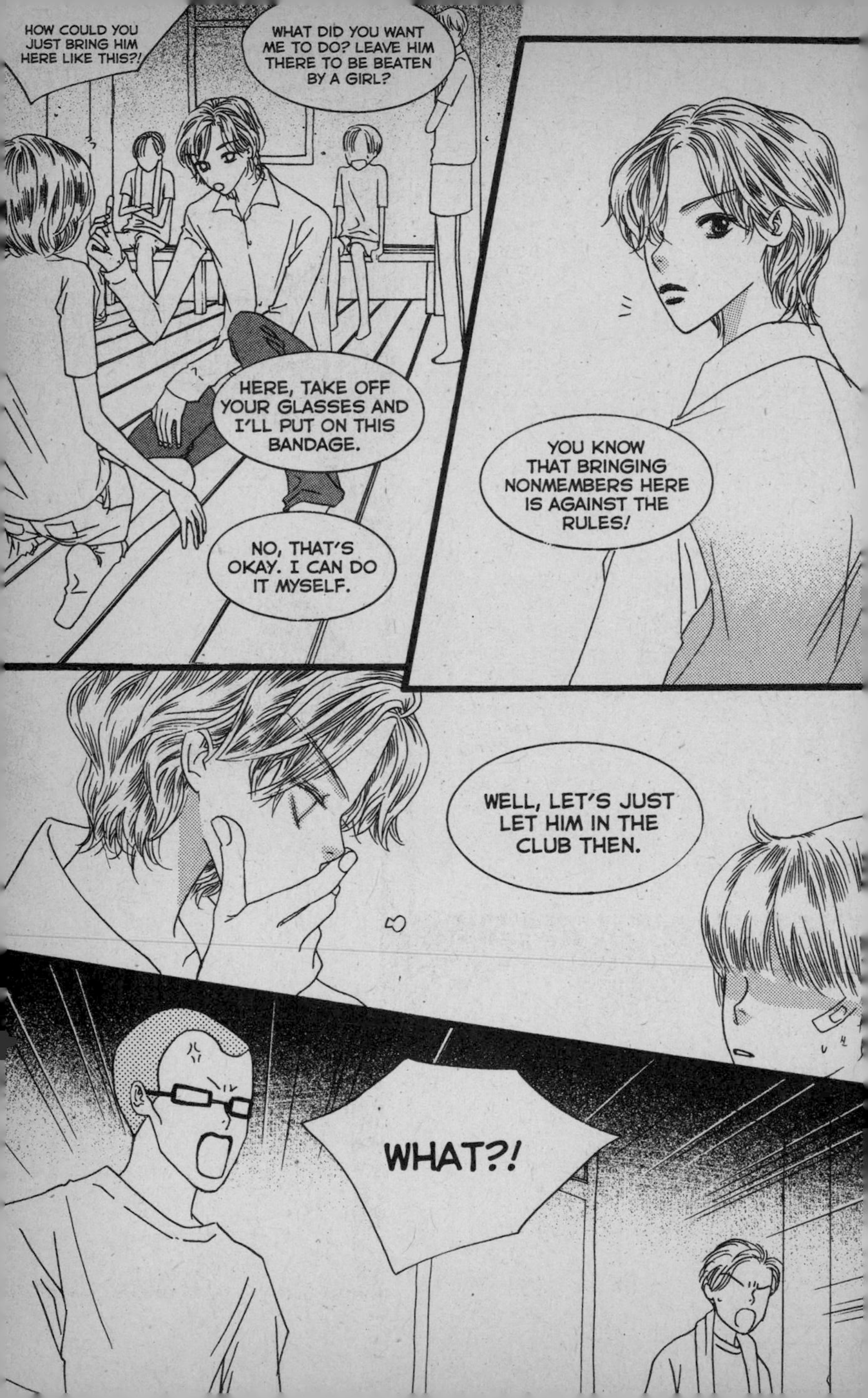
HOW COULD YOU JUST BRING HIM HERE LIKE THIS?!
WHAT DID YOU WANT ME TO DO? LEAVE HIM THERE TO BE BEATEN BY A GIRL?
HERE, TAKE OFF YOUR GLASSES AND I'LL PUT ON THIS BANDAGE.
NO, THAT'S OKAY. I CAN DO IT MYSELF.
YOU KNOW THAT BRINGING NONMEMBERS HERE IS AGAINST THE RULES!
WELL, LET'S JUST LET HIM IN THE CLUB THEN.
WHAT?!

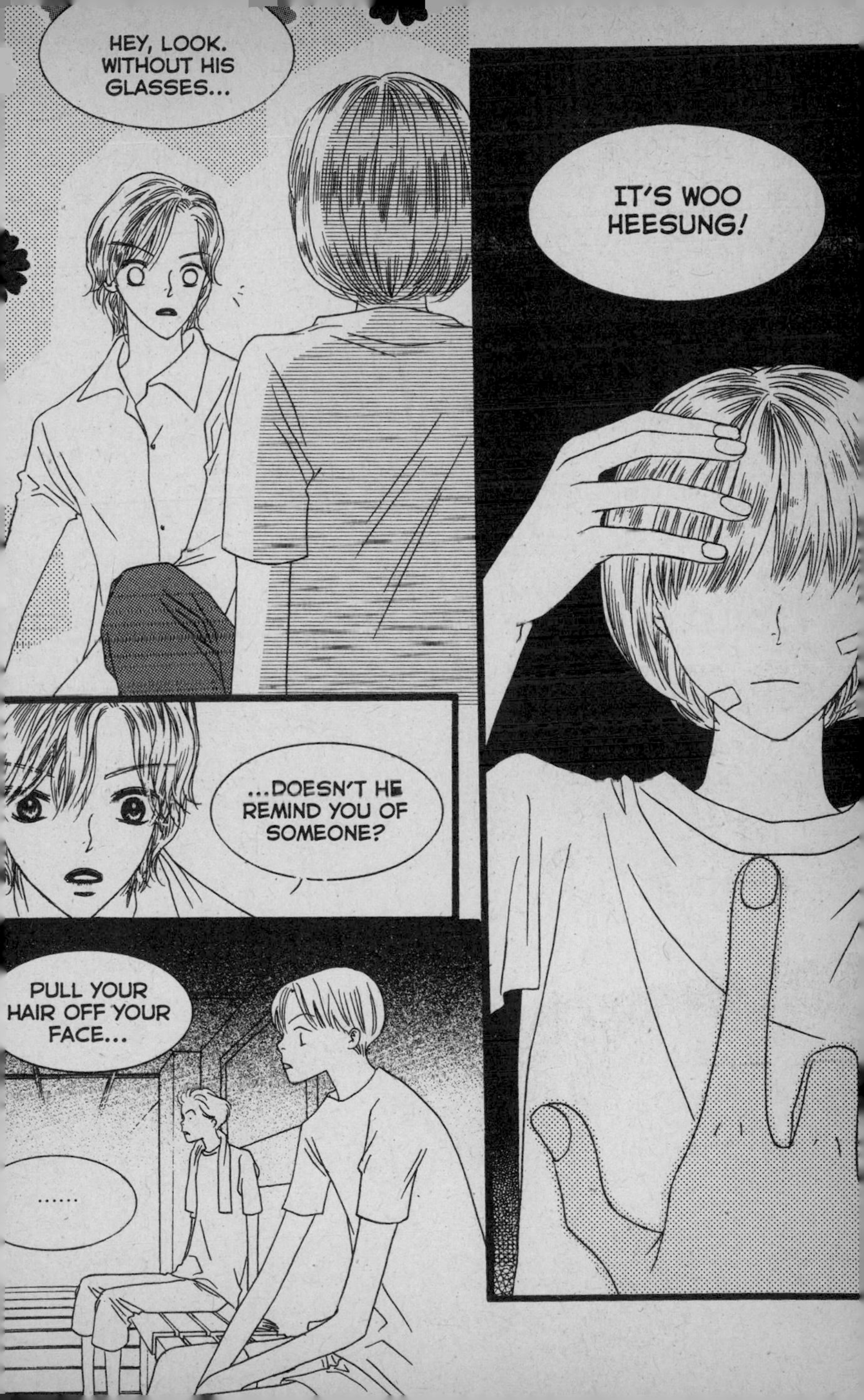
HEY, LOOK. WITHOUT HIS GLASSES...
...DOESN'T HE REMIND YOU OF SOMEONE?
PULL YOUR HAIR OFF YOUR FACE...
......
IT'S WOO HEESUNG!

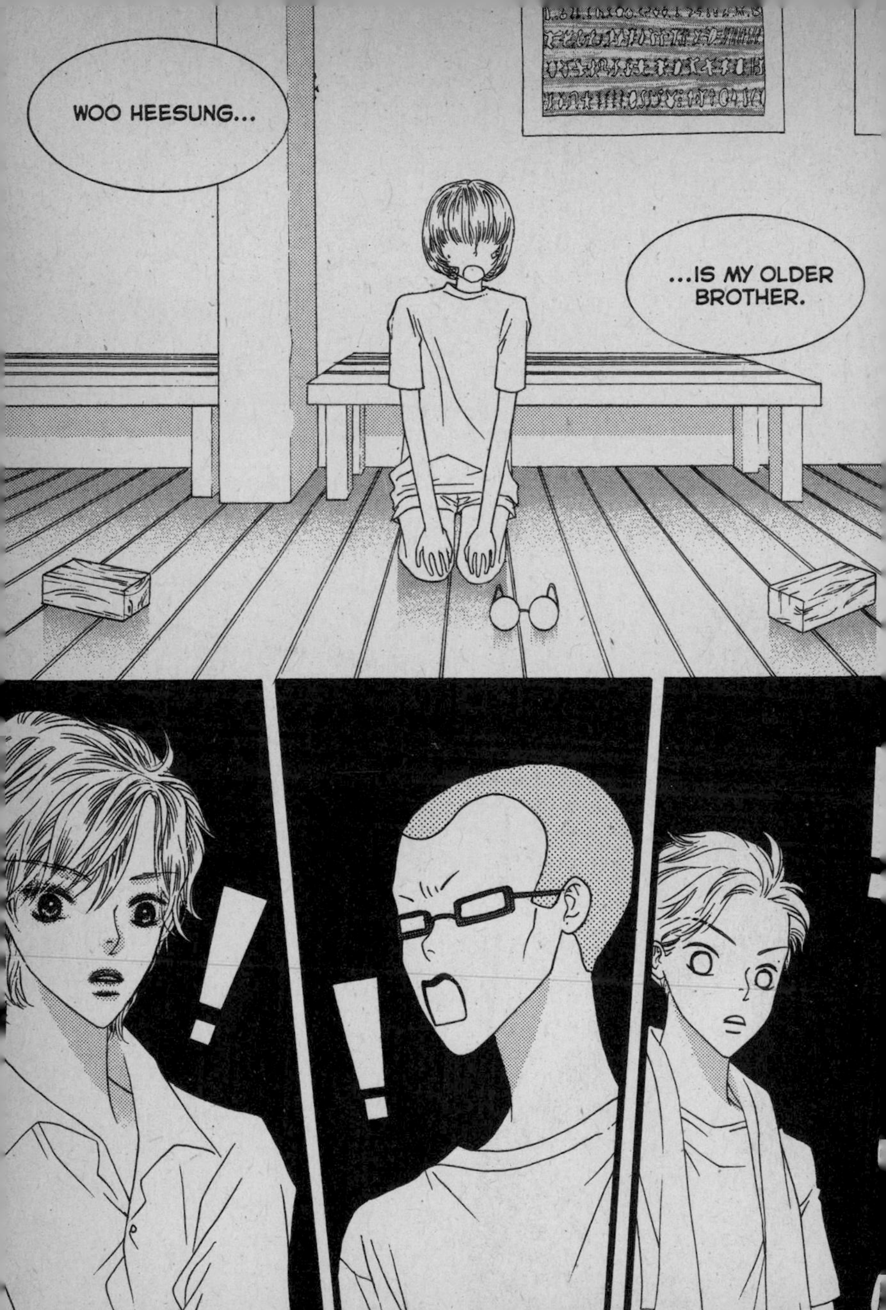
WOO HEESUNG...
...IS MY OLDER BROTHER.

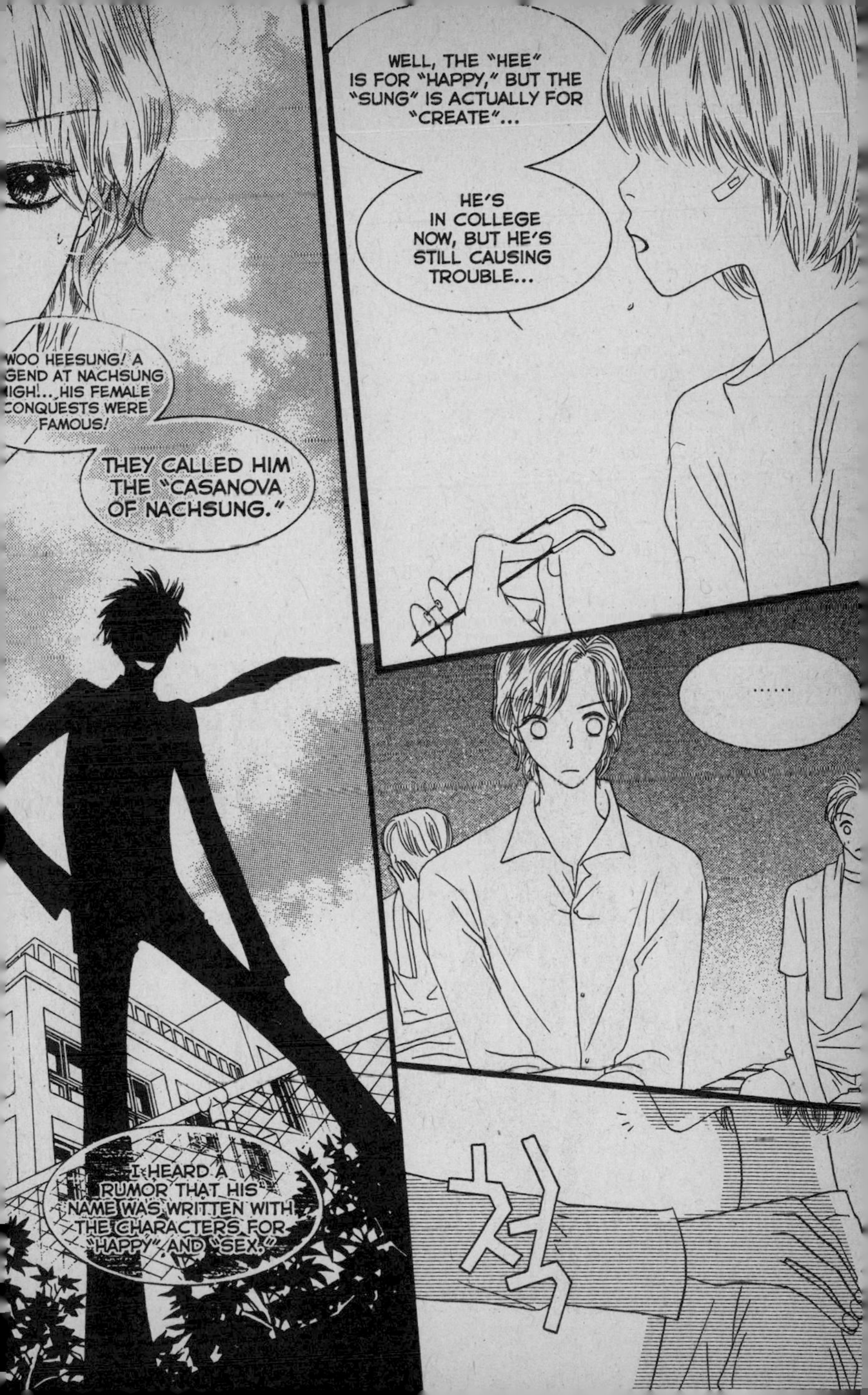
WOO HEESUNG! A GEND AT NACHSUNG IGH!... HIS FEMALE CONQUESTS WERE FAMOUS!
THEY CALLED HIM THE "CASANOVA OF NACHSUNG."
I HEARD A RUMOR THAT HIS NAME WAS WRITTEN WITH THE CHARACTERS FOR "HAPPY" AND "SEX."
WELL, THE "HEE" IS FOR "HAPPY," BUT THE "SUNG" IS ACTUALLY FOR "CREATE"...
HE'S IN COLLEGE NOW, BUT HE'S STILL CAUSING TROUBLE...
......

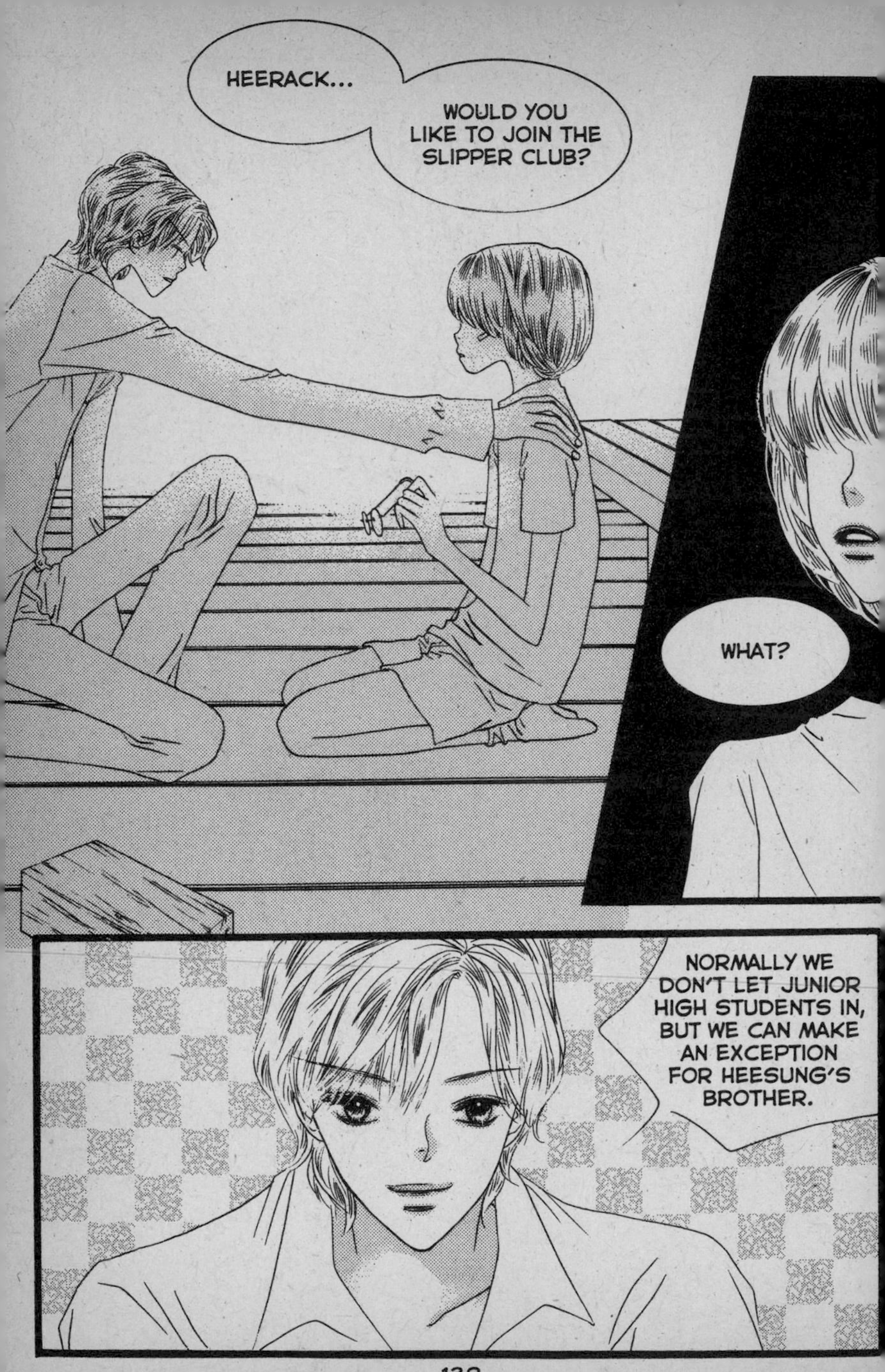
HEERACK...
WOULD YOU LIKE TO JOIN THE SLIPPER CLUB?
WHAT?
NORMALLY WE DON'T LET JUNIOR HIGH STUDENTS IN, BUT WE CAN MAKE AN EXCEPTION FOR HEESUNG'S BROTHER.

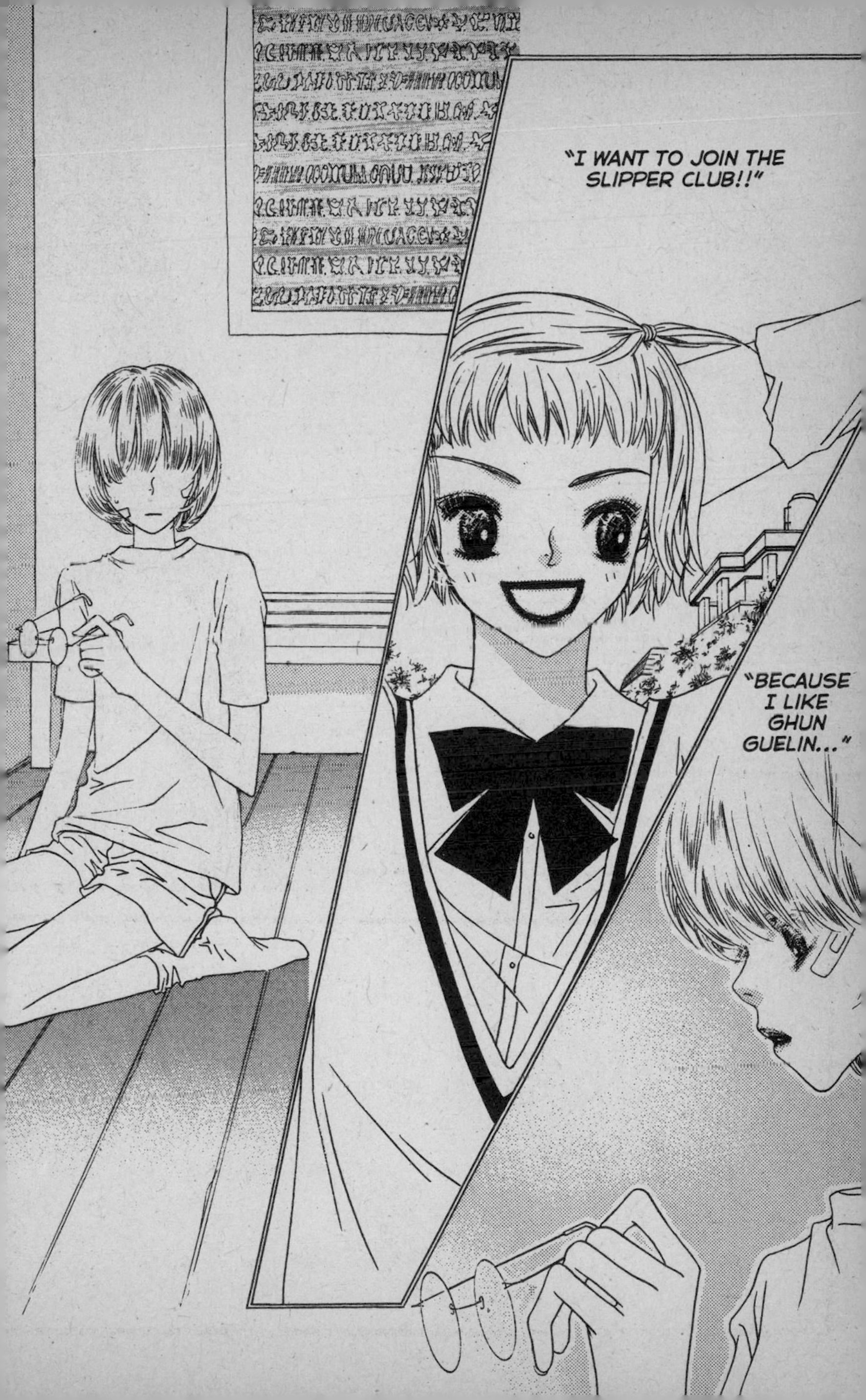
"I WANT TO JOIN THE SLIPPER CLUB!!"
"BECAUSE I LIKE GHUN GUELIN..."

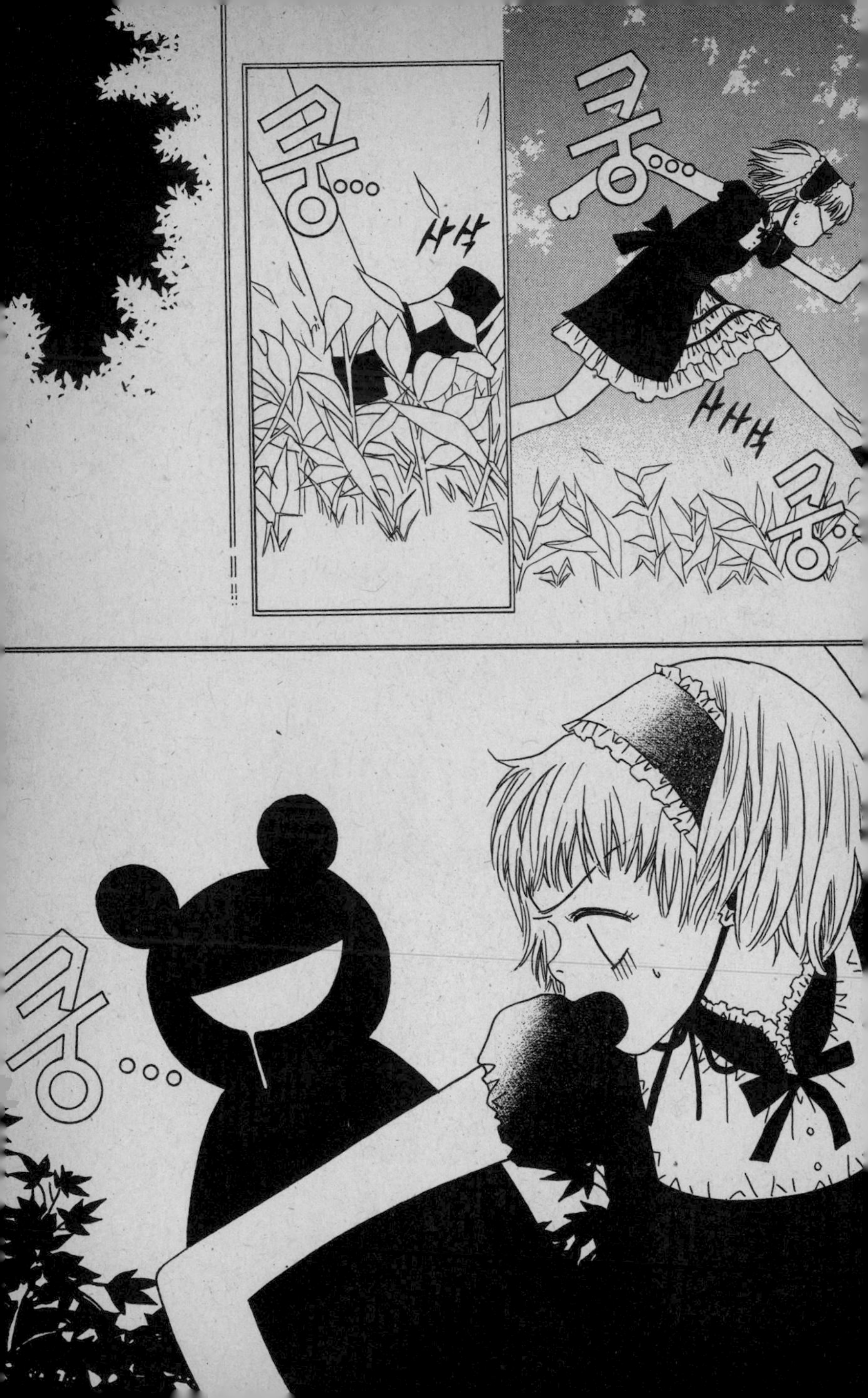
쿵···
사삭
쿵···
사사삭
쿵···
쿵···

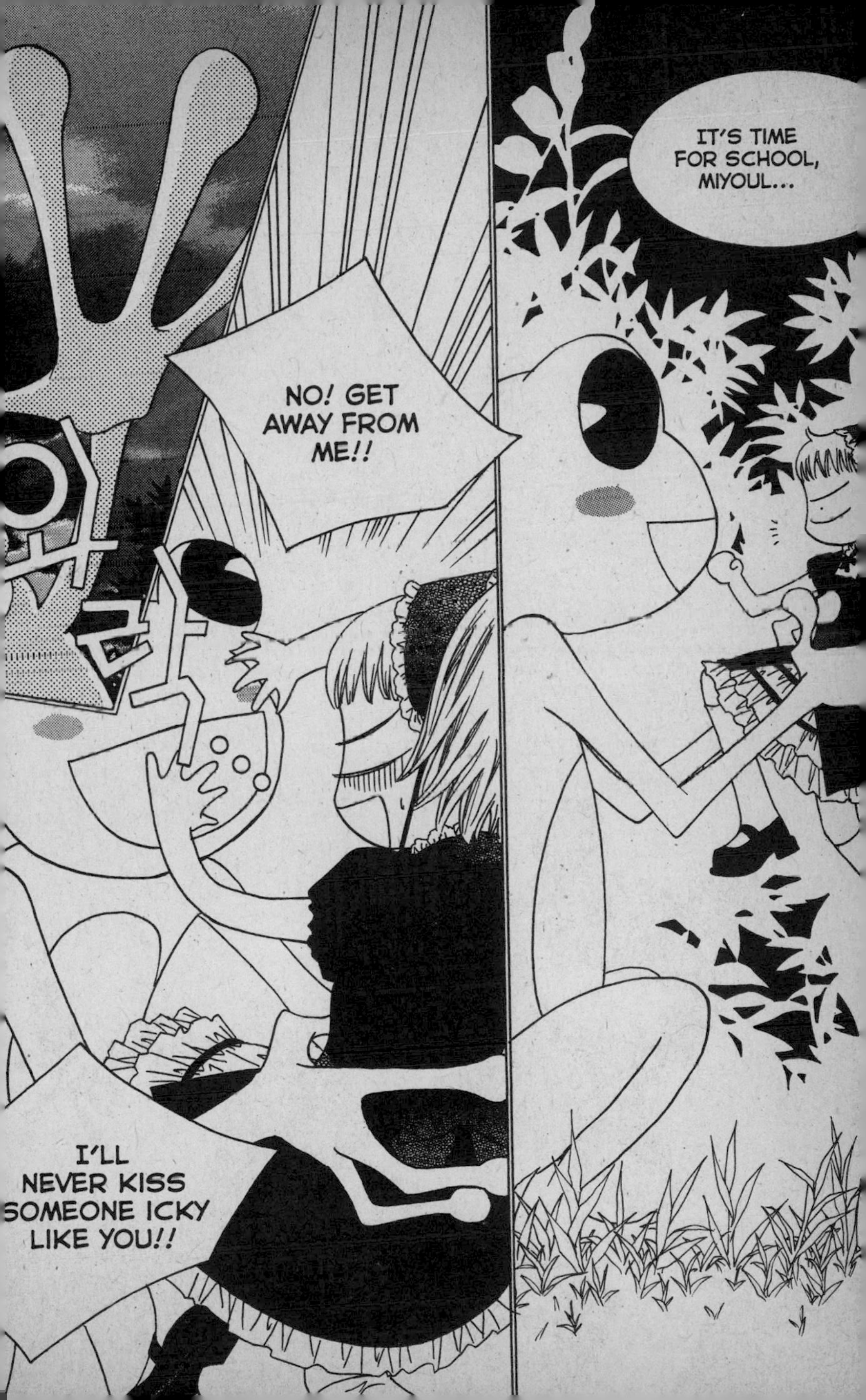
NO! GET AWAY FROM ME!!
I'LL NEVER KISS SOMEONE ICKY LIKE YOU!!
IT'S TIME FOR SCHOOL, MIYOUL...

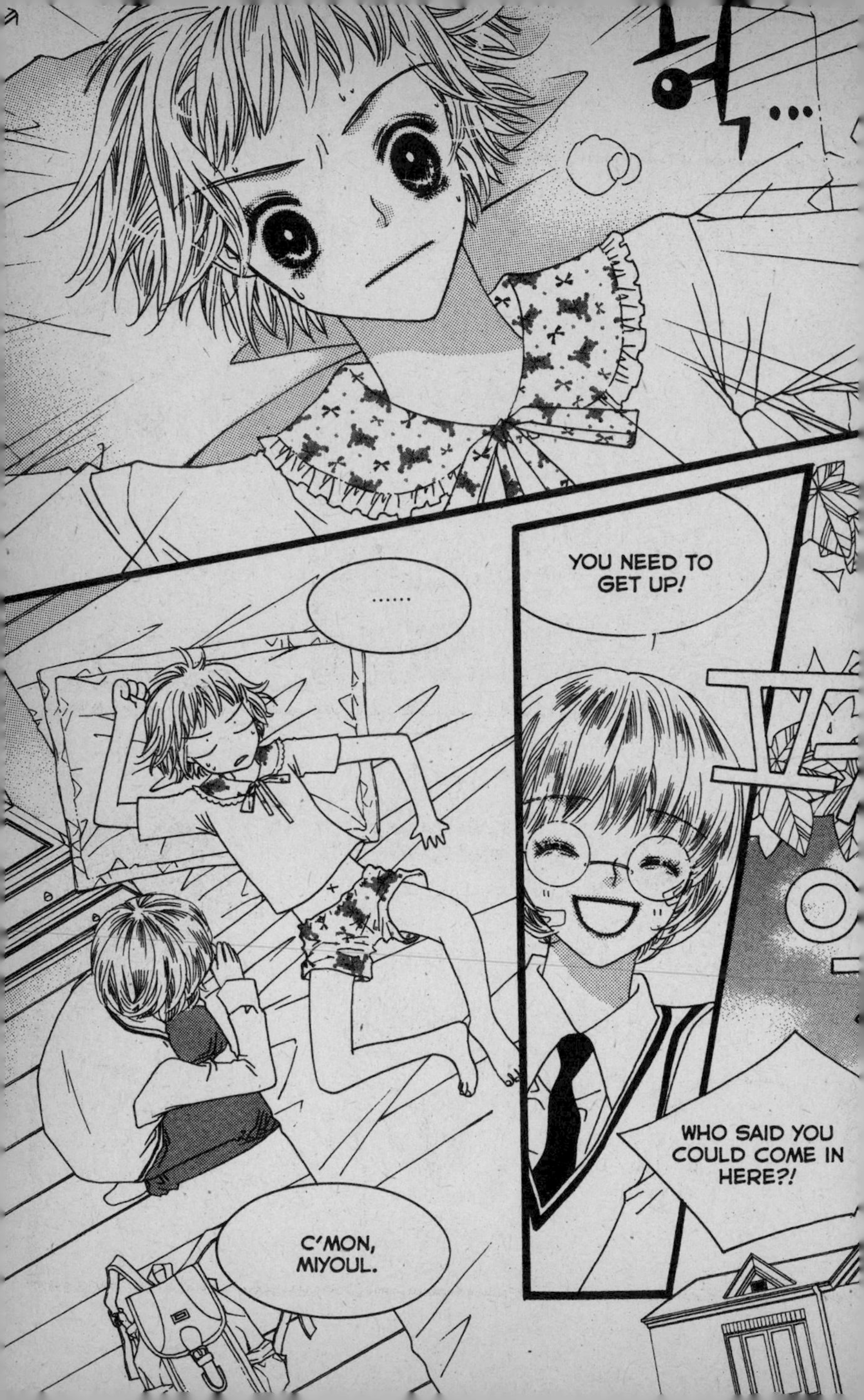
헉...
......
C'MON, MIYOUL.
YOU NEED TO GET UP!
WHO SAID YOU COULD COME IN HERE?!

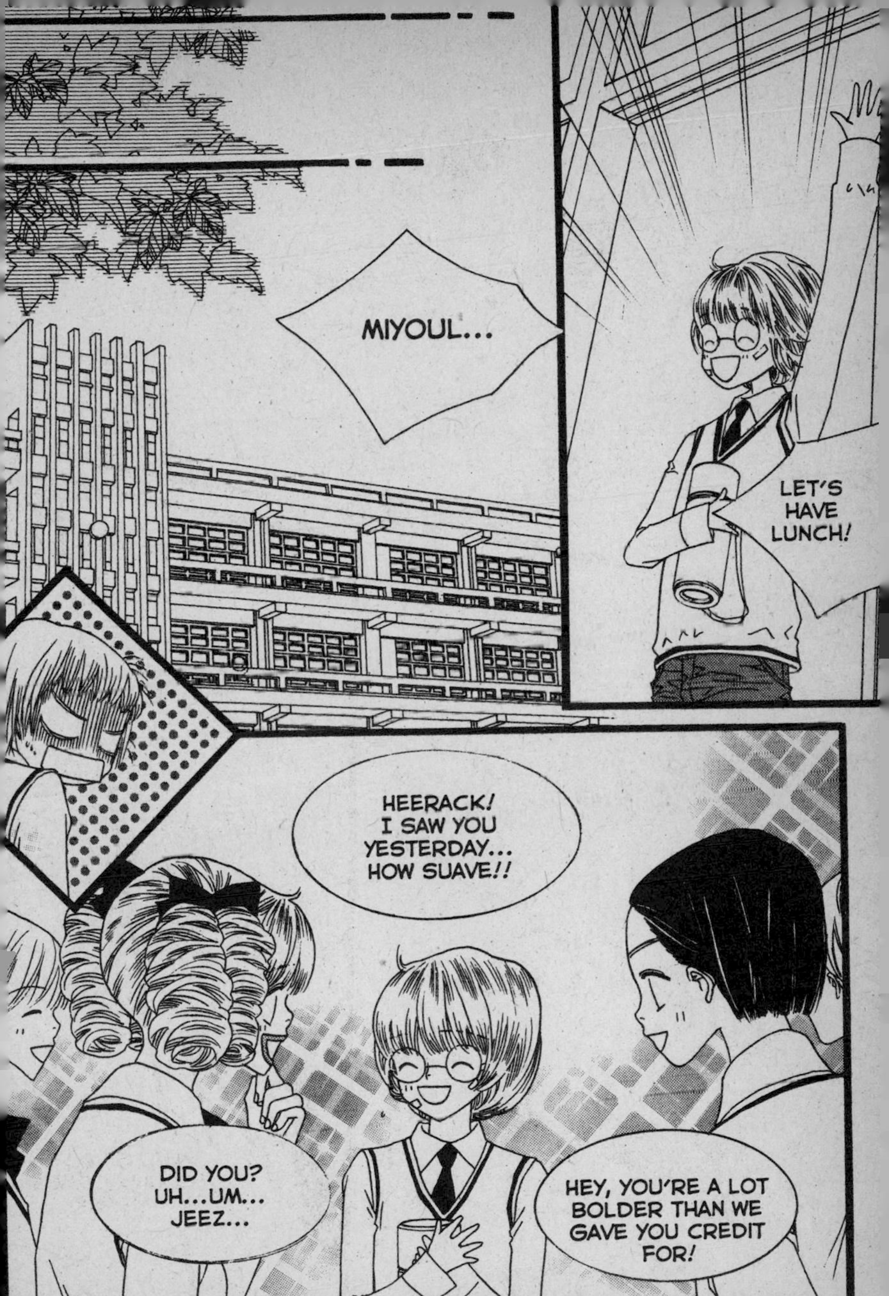
MIYOUL...
LET'S HAVE LUNCH!
HEERACK! I SAW YOU YESTERDAY... HOW SUAVE!!
DID YOU? UH...UM... JEEZ...
HEY, YOU'RE A LOT BOLDER THAN WE GAVE YOU CREDIT FOR!

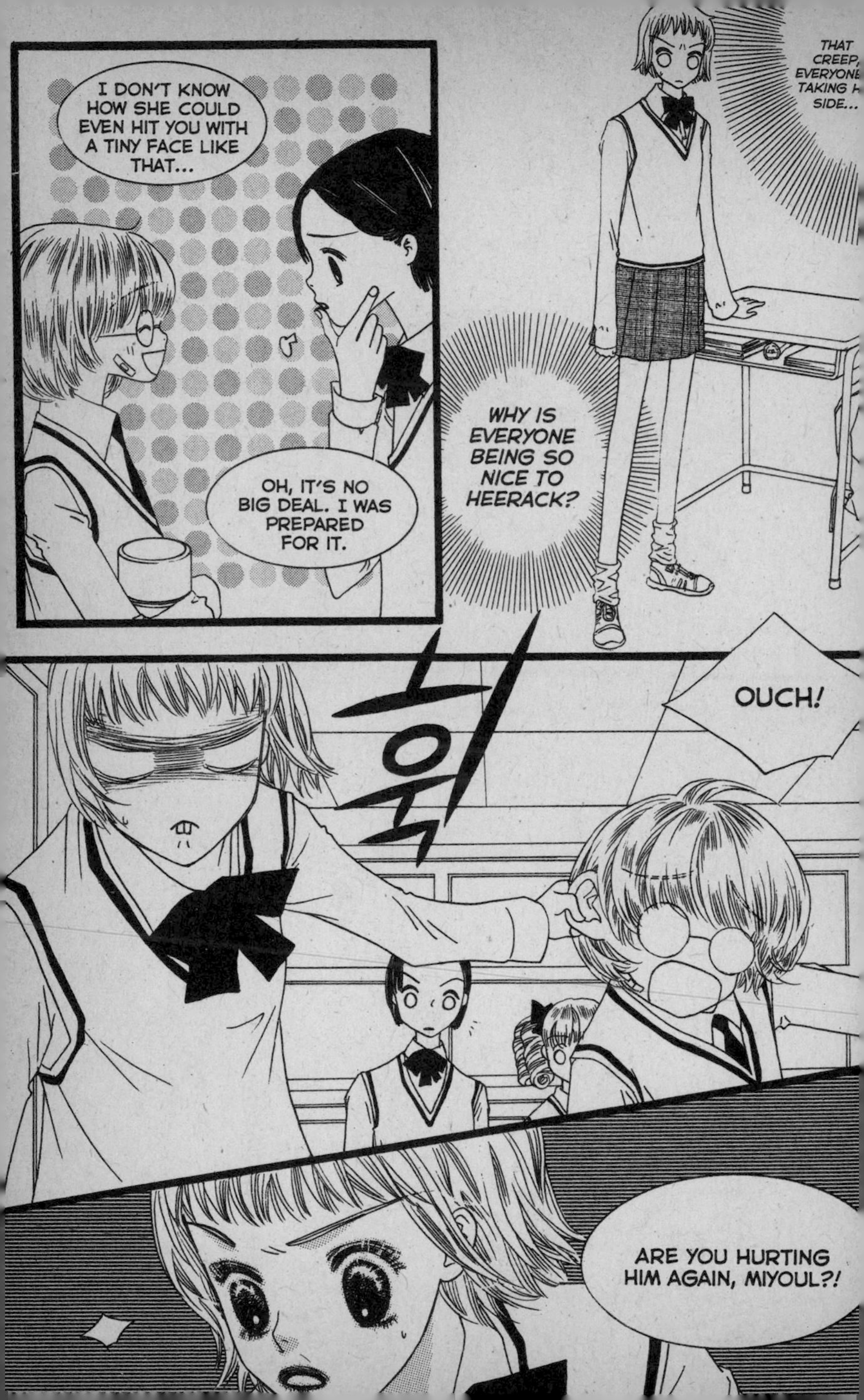
I DON'T KNOW HOW SHE COULD EVEN HIT YOU WITH A TINY FACE LIKE THAT...
OH, IT'S NO BIG DEAL. I WAS PREPARED FOR IT.
THAT CREEP,
WHY IS EVERYONE BEING SO NICE TO HEERACK?
OUCH!
ARE YOU HURTING HIM AGAIN, MIYOUL?!

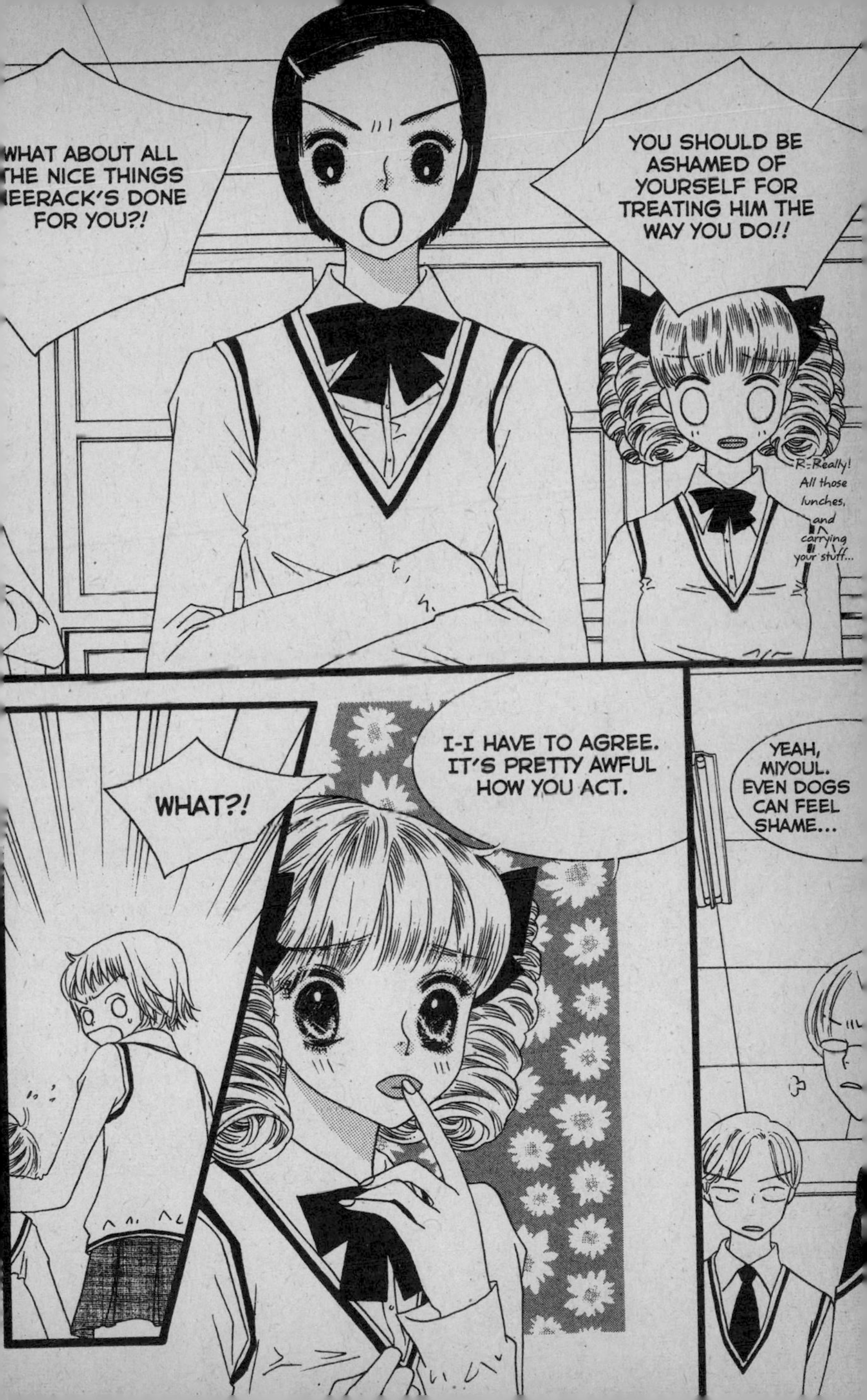
WHAT ABOUT ALL THE NICE THINGS EERACK'S DONE FOR YOU?!
YOU SHOULD BE ASHAMED OF YOURSELF FOR TREATING HIM THE WAY YOU DO!!
R-Really! All those lunches, and carrying your stuff...
WHAT?!
I-I HAVE TO AGREE. IT'S PRETTY AWFUL HOW YOU ACT.
YEAH, MIYOUL. EVEN DOGS CAN FEEL SHAME...

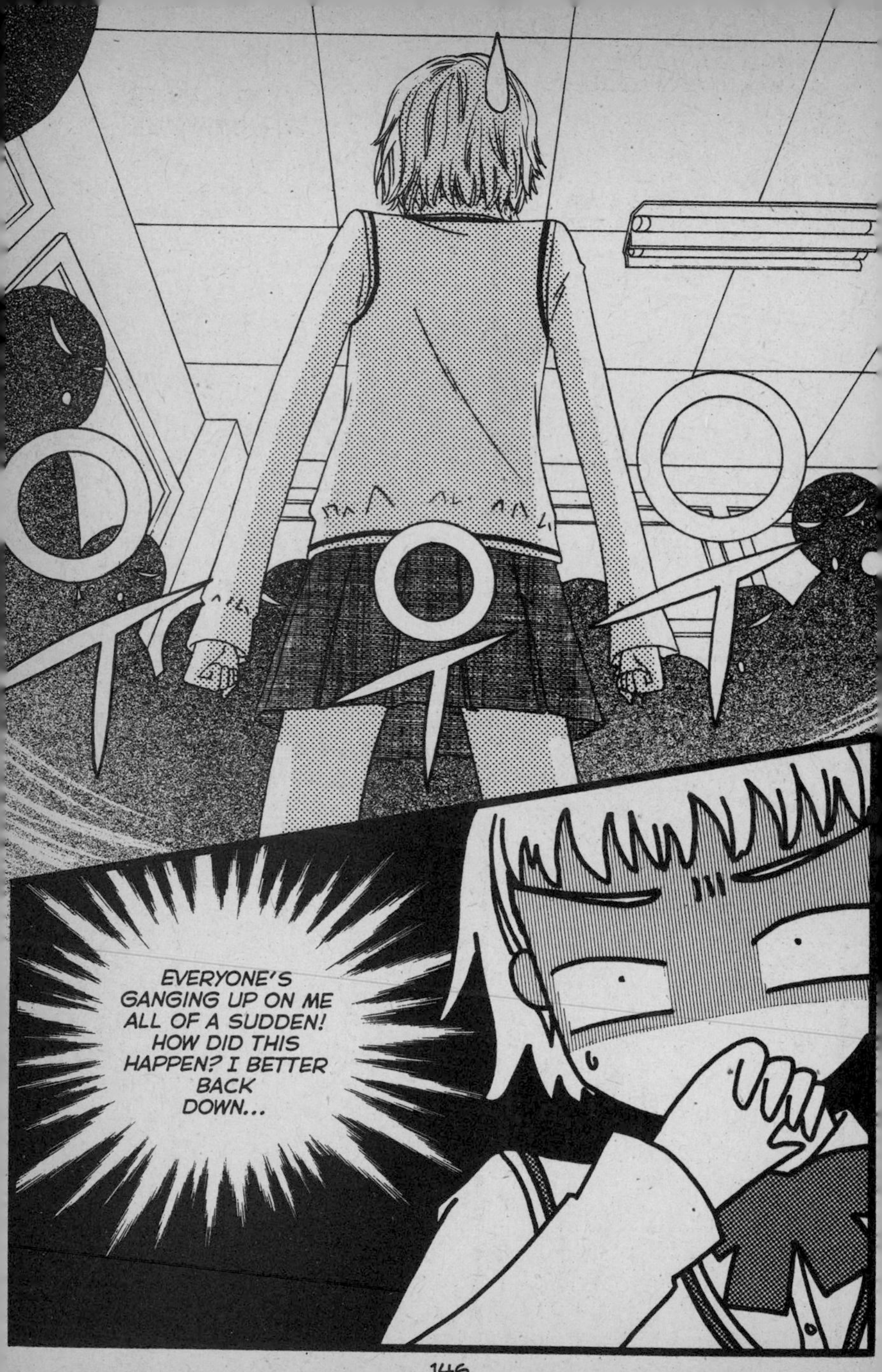
EVERYONE'S GANGING UP ON ME ALL OF A SUDDEN! HOW DID THIS HAPPEN? I BETTER BACK DOWN...

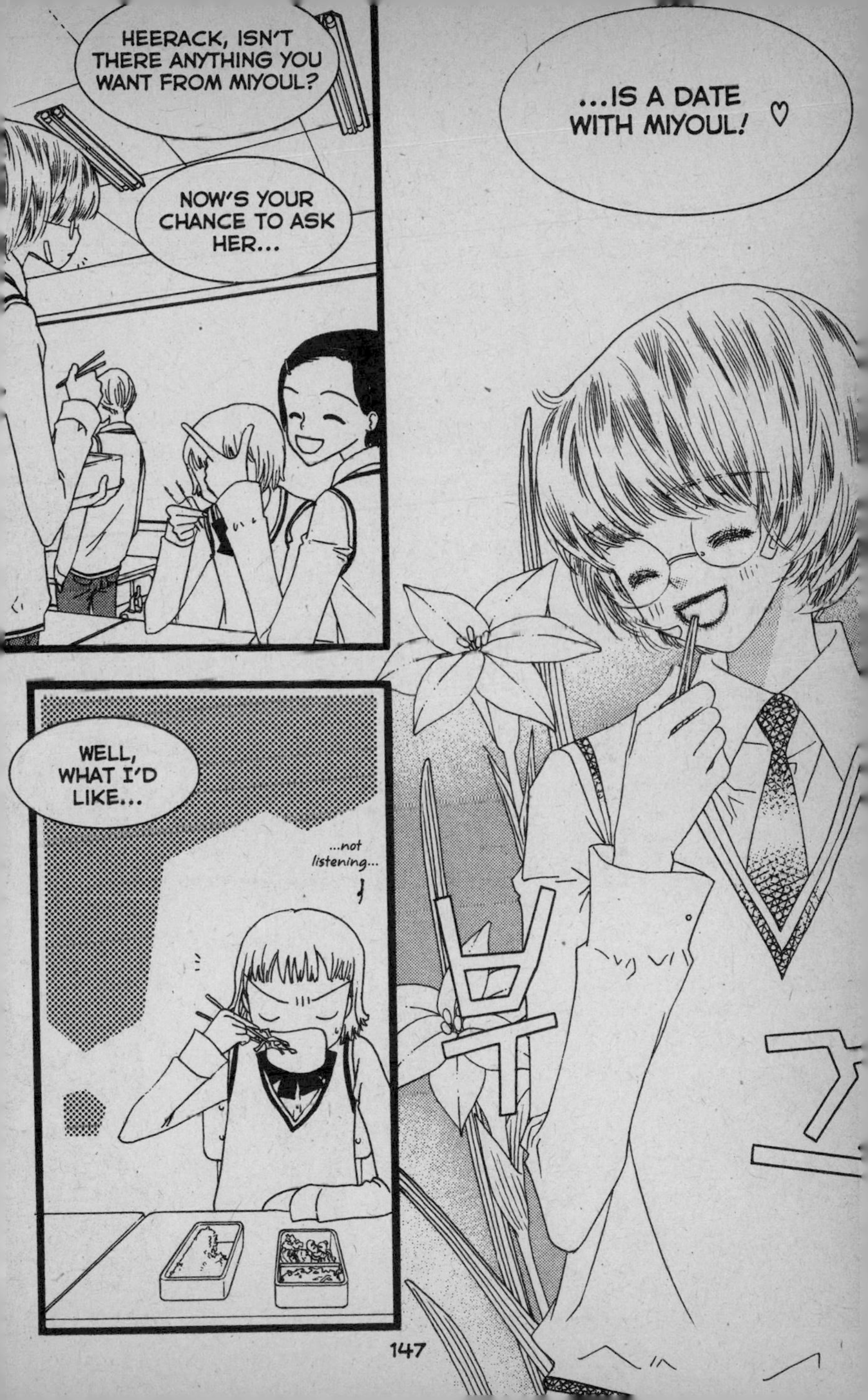
HEERACK, ISN'T THERE ANYTHING YOU WANT FROM MIYOUL?
NOW'S YOUR CHANCE TO ASK HER...
WELL, WHAT I'D LIKE...
...not listening...
...IS A DATE WITH MIYOUL! ♡

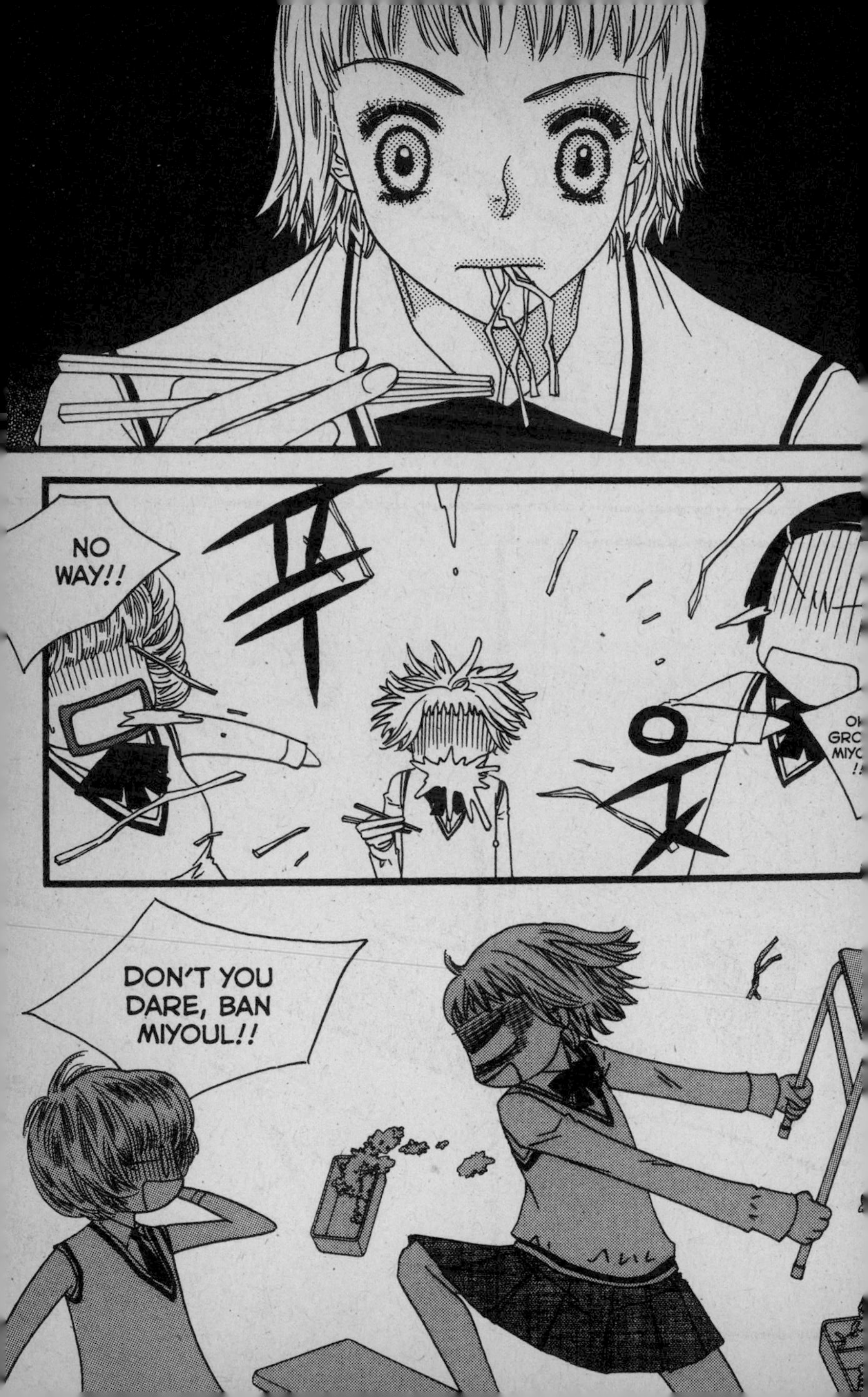
NO WAY!!
DON'T YOU DARE, BAN MIYOUL!!

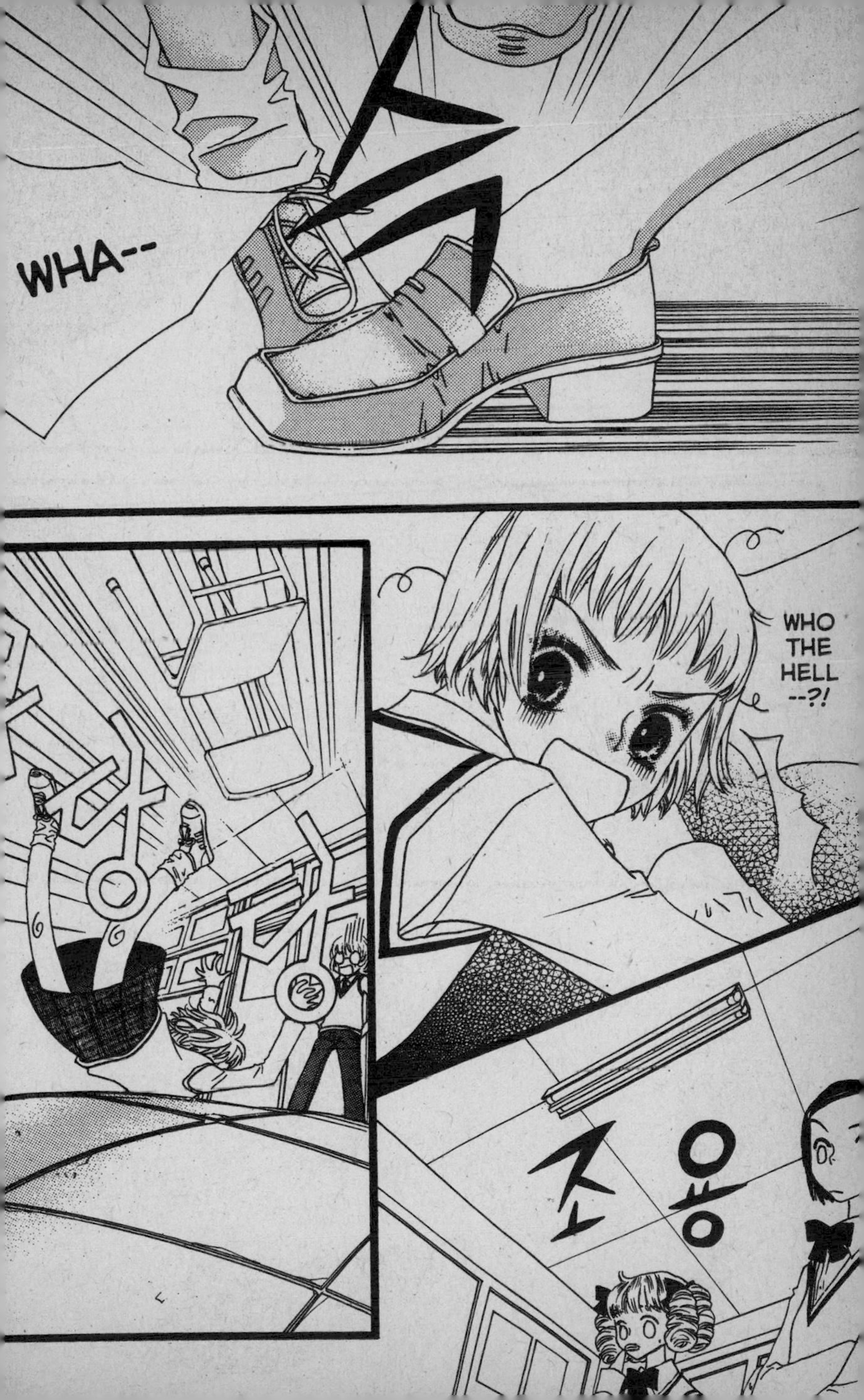
WHA--
WHO THE HELL --?!

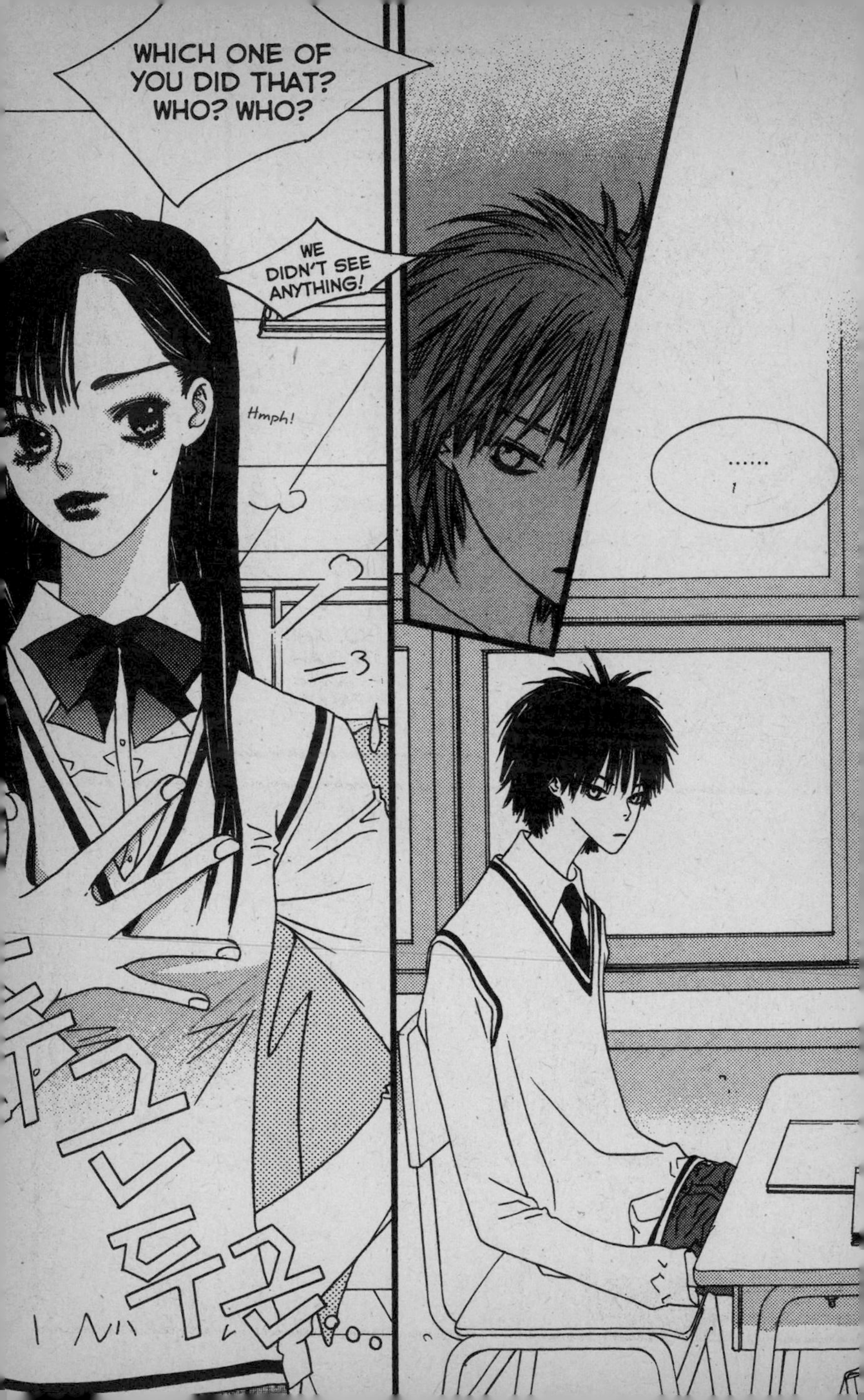
WHICH ONE OF YOU DID THAT? WHO? WHO?
WE DIDN'T SEE ANYTHING!
Hmph!
......

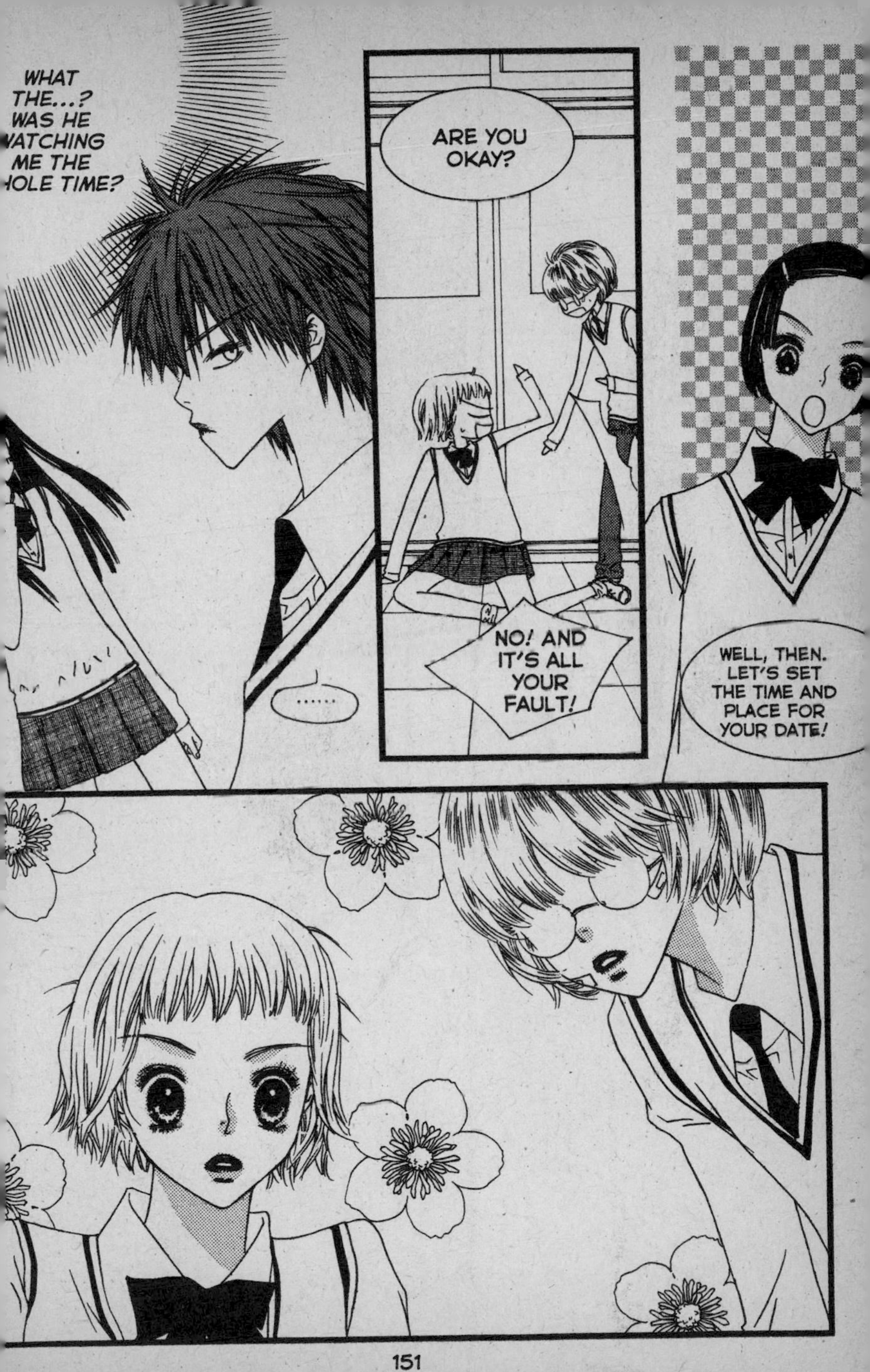
WHAT THE...? WAS HE WATCHING ME THE WHOLE TIME?
......
ARE YOU OKAY?
NO! AND IT'S ALL YOUR FAULT!
WELL, THEN. LET'S SET THE TIME AND PLACE FOR YOUR DATE!

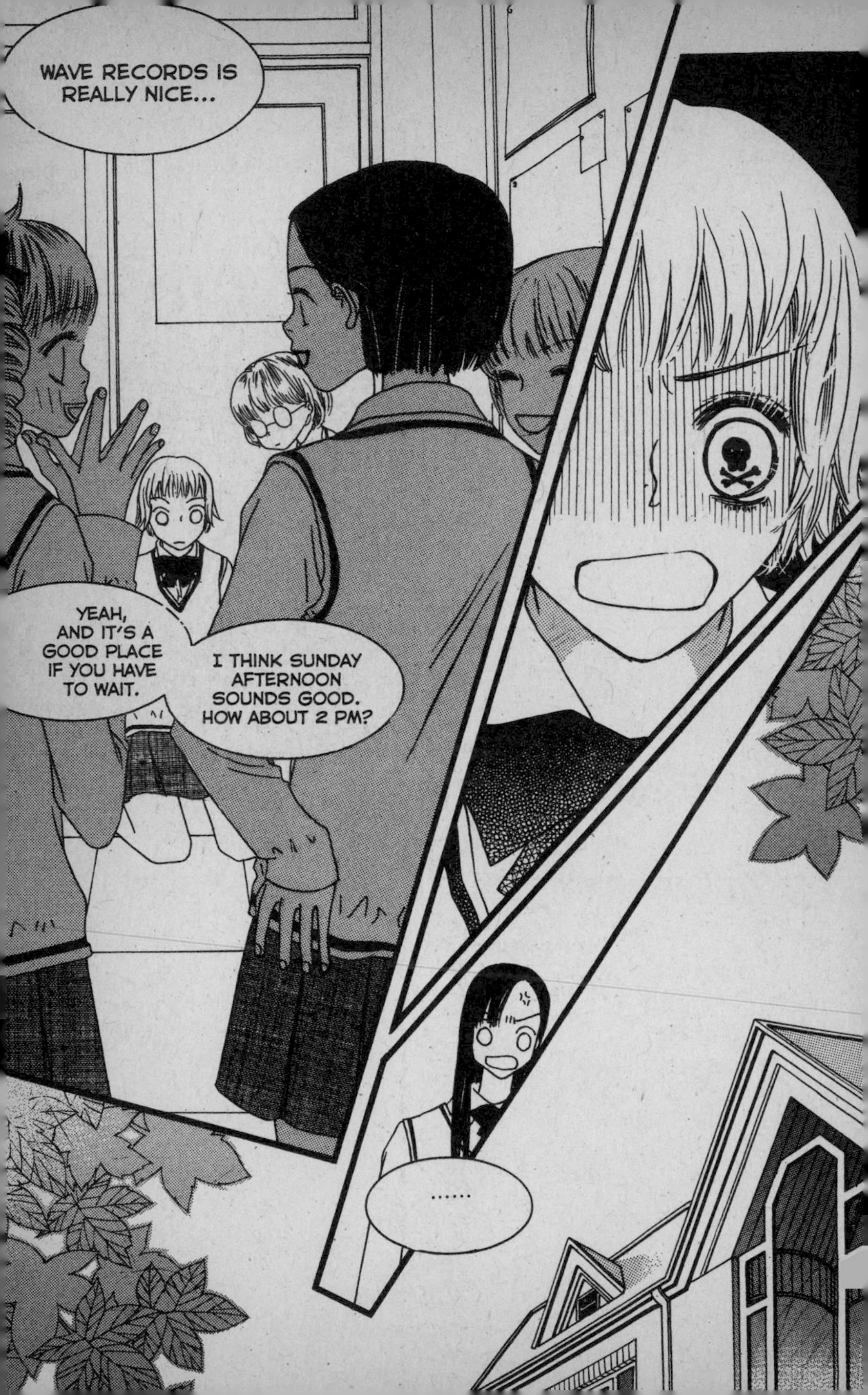
WAVE RECORDS IS REALLY NICE...
YEAH, AND IT'S A GOOD PLACE IF YOU HAVE TO WAIT.
I THINK SUNDAY AFTERNOON SOUNDS GOOD. HOW ABOUT 2 PM?
......

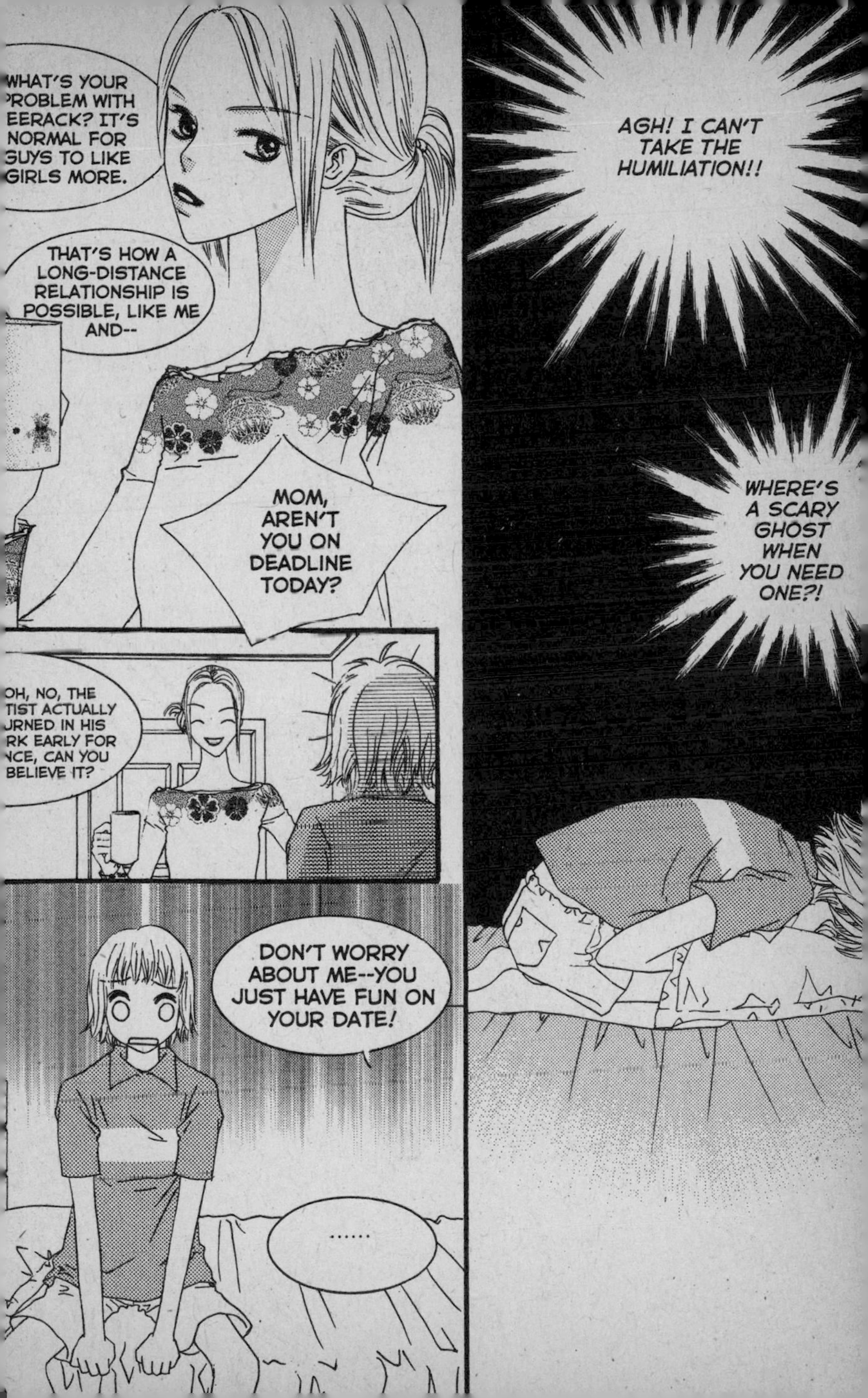
WHAT'S YOUR PROBLEM WITH EERACK? IT'S NORMAL FOR GUYS TO LIKE GIRLS MORE.
THAT'S HOW A LONG-DISTANCE RELATIONSHIP IS POSSIBLE, LIKE ME AND--
MOM, AREN'T YOU ON DEADLINE TODAY?
OH, NO, THE TIST ACTUALLY URNED IN HIS RK EARLY FOR NCE, CAN YOU BELIEVE IT?
DON'T WORRY ABOUT ME--YOU JUST HAVE FUN ON YOUR DATE!
......
AGH! I CAN'T TAKE THE HUMILIATION!!
WHERE'S A SCARY GHOST WHEN YOU NEED ONE?!

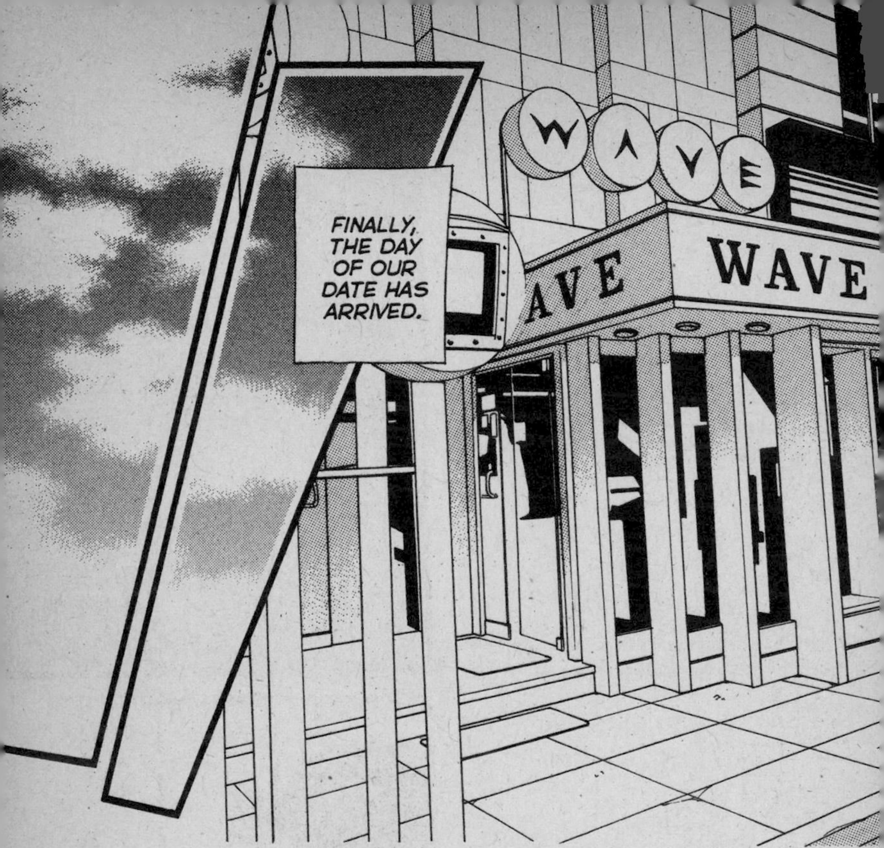
WAVE
FINALLY, THE DAY OF OUR DATE HAS ARRIVED.
AVE
WAVE

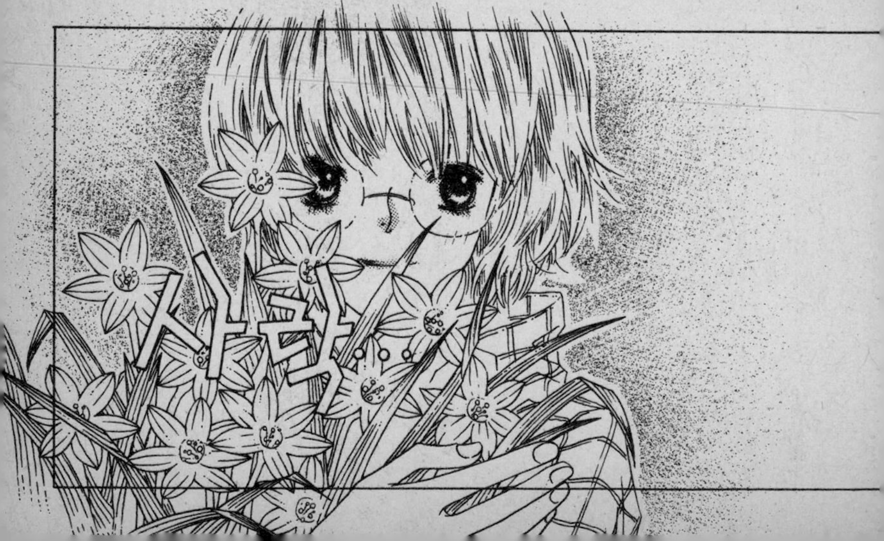

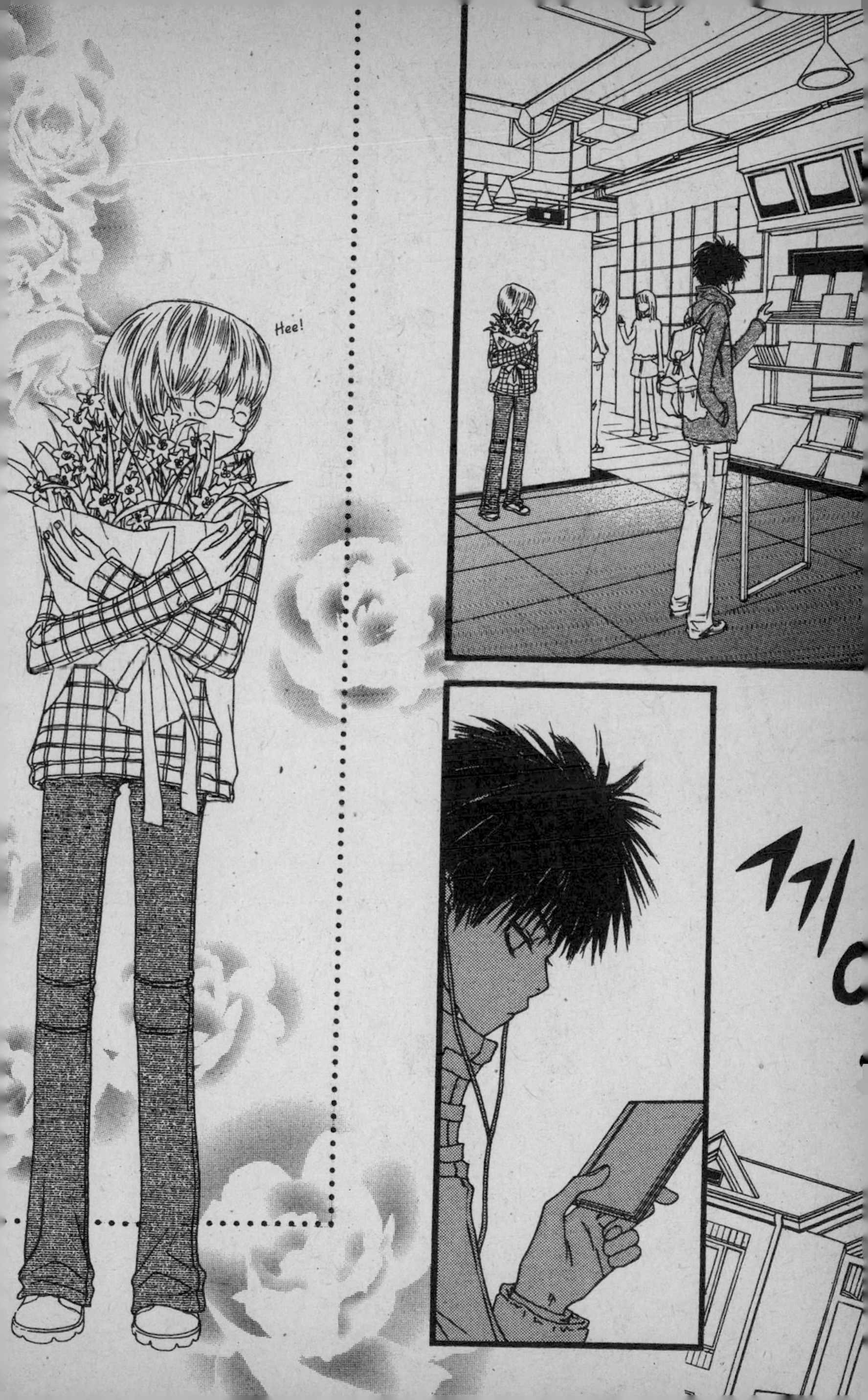
Hee!

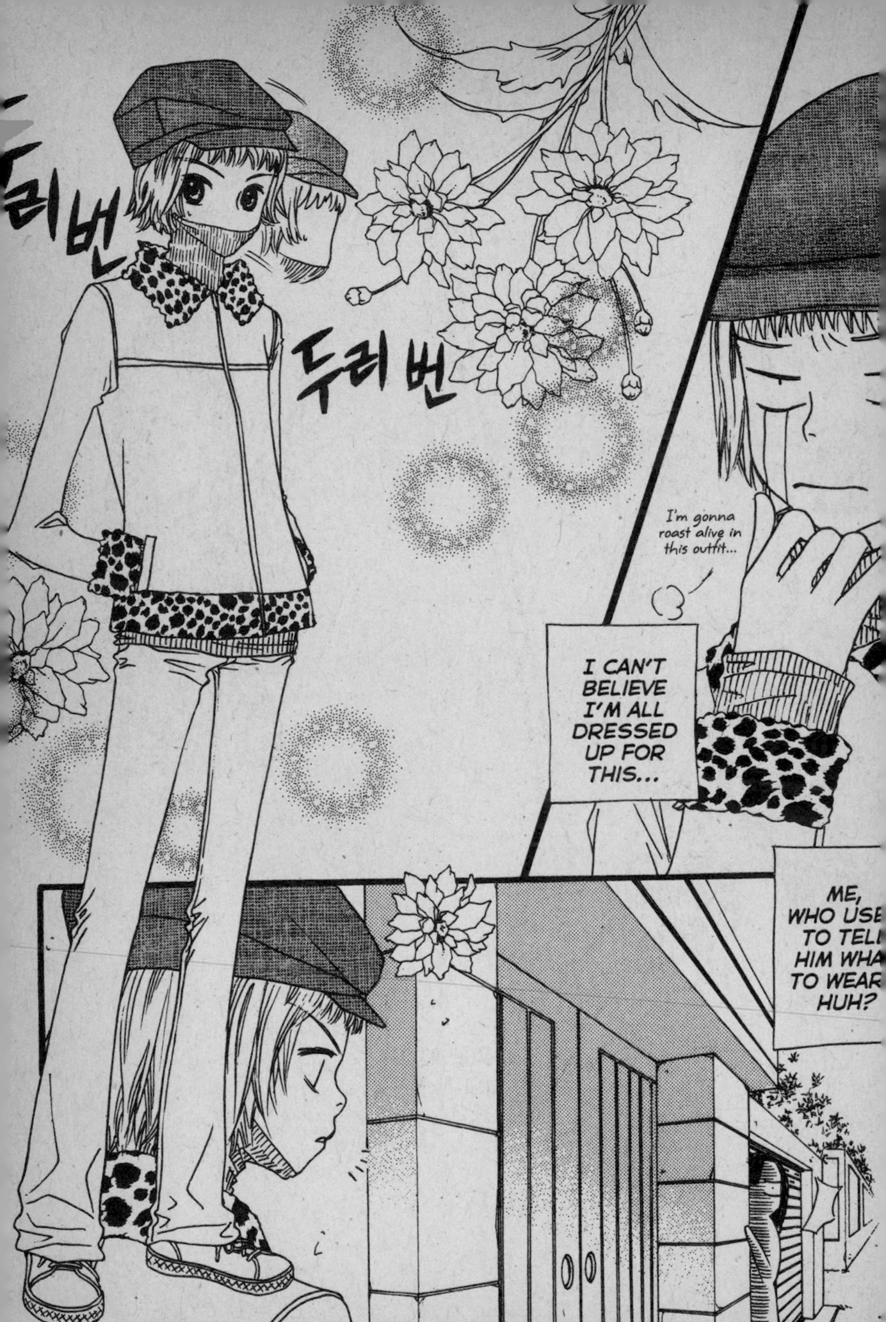
두리번
두리번
I'm gonna roast alive in this outfit...
I CAN'T BELIEVE I'M ALL DRESSED UP FOR THIS...
ME, WHO USE TO TELL HIM WHA TO WEAR HUH?

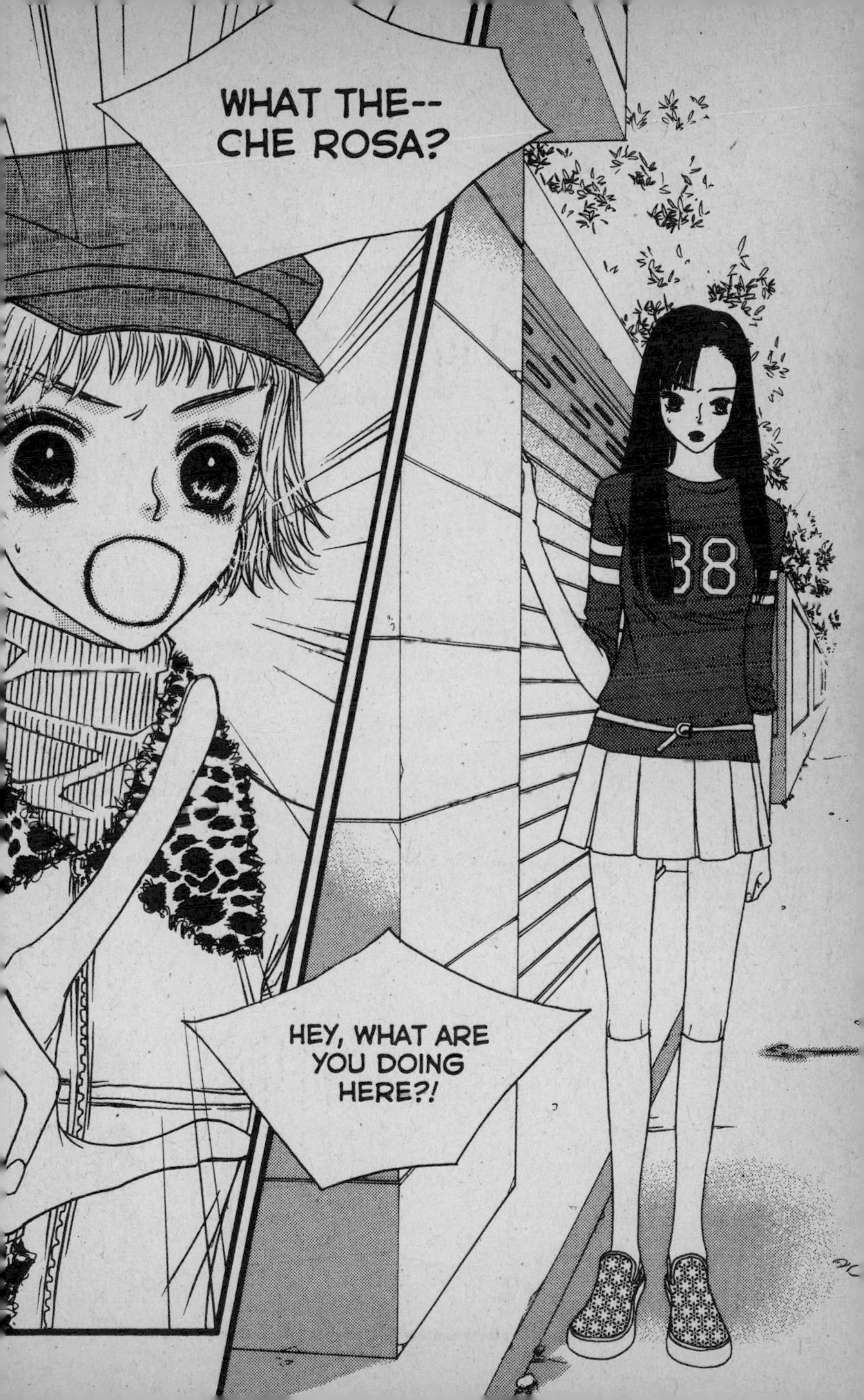
WHAT THE--
CHE ROSA?
HEY, WHAT ARE
YOU DOING
HERE?!

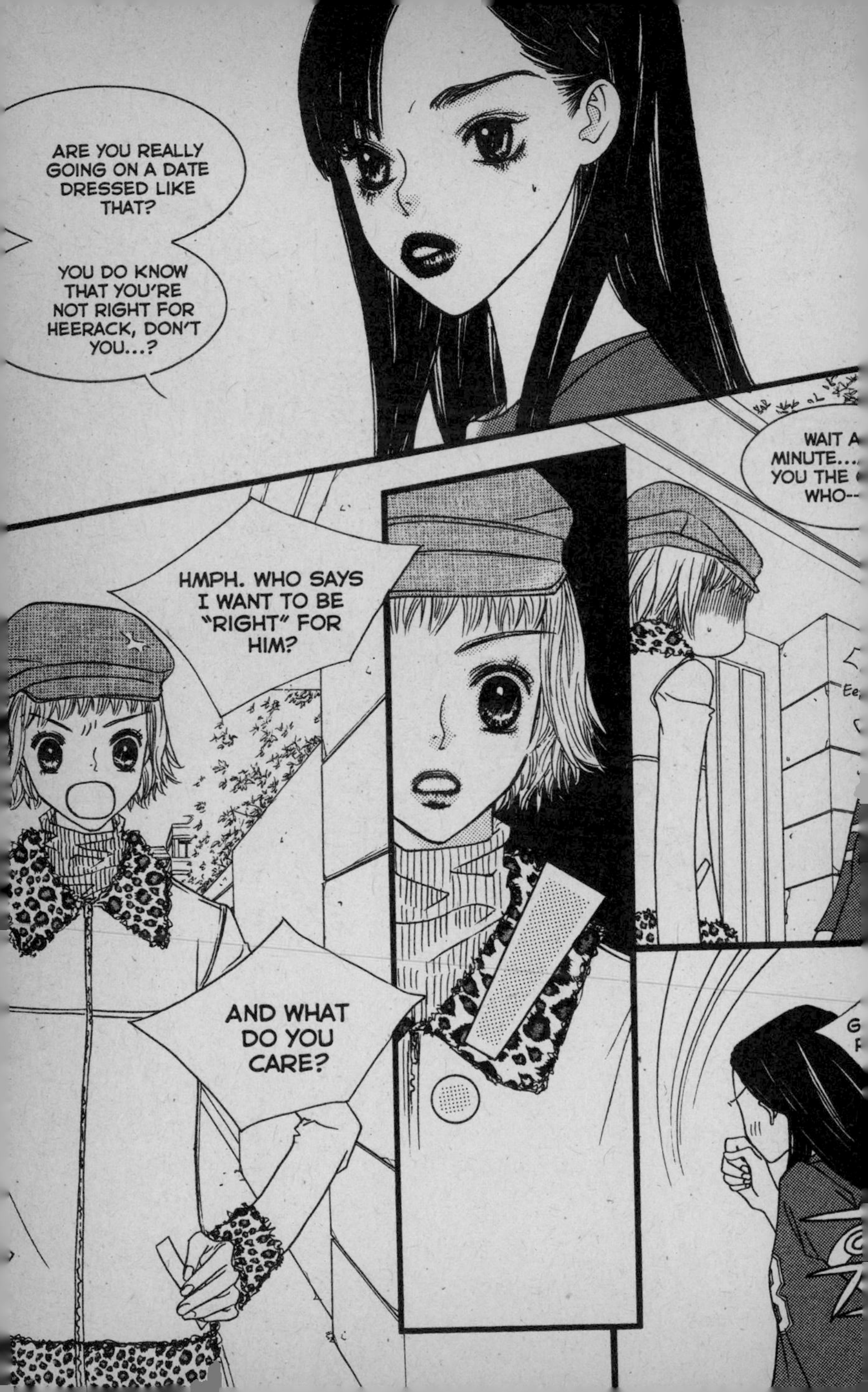
ARE YOU REALLY GOING ON A DATE DRESSED LIKE THAT?
YOU DO KNOW THAT YOU'RE NOT RIGHT FOR HEERACK, DON'T YOU...?
HMPH. WHO SAYS I WANT TO BE "RIGHT" FOR HIM?
AND WHAT DO YOU CARE?
WAIT A MINUTE.... YOU THE WHO--

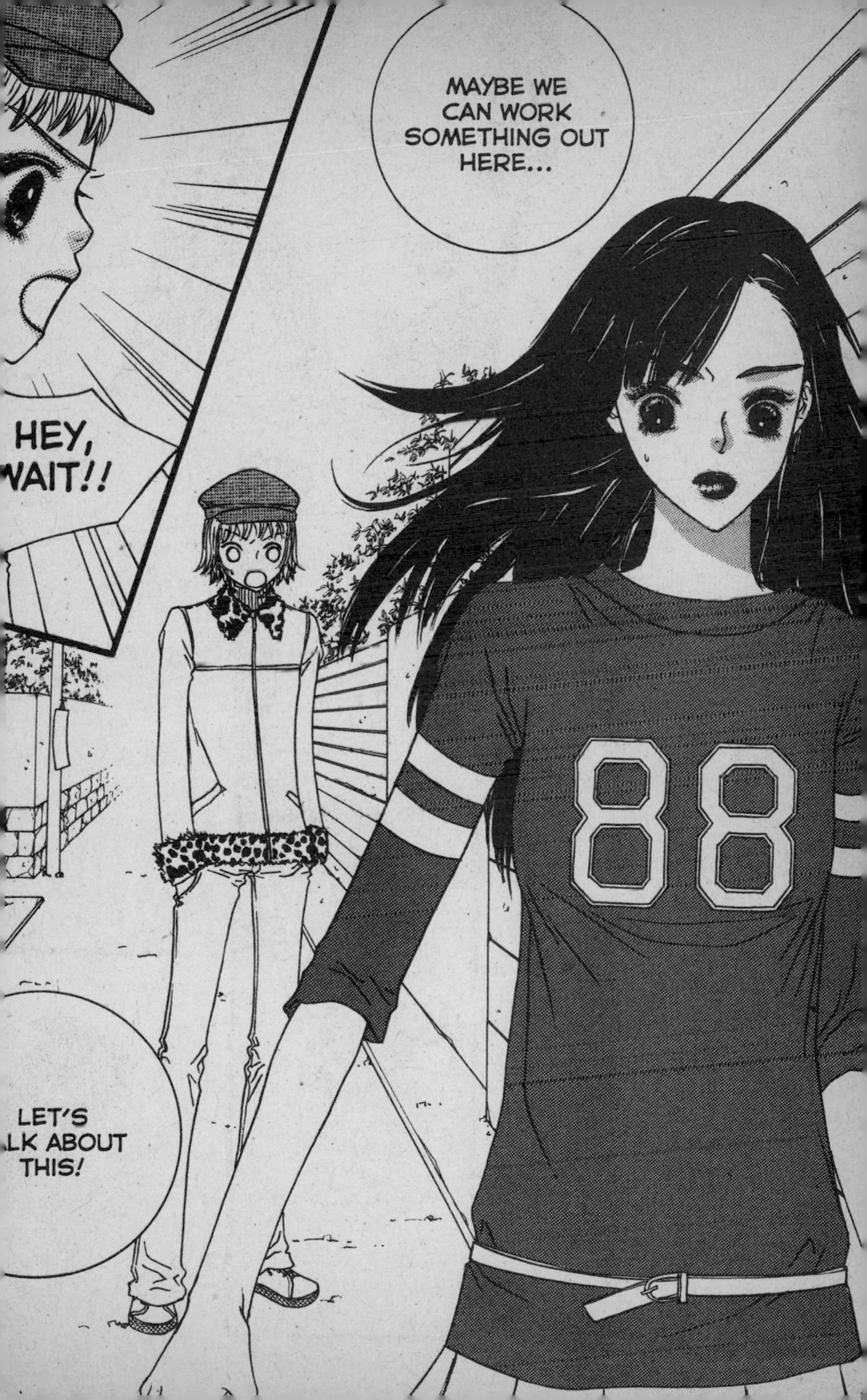
HEY, WAIT!!
MAYBE WE CAN WORK SOMETHING OUT HERE...
LET'S LK ABOUT THIS!

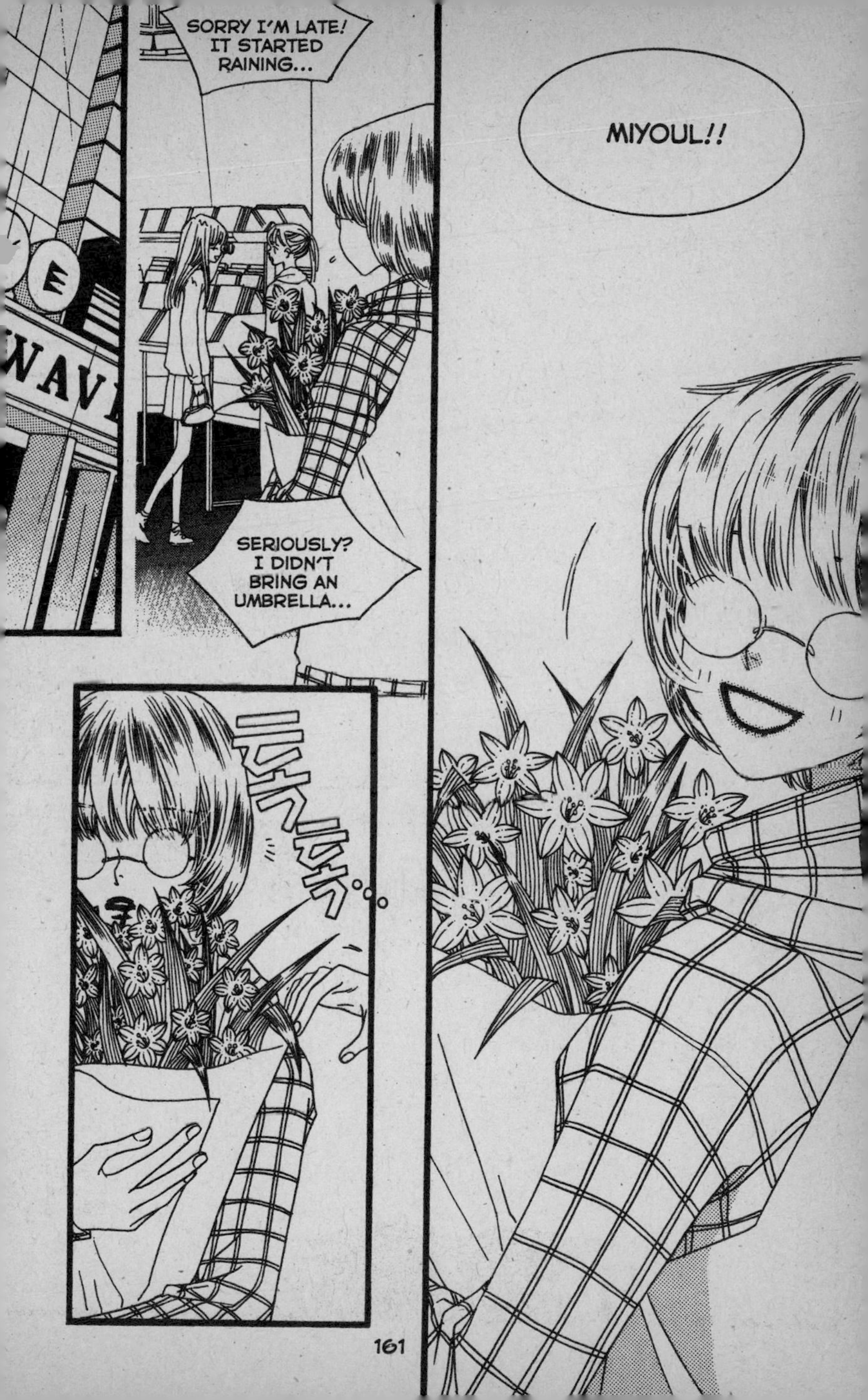
SORRY I'M LATE! IT STARTED RAINING...
SERIOUSLY? I DIDN'T BRING AN UMBRELLA...
MIYOUL!!

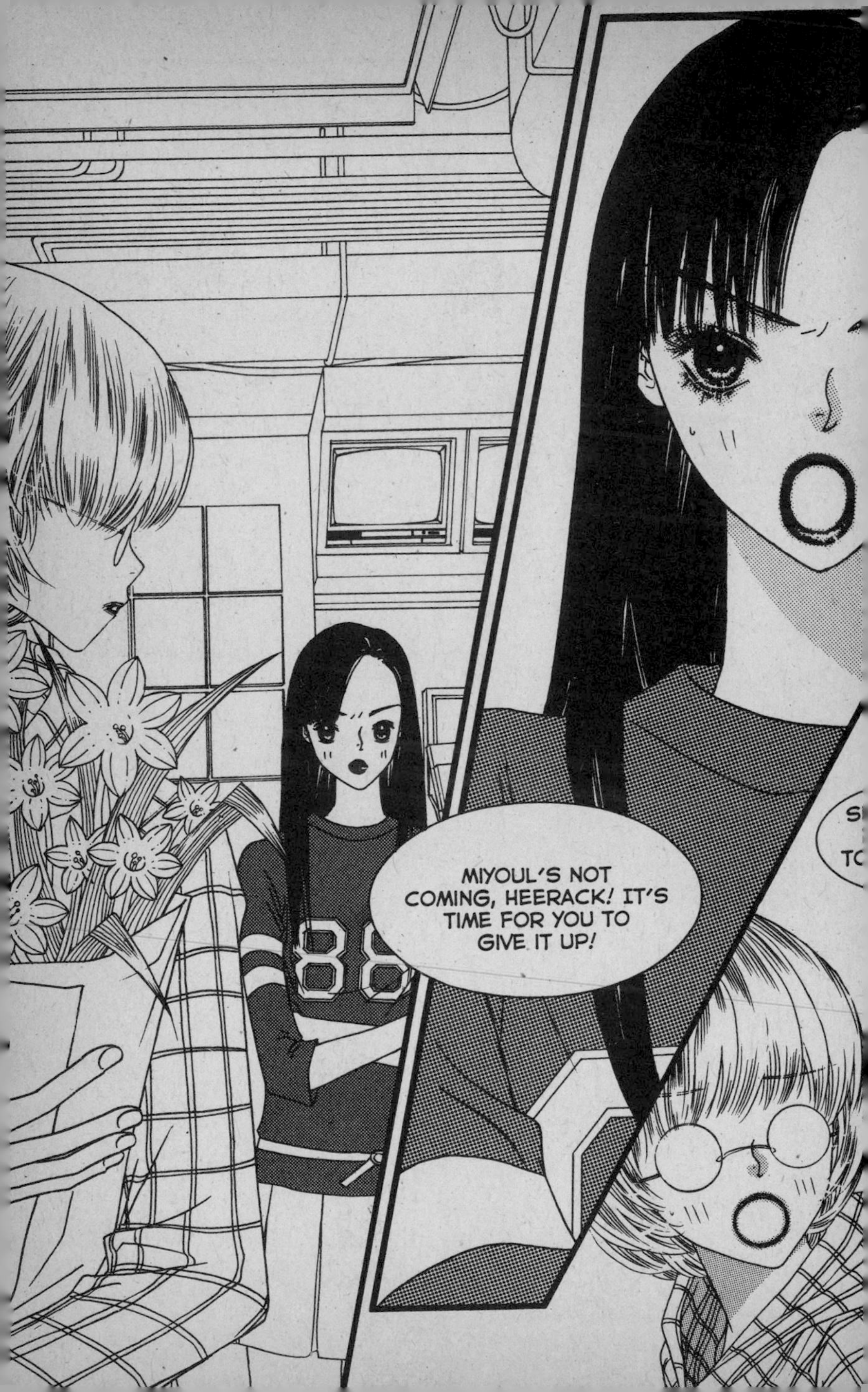
MIYOUL'S NOT COMING, HEERACK! IT'S TIME FOR YOU TO GIVE IT UP!

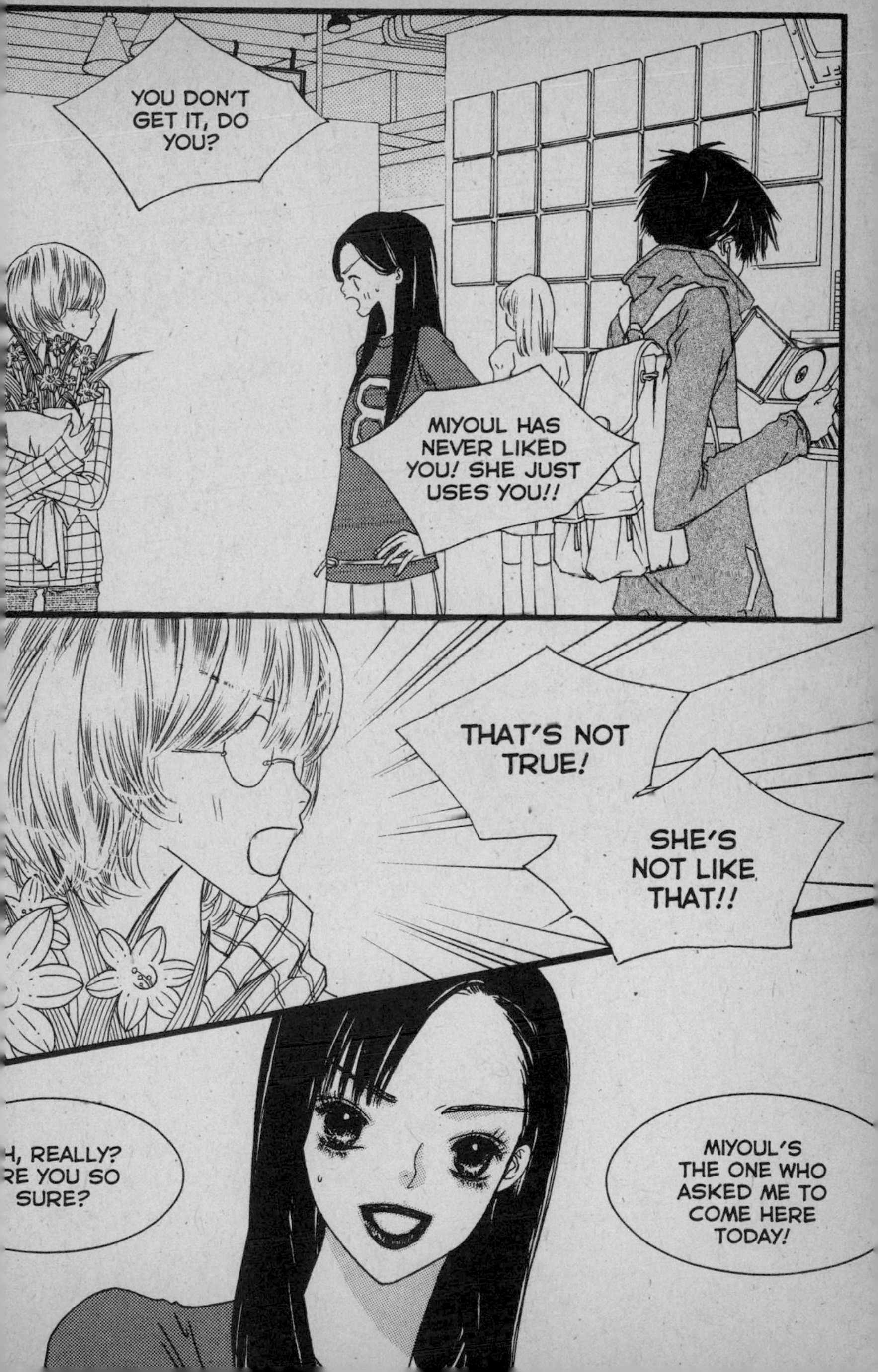
YOU DON'T GET IT, DO YOU?
MIYOUL HAS NEVER LIKED YOU! SHE JUST USES YOU!!
THAT'S NOT TRUE!
SHE'S NOT LIKE THAT!!
H, REALLY? RE YOU SO SURE?
MIYOUL'S THE ONE WHO ASKED ME TO COME HERE TODAY!

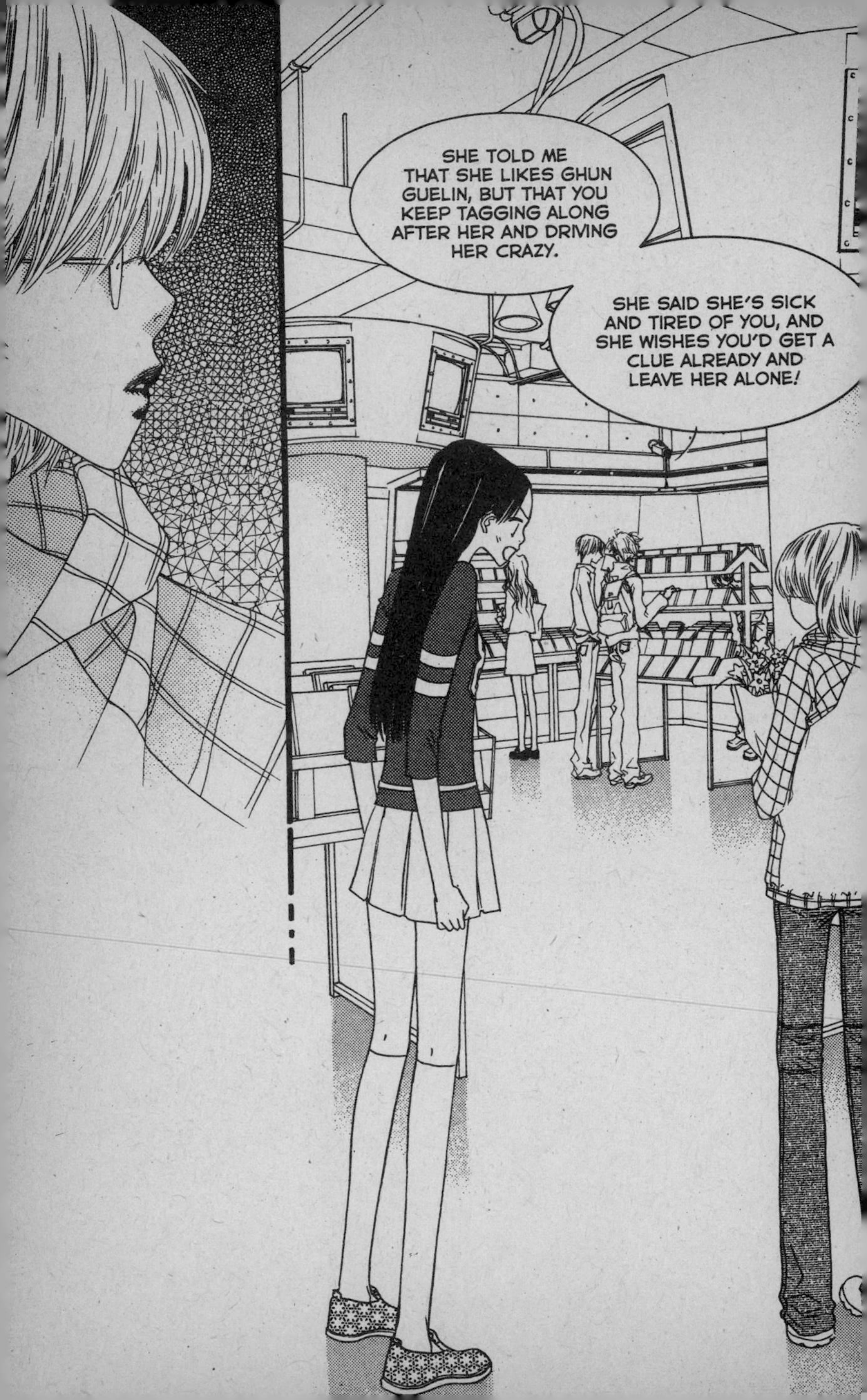
SHE TOLD ME THAT SHE LIKES GHUN GUELIN, BUT THAT YOU KEEP TAGGING ALONG AFTER HER AND DRIVING HER CRAZY.
SHE SAID SHE'S SICK AND TIRED OF YOU, AND SHE WISHES YOU'D GET A CLUE ALREADY AND LEAVE HER ALONE!

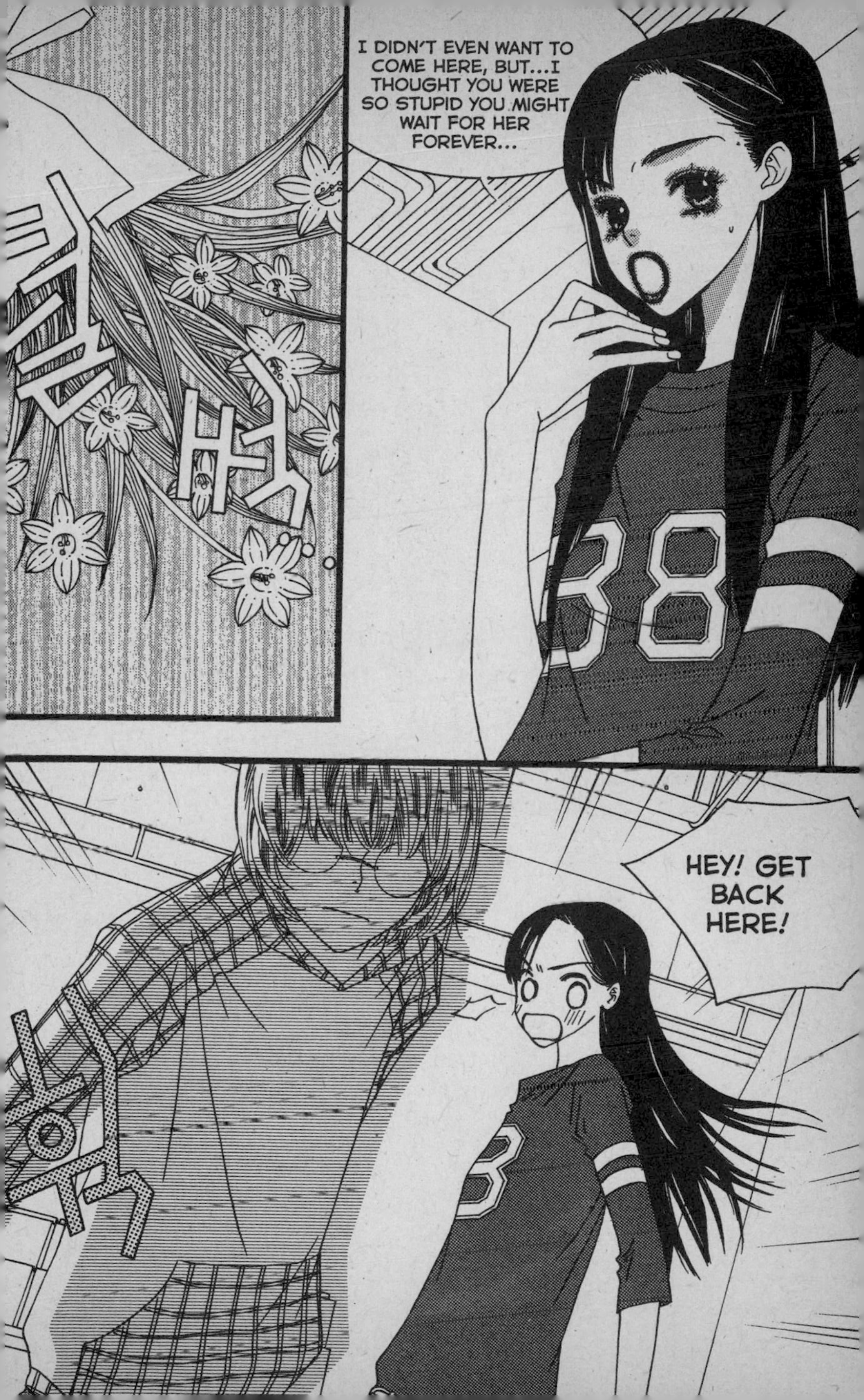
I DIDN'T EVEN WANT TO COME HERE, BUT...I THOUGHT YOU WERE SO STUPID YOU MIGHT WAIT FOR HER FOREVER...
HEY! GET BACK HERE!

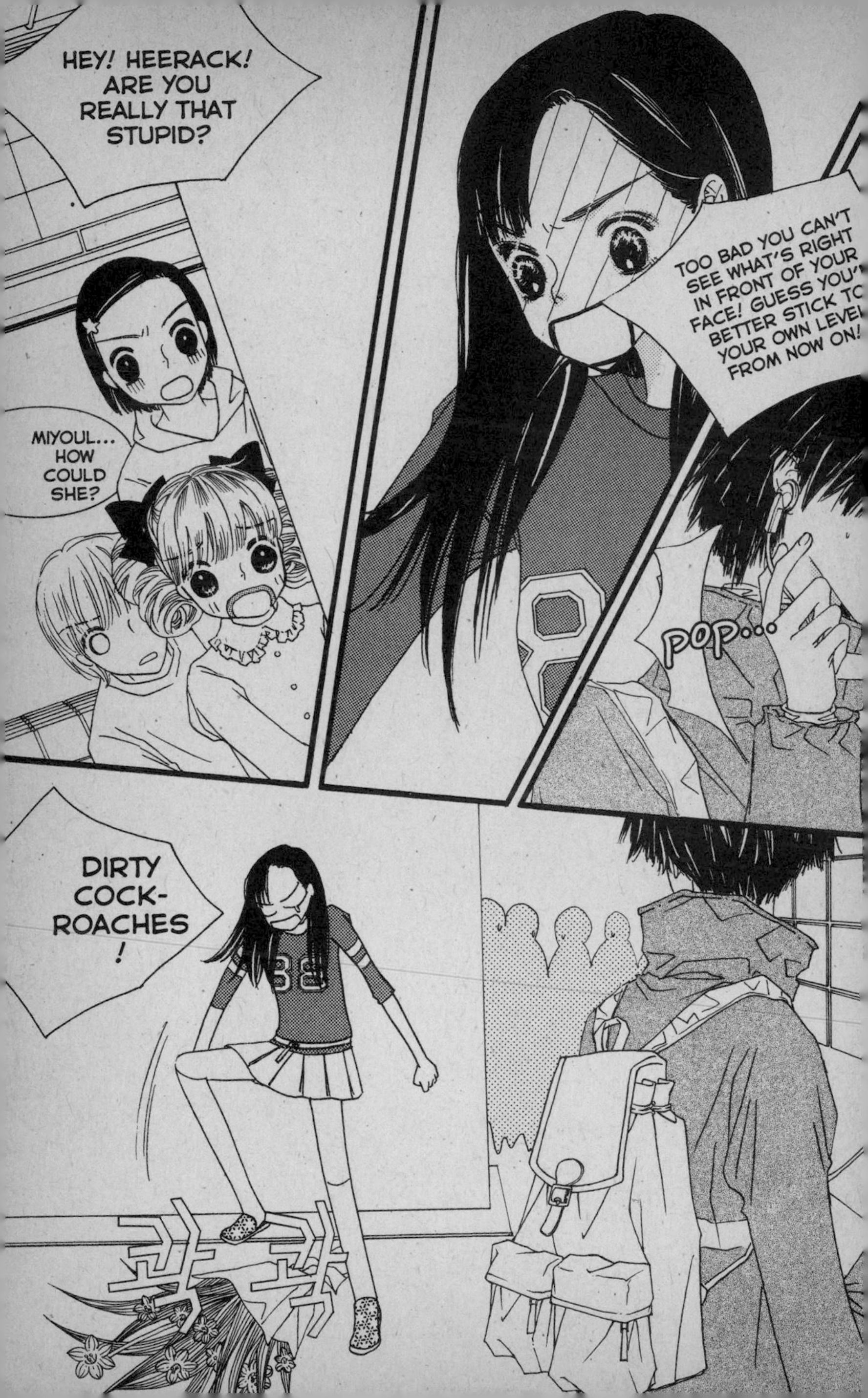
HEY! HEERACK! ARE YOU REALLY THAT STUPID?
MIYOUL... HOW COULD SHE?
TOO BAD YOU CAN'T SEE WHAT'S RIGHT IN FRONT OF YOUR FACE! GUESS YOU' BETTER STICK TO YOUR OWN LEVE FROM NOW ON!
POP...
DIRTY COCK-ROACHES!

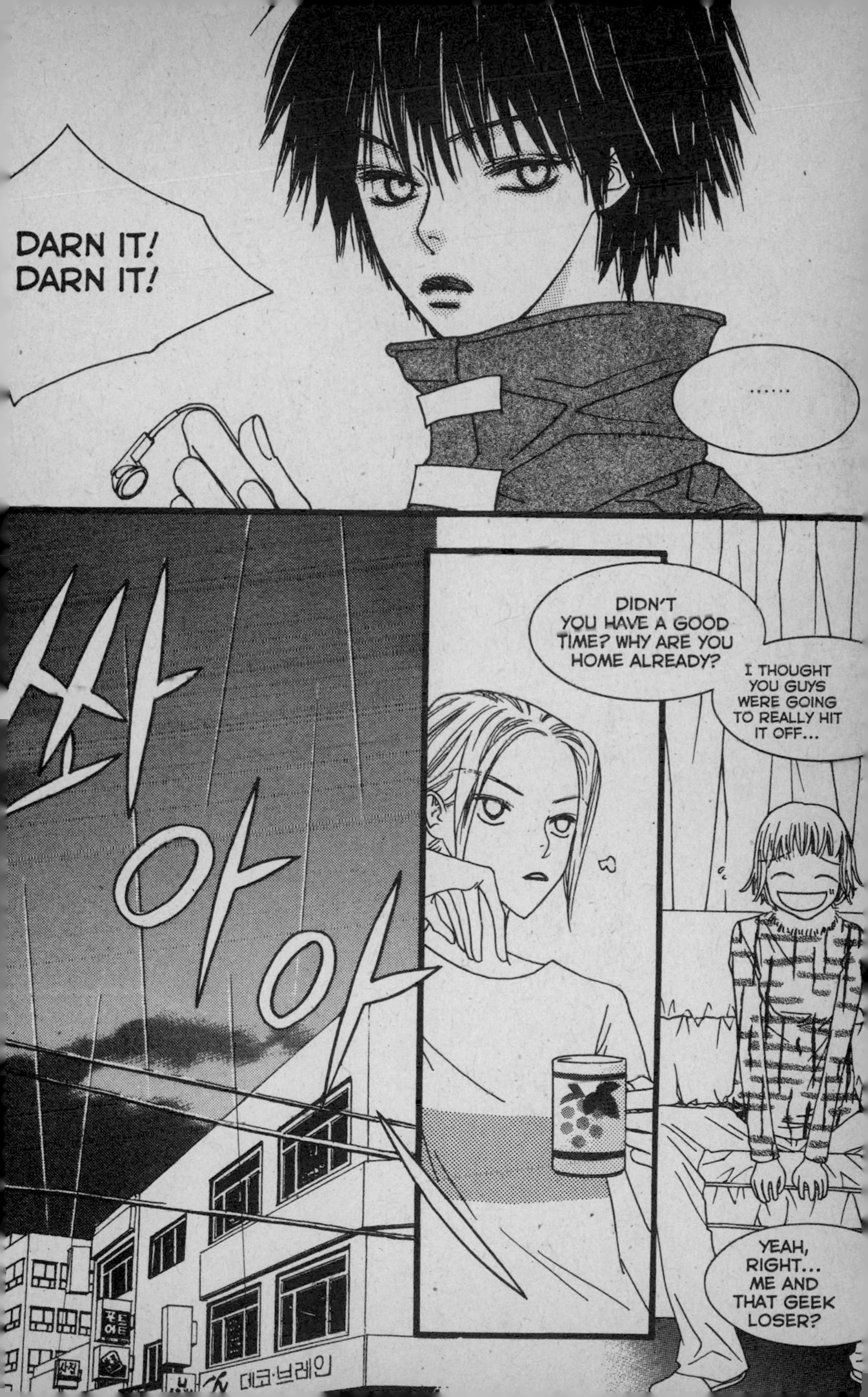
DARN IT! DARN IT!
......
쏴아아
데코·브레인
DIDN'T YOU HAVE A GOOD TIME? WHY ARE YOU HOME ALREADY?
I THOUGHT YOU GUYS WERE GOING TO REALLY HIT IT OFF...
YEAH, RIGHT... ME AND THAT GEEK LOSER?

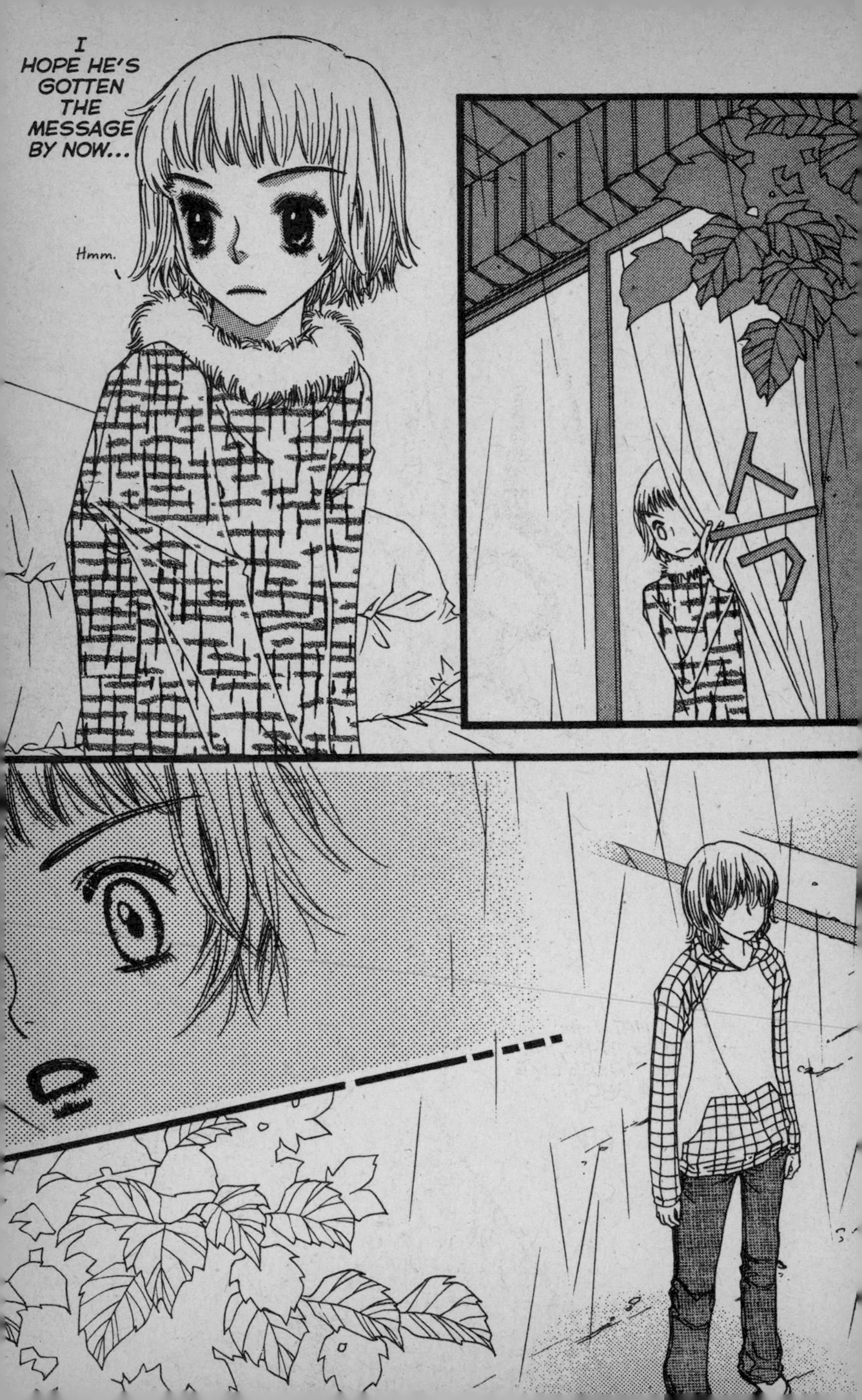
I HOPE HE'S GOTTEN THE MESSAGE BY NOW...
Hmm.

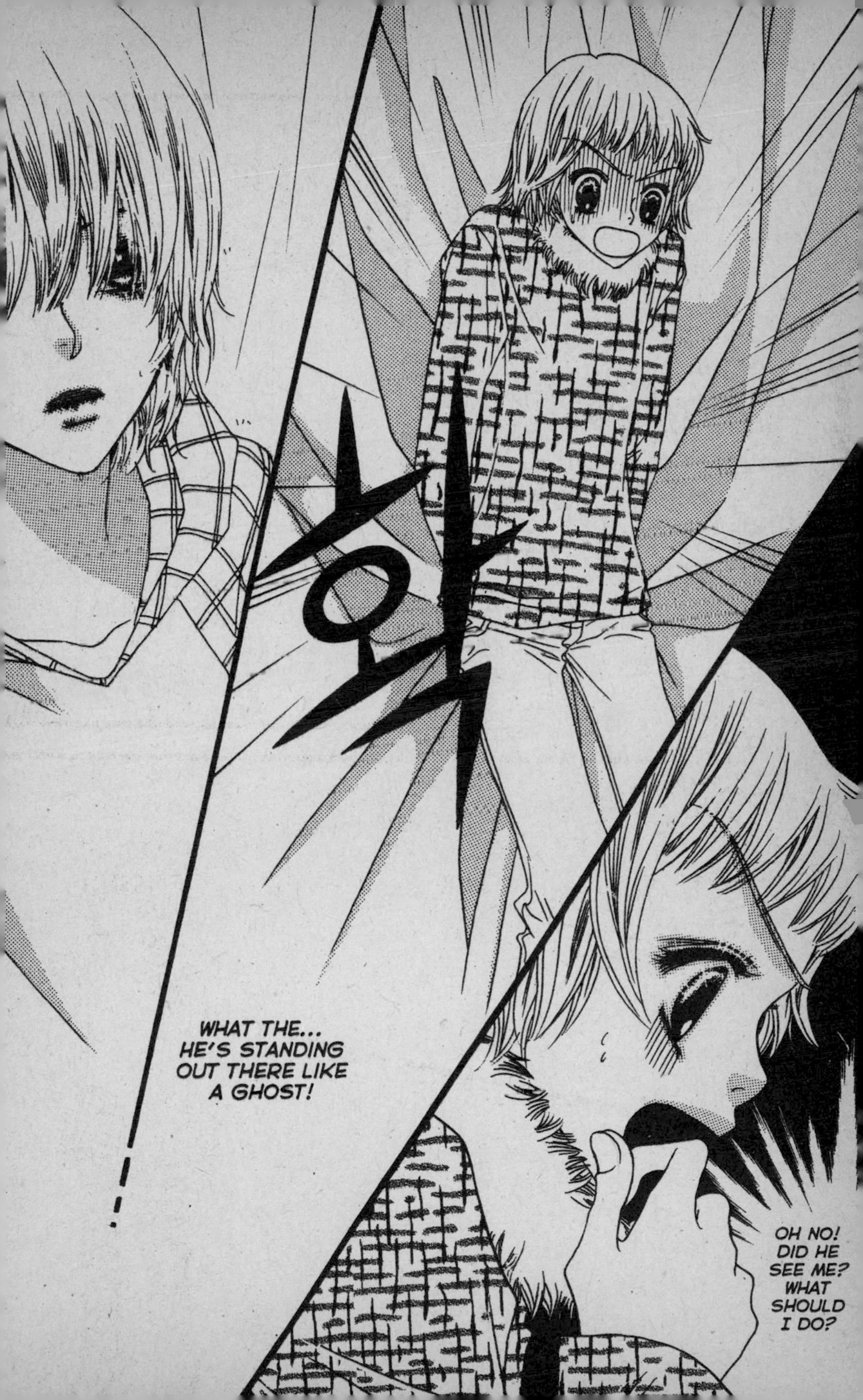
WHAT THE... HE'S STANDING OUT THERE LIKE A GHOST!
OH NO! DID HE SEE ME? WHAT SHOULD I DO?

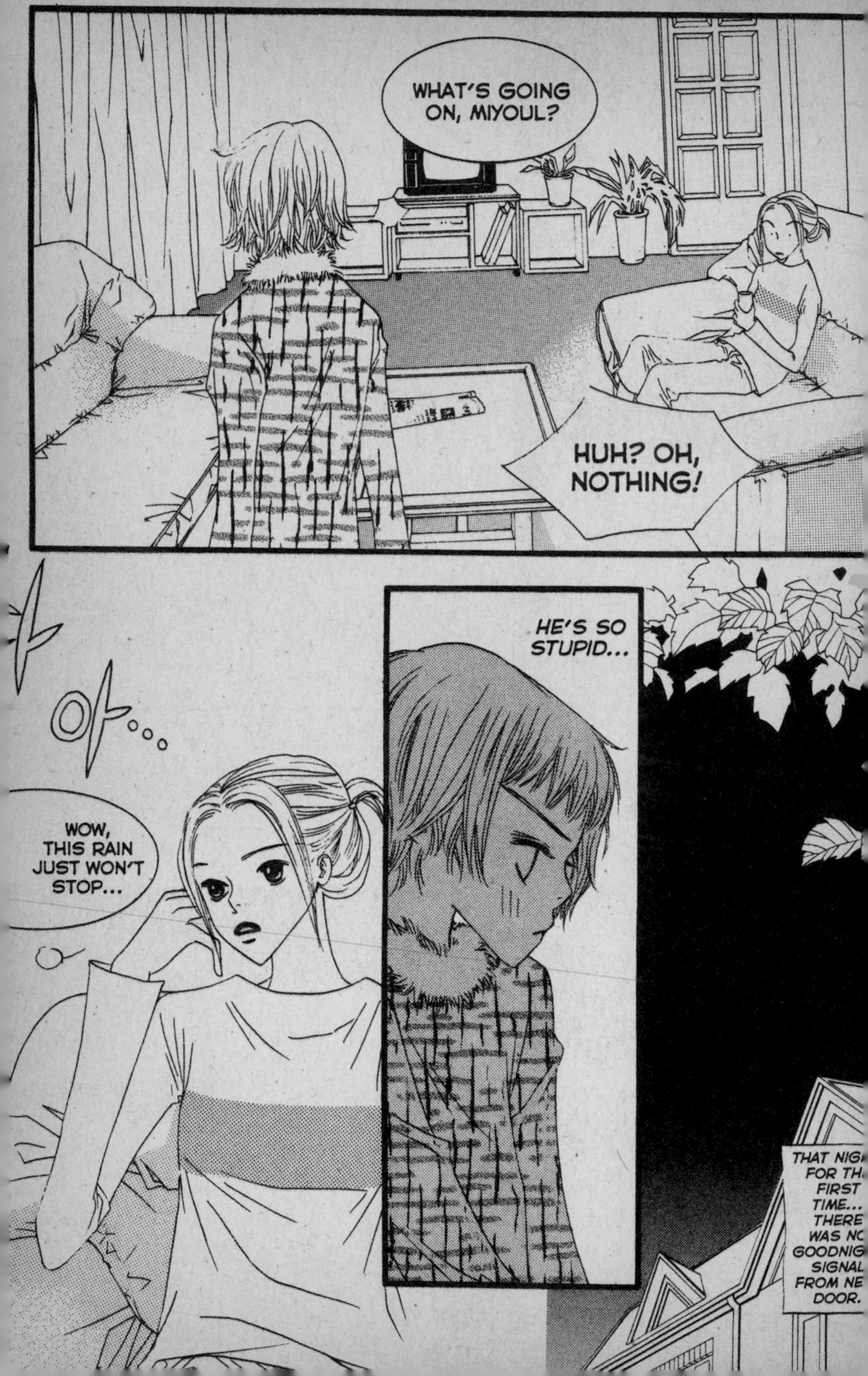
WHAT'S GOING ON, MIYOUL?
HUH? OH, NOTHING!
아...
WOW, THIS RAIN JUST WON'T STOP...
HE'S SO STUPID...
THAT NIG FOR TH FIRST TIME... THERE WAS N GOODNIG SIGNAL FROM NE DOOR.

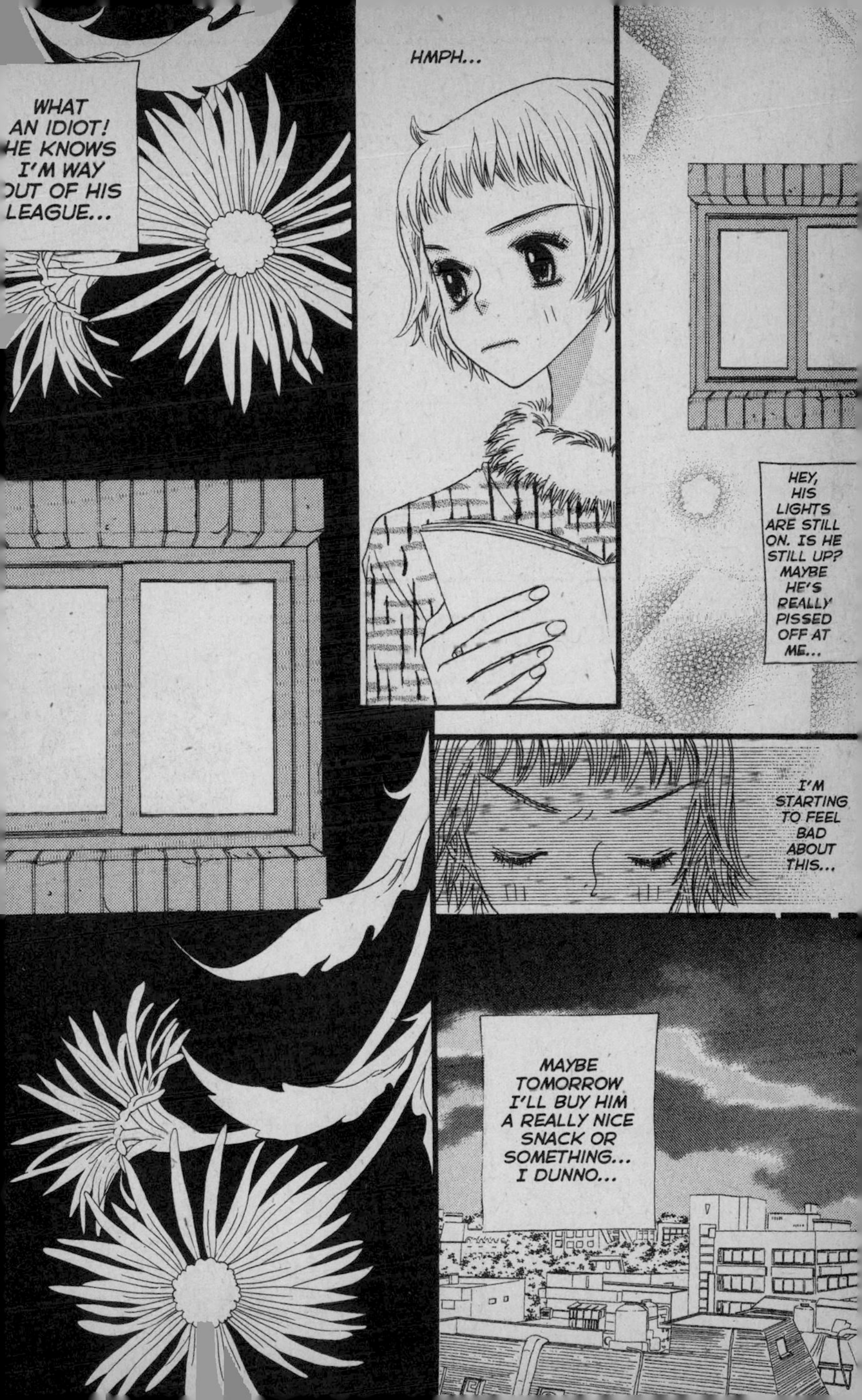
WHAT AN IDIOT! HE KNOWS I'M WAY OUT OF HIS LEAGUE...
HMPH...
HEY, HIS LIGHTS ARE STILL ON. IS HE STILL UP? MAYBE HE'S REALLY PISSED OFF AT ME...
I'M STARTING TO FEEL BAD ABOUT THIS...
MAYBE TOMORROW I'LL BUY HIM A REALLY NICE SNACK OR SOMETHING... I DUNNO...

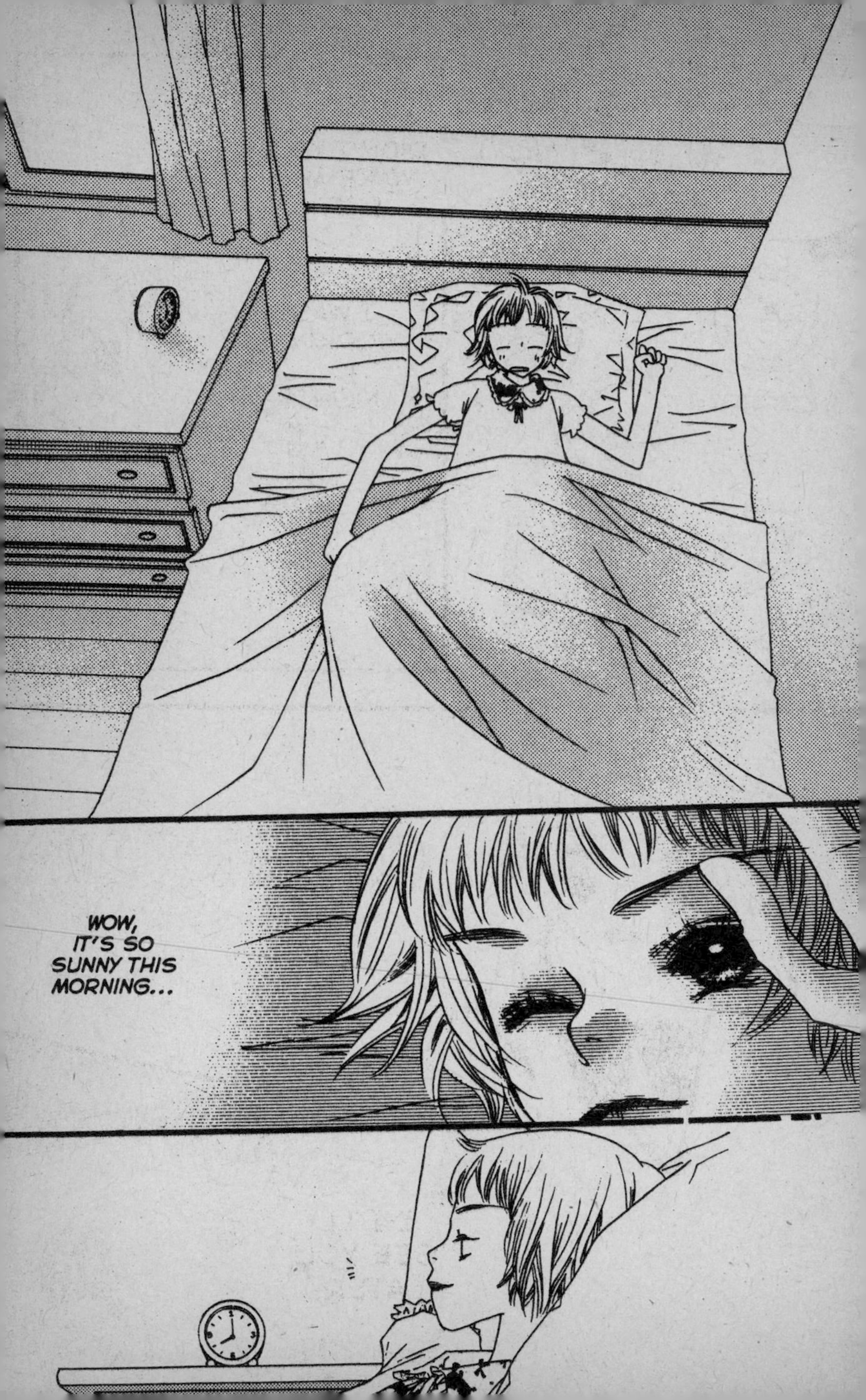
WOW, IT'S SO SUNNY THIS MORNING...

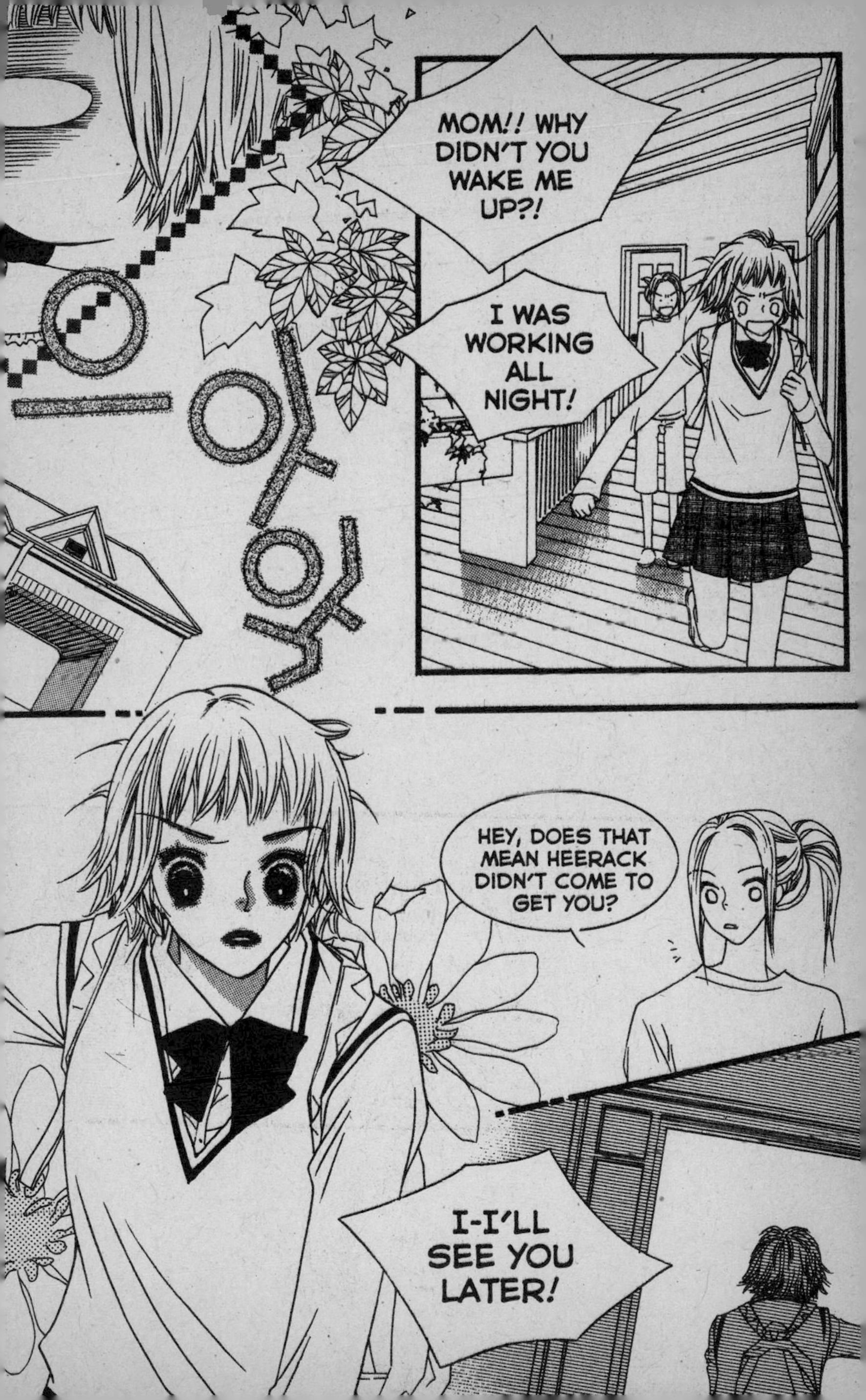
MOM!! WHY DIDN'T YOU WAKE ME UP?!
I WAS WORKING ALL NIGHT!
HEY, DOES THAT MEAN HEERACK DIDN'T COME TO GET YOU?
I-I'LL SEE YOU LATER!

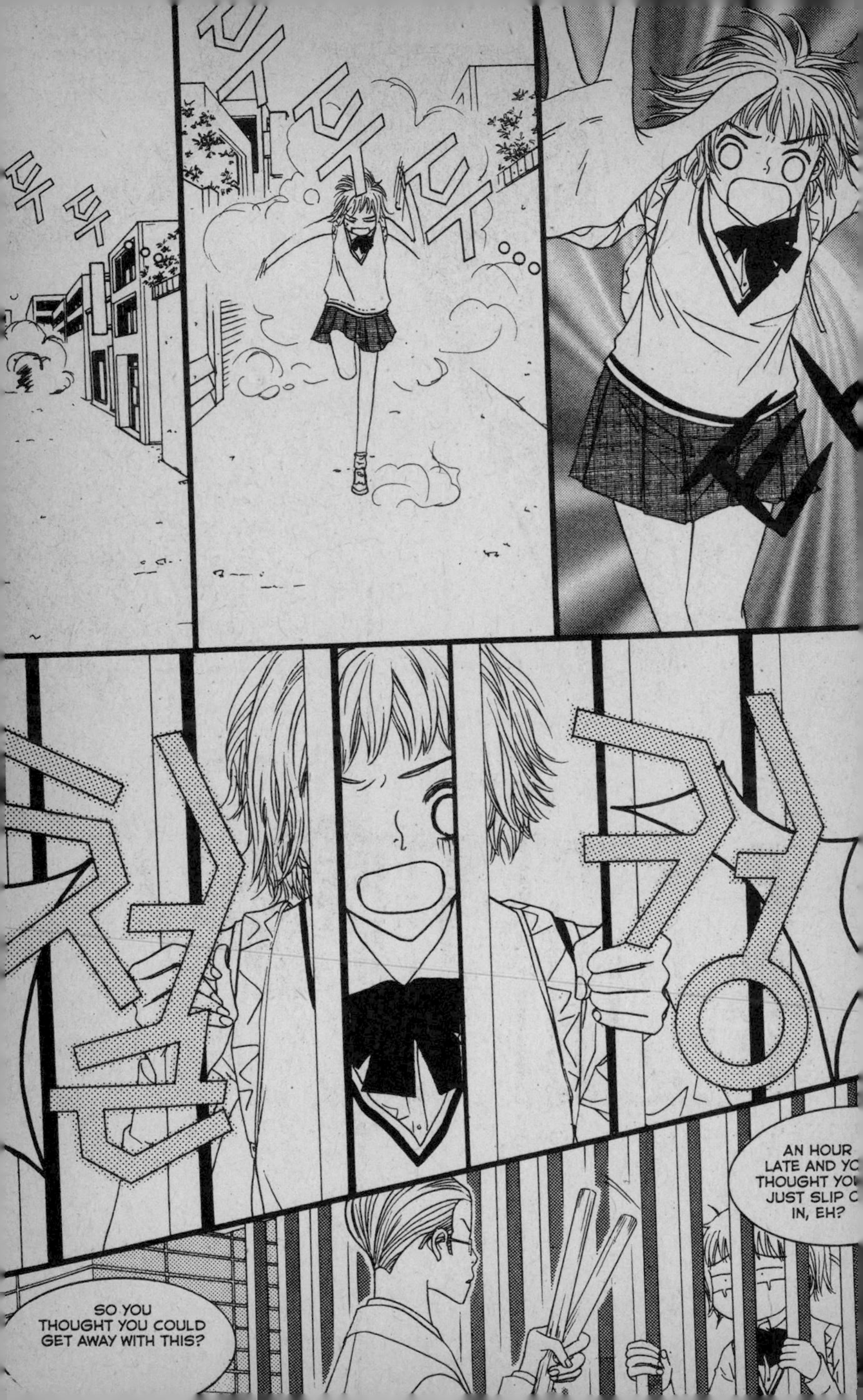
SO YOU THOUGHT YOU COULD GET AWAY WITH THIS?
AN HOUR LATE AND YO THOUGHT YOU JUST SLIP C IN, EH?

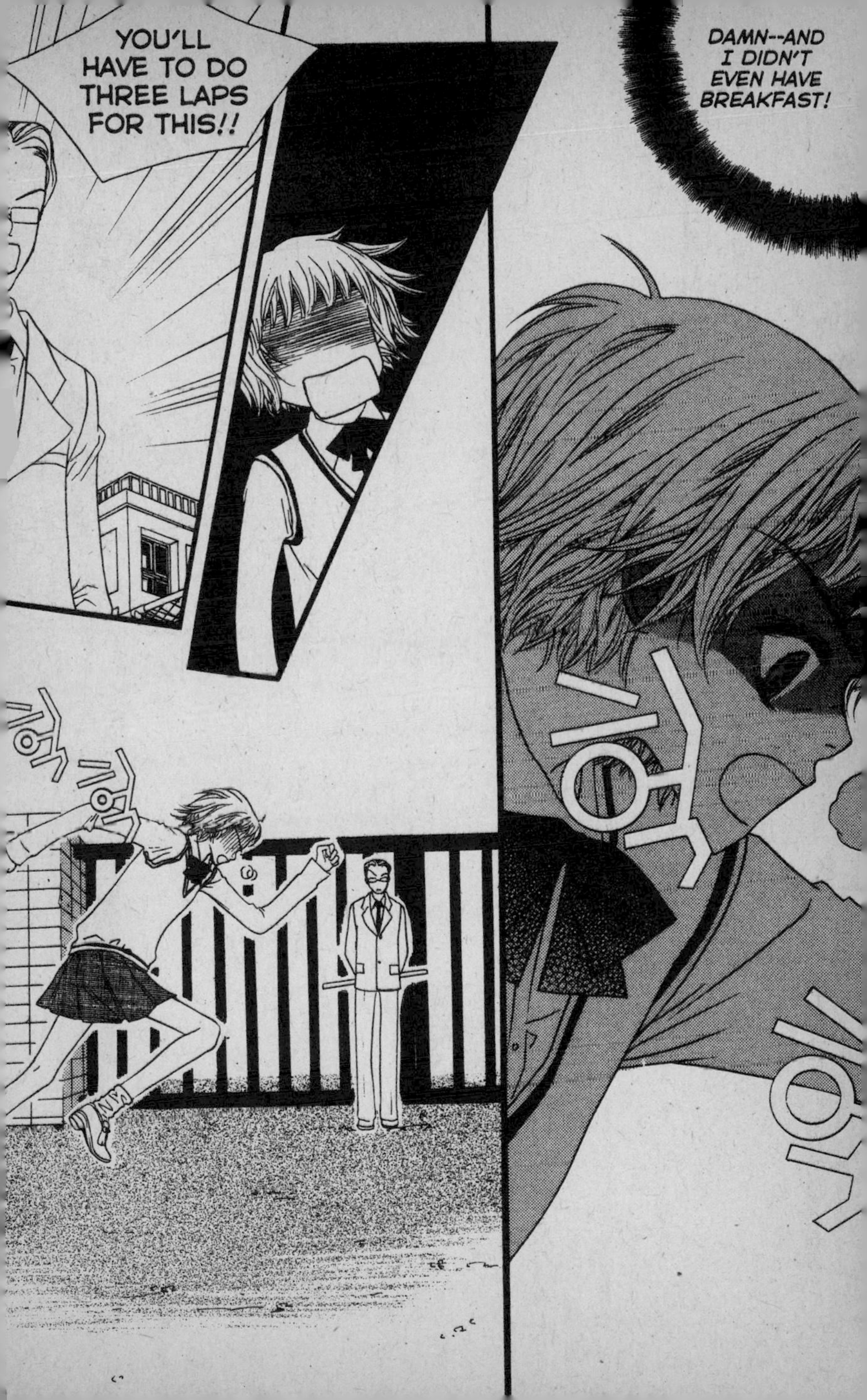
YOU'LL HAVE TO DO THREE LAPS FOR THIS!!
DAMN--AND I DIDN'T EVEN HAVE BREAKFAST!

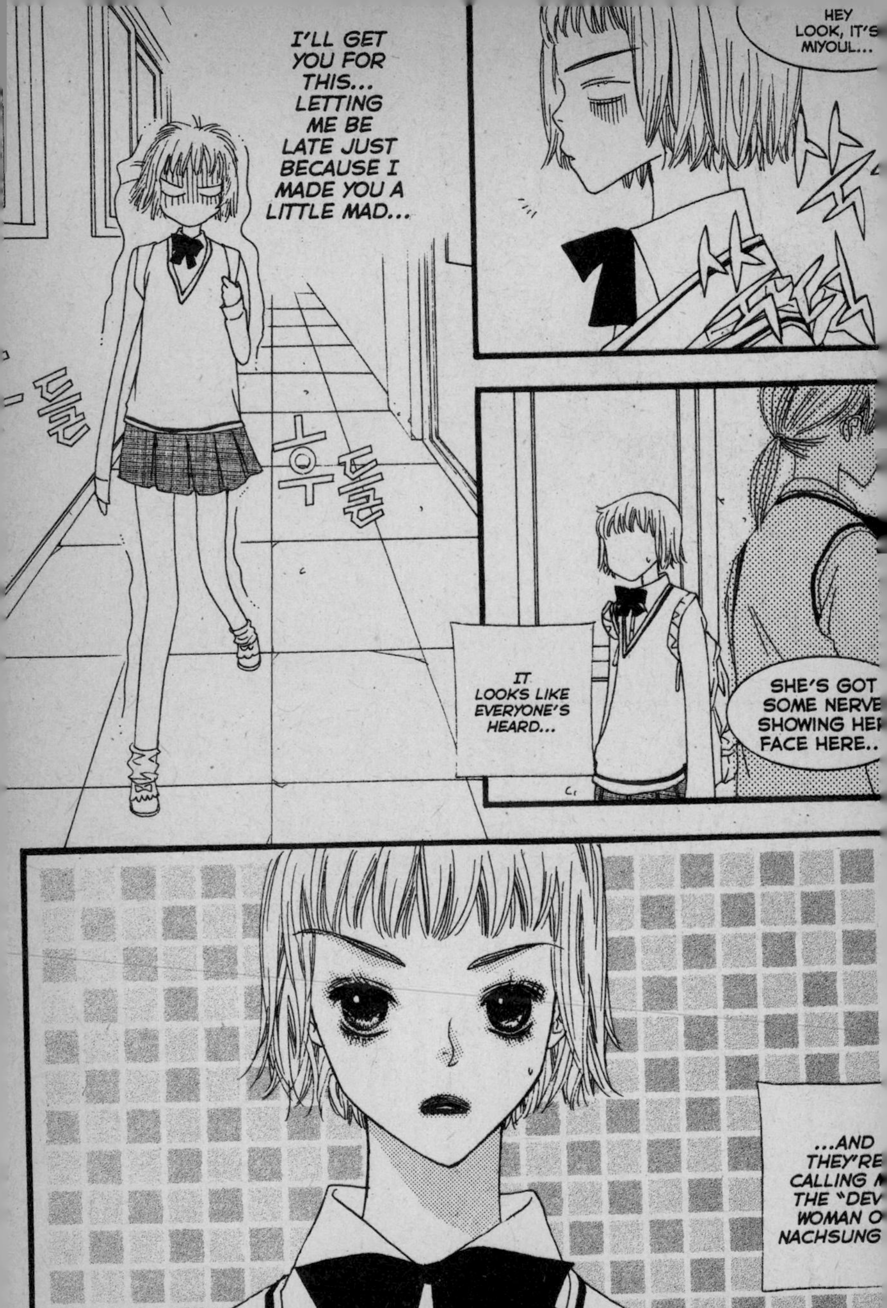
I'LL GET YOU FOR THIS... LETTING ME BE LATE JUST BECAUSE I MADE YOU A LITTLE MAD...
HEY LOOK, IT'S MIYOUL...
IT LOOKS LIKE EVERYONE'S HEARD...
SHE'S GOT SOME NERVE SHOWING HE FACE HERE..
...AND THEY'RE CALLING M THE "DEV WOMAN O NACHSUNG

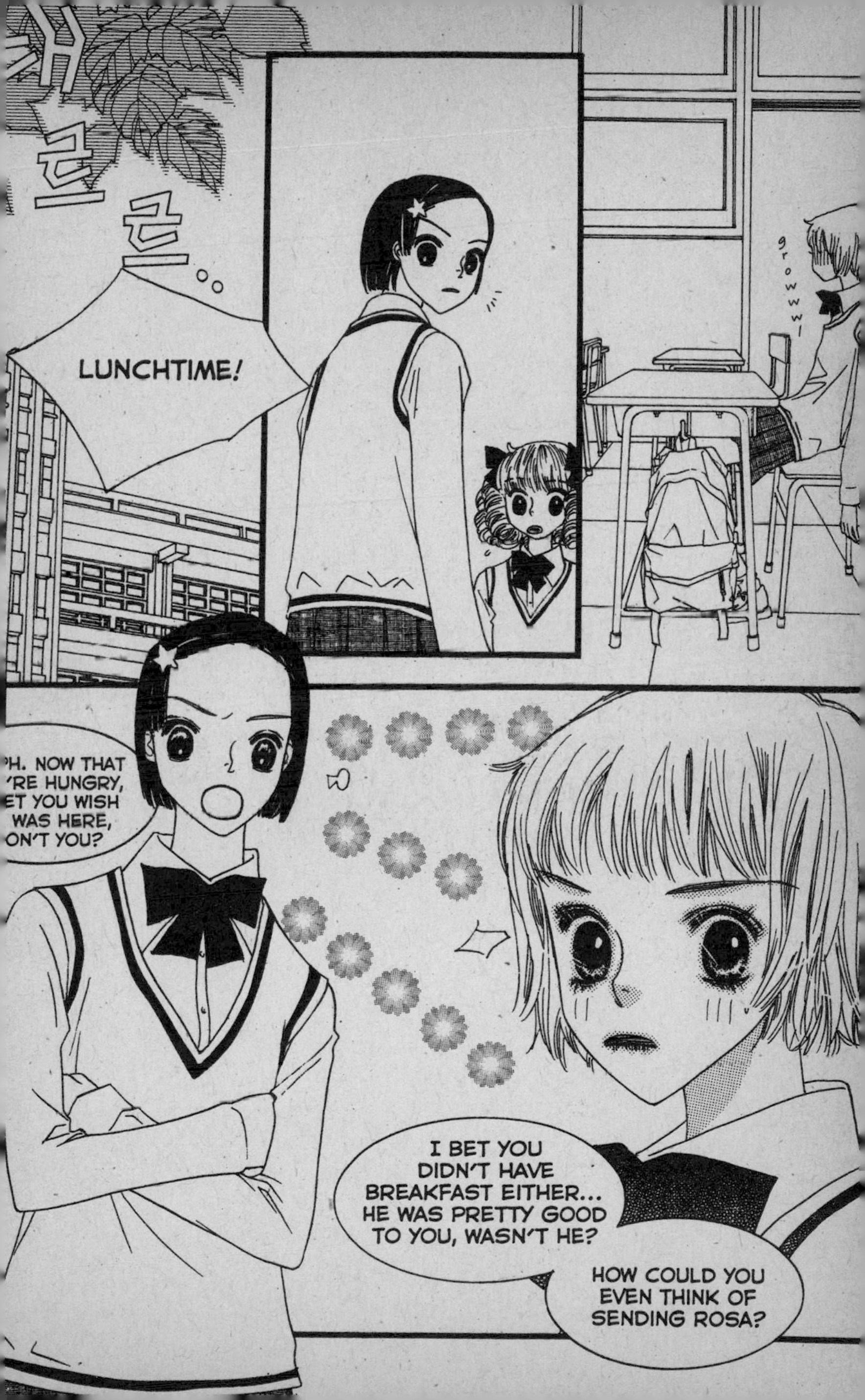
LUNCHTIME!
growwwl
PH. NOW THAT 'RE HUNGRY, ET YOU WISH WAS HERE, ON'T YOU?
I BET YOU DIDN'T HAVE BREAKFAST EITHER... HE WAS PRETTY GOOD TO YOU, WASN'T HE?
HOW COULD YOU EVEN THINK OF SENDING ROSA?

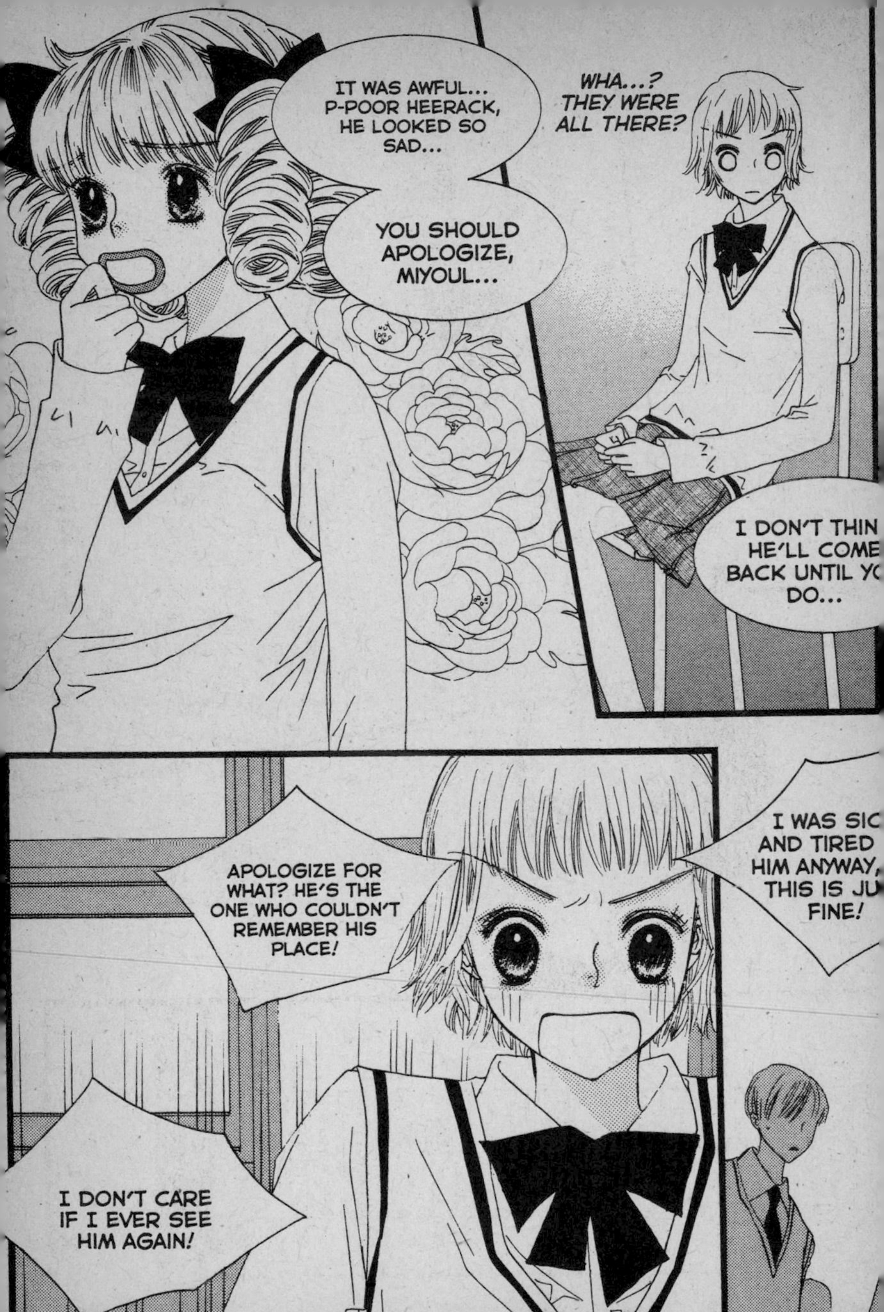
IT WAS AWFUL... P-POOR HEERACK, HE LOOKED SO SAD...
YOU SHOULD APOLOGIZE, MIYOUL...
WHA...? THEY WERE ALL THERE?
I DON'T THIN HE'LL COME BACK UNTIL Y DO...
APOLOGIZE FOR WHAT? HE'S THE ONE WHO COULDN'T REMEMBER HIS PLACE!
I WAS SIC AND TIRED HIM ANYWAY, THIS IS JU FINE!
I DON'T CARE IF I EVER SEE HIM AGAIN!

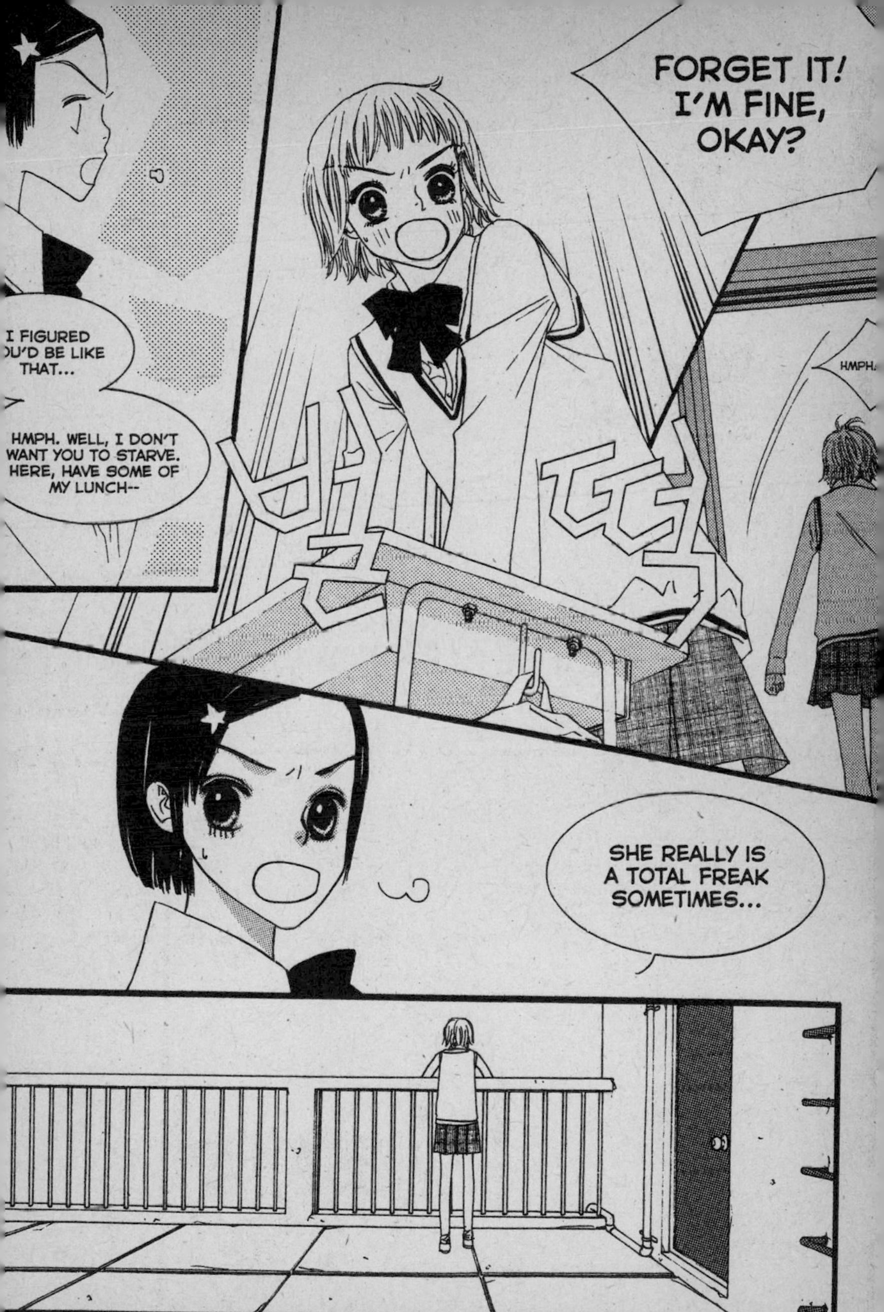
I FIGURED
OU'D BE LIKE THAT...
HMPH. WELL, I DON'T WANT YOU TO STARVE. HERE, HAVE SOME OF MY LUNCH--
FORGET IT! I'M FINE, OKAY?
HMPH.
SHE REALLY IS A TOTAL FREAK SOMETIMES...

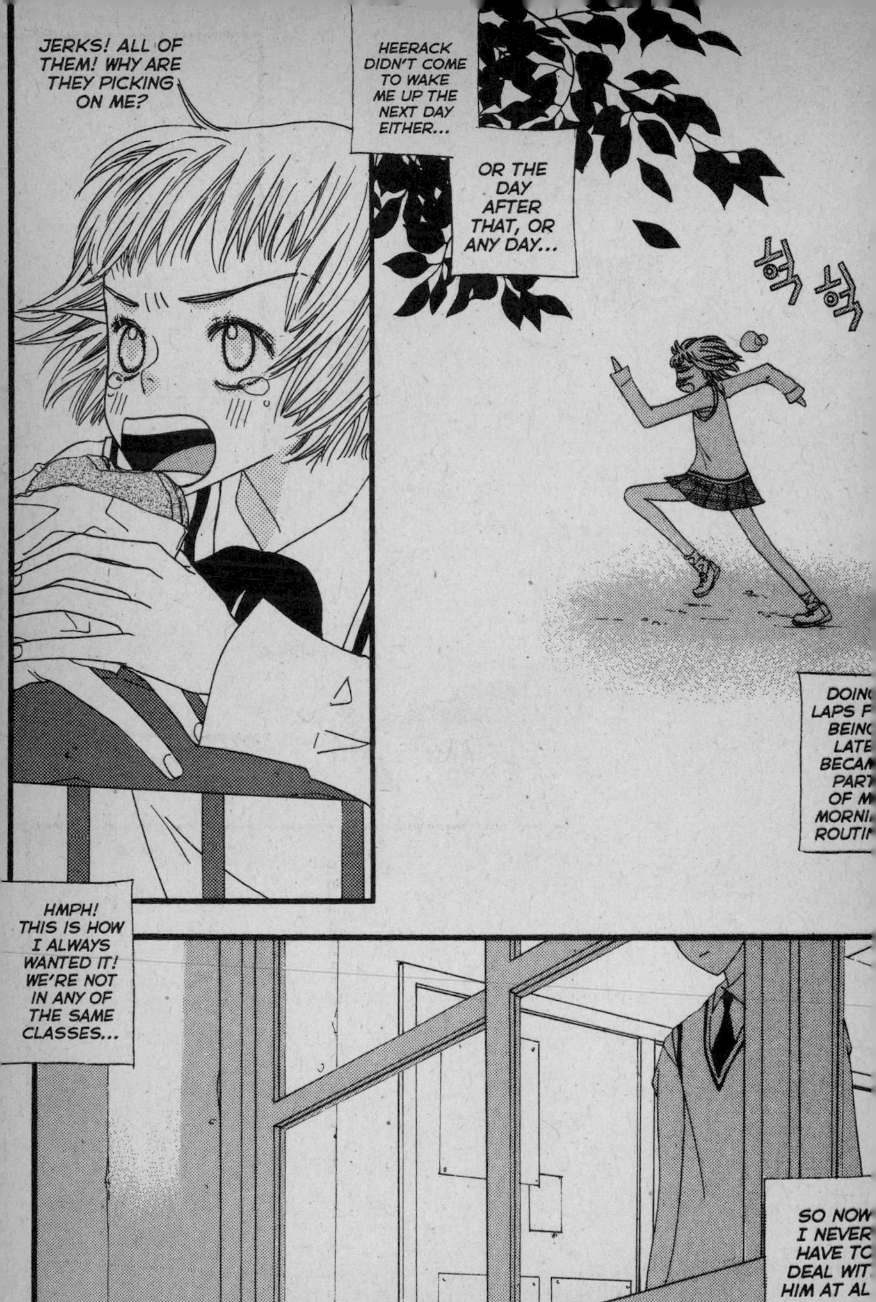
JERKS! ALL OF THEM! WHY ARE THEY PICKING ON ME?
HEERACK DIDN'T COME TO WAKE ME UP THE NEXT DAY EITHER...
OR THE DAY AFTER THAT, OR ANY DAY...
헉 헉
DOIN LAPS F BEIN LATE BECAM PART OF M MORNI ROUTI
HMPH! THIS IS HOW I ALWAYS WANTED IT! WE'RE NOT IN ANY OF THE SAME CLASSES...
SO NOW I NEVER HAVE TO DEAL WIT HIM AT AL

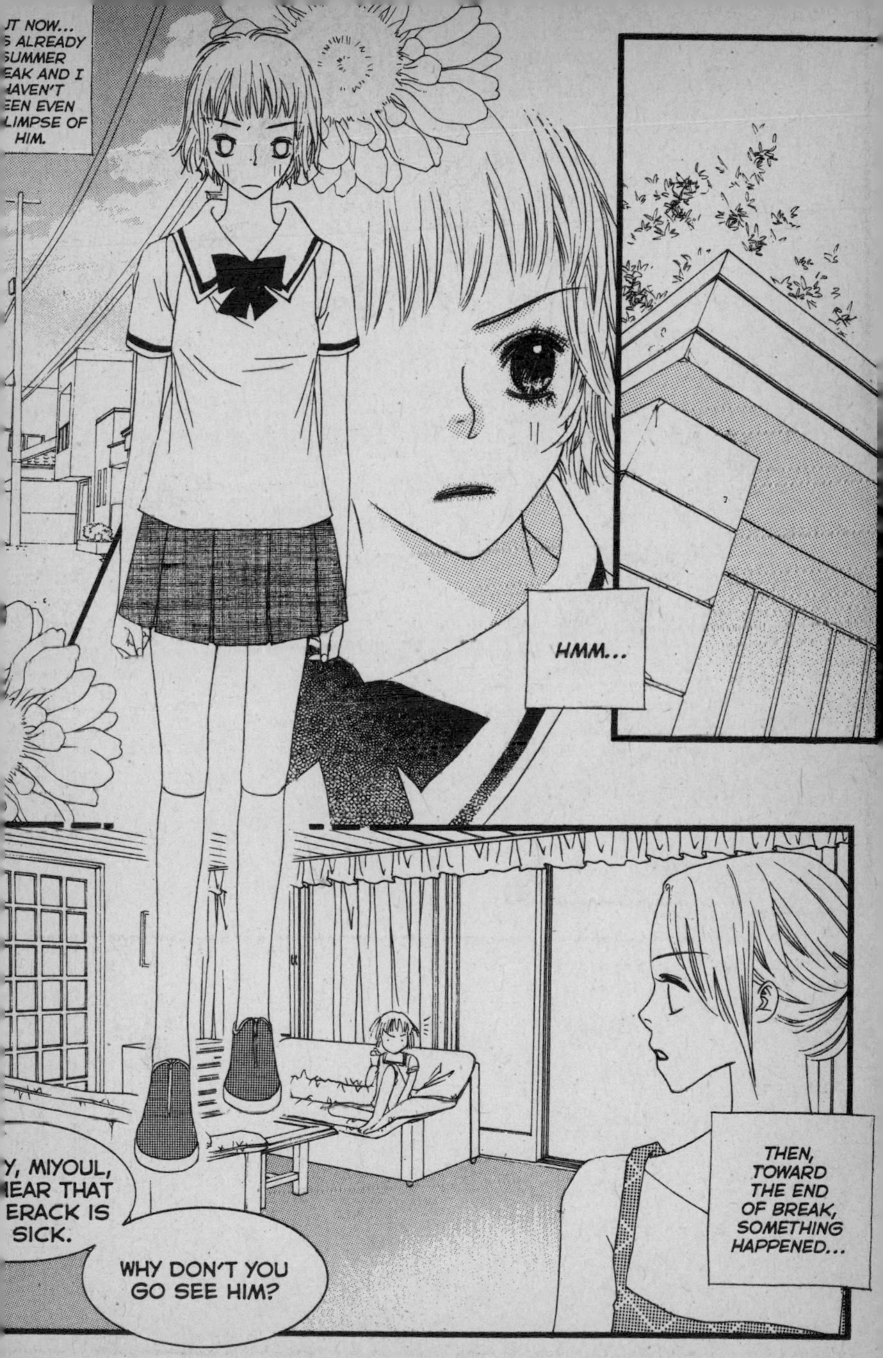

JT NOW... S ALREADY SUMMER EAK AND I HAVEN'T EEN EVEN LIMPSE OF HIM.
HMM...
Y, MIYOUL, HEAR THAT ERACK IS SICK.
WHY DON'T YOU GO SEE HIM?
THEN, TOWARD THE END OF BREAK, SOMETHING HAPPENED...

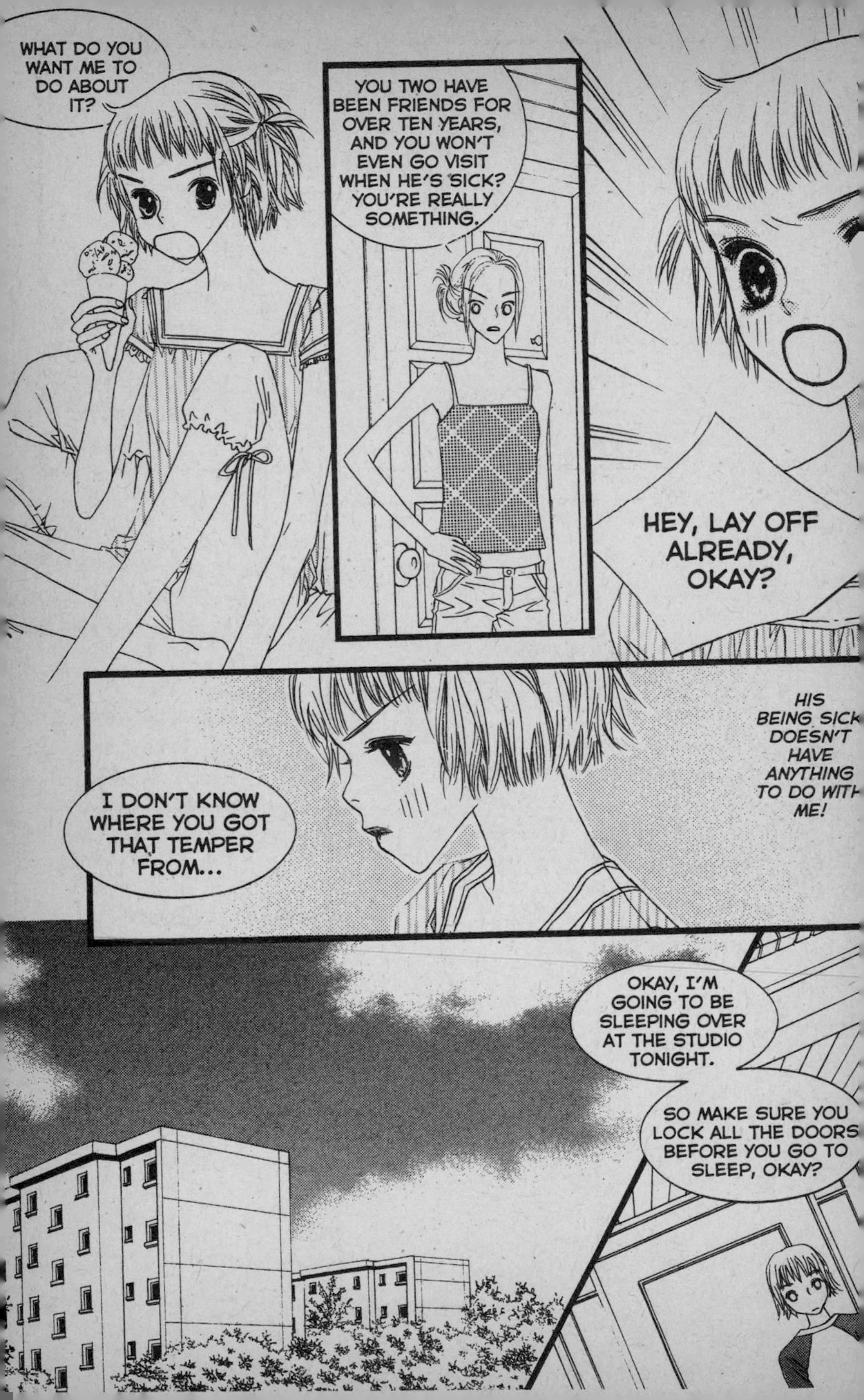
WHAT DO YOU WANT ME TO DO ABOUT IT?
YOU TWO HAVE BEEN FRIENDS FOR OVER TEN YEARS, AND YOU WON'T EVEN GO VISIT WHEN HE'S SICK? YOU'RE REALLY SOMETHING.
HEY, LAY OFF ALREADY, OKAY?
I DON'T KNOW WHERE YOU GOT THAT TEMPER FROM...
HIS BEING SICK DOESN'T HAVE ANYTHING TO DO WITH ME!
OKAY, I'M GOING TO BE SLEEPING OVER AT THE STUDIO TONIGHT.
SO MAKE SURE YOU LOCK ALL THE DOORS BEFORE YOU GO TO SLEEP, OKAY?

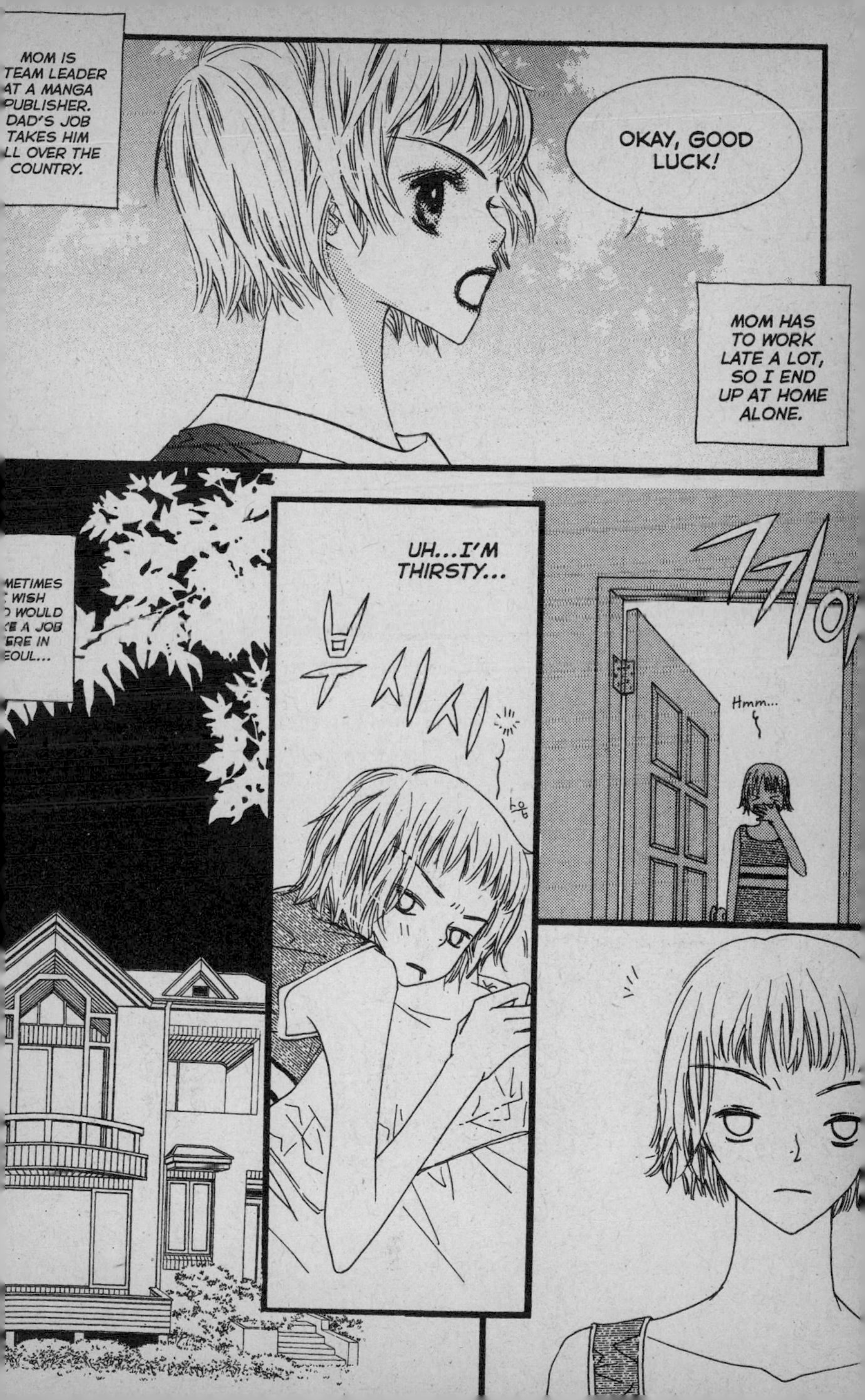
MOM IS TEAM LEADER AT A MANGA PUBLISHER. DAD'S JOB TAKES HIM LL OVER THE COUNTRY.
OKAY, GOOD LUCK!
MOM HAS TO WORK LATE A LOT, SO I END UP AT HOME ALONE.
METIMES WISH D WOULD E A JOB ERE IN EOUL...
UH...I'M THIRSTY...
Hmm...

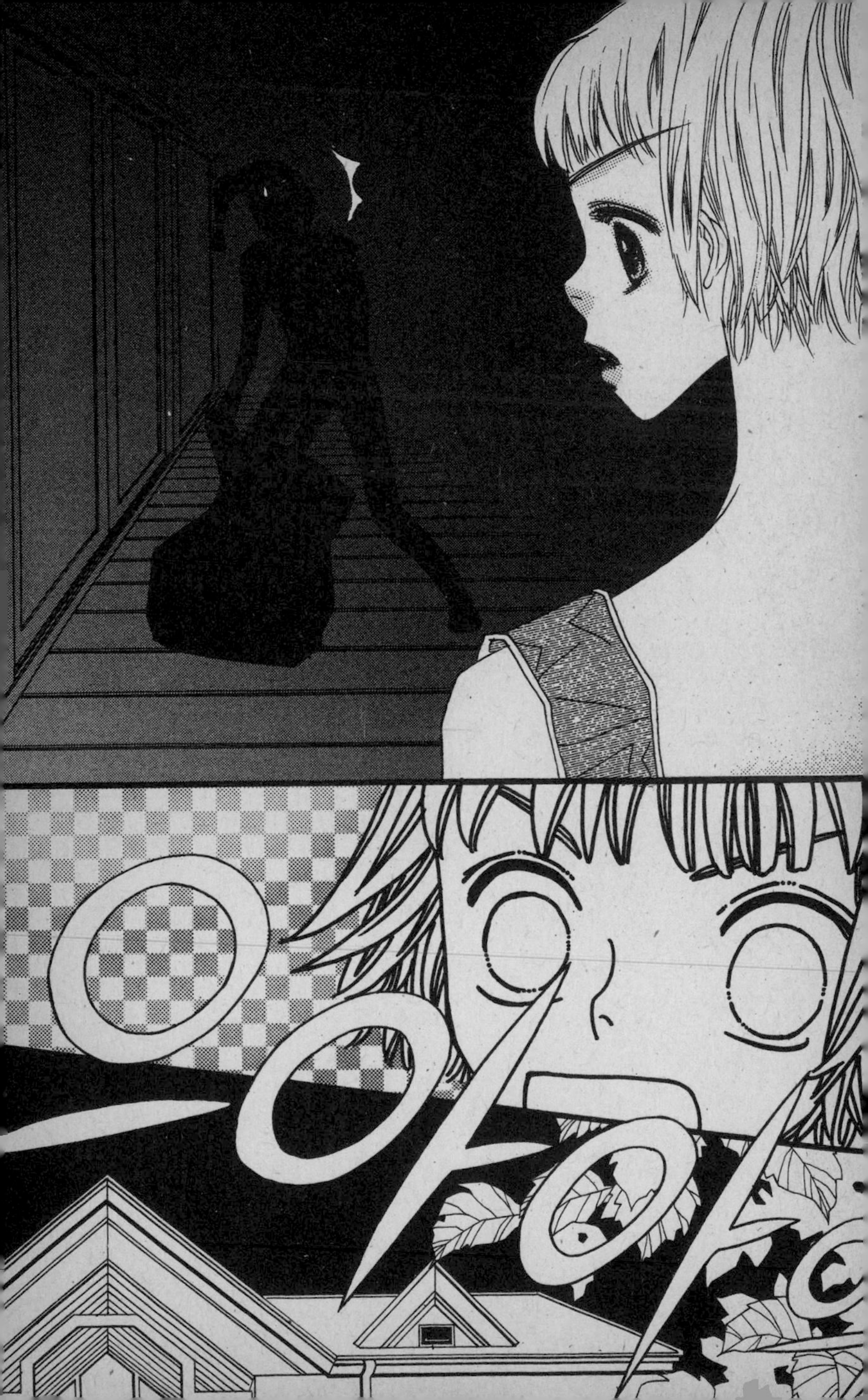

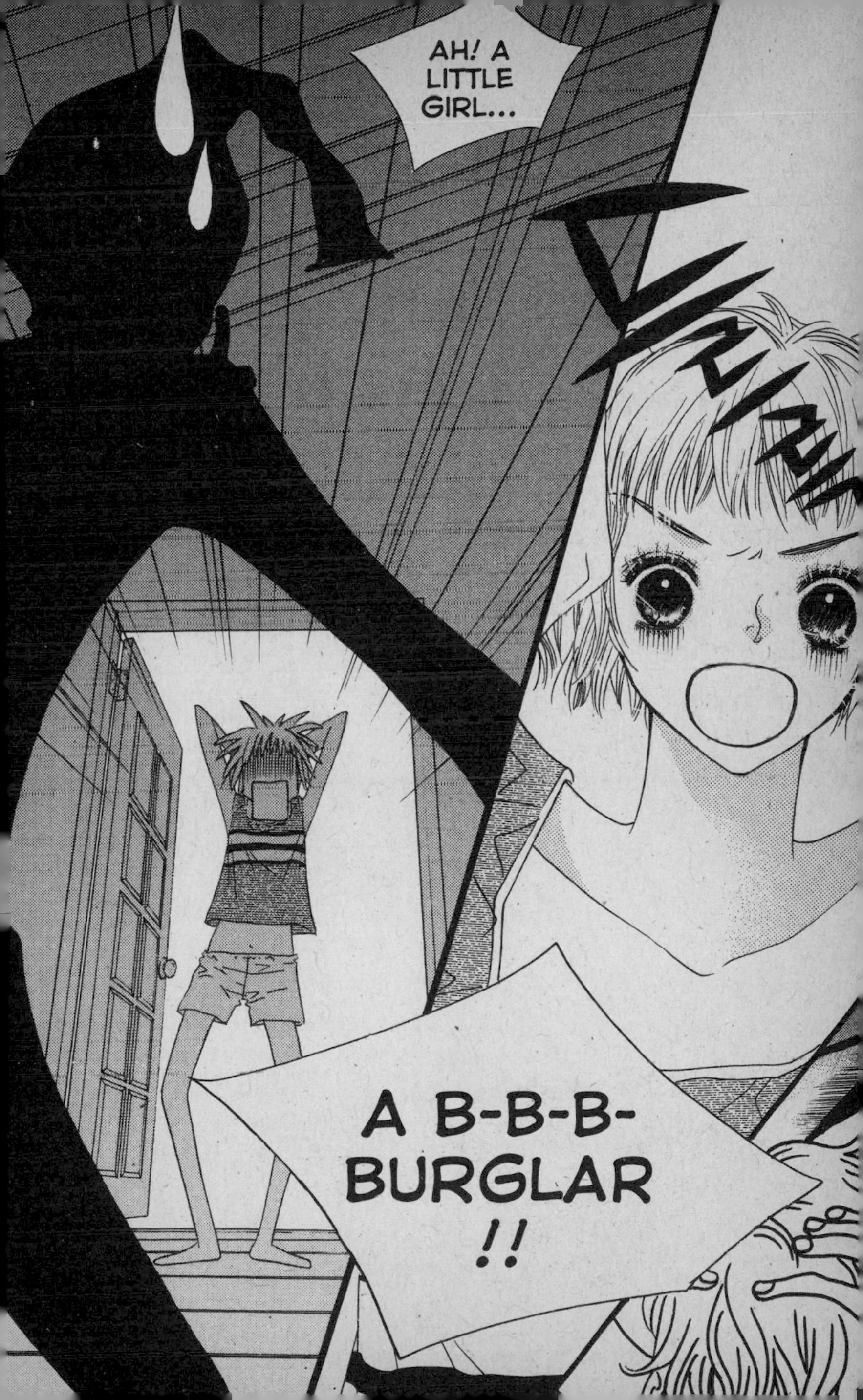
AH! A LITTLE GIRL...
A B-B-B-BURGLAR !!

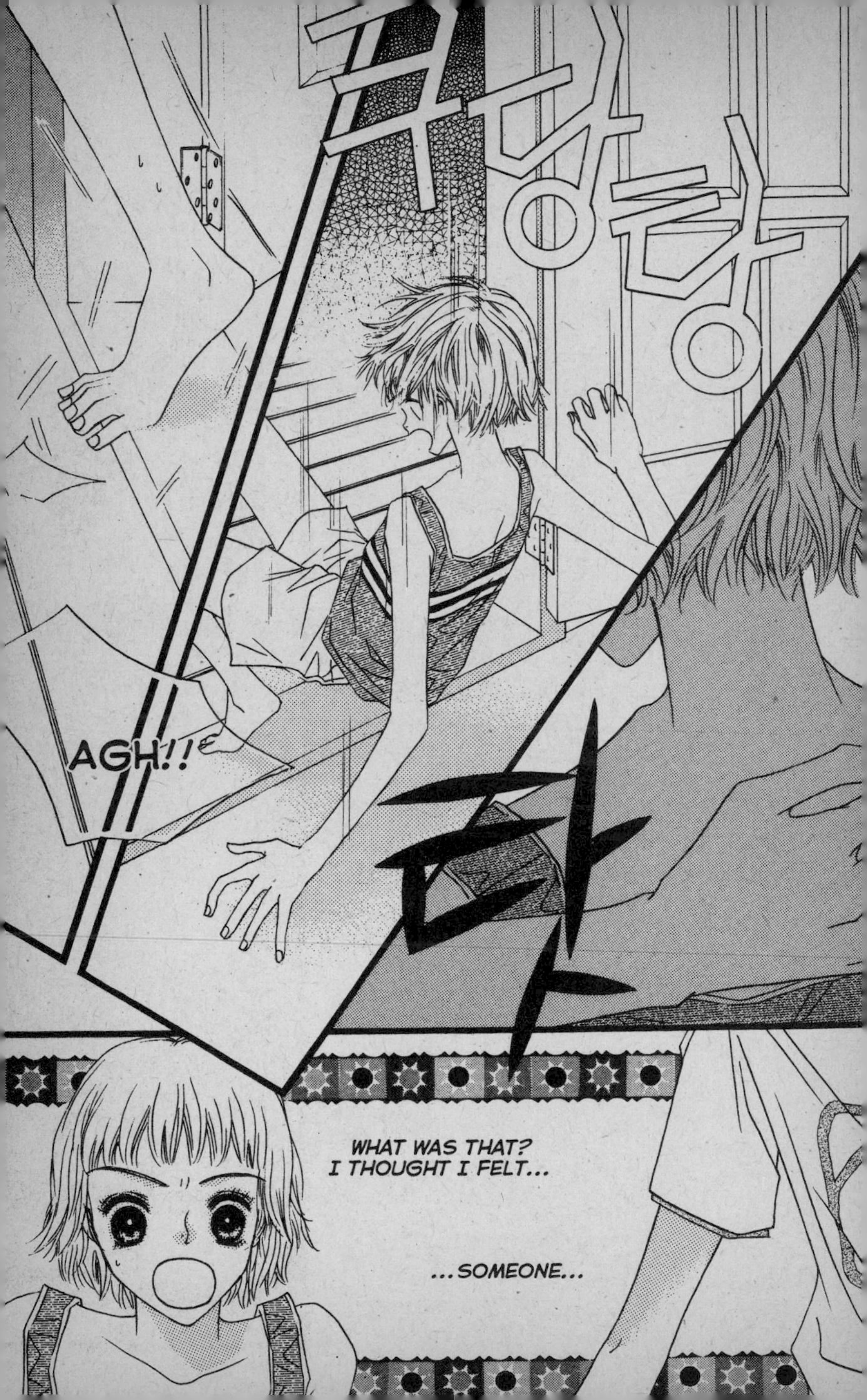
AGH!!
WHAT WAS THAT? I THOUGHT I FELT...
...SOMEONE...

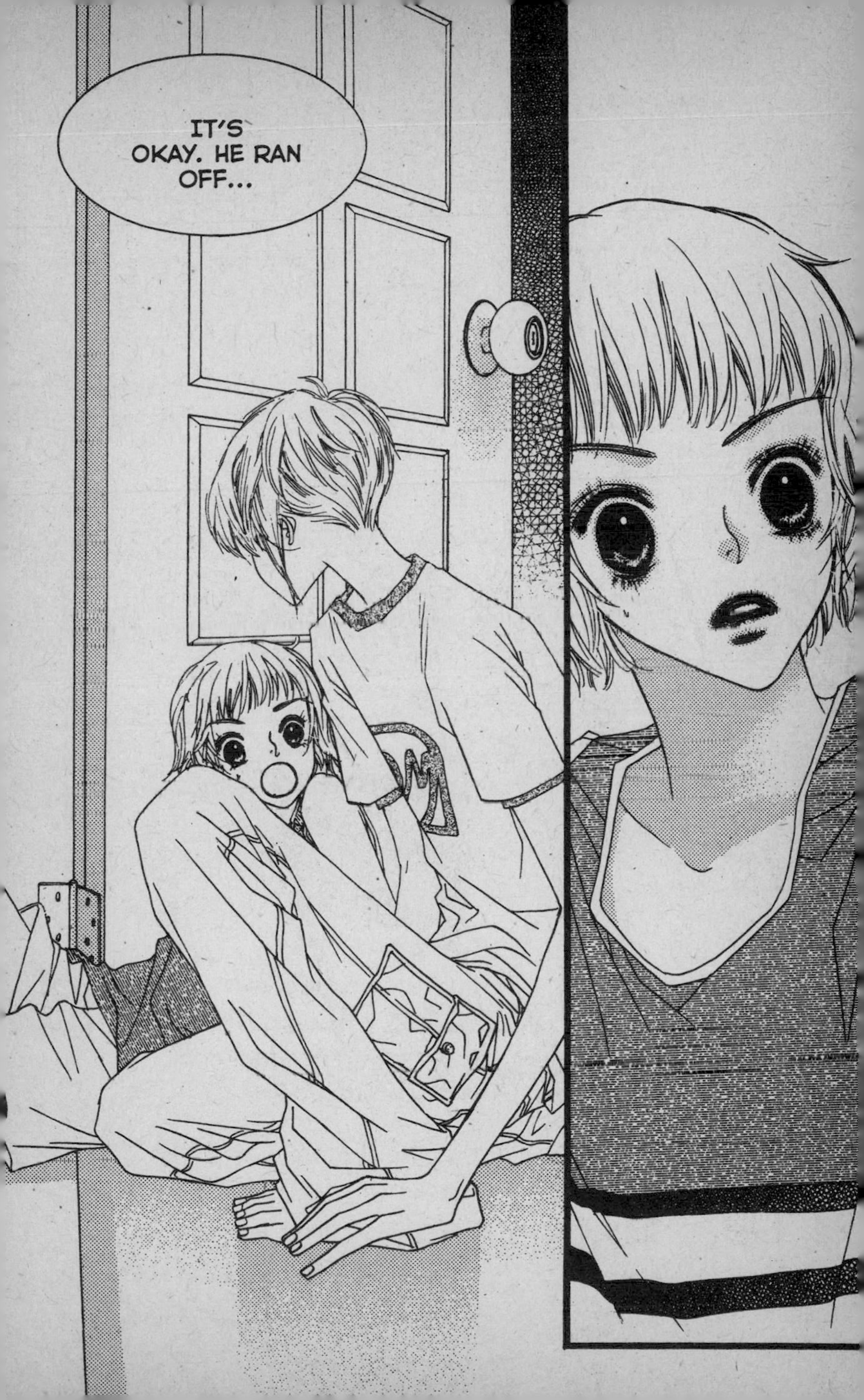
IT'S OKAY. HE RAN OFF...

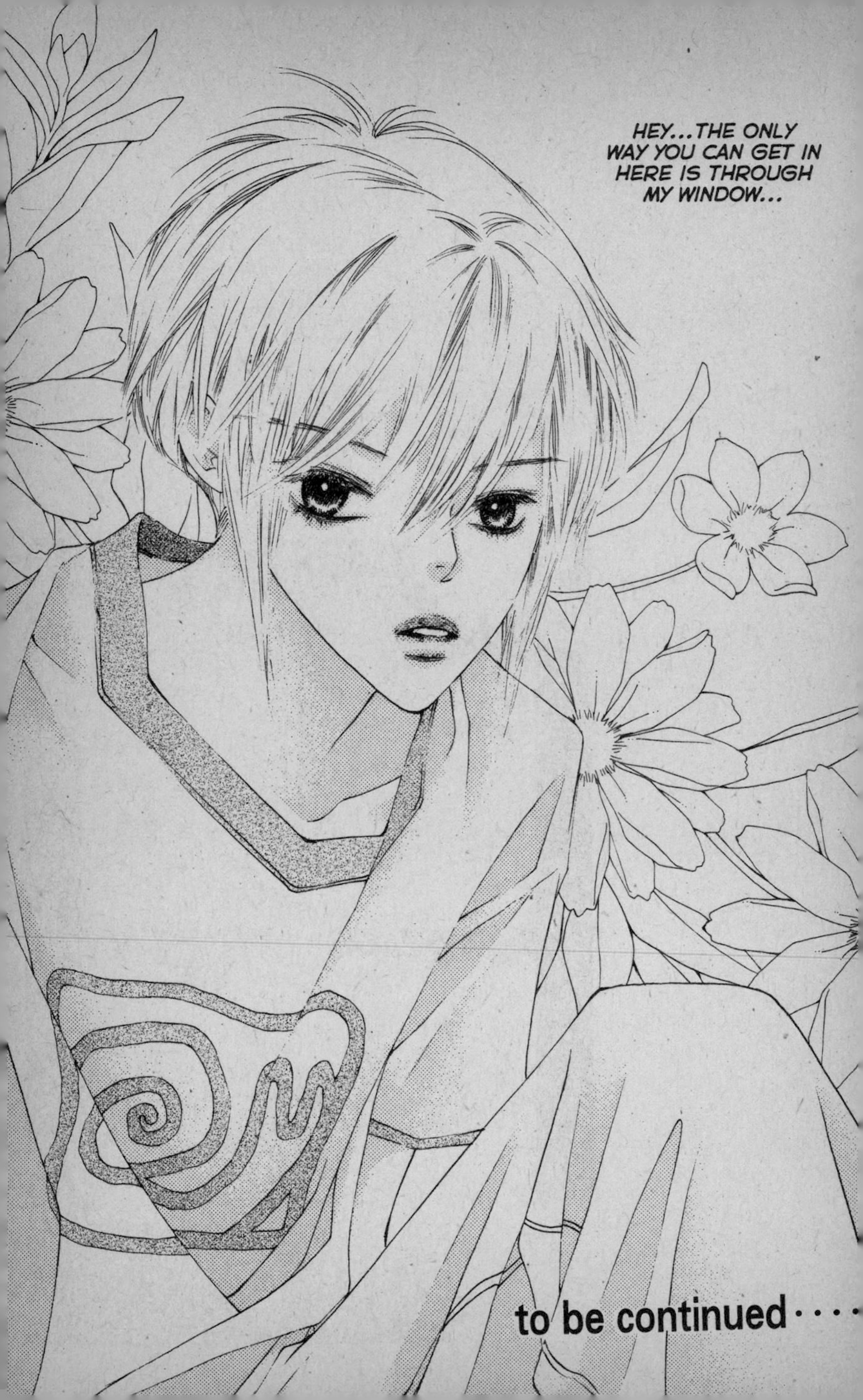
HEY...THE ONLY WAY YOU CAN GET IN HERE IS THROUGH MY WINDOW...
to be continued....

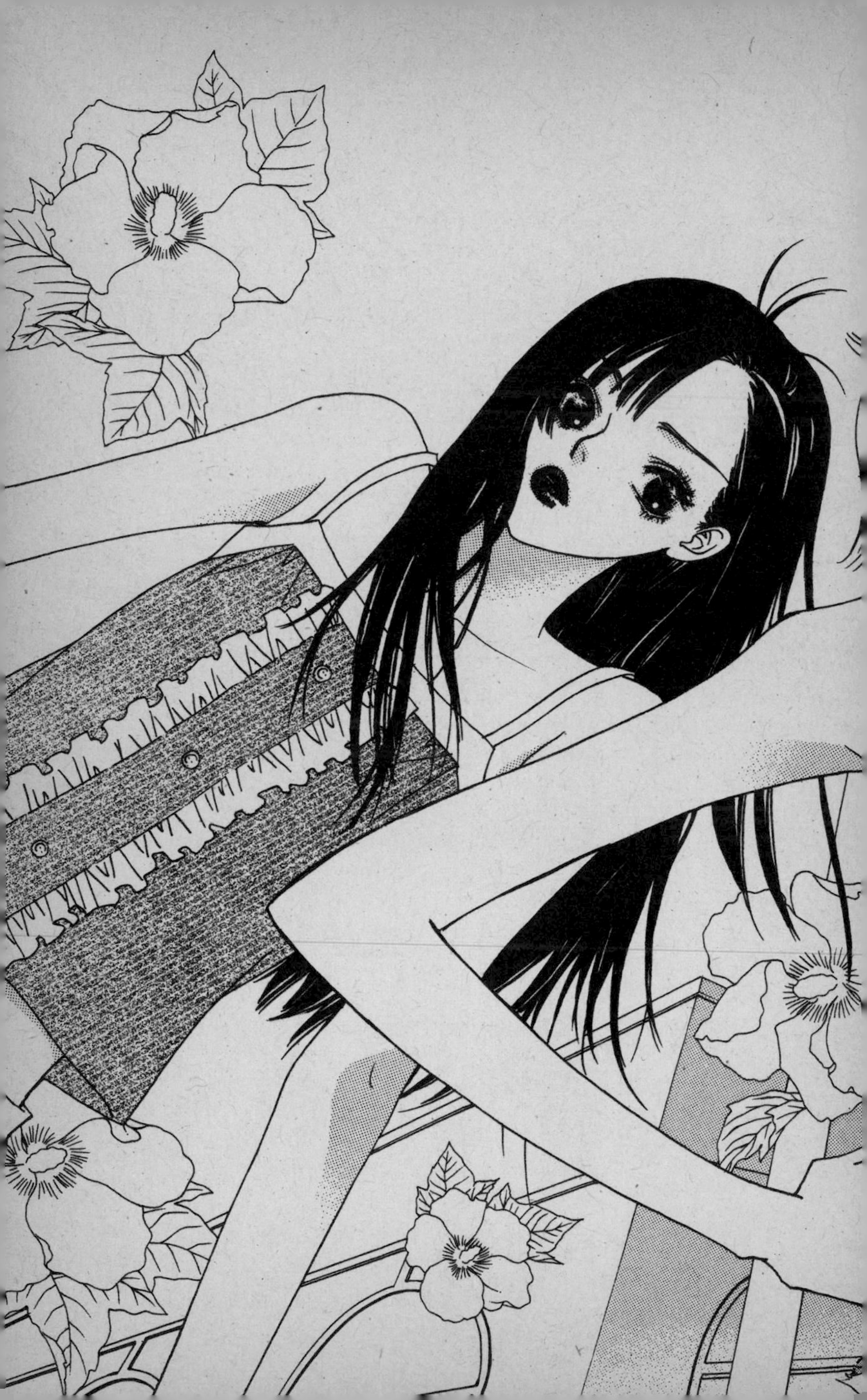

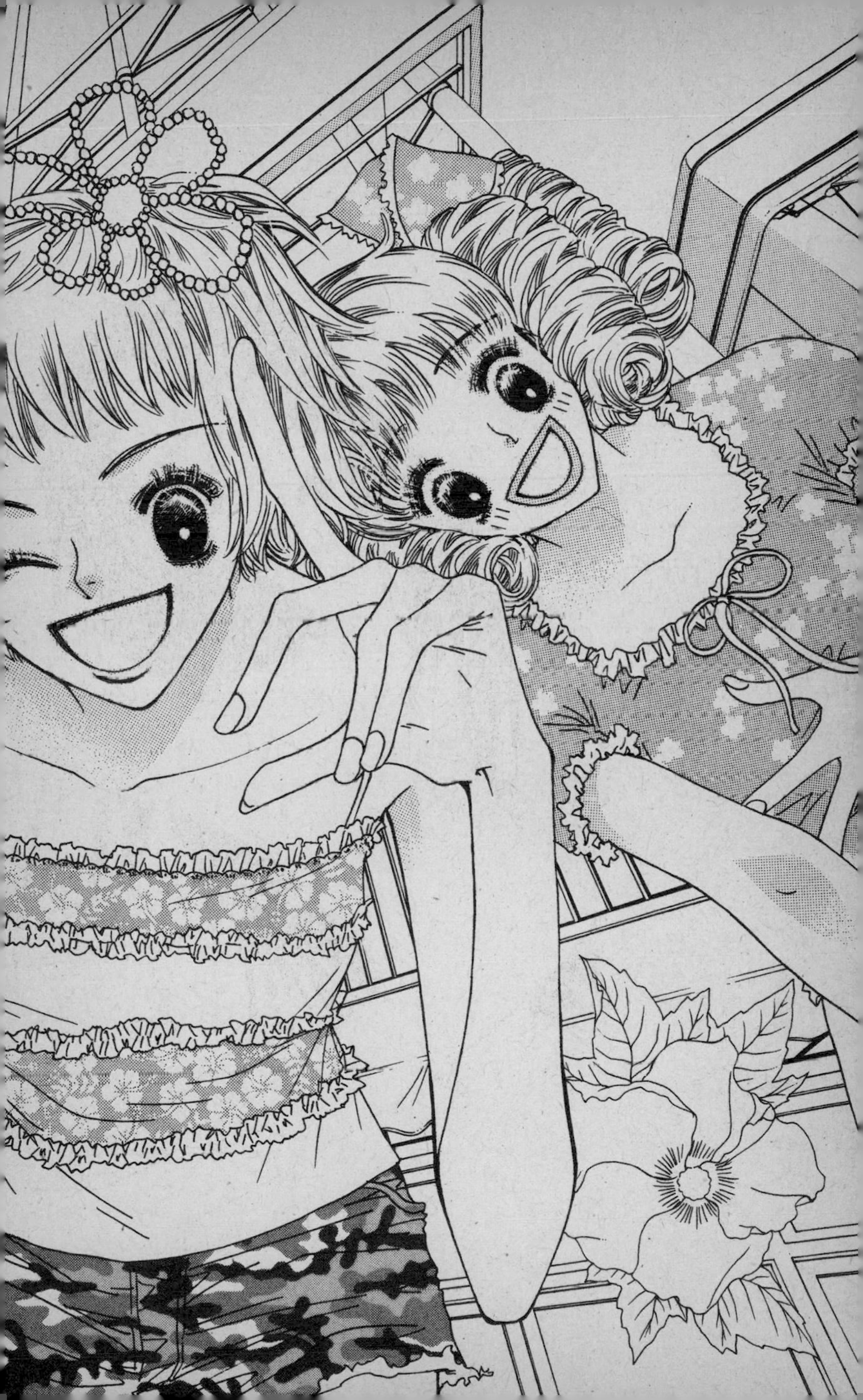

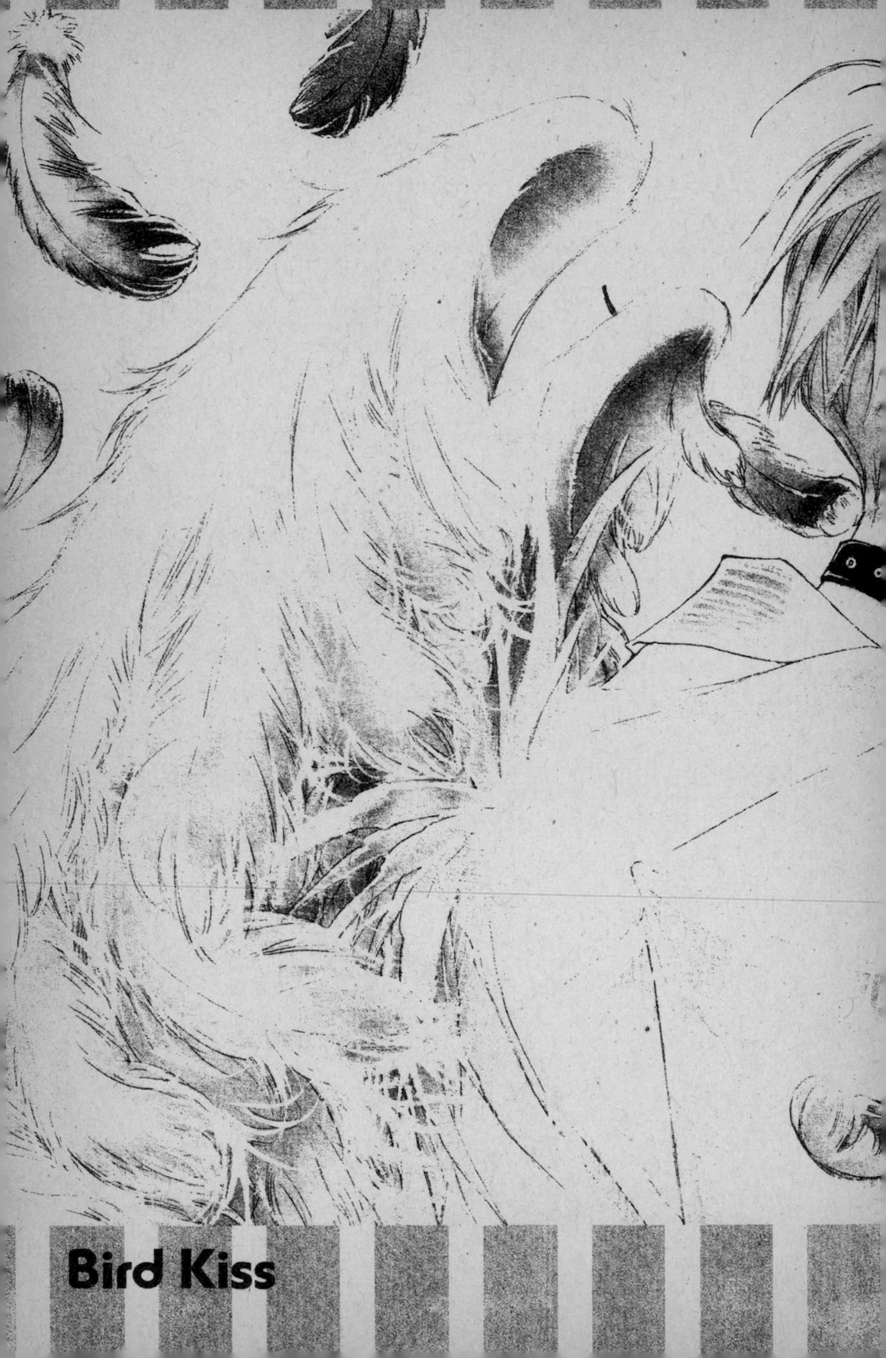

# Bird Kiss

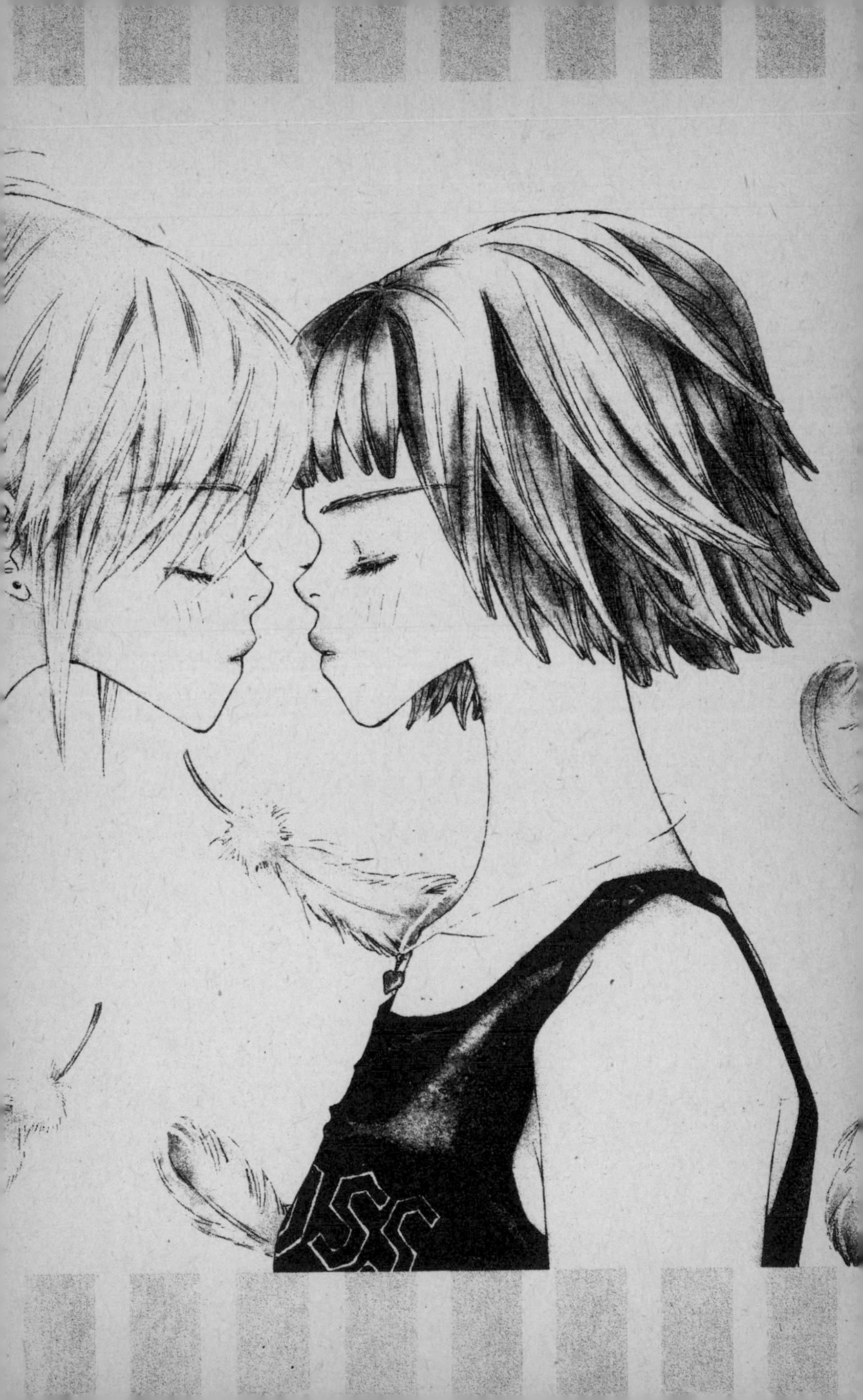

# In the Next Volume of

# BirdKiss

When the frog becomes the prince, what is the little princess to do? Miyoul tries to pretend nothing has changed after the robbery incident and Heeracks transformation, but when she learns her admirer is being courted by Guelin for the Slipper Club, shes thrown into a jealous rage...but who or what is she jealous about?

Find out in the next chapter of Bird Kiss!

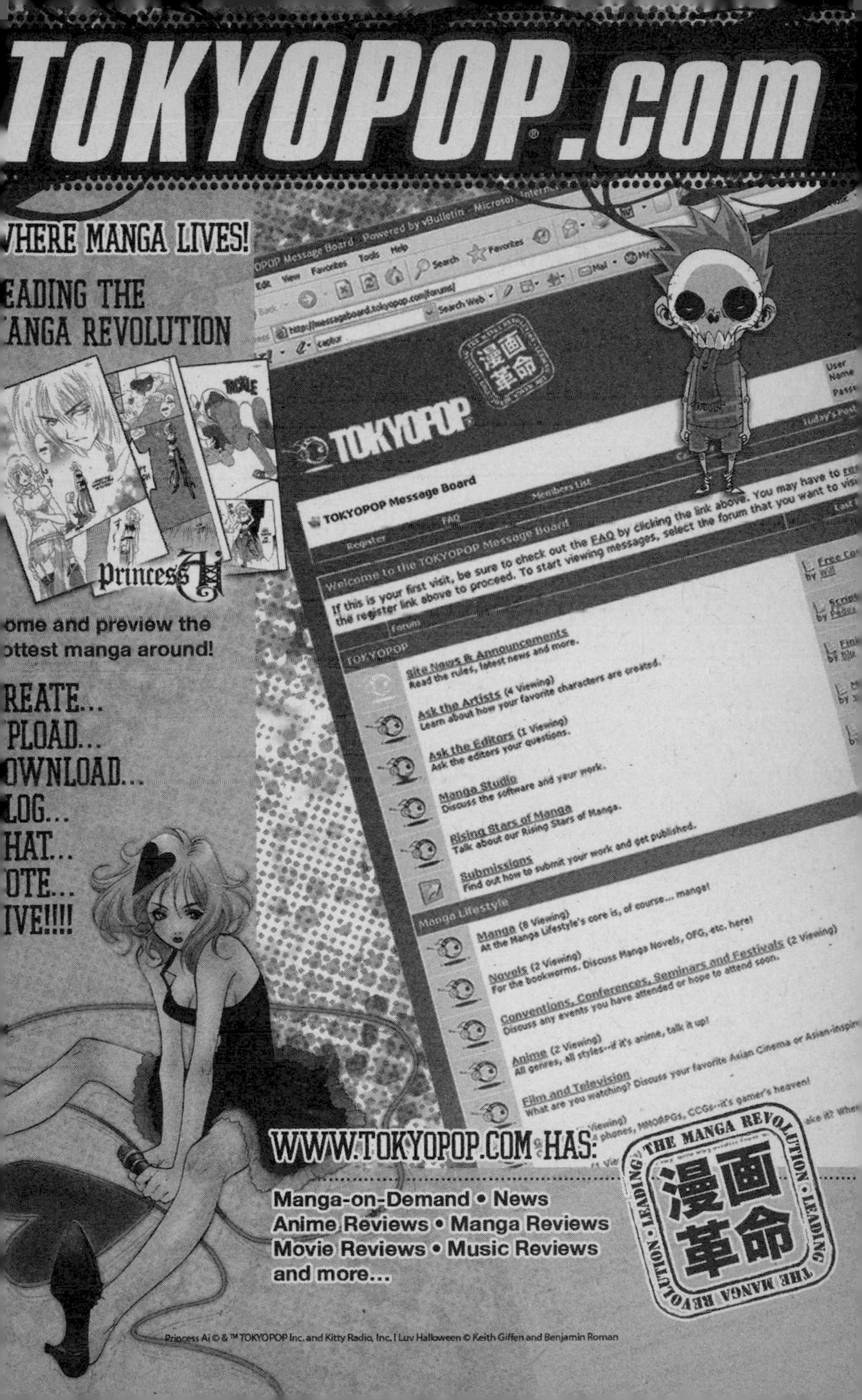
TOKYOPOP®.com
WHERE MANGA LIVES!
LEADING THE
MANGA REVOLUTION
Princess Ai
Come and preview the
hottest manga around!
CREATE...
UPLOAD...
DOWNLOAD...
BLOG...
CHAT...
VOTE...
LIVE!!!!
TOKYOPOP Message Board
Welcome to the TOKYOPOP Message Board
If this is your first visit, be sure to check out the FAQ by clicking the link above. You may have to register before you can post: click the register link above to proceed. To start viewing messages, select the forum that you want to visit
Site News & Announcements
Read the rules, latest news and more.
Ask the Artists (4 Viewing)
Learn about how your favorite characters are created.
Ask the Editors (1 Viewing)
Ask the editors your questions.
Manga Studio
Discuss the software and your work.
Rising Stars of Manga
Talk about our Rising Stars of Manga.
Submissions
Find out how to submit your work and get published.
Manga Lifestyle
Manga (8 Viewing)
At the Manga Lifestyle's core is, of course... manga!
Novels (2 Viewing)
For the bookworms. Discuss Manga Novels, OFG, etc. here!
Conventions, Conferences, Seminars and Festivals (2 Viewing)
Discuss any events you have attended or hope to attend soon.
Anime (2 Viewing)
All genres, all styles--if it's anime, talk it up!
Film and Television
What are you watching? Discuss your favorite Asian Cinema or Asian-inspired
WWW.TOKYOPOP.COM HAS:
Manga-on-Demand • News
Anime Reviews • Manga Reviews
Movie Reviews • Music Reviews
and more...
LEADING • THE MANGA REVOLUTION • LEADING • THE MANGA REVOLUTION
漫画革命
Princess Ai © & ™ TOKYOPOP Inc. and Kitty Radio, Inc. I Luv Halloween © Keith Giffen and Benjamin Roman

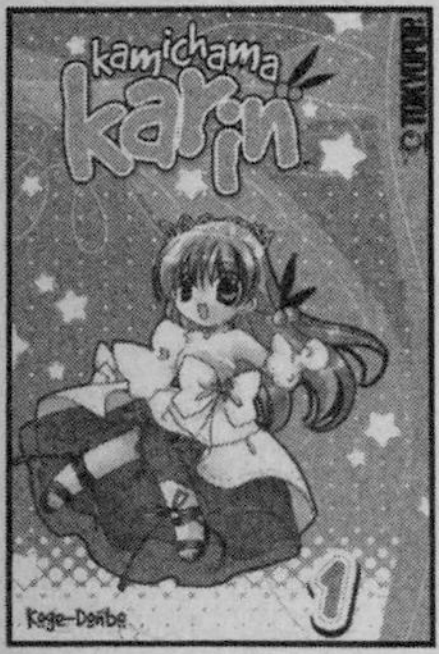
kamichama
karin
TOKYOPOP
Koge-Donbo
1

ROMANCE

YOUTH AGE 10+

## KAMICHAMA KARIN

BY KOGE-DONBO

This one was a surprise. I mean, I knew Koge-Donbo drew insanely cute characters, but I had no idea a magical girl story could be so darn clever. *Kamichama Karin* manages to lampoon everything about the genre, from plushie-like mascots to character archetypes to weapons that appear from the blue! And you gotta love Karin, the airheaded heroine who takes guff from no one and screams "I AM GOD!" as her battle cry. In short, if you are looking for a shiny new manga with a knack for hilarity and a penchant for accessories, I say look no further.

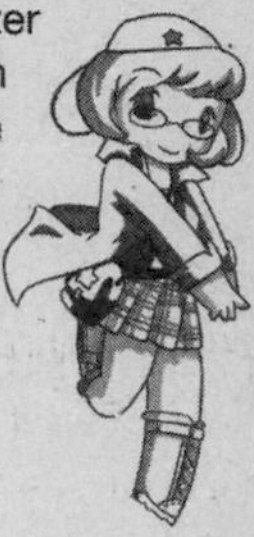

~Carol Fox, Editor

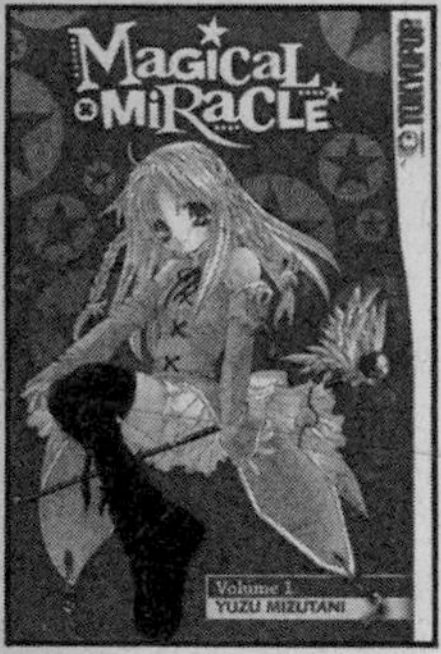
Magical
x Miracle
TOKYOPOP
Volume 1
YUZU MIZUTANI

FANTASY

TEEN AGE 13+

## MAGICAL X MIRACLE

BY YUZU MIZUTANI

*Magical X Miracle* is a quirky—yet uplifting—tale of gender-bending mistaken identity! When a young girl must masquerade as a great wizard, she not only finds the strength to save an entire kingdom...but, ironically, she just might just find herself, too. Yuzu Mizutani's art is remarkably adorable, but it also has a dark, sophisticated edge.

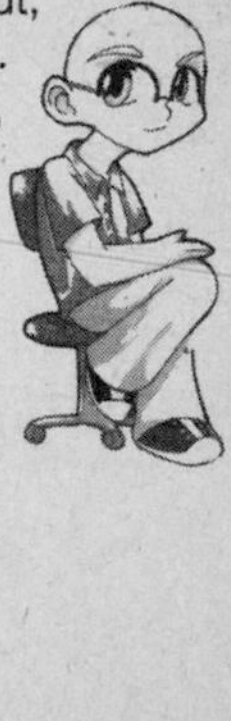

~Paul Morrissey, Editor

Every life has a story...
Every story has a life of its own.

# LIFE™

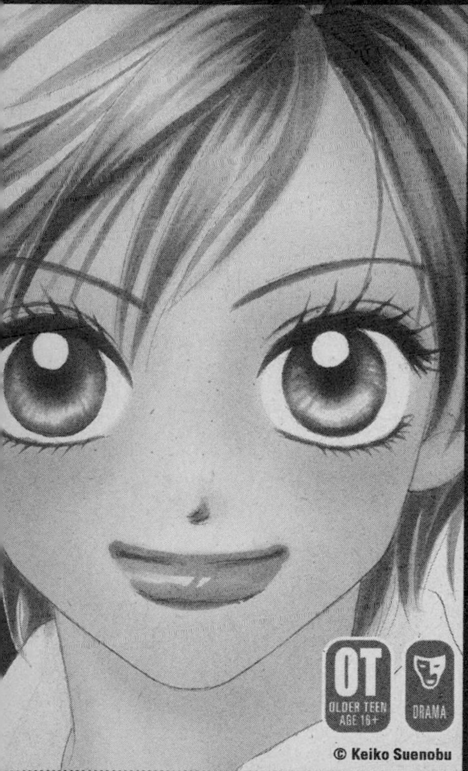
OT
OLDER TEEN AGE 16+
DRAMA



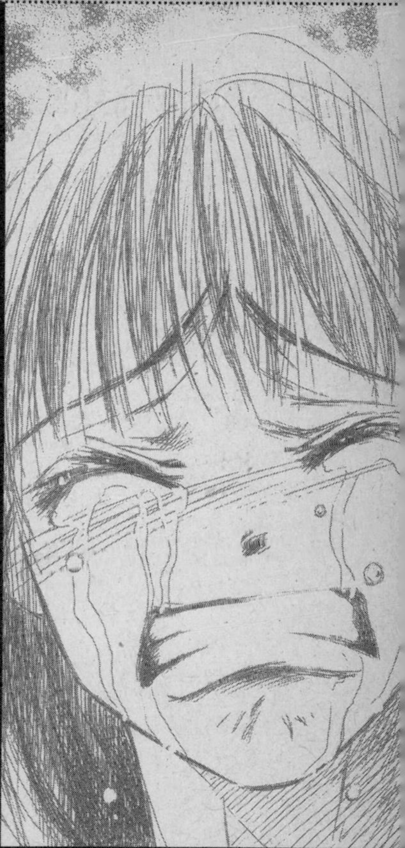

When Ayumu gets in the school of her choice but her best bud does not, the pain of being separated from her friend is too much to handle...But a new school year begins and a fresh start is presented to her, until she takes solace in her new friend Manami...

Volumes 1 and 2 Available Now!

FOR MORE INFORMATION VISIT: WWW.TOKYOPOP.COM

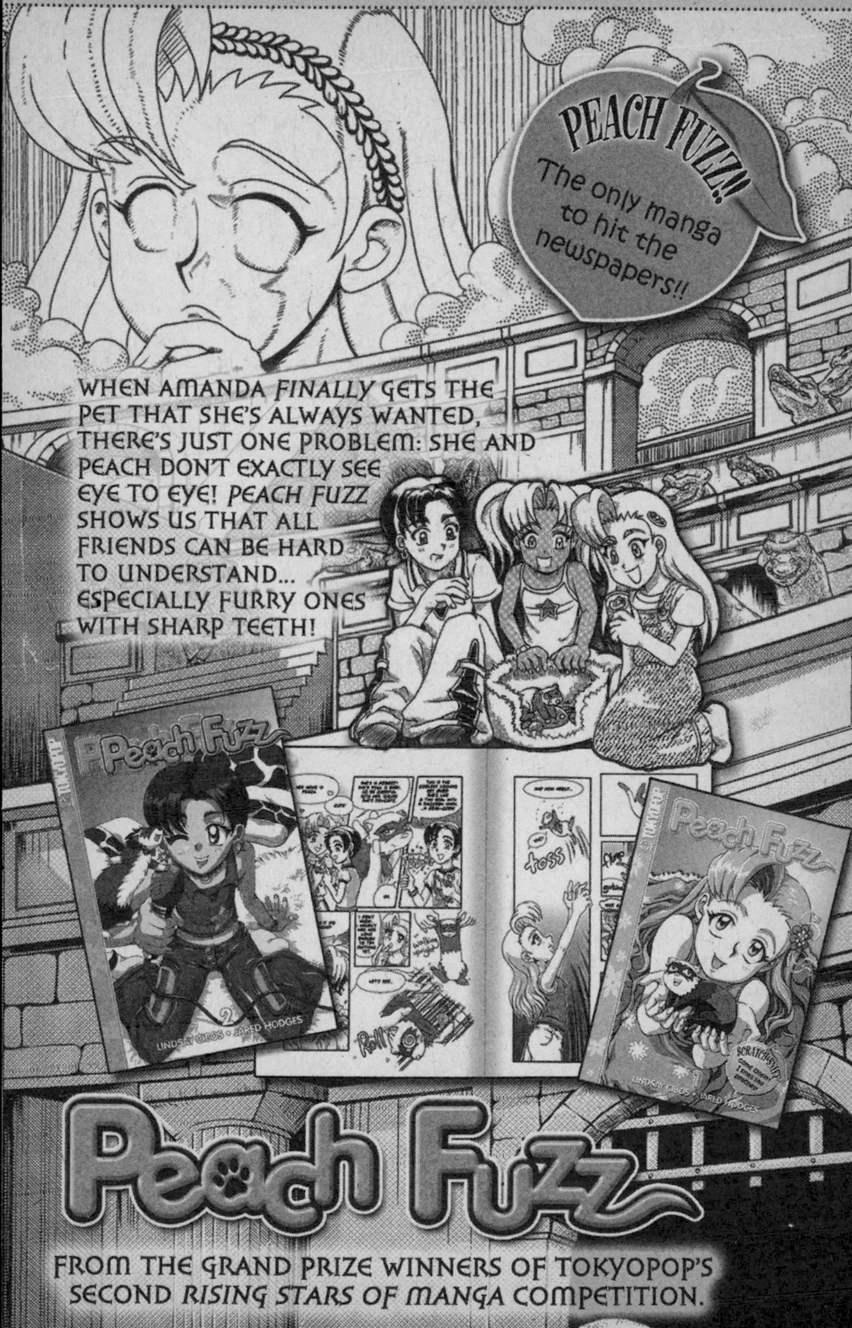
PEACH FUZZ!!
The only manga to hit the newspapers!!
WHEN AMANDA *FINALLY* GETS THE PET THAT SHE'S ALWAYS WANTED, THERE'S JUST ONE PROBLEM: SHE AND PEACH DON'T EXACTLY SEE EYE TO EYE! *PEACH FUZZ* SHOWS US THAT ALL FRIENDS CAN BE HARD TO UNDERSTAND... ESPECIALLY FURRY ONES WITH SHARP TEETH!
Peach Fuzz
LINDSAY CIBOS • JARED HODGES
toss
Roll
Peach Fuzz
LINDSAY CIBOS • JARED HODGES
Peach Fuzz
FROM THE GRAND PRIZE WINNERS OF TOKYOPOP'S SECOND *RISING STARS OF MANGA* COMPETITION.

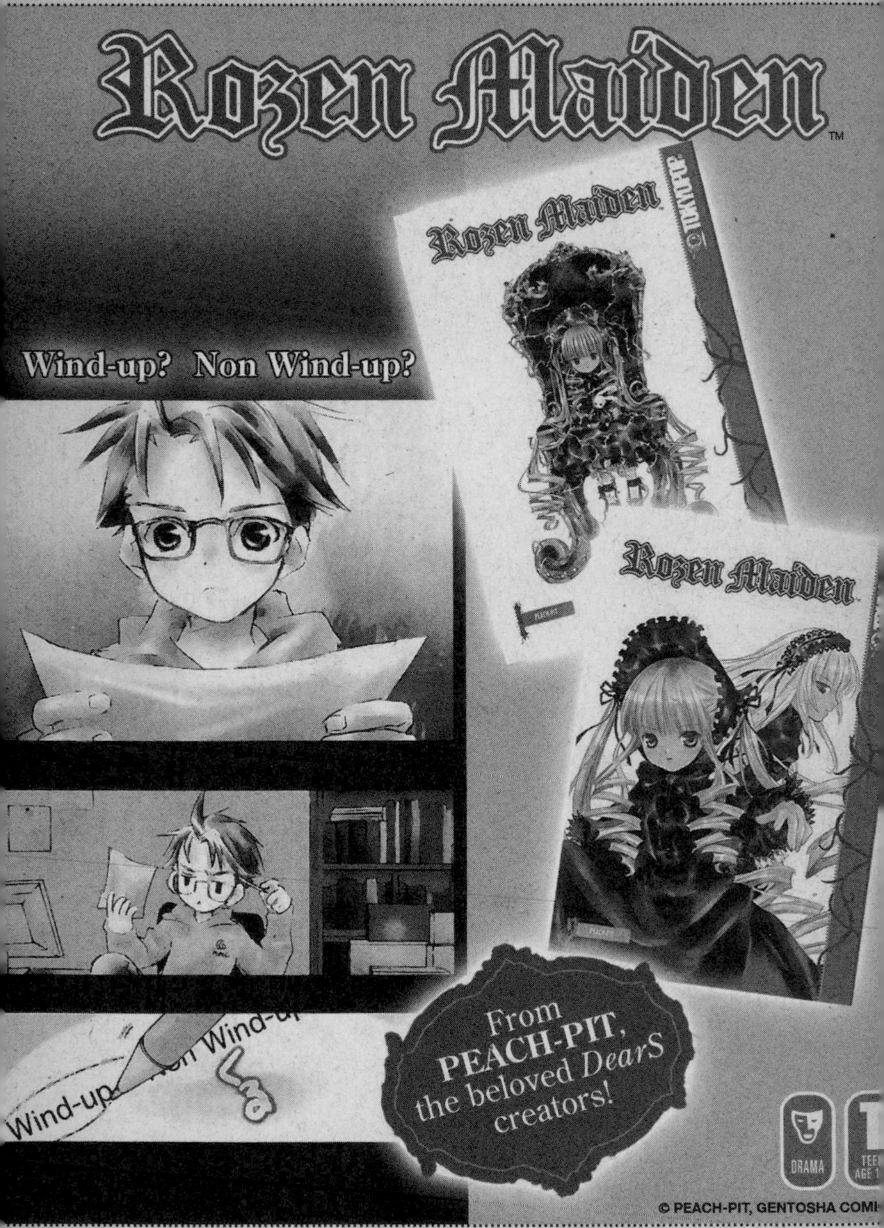
Rozen Maiden™
Wind-up? Non Wind-up?
Rozen Maiden
Rozen Maiden
From PEACH-PIT, the beloved *DearS* creators!
DRAMA
© PEACH-PIT, GENTOSHA COMI

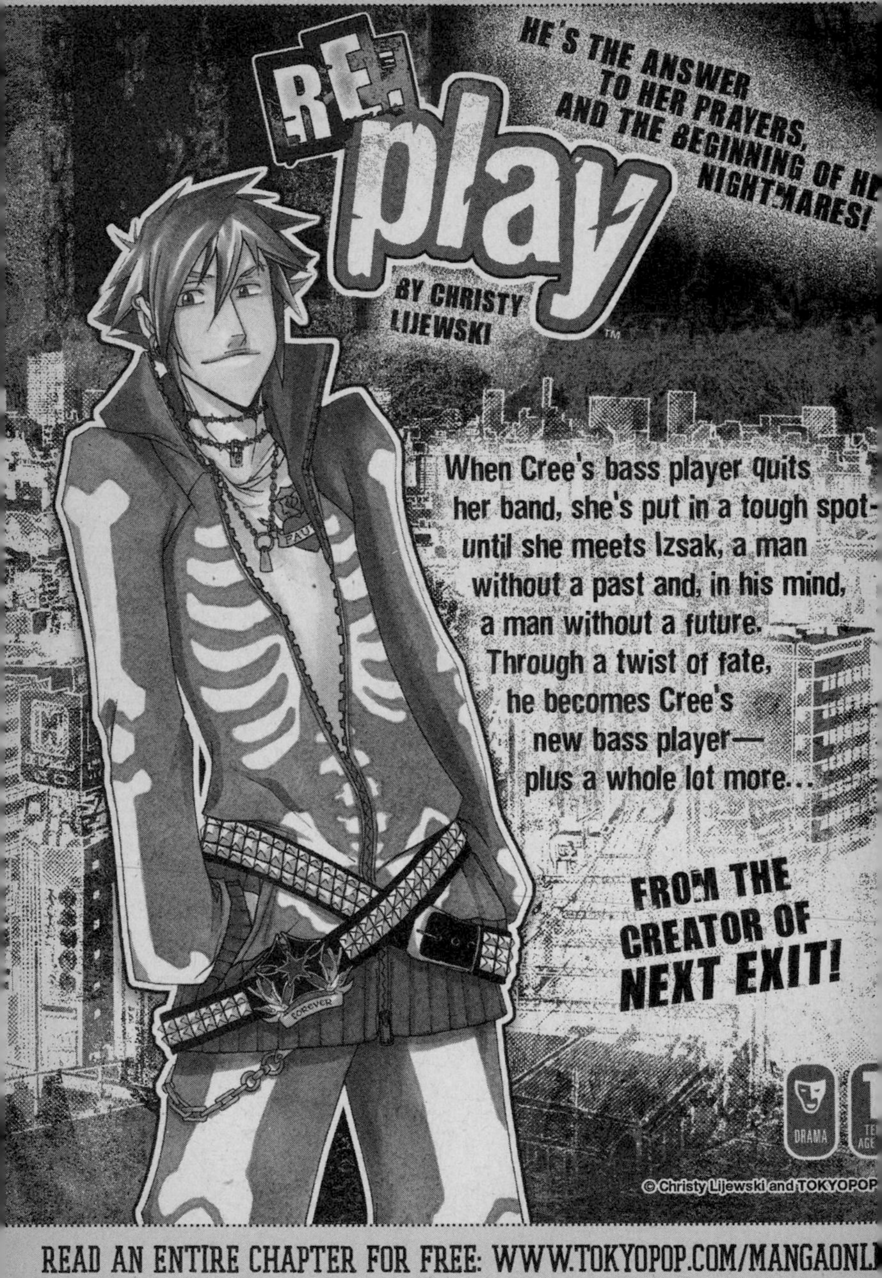
RE: play
HE'S THE ANSWER TO HER PRAYERS, AND THE BEGINNING OF HE NIGHTMARES!
BY CHRISTY LIJEWSKI
When Cree's bass player quits her band, she's put in a tough spot-until she meets Izsak, a man without a past and, in his mind, a man without a future. Through a twist of fate, he becomes Cree's new bass player—plus a whole lot more...
FROM THE CREATOR OF NEXT EXIT!
DRAMA
© Christy Lijewski and TOKYOPOP